TRIALS FOR INTERNATIONAL CRIMES IN ASIA

The issue of international crimes is highly topical in Asia, with still-resonant claims against the Japanese for war crimes, and deep schisms resulting from crimes in Bangladesh, Cambodia and East Timor. Over the years, the region has hosted a succession of tribunals, from Manila, Singapore and Tokyo after the Asia-Pacific War to those currently at work in Dhaka and Phnom Penh. This book draws on extensive new research and offers the first comprehensive legal appraisal of the Asian trials. As well as the famous tribunals, it also considers lesser-known examples, such as the Dutch and Soviet trials of the Japanese, the Cambodian trial of the Khmer Rouge, and the Indonesians' trials of their own military personnel. It focuses on their approach to the elements of international crimes, and their contribution to general theories of liability. In the process, the book challenges some of the prevailing orthodoxies about the development of international criminal law.

KIRSTEN SELLARS is Assistant Professor at the Faculty of Law, The Chinese University of Hong Kong.

TRIALS FOR INTERNATIONAL CRIMES IN ASIA

Edited by

KIRSTEN SELLARS

The Chinese University of Hong Kong

CAMBRIDGE
UNIVERSITY PRESS

CAMBRIDGE
UNIVERSITY PRESS

University Printing House, Cambridge CB2 8BS, United Kingdom

Cambridge University Press is part of the University of Cambridge.

It furthers the University's mission by disseminating knowledge in the pursuit of education, learning and research at the highest international levels of excellence.

www.cambridge.org
Information on this title: www.cambridge.org/9781107104655

First published 2016

A catalogue record for this publication is available from the British Library.

Library of Congress Cataloguing in Publication data
Trials for international crimes in Asia / edited by Kirsten Sellars.
pages cm
ISBN 978-1-107-10465-5 (hardback)
1. War crime trials – Asia. 2. International crimes – Asia. 3. International criminal courts – Asia. I. Sellars, Kirsten, editors.
KZ7230.T79 2015
341.6′90268–dc23
2015021264

ISBN 978-1-107-10465-5 Hardback

CONTENTS

CONTRIBUTORS

REHAN ABEYRATNE, Associate Professor, Jindal Global Law School, Haryana.

MARK CAMMACK, Professor of Law, Southwestern Law School, Los Angeles.

CHEAH WUI LING, Assistant Professor, Faculty of Law, National University of Singapore.

SIMON CHESTERMAN, Dean and Professor of Law, Faculty of Law, National University of Singapore.

ROBERT CRYER, Professor of International and Criminal Law, Birmingham Law School, University of Birmingham.

TARA H. GUTMAN, ANU College of Law, Australian National University, Canberra.

M. RAFIQUL ISLAM, Professor of Law, Macquarie Law School, Macquarie University, Sydney.

NEHA JAIN, Associate Professor, University of Minnesota Law School, Minneapolis.

BING BING JIA, Professor of International Law, Law School, Tsinghua University, Beijing.

NINA H.B. JØRGENSEN, Professor, Faculty of Law, The Chinese University of Hong Kong.

ŌSAWA TAKESHI, Associate Professor, Faculty of Foreign Studies, Kumamoto Gakuen University, Kumamoto.

VALENTYNA POLUNINA, Doctoral Candidate, Cluster of Excellence, 'Asia and Europe in a Global Context', University of Heidelberg.

ABDUR RAZZAQ, Senior Advocate, Supreme Court of Bangladesh, and Chief Defence Counsel, International Crimes Tribunal, Dhaka.

LISETTE SCHOUTEN, Doctoral Candidate, Cluster of Excellence, 'Asia and Europe in a Global Context', University of Heidelberg.

KIRSTEN SELLARS, Assistant Professor, Faculty of Law, The Chinese University of Hong Kong.

FOREWORD

Some of the earliest rules intended to limit the conduct of hostilities can be traced back two and a half thousand years to Asia. The Chinese general Sun Tzu's *The art of war*, written in the sixth century BC, is now a classic text of military strategy and tactics. But it is more than that. For alongside the discussions of attack and defence, the laying of traps and the burning of arsenals, it also explores commanders' responsibilities to both sovereigns and subordinates when engaged in warfare. Sun placed the onus squarely on the shoulders of commanders to impose discipline on their troops or else take responsibility for their actions, and insisted that they should make the best use of information and resources that came their way, so as not to prolong conflict unnecessarily – for to do otherwise would be inhumane.

Yet despite these antecedents, Asia today is often regarded as the region with the least experience of or respect for international criminal law. The dominant story tends to be a European one, from the trial of the Alsatian Peter von Hagenbach for crimes committed at Breisach; to the Allies' trials of the Germans at Nuremberg, Hamburg, Rastatt and East Berlin; to the ad hoc tribunal trying those responsible for the killing fields in Bosnia; to the Rome Statute of the International Criminal Court, which now sits in The Hague. Other regions do feature, of course. The United States, for example, was instrumental in ensuring that Nazi atrocities were punished in a court of law rather than through summary execution. Latin America contributed much to the development of transitional justice, as did South Africa. Though some African nations now protest at being on the receiving end of a disproportionate amount of international criminal justice, they are without question active participants. Asia, by contrast, is rarely mentioned.

Indeed, it is striking that while two-thirds of African states and three-quarters of other regions have accepted the jurisdiction of the International Criminal Court, less than one-third of the countries in Asia have done so. The reasons for this are complex and linked to a more general wariness of accepting international obligations. Nevertheless, it seems probable that part of the hesitation in embracing a permanent tribunal with jurisdiction over war crimes, crimes against humanity, genocide, and, potentially, aggression, can be traced to the region's experience of international criminal law.

As this volume demonstrates, far from being bypassed by international criminal law or ignorant of its content, there is in fact a rich history to be discovered. In the aftermath of the Second World War in particular, around a thousand trials were conducted across Asia. In some cases, the trials were minimally documented; in others, the trial records have only come to light long after the event. Even the 1948 Majority Judgment in the highest profile post-war case in the region – that of Japan's leaders before the International Military Tribunal for the Far East – took time to emerge: it was published in Japanese and Russian at the time, but the English-language version was available only in mimeograph until it was eventually published in 1977. By contrast, the Judgment of the Nuremberg Tribunal was published in English, French, Russian and German within a year of the decision being released.

The relative ignorance about the Tokyo Tribunal was not entirely accidental. Even at the time, it was regarded as being somewhat embarrassing. When the trial opened in 1946, *Time* magazine, while likening the Nuremberg trial to the portentous drama of a Wagnerian opera, contrasted its counterpart in Japan to the 'opéra bouffe' qualities of Gilbert and Sullivan musicals. After the Tokyo Tribunal closed, the international lawyer Georg Schwarzenberger wrote that the 'legal standards – or their absence – of the Tokyo Trial were such as to make lawyers wish to forget all about it at the earliest possible moment'.

In more recent years, legal scholars, not succumbing to the desire to forget, have rightly stressed the Tribunal's many shortcomings, such as its selective focus, retroactive charges, evidentiary failings and other flaws. But there has been less examination – at least outside Japan – of the manner in which colonialism and race figured in this and other post-war trials. Given the fast-changing political environment after the conclusion of hostilities in the Pacific theatre, it is not surprising that the trials quickly became caught up in the liberation struggles around the region – nor that the United States and the European powers preferred to frame the legal proceedings in a manner that emphasised Japanese atrocities rather than colonialism. Race was also a feature, with the Allied powers claiming the right to speak on behalf of 'civilisation' in prosecuting the trials. Though many of those on trial had clearly violated the norms of any society calling itself civilised, it was evident that 'civilisation' in this context meant *Western* civilisation.

A further complication with long-term implications was the political decision to protect the Japanese Emperor from prosecution. This assisted the short-term occupation of Japan, but created a more enduring problem bound up with the Japanese failure to accept responsibility for their actions during the fifteen-year war against China and the Allies. The repercussions of that decision continue to be felt today, as China, South Korea and other Asian states call on Japan to apologise for its wartime activities – even as nationalists within Japan press for ritualistic visits to the Yasukuni shrine to Japan's war dead, which include some leading figures convicted of war crimes and crimes against peace at the Tokyo Tribunal.

Given this history, it is not hard to see how international criminal law might come to be seen in Asia as a tool to be used for selected political ends, rather than as a manifestation of the rule of law applicable equally to all. The various trials are interesting not only for their political significance, however. They also offered what Kirsten Sellars rightly describes as a 'proving-ground' for legal innovation. This was especially true in the area of 'common plan or conspiracy' and the doctrine of command responsibility. The innovative approach was in part driven by the facts before the post-war tribunals. In Nuremberg, the Nazi leadership had left behind evidence that clearly documented orders to commit international crimes. Such evidence was not available in Tokyo, meaning that charges could not be based solely on explicit orders. To fill this gap, defendants were charged not only with ordering, authorising and permitting war crimes, but also with participating in a grand conspiracy and failing to prevent violations by the soldiers under their command. The limits of these doctrines continue to be a subject of debate today.

This book also provides an account of other trials that took place after the Second World War, ranging from Singapore and the Dutch East Indies to China and the Soviet Union. In addition it examines the more recent experiments with trials for international crimes in Asia, which can be traced back to events in the 1970s but which often took a generation to reach the courtroom. First in Bangladesh, where the experience of the bloody war of separation from Pakistan in 1971 gave rise to calls for the creation of a domestic 'international crimes tribunal'. These plans were halted by a coup and instability, but revived in 2009. Second in Cambodia, where the Khmer Rouge's reign of terror from 1975 to 1979 became the focus, three decades later, of mixed 'extraordinary chambers' within the national courts. And finally in Timor-Leste, where Indonesia's occupation, beginning in 1975, was reversed by plebiscite in 1999 amidst violence and destruction, which in turn gave rise to an unusual hybrid court convened in Dili under the auspices of the UN transitional administration.

Some of the issues confronted in these various trials are consistent with experience in other regions, though some appear unique to Asia. This is, perhaps, to be expected. The application of 'universal' principles in specific jurisdictions often highlights the inherent tension between legitimacy and effectiveness in international criminal trials. Such trials must, of course, aspire to a legitimacy that goes beyond the state, particularly when it is the very leaders of that state who may have orchestrated unspeakable acts. At the same time, however, those trials must be sensitive to the local context if their results are to be effective. Unless the population regards the legal process as tailored to their needs and concerns, any resolution they seek to impose is unlikely to endure.

Kirsten Sellars and her contributors bring together a wealth of expertise on these and many other topics. It is hoped that this volume will contribute to a deeper understanding of the significance of international criminal trials for Asia, and of Asia for the future of international criminal law.

Simon Chesterman

ACKNOWLEDGEMENTS

This book is a collective enterprise. My thanks to Julien Anglade, Chen Chi, Kam Kai Qi, Li Danyang, Lucy North, Peng Yiyun, Valentyna Polunina and Alainna Wrigley for their translations of Chinese, Japanese, Russian and French materials. Thanks, too, to Finola O'Sullivan, Elizabeth Spicer, Clare Dennison and Sarah Green at Cambridge University Press for guiding the book through the publication process. And special thanks to Simon Chesterman at the Faculty of Law, National University of Singapore, and Andrew Harding at the Faculty's Centre for Asian Legal Studies, for encouragement and financial support for the research and conference that set this project in motion.

Finally, I must, of course, express my deep gratitude to the contributors, whose research on the trials in Asia shines a bright light on a compelling subject.

Kirsten Sellars

Introduction

KIRSTEN SELLARS

The issue of international crimes is highly topical in Asia today, and it is likely to remain so, given the still-resonant claims against the Japanese for crimes committed in the 1930s and 1940s, and the deep political schisms caused by later crimes carried out in Bangladesh, Cambodia and East Timor. Over the years, the region has hosted a succession of tribunals for such crimes, from those established in Manila, Singapore and Tokyo just after the Asia-Pacific War to those currently hearing cases in Dhaka and Phnom Penh. Some of these tribunals were established at the behest of Asian governments, and others by non-Asian states or international organisations. Some are well known, while others – such as the Dutch and Soviet trials of the Japanese, the Cambodian trial of the Khmer Rouge and the Indonesians' trials of their own military personnel – are less frequently discussed. This book assesses these tribunals' approach to international crimes: crimes against peace, war crimes, crimes against humanity and genocide. And it considers the development of general theories of liability, to which the Asian trials have made especially important contributions.

As the low take-up of International Criminal Court membership demonstrates, many Asian states are wary about bringing cases before international or hybrid courts, not least because of the accompanying loss of control over the process. They have, however, been willing to mount trials themselves. The Indonesian authorities charged their own military personnel for crimes committed in East Timor rather than hand them over to a proposed UN-mandated tribunal, and the Bangladeshi authorities have pushed ahead with the current trials, despite these provoking lethal clashes on the streets and widespread criticism from international observers.

When examining trials across the decades since 1945, some intriguing themes emerge. Consider, for example, the reasons for establishing trials in Asia. These were usually justified as a means to punish, deter and leave an official record. They might in addition have had the benefit of reassuring the public that they had fought a good war or that an enemy had been expelled for good. But the trials were also motivated by unheralded agendas, such as underwriting the *status quo*, justifying violence, winning allies and silencing critics. These more political functions bore down heavily on the proceedings, and prosecution and defence lawyers occasionally accommodated to them. At Khabarovsk, for example, both sides strove to establish the Japanese defendants' guilt, while at Jakarta, both sides sought to demonstrate the Indonesian defendants' innocence.

The sponsoring powers' approaches to indictments also reveal interesting patterns. Some trials were as notable for who they omitted as for who they included. The Tokyo prosecution declined to indict the Emperor Shōwa (who, under American tutelage, had been transformed into an obliging constitutional monarch); and the People's Revolutionary Tribunal decided not to charge Khmer Rouge leaders Khieu Samphan and Nuon Chea (in the hope that they would participate in a post-Kampuchea settlement). Sometimes potential prosecution targets escaped the net: the Japanese biological warfare chiefs who fled to the Americans after the Second World War, the Pakistani generals who fled to the Indians after the secession of Bangladesh and, famously, Pol Pot, who long evaded capture, and then, days before he was due to be arrested, made the ultimate escape, through death.

The Asian trials have seen both judicial activism and judicial restraint – often in counterpoint to concurrent trial programmes in Europe. At the Tokyo Tribunal, for example, prosecutors relied more heavily on 'common plan or conspiracy' than did their opposite numbers at Nuremberg, alleging, among other things, that the Japanese conspired to dominate not just East Asia but all the states within and bordering the Pacific and Indian oceans.[1] In recent decades, European jurists dealing with cases arising from the war in Bosnia have adopted a more sweeping approach to modes of liability: the Appeals Chamber of the International Criminal Tribunal for the former Yugoslavia, in *Prosecutor* v. *Tadić*, advanced a highly innovative approach to joint criminal enterprise (JCE), while the Extraordinary Chambers in the Courts of Cambodia exercised greater caution, declining to apply the 'extended' third form of the doctrine to cases dating back to the 1970s.

[1] International Military Tribunal for the Far East, *The Tokyo major war crimes trial*, R.J. Pritchard (ed.), 124 vols. (Lewiston: Edwin Mellen Press, 1998), Indictment, vol. 2, p. 2.

Finally, the prosecuting powers' policies towards the punishment of those convicted have thrown up exceptions – but exceptions that prove the rule. Most have publicly adopted a 'firm but fair' position, up to and including the death penalty. The Allies executed Japanese war criminals in Singapore, Batavia, Saigon, Yokohama, Rabaul, Manila and scores of other places after the war, and the Bangladesh authorities are executing people to this day. But some powers have on occasion played the magnanimity card. The Chinese, for example, stressing the leniency of their policies, declined to execute those Japanese convicted at Shenyang and Taiyuan. This 'leniency' was relative, of course, as some of the accused had been held without trial for as long as a decade. During their incarceration the Chinese took steps to 're-educate' the Japanese with the aim of inculcating remorse and encouraging the prisoners to spread the word about Chinese benevolence on their return to Japan. Examples such as this are unusual, though, and talk of any kind of rehabilitation, whether politically motivated or not, is still extremely rare.

The problem of legitimacy

The origins of the charges brought at the Asian trials can be traced back to the late nineteenth and early twentieth century. As this author argues in her opening chapter about treasonable conspiracies, the formation of international criminal law was driven by concerns about security rather than justice. Just as national security law dealt with assaults on the integrity of the state, so international criminal law (which drew heavily on national security law) was designed to deal with assaults on the integrity of the society of states. These ideas bore fruit after the Second World War. The International Military Tribunal for the Far East was thus established primarily to underwrite the post-war *status quo* in Asia, and its central charge – 'crimes against peace' – was presented as a form of treason against the international order.

Ironically, the charges of 'crimes against peace' against Japan's former leaders were framed just as the prosecuting powers were themselves fighting their way back into their old colonial possessions. In a few places, such as Indo-China, the Europeans were even assisted by the departing Japanese – a baton-change from one occupying power to another. When French colonial officials (ousted by the Japanese in 1941) returned to Hanoi in August 1945, they were greeted by violent anti-French demonstrations, which were held back by Japanese troops.[2]

[2] R.J. Aldrich, *Intelligence and the war against Japan: Britain, America and the politics of secret service* (Cambridge University Press, 2000), p. 345.

The following month, American war crimes investigators, who had arrived in Saigon with the intention of arresting members of the Japanese *Kempeitai* for war crimes, postponed their plans when they discovered that the French, British and Indian forces occupying the country had given the *Kempeitai* their guns back so that they could help fight a common enemy: the Viet Minh.[3]

A similar thing happened in Netherlands East Indies. At the end of the war, the invading British used the retreating Japanese troops to protect oil installations against a new military threat: the Indonesian nationalist forces.[4] When the Dutch returned to reclaim their old colony, the British withdrew, leaving them to fight the Indonesians and try the Japanese for crimes committed during the occupation. But convening war crimes trials in the midst of a colonial insurgency raised significant problems, the greatest of which was the legitimacy of the trials themselves. As Lisette Schouten shows in her chapter, the Dutch attempted, among other things, to use the trials to present themselves as liberators of the colony, and to positively contrast their 'lawful' colonialism with the 'criminal' variety previously imposed by the Japanese. This message may have reassured the Dutch, but it made little impact on Indonesians, who, notwithstanding their experiences at the hands of the Japanese, had no desire to be liberated by anyone but themselves. In the event, on 26 December 1949, the Dutch escorted the remaining Japanese accused and convicted onto the M.S. *Tjisadane*, bound for Japan. The following day, they ceded power to the Republic of Indonesia, and departed their former colony for good.

Half a century later, it was the turn of the Indonesians to be ejected from part of the archipelago. In 1999, in response to East Timorese demands for independence, the Indonesians and their paramilitary proxies pursued a campaign of terror in the province. In 2002, the ad hoc Human Rights Court in Jakarta (convened to pre-empt the threat of an international tribunal) began to hear the cases of eighteen defendants accused of coordinating the violence. All the indictments alleged crimes against humanity and charged the defendants on the basis of command

[3] Ibid., p. 347.

[4] See, for example, Mountbatten's telegram to London, requesting guidance over whether he should use Japanese troops to guard the oil refineries at Palembang in light of American press complaints about the British use of Japanese forces. (Chiefs of Staff Committee Joint Planning Staff (14 December 1945), p. 227: CAB 79/42, TNA.) It was agreed he could use Japanese troops if none other were available. (Chiefs of Staff Committee Joint Planning Staff (23 December 1945), Annex 2, p. 332: CAB 79/42, TNA.)

responsibility for acts committed by subordinates. Six defendants were convicted; all were acquitted on appeal.

As Mark Cammack shows in his chapter, the ad hoc Court, operating under the nose of the powerful Indonesian military, was engaged in an exceptionally delicate task. The prosecutors were expected to bring cases against still-serving Army officers who enjoyed the support of not only their military superiors but also the uniformed cadres packed into the Court's public gallery. In the event, they constructed a weak case on grounds of crimes against humanity, and did what they could to minimise the likelihood of defendants being found guilty. Legal slips, calculated or otherwise, abounded: in the *Eurico Guterres* case, the accused was charged on grounds of command responsibility although he held no formal position of power, and in *Timbul Silaen* case, the prosecutors treated the *mens rea* and *actus reus* requirements as independent crimes. At times, prosecutors and defence lawyers put forward similar arguments, both of which were favourable to the accused. It took the intervention of some of the judges to bring more incriminating testimony and evidence to light.

The command responsibility doctrine

The trials in the region have contributed greatly to the evolution of the general principles of law, and particularly to the theory of command responsibility, a doctrine developed to settle accounts for wars in Asia. It first emerged at the trials of Yamashita Tomoyuki, Toyoda Soemu and the Tokyo Tribunal defendants after the Asia-Pacific War. It was redeployed at the American *Medina* case in the wake of the My Lai massacre, then inserted into Additional Protocol I of the Geneva Conventions after the Vietnam War, and finally deployed at the recent trials at Jakarta, Dili, Phnom Penh and Dhaka to deal with violence of a non-international character.

The first post-war development occurred at the 1945 trial, conducted under American auspices in Manila, of General Yamashita for failing to control the troops under his command. A defence appeal to the US Supreme Court produced a majority opinion upholding the Judgment and two famous dissents from Justices Wiley Rutledge and Frank Murphy, who described its deployment of the doctrine as vacuous and without precedent.[5] Robert Jackson, a fellow Supreme Court judge who

5 *In re Yamashita*, 327 US 1 (1946), 51, 40.

had served as American Chief Prosecutor at the Nuremberg Tribunal, later made reference to the law and politics of the *Yamashita* case. He wrote, 'Of course, the charges against Yamashita that he failed to prevent atrocities went somewhat beyond our Nurnberg precedent, in which we prosecuted only those who had affirmatively ordered or incited atrocities.'[6] Then, in political mode, he added, 'I have always thought it a very unfortunate thing for the United States that members of the [Supreme] Court saw fit to write as they did in the Yamashita case, for it has provided most damaging propaganda against our entire policy in the orient.'[7]

As Rehan Abeyratne explains in his chapter, the trial of Admiral Toyoda Soemu further clarified the concept of command responsibility. The Judgment stated that in a case where a commander had ordered crimes to be carried out, a court would have to establish, first, that the crimes had been committed by troops under the accused's command and, second, that the accused had ordered their commission. Where there was no proof beyond reasonable doubt that the accused had issued such orders, the court set out five criteria for a finding of command responsibility, and this represented an important step towards the modern concept of 'effective control'. The criteria were:

1. [T]hat atrocities were actually committed;
2. Notice of the commission thereof. This notice may be either:
   a. Actual, as in the case of an accused who sees their commission or who is informed thereof shortly thereafter; or
   b. Constructive. That is, the commission of such a great number of offenses within his command that a reasonable man could come to no other conclusion than that the accused must have known of the offenses or of the existence of an understood and acknowledged routine for their commission.
3. Power of command. That is, the accused must be proved to have had actual authority over the offenders to issue orders to them not to commit illegal acts, and to punish offenders.
4. Failure to take such appropriate measures as are within his power to control the troops under his command and to prevent acts which are [in] violation of the laws of war.
5. Failure to punish offenders.[8]

[6] Jackson to Lyon (11 July 1950): Box 113, Jackson Papers, Library of Congress. [7] Ibid.

[8] 'Judgement of the GHQ War Crimes Tribunal in the Case of U.S.A. v. Toyoda Soemu' (Tokyo: General Headquarters, Supreme Commander for the Allied Powers, 1949), pp. 5005–5006.

Setting aside command responsibility for the moment, the *Toyoda* trial also demonstrated how the Allies saw 'civilised' values as being integral to the rule of law. As the judges stated, 'When some of the participants in war, whether in high or low places, violate those principles of decency, honor, fair play, and humanity which we have come to know as "civilized," they must be punished.'[9] The concept of 'civilisation' is necessarily exclusive, however, and undermines the law's pretention to universal application. Radhabinod Pal, the Indian judge at the Tokyo Tribunal, made precisely this point when he questioned the existence of a genuine international community, and posited instead a world divided into dominating and dominated states.[10] He questioned the Allies' motives for advancing the crimes against peace charge – which effectively froze the post-war international *status quo* and potentially criminalised struggles for independence – and concluded that colonies could not be compelled 'to submit to eternal domination only in the name of peace'.[11]

Even when Allied jurists strained towards the idea of common humanity governed by universal precepts, they fell short. The *Toyoda* judges did manage to evoke commonality, but only on the grounds of shared 'civilisation'. They observed,

> [T]he accused is a Japanese. As a result of its almost daily observations of him during the long course of the trial, the Tribunal has little hesitation in accepting him as an advanced embodiment of the results of the development of Japanese culture and character from its very beginning to the present time. This development proceeded separately and unrelated to parallel growth in Western civilization, except during the recent decades. It is but natural that such separation should have produced a national character and culture that shows considerable differences from what we, as Occidentals, are familiar. But the accused is not being tried as a Japanese nor because he is a Japanese. He is being tried only on grounds that are common to the two civilizations.[12]

It might further be noted that as soon as the Allied powers encountered problems in the application of justice in Asia, they reverted back to the old idea of 'the West'. Informed of the split on the Tokyo Tribunal bench over the validity of some of the charges, the British Foreign Office Assistant Under-Secretary Esler Dening wrote: 'If the tribunal fails to fulfil its task, Western justice will become the laughing-stock not only of

[9] Ibid., p. 5004. [10] IMTFE, Pal Dissent, vol. 105, p. 103. [11] Ibid., p. 239.

[12] 'Judgement of the GHQ War Crimes Tribunal in the Case of *U.S.A.* v. *Toyoda Soemu*' (Tokyo: General Headquarters, Supreme Commander for the Allied Powers, 1949), pp. 5008–5009.

Japan but of the Far East in general.'[13] His colleague Frederick Garner agreed: the trial's failure would be 'a shattering blow to European prestige'.[14] In short, the Tribunal, convened to deal with two earlier crises of Western authority – Pearl Harbor and the fall of Singapore – would, if it collapsed, create another crisis of Western authority.

Returning to the issue of command responsibility, lawyers for the now-deceased Ieng Sary, one of the accused in Case 002 before the Extraordinary Chambers in the Courts of Cambodia, claimed in 2011 that command responsibility was not customarily recognised as a basis of liability in the late 1970s, and that holding him responsible for his subordinates' actions during this period was therefore a retroactive enactment. 'The concept of command responsibility was not defined with sufficient clarity in 1975–79 for liability to be foreseeable to Mr. Ieng Sary,' they wrote. 'This is evident from the lack of clarity with regard to the requisite *mens rea* and whether it may apply to non-international conflicts and to civilian superiors.'[15] The Pre-Trial Chamber rejected their argument, relying, among other things, on the *Yamashita*, *Toyoda*, and Tokyo judgments.[16]

These are important sources, but as Robert Cryer shows in his chapter, there are equally significant, but overlooked, appraisals of the command responsibility doctrine to be found within the dissenting judgments at the Tokyo Tribunal. These address, among other things, the problem of the various gradations of liability implicit within the doctrine. The Dutch judge Bernard Röling tackled the distinction between 'permitted', as set out in Count 54, and 'deliberately and recklessly disregarded', as set out in Count 55,[17] while his French colleague Henri Bernard attempted to draw a line between intentional, and reckless or negligent, manifestations of command responsibility.[18] (Some six decades before the contemporary discussion, Bernard also touched on the different facets of command responsibility, as a form of liability and as a separate offence.)

Judges at the current ad hoc tribunals have paid no attention to these sources, despite their having been easily accessible for decades. (Röling

[13] Dening to Sargent (30 April 1947): FO 371/66552, TNA.

[14] Garner (20 May 1947): FO 371/66553, TNA.

[15] *Nuon et al.*, 002/19-09-2007-ECCC/OCIJ (PTC 75), Ieng Sary's Appeal against the Closing Order (25 October 2010), par. 134.

[16] *Nuon et al.*, 002/19-09-2007-ECCC/OCIJ (PTC75), Decision on Ieng Sary's Appeal against the Closing Order (11 April 2011), par. 460.

[17] IMTFE, vol. 109, Röling Dissent, p. 56.

[18] IMTFE, vol. 105, Bernard Dissent, pp. 16–17.

and Bernard's dissents were published in 1977, and Pal's dissent was published even earlier, in 1953.)[19] Perhaps the many criticisms of Tokyo Tribunal – for example, for its self-serving imperial predilections, its slipshod approach to individual liability and its failure to adhere to fair trial principles – have counted against it in other areas as well. If this is the case, then the other post-war touchstones for the doctrine – *Yamashita*, with its nebulous approach to *mens rea*, and *Toyoda*, with its jarring invocations of 'civilisation' – are scarcely an improvement. None had impeccable credentials, and none provided all the answers, but modern jurisprudence is impoverished by its failure to engage with some of the doctrinal contributions made in the past.

Legal remedies in China

The literature on international criminal law has tended to focus on Western, or international, contributions to jurisprudence in the Asian context; but what of local, or intra-regional justice? In early 1947, a Chinese military tribunal in Shanghai found Yonemura Haruchi guilty of burying Chinese victims alive, and Shimoto Jiro guilty of torture, rape and plunder. Both were sentenced to death. Six months later, they were driven along the Bund and Nanking Road in open-backed vehicles before being shot at the Kiangwan Execution Ground in front of a vast crowd. It was the first public execution of Japanese war criminals to take place in the city.

The British Consul-General in Shanghai, A.G.N. Ogden, reported all this to the British Ambassador in Nanking:

> It had been announced that the two Japanese were to be paraded in Chinese carts, but possibly owing to a delay in the start, the procession actually consisted of military motor vehicles, with the Japanese in an open truck under a heavy armed-guard. Crowds estimated at about 150,000 in all shouted and cheered as the parade passed and it is said that at some points stones were thrown at the condemned men, who preserved a stolid and unmoved attitude throughout, although they had refused a narcotic injection offered to them before the procession set out.[20]

[19] B.V.A. Röling and C.F. Rüter (eds.), *The Tokyo judgment: the International Military Tribunal for the Far East*, 2 vols. (University Press Amsterdam BV, 1977); R. Pal, *International Military Tribunal for the Far East: dissentient judgment of Justice R.B. Pal* (Calcutta: Sanyal, 1953).

[20] Ogden (Shanghai) to UK Mission (Nanking) (25 June 1947): FO 371/66554, TNA. See also, K. Sellars, *The rise and rise of human rights* (Stroud: Sutton, 2002), pp. 47–48.

Shanghai's English-language newspapers condemned this public spectacle, expressing surprise that the Chinese authorities still regarded such exhibitions as acceptable.[21] Ogden was himself critical of a perceived double standard in the Chinese treatment of former enemies: 'It is interesting to compare the relentless attitude of the Chinese authorities towards Japanese accused of war crimes and Chinese "traitors" . . . with their complacency regarding the continued presence in this country of certain Germans who, although objectionable on political grounds, were granted exemption from deportation presumably because they were regarded as being useful in post-war trade activity.'[22]

Yet when Ogden's report was forwarded to London, it elicited a sharp retort from the aforementioned Frederick Garner in the Foreign Office's War Crimes Section:

> As a matter of fact the Chinese have been quite moderate about Japanese war criminals. Considering the immense number of crimes committed they have executed very few. They have preferred to make a public example of notorious cases rather than execute large numbers privately. I do not consider that the Chinese have behaved any worse than many European countries – in fact they have I think behaved better. The Pacific Sub-Commission of the United Nations War Crimes Commission was able to wind up in March last but the parent body still drags on. As regards letting useful Germans stay on in China, what about von Paulus in Russia and the German 'rocket' scientists in the USA and in this country?[23]

The Kuomintang were not the only ones to try and punish the Japanese for crimes committed during the occupation of China. After the Tokyo Tribunal, the Soviet Union convened a trial at Khabarovsk in 1949 to try defendants who had previously run the biological warfare research centres, and the People's Republic convened trials at Shenyang and Taiyuan in 1956 to try defendants accused of war crimes. Both the Soviet and Chinese initiatives were carefully calibrated to emphasise communist magnanimity towards a former enemy, in contrast to the brute force exercised by the Americans and their Western acolytes.

The trial at Khabarovsk could reasonably be described as the first revisionist response to the Tokyo Tribunal. Many have claimed that the Tokyo Tribunal went too far – especially with its catch-all 'common plan or conspiracy' and 'murder' charges. But the Soviets were the first to claim that the Tribunal *did not go far enough* – in this case, for failing to target the orchestrators of Japan's bacteriological warfare programme in

[21] Ibid. [22] Ibid. [23] Garner (31 July 1947): FO 371/66554, TNA.

China. These Japanese germ warriors, like the German rocket scientists, had escaped into the arms of the Americans at the end of the war; the latter, after striking information-for-amnesty deals, shielded them from prosecution. The Soviets decided to convene the trial of the less senior figures – mostly military and medical personnel who had served at the Japanese human experimentation facilities at Harbin and Shanghai – after the Tribunal handed down its Majority Judgment. This served several purposes: as a riposte to Tokyo's equivocal judgment on Japan's crimes against the Soviets, as a gesture of goodwill to Mao's new government, and as a poke in the eye to Washington. If Tokyo was for the Allies, their logic ran, then Khabarovsk was for the true 'peace-loving peoples'.

At the trial itself, the Japanese defendants were charged with: 'Formation of special units for the preparation and prosecution of bacteriological warfare', 'Criminal experiments on human beings', 'Employment of the bacteriological weapon in the war against China' and 'Intensification of preparations for bacteriological warfare against the U.S.S.R'.[24] The first and fourth counts thus dealt with crimes that had been planned but not executed; the second and third with those that had actually been carried out.

Under the international jurisprudence of the time, 'criminal experiments on human brings' resulting in death were unlawful under the 1907 Hague Convention, which set out the duties of occupying armies, including the preservation of life, and under the 1929 Geneva Convention, which set out the duties of states towards prisoners of war. The charge of *employment* of bacteriological weapons against China was less clear-cut, however. While the 1925 'Geneva Protocol for the Prohibition of the Use in War of Asphyxiating, Poisonous or Other Gases, and of Bacteriological Methods of Warfare' dealt with their use, neither Japan nor China were parties to it.[25] The charges dealing with the *preparation* for bacteriological warfare against the Soviet Union had even less basis in international law: the 1925 Geneva Protocol did not address research on, or the development or stockpiling of, biological weapons. Furthermore, the Protocol, which had attracted reservations from the Soviet Union and British Commonwealth to the effect that they would not apply it against

[24] *Materials on the trial of former servicemen of the Japanese Army charged with manufacturing and employing bacteriological weapons* (Moscow: Foreign Languages Publishing House, 1950), pp. 9, 15, 22, 25.

[25] Protocol for the Prohibition of the Use in War of Asphyxiating, Poisonous or Other Gases, and of Bacteriological Methods of Warfare, signed 17 June 1925, entered into force on 8 February 1928, 94 LNTS, 65.

non-ratifiers, had prevented it from acquiring the status of customary international law.[26]

From the Soviets' point of view, the legal irregularities could not be allowed to undermine the purpose of the trial, which was to draw attention to those who were *not* standing in the dock. The prosecution stressed that the defendants in Khabarovsk, though entirely deserving of punishment, were not the most important players in the conspiracy to unleash a bacteriological cataclysm against the world. Those most responsible, they argued, were the leaders of Japan's biological warfare programme, and their political master, the Emperor Shōwa – all of whom had been rendered untouchable by the Americans. The defence, assisted by the defendants themselves, embellished the prosecutors' arguments, suggesting that they had merely been following the orders of their superiors, who, in a chain of command leading right up to the Imperial Throne, had been the true instigators and organisers of the conspiracy. These ostensibly legal arguments, advanced in the Khabarovsk courtroom, acquired political form a month later, when the Soviets proposed to their former Western allies that they jointly convene an international tribunal to try the Emperor and four leading figures in the biological warfare programme for crimes against humanity. As Alvary Gascoigne, the British Ambassador in Tokyo, suggested, the Soviets' motives were

> First and foremost to distract the attention of the Japanese people from the much publicised action of the Allied Council for Japan calling for the repatriation of some 375,000 Japanese prisoners from Siberia . . . Secondly to make the United States and Great Britain unpopular in the eyes of the Chinese Communists by reason of the former's refusal to comply with the Russian request [to indict the Emperor and others] . . . Thirdly to give the Japanese Communist party something to bite on, and further to test their allegiance to Moscow.[27]

The trials convened in China some seven years later were also designed to send signals to Japan. As Ōsawa Takeshi explains in his chapter, the People's Republic's 'lenient treatment' policy towards alleged Japanese war criminals drew inspiration from earlier policies, dating back to the 1920s, of magnanimity towards captured Kuomintang troops, and acquired its most developed form in the mid-1950s, when Zhou Enlai began to court Tokyo with the aim of pulling Japan out of the embrace of

[26] See, for example, New Zealand Department of External Affairs, 'Note concerning Soviet request for International Military Tribunal' (28 April 1950), p. 2: EA W2619 106/3/37 Pt. 1, National Archives of New Zealand (NANZ).

[27] Gascoigne to Foreign Office (6 February 1950), pp. 1–2: EA W2619 106/3/37 Pt. 1, NANZ.

the United States. Many of the Japanese prisoners were Kwantung Army officers and senior officials who had been swept up by the Soviet forces in Manchuria in 1945 and held in the Soviet Far East before being sent back to China in 1950. Other Japanese remnants had fought on in China as members of anti-communist militias during the civil war period ending in 1949. The Chinese held them for years without charge or trial, before finally deciding to use them to prop open the door to dialogue with Japan.

There was disagreement within the top echelons of the Chinese Communist Party and government about how many people to indict, and what prison terms to dispense (this before any case was brought to court). Some officials were also concerned that the prisoners' confessions alone might not provide sufficient basis for prosecution. It was then that Mei Ru'ao, the former Chinese judge at the Tokyo Tribunal, stepped into the debate. His advice was to avoid getting tied up by the legal technicalities, and to simply declare that Beijing was releasing most of the prisoners as a grand political gesture. (One cannot help but be reminded of Philander Knox's response to Teddy Roosevelt's attempts to justify irregularities over the Panama Canal: 'Oh, Mr. President, do not let so great an achievement suffer from any taint of legality!')[28]

After some senior officials raised the possibility that the Chinese public might be hostile to the 'lenient treatment' of their former tormentors, the Japanese prisoners were paraded around the countryside to sell the policy. Unsurprisingly, these prisoners apologised profusely for their actions. They also offered up an explanation that accorded conveniently with the Chinese government's propagandist priorities: that they had been raised in a culture of militarism, but had seen the error of their ways and would now campaign against the vestiges of that culture in their homeland. Many of the prisoners were consequently released and repatriated, but despite the efforts of the Chinese authorities to nurture better relations with Japan, the rapprochement lasted barely a year longer, and was eventually swept away by Kishi Nobusuke and the Great Leap Forward.

The superior orders defence

The most common defence raised in war crimes trials convened at the end of the Asia-Pacific War was obedience to superior orders. Before the

[28] D. McCullough, *The path between the seas: the creation of the Panama Canal, 1870–1914* (New York: Simon and Schuster, 1977), p. 383.

war, the traditional doctrinal emphasis had been on *respondeat superior* – 'let the master answer' – which, by imposing responsibility on the commander, had the effect of screening the subordinate from responsibility. But from 1942 onwards, as German and Japanese atrocities escalated, the Allies began to consider trying subordinates as well. The initial impetus for the recasting of the doctrine seems to have come from the United States. In February 1943, the American Judge Advocate General for the European Theatre Colonel Edward C. Betts sounded out the British Judge Advocate General Sir Henry MacGeagh about the possibility of amending their respective military manuals. MacGeagh's view, shared by the other departments' Law Officers, was that superior orders were no longer a defence, 'except possibly where an accused was a mere automaton such as a member of a firing squad who really had no discretion and would himself probably be shot if he disobeyed the order'.[29]

The Moscow Declaration of November 1943, and the opening of the trial against three German defendants and a local collaborator in the city of Kharkov the following month, were further spurs to action. When dealing with their own military personnel, the Soviets adhered to a strictly orthodox line: orders were orders. As Section 8 of the Disciplinary Code of the Red Army (1940) stated, 'The order of the commander and the superior is law for the subordinate. He must execute it without reservation, precisely and in time. Failure to execute the order is a crime.'[30] But when prosecuting the German defendants at the Kharkov trial, they expressly excluded the superior orders defence from consideration. As the jurist Aron Trainin explained, criminal orders, unlike military orders, were not to be obeyed: 'An order to cast women and children into the fire ... is essentially *not a military order*; it is an *instigation to evil-doing*.'[31]

The British and Americans followed suit. As MacGeagh wrote to the British Solicitor-General David Maxwell Fyfe in December 1943, 'I am bring pressed now from various quarters for the Manual to be appropriately amended ... Sorry to be a nuisance, but in view of the Kharkov

29 MacGeagh to Betts (22 February 1943): LCO 53/78, TNA.

30 Section 8 of the Disciplinary Code of the Red Army (1940), stated, 'The order of the commander and the superior is law for the subordinate. He must execute it without reservation, precisely and in time. Failure to execute the order is a crime.' Quoted in: Office of Strategic Services Research and Analysis Branch, 'Soviet intentions to punish war criminals' (30 April 1945), p. 49: William J. Donovan Papers, Cornell Law Library's Donovan Nuremberg Trials Collection.

31 Ibid. Original emphasis.

trials I think it is quite time we got this matter put right.'[32] Hersch Lauterpacht was asked to draft an amendment to Paragraph 443, which was inserted into the British *Manual of military law* in April 1944. As Cheah Wui Ling explains in her chapter on the British-run trials in Singapore, this amendment was the touchstone for the debates about criminal liability of the low- and middle-ranking Japanese personnel accused of committing war crimes in Burma, Borneo, Malaya, Singapore, the Andaman and Nicobar islands and other parts of Southeast Asia.

The recalibration of 'superior orders' also led to the revision in November 1944 of Article 347 in the American *Basic field manual: rules of land warfare*. This Article had previously stated: 'Individuals of the armed forces will not be punished for these offences [war crimes] in case they are committed under the orders or sanction of their government or commanders.'[33] This was rescinded and replaced with Article 345.1, which stated,

> Individuals and organizations who violate the accepted laws and customs of war may be punished therefor. However, the fact that the acts complained of were done pursuant to order of a superior or government sanction may be taken into consideration in determining culpability, either by way of defense or in mitigation of punishment. The person giving such orders may also be punished.[34]

Thereafter, as Bing Bing Jia explains in his chapter on superior orders, the doctrine has developed along two different lines within international criminal law. One of these, arising out of the Nuremberg Charter and later endorsed by the ad hoc tribunals on former Yugoslavia and Rwanda, upheld the idea that superior orders could not be considered as a defence, but only as a mitigating factor in sentencing. The other, revived by the International Criminal Court, readmitted the idea that superior orders might be considered a defence in some circumstances.

Whichever line was pursued, the delegates at the negotiations that created the founding charters of these courts, from the 1945 London Conference to the 1998 Rome Conference, were compelled to acknowledge three overlapping concerns on the issue of superior orders: the obligation to uphold the laws of war, the desire to maintain military

32 MacGeagh to Maxwell Fyfe (21 December 1943): LCO 53/78, TNA.

33 Rule 347 in War Department, *Basic field manual: rules of land warfare* (Washington, DC: US Government Printing Office, 1940).

34 Rule 345.1 (15 November 1944), ibid.

discipline through obedience to orders, and the need to avoid injustice to the accused. Sometimes the task of striking a balance between these considerations proved too great. Just after the Vietnam War, for example, delegates drafting the Additional Protocols to the Geneva Conventions – while recognising that an international standard on superior orders would be an improvement on the vagaries of the domestic penal laws of a detaining power – were still unable to agree a suitable formula. They eventually voted out the article dealing with superior orders, leaving a gaping hole in the laws of war concerning the liability of subordinates.

Trying Khmer Rouge leaders

While the Geneva negotiations were in progress, the Khmer Rouge took power in Democratic Kampuchea. The Vietnamese ousted them in January 1979, and eight months later the new Cambodian government convened the People's Revolutionary Tribunal to try Pol Pot and Ieng Sary *in absentia* for crimes committed by the regime. Genocide charges were still exceedingly rare at the time, making the trial a highly unusual event. Despite this, the Tribunal has been almost completely overlooked in the legal literature (in marked contrast to the much-discussed first genocide trial, of Adolf Eichmann in 1961).

The two Khmer Rouge leaders were charged with instigating and committing genocide, but, as Tara Gutman argues in her chapter, the case against them was not as straightforward as it might seem, because the regime's crimes did not fit neatly into the genocide mould.[35] Although Buddhist, Muslim, and Vietnamese and Chinese communities suffered greatly from their actions, the Khmer Rouge tended to prioritise the elimination of *social classes* over the 'national, ethnical, racial or religious' groups specified by the 1948 Genocide Convention.[36] Why, then, did the prosecution focus on genocide rather than on crimes against humanity, which was a more capacious charge with a lower threshold of intent? The most likely explanation is that genocide was codified by the aforementioned Convention, which, crucially, applied to crimes carried out 'in time of peace'.[37] By contrast, crimes against humanity had, at the

[35] Indictment, H.J. De Nike, J. Quigley and K.J. Robinson (eds.), *Genocide in Cambodia: documents from the trial of Pol Pot and Ieng Sary* (*Documents*) (Philadelphia: University of Pennsylvania Press, 2000), pp. 463–488.

[36] Article 1, Convention on the Prevention and Punishment of the Crime of Genocide: treaties.un.org.

[37] Ibid., Article 2.

Nuremberg and Tokyo tribunals, been explicitly linked with armed conflict. When the People's Revolutionary Tribunal was conceived in 1979 it was far from clear whether crimes against humanity had acquired the status of customary international law, and if it had, whether this 'war nexus' still existed. The latter question was no clearer more than a decade later, when both the Statute of the International Criminal Tribunal for former Yugloslavia and the *Tadić* Judgment suggested that the connection with armed conflict was still extant.[38] It was only when the ICTY Appeals Chamber disagreed that the link was broken.[39]

The People's Revolutionary Tribunal clearly denied the defendants a fair trial – there was, for example, no presumption of innocence and few of the usual protections. Even so, some of the criticisms of the proceedings have been superficial. Common law commentators, for example, have fixed on the defendants' absence from court,[40] while failing to acknowledge that French civil law, from which Cambodian law is derived, admits *in absentia* trials. Others drew attention to the weakness of the defence, citing in particular the speech of the American defence lawyer Hope R. Stevens (not, as they assume, a female advocate, but the New York–based pan-Africanist lawyer, well known for taking on civil rights cases, who originally hailed from the West Indies).[41] Whatever the flaws of the speech, the defence had little, if any, exculpatory material to work with: the defendants were absent and their crimes were all too present. Given this, they might have challenged the jurisdiction of the court, challenged the genocide charge or attempted to mitigate punishment on grounds of superior orders. In the event, they admitted the accused's responsibility for genocide but tilted towards the last strategy

38 Article 5, Updated Statute of the International Criminal Tribunal for the Former Yugoslavia, September 2009 (originally adopted by Security Council Resolution 827 on 25 May 1993), stating with respect to crimes against humanity that the Tribunal 'shall have the power to prosecute persons responsible for the following crimes when committed in armed conflict'; *Prosecutor* v. *Tadić*, IT-94-1-T, Trial Chamber Judgment (7 May 1997), par. 659, stating, 'the act [crimes against humanity] must not be taken for purely personal reasons unrelated to the armed conflict'.

39 *Prosecutor* v. *Tadić*, IT-94-1-A, Appeals Chamber Judgment (15 July 1999), par. 251: 'A nexus between the accused's acts and the armed conflict is not required, as is instead suggested by the Judgement.'

40 See, for example, S. Luftglass, 'Crossroads in Cambodia: the United Nation's responsibility to withdraw involvement from the establishment of a Cambodian tribunal to prosecute the Khmer Rouge', *Virginia Law Review* 90 (2004), 902.

41 See, for example, C. Etcheson, *After the Killing Fields: lessons from the Cambodian genocide* (Praeger: Westport, CT, 2005), p. 14; P.H. Maguire, *Facing death in Cambodia* (New York: Columbia University Press, 2013), p. 66.

by trying to portray the defendants as dancing to the tune of 'the false socialist leaders of fascist China'.[42] Perhaps, as one commentator has speculated, they were following the brief of an East German advisor to the Cambodian government.[43]

If the People's Revolutionary Tribunal was the unsound sequel to the Eichmann trial, it was also the overlooked prequel to the Extraordinary Chambers in the Courts of Cambodia (ECCC). This latter court, established in 2006 at the behest of the United Nations and the Cambodian government, was intended to call to account Khmer Rouge leaders and those most responsible for the atrocities committed under the regime. A central plank of the prosecution's strategy was joint criminal enterprise – the mode of liability *de nos jours*. Deriving from common law, and first articulated in *Prosecutor* v. *Tadić*, this doctrine assumes three forms, which have the same *actus reus* elements but different *mens rea* requirements. It was the third form of joint criminal enterprise that aroused particular concern at the ECCC. In this, the *mens rea* requirement is satisfied if the accused not only intended to participate in and further the group's criminal purpose but did so despite having *foreseen* that further crimes would be committed beyond the scope of the common plan. As Neha Jain explains in her analysis of the JCE jurisprudence at the ECCC, the Pre-Trial Chamber concluded that the sources relied on by *Tadić* were insufficient to establish its existence in customary international law at the time the crimes were committed in the late 1970s.[44]

This repudiation of the third form was grist to the mill of those who have questioned the efficacy of the joint criminal enterprise doctrine in capturing the conduct and intent of those who commit collective crimes. As Nina Jørgensen indicates in her chapter about the deployment of latter-day modes of liability in Asia, some have suggested that a better approach might be co-perpetratorship – another method for ascribing liability when more than one person commits a crime. As well as its intrinsic merits, co-perpetratorship, which arises out of civil law (unlike JCE, which draws on common law traditions), is particularly useful in jurisdictions such as Cambodia, where it is already available under domestic law.

[42] Closing Argument of Hope R. Stevens, *Documents*, p. 507.

[43] H. De Nike, 'East Germany's legal advisor to the 1979 tribunal in Cambodia', *Searching for the Truth* (Phnom Penh: Documentation Center of Cambodia, 2nd quarter, 2008), 43.

[44] *Nuon et al.*, 002/19-09-2007-ECCC-OCIJ, Pre-Trial Chamber Decision on the Appeals against the Co-Investigative Judges Order on Joint Criminal Enterprise (JCE) (20 May 2010), par. 83.

The Bangladesh experience

The trials in Bangladesh grew out of the poisoned soil of the 1971 war of independence, when Pakistan attempted to prevent the secession of its eastern province, and millions were killed or displaced. Once the Pakistan Army had surrendered to Indian forces in December, the new leader of Bangladesh, Mujibur Rahman, hoping to stop the bloodshed and prevent further communal violence, proposed two sets of trials: one to deal with Pakistanis accused of committing international crimes, and the other to deal with local collaborators. Bangladesh eventually yielded to international pressure to forego the trials of Pakistanis in return for Pakistan's recognition of Bangladesh, but the trials of collaborators went ahead. The current trials, which deal with citizens of Bangladesh accused of orchestrating international crimes at the behest of the Pakistani forces in 1971, can be seen as the completion of the earlier project.

As early as February 1972, just a month or so after Pakistan's surrender, the provisional government in Bangladesh was already planning to establish an international tribunal to try leading Pakistani figures. They envisaged genocide charges (although Bangladesh was not yet a signatory of the Genocide Convention), and *in absentia* trials of, for example, former Pakistani President Yahya Khan and General Tikka Khan.[45] The following month it approached, among others, Niall MacDermot, the British Secretary-General of the International Commission of Jurists, for further advice. In a meeting with the Minister of Law Kamal Hossein, and in a memorandum produced by the Commission, MacDermot urged the establishment of an international court loosely modelled on the Nuremberg Tribunal, which he thought would carry greater authority than a domestic one.[46] Yet he cautioned against following Nuremberg too closely by allowing *in absentia* proceedings, which he thought would deter foreign lawyers from taking part.[47] In reality, the formation of the court, which would have been established by Presidential decree, would have more closely resembled the Tokyo Tribunal (decreed by Douglas MacArthur) than Nuremberg (convened jointly by the four Allies). But MacDermot's general advice appeared to

[45] Walker to Davidson, 'International Commission of Jurists' (22 February 1972): FCO 37/1056, TNA.

[46] Garvey (Delhi) (16 March 1972): FCO 37/1056, TNA; International Commission of Jurists, 'Memorandum on the trial of war criminals in Bangladesh' (c. March 1972), pp. 1, 2: FCO 37/1056, TNA.

[47] Ibid., p. 3.

have been heeded, and Dhaka moved towards what one British official dubbed the 'Asian Nuremberg'.[48]

The first step was to draw up the court's charter, entitled 'War Crimes Tribunal Order, 1972'. This was designed to provide the legal framework for the trials of Pakistani civilian and military officials in the custody of Bangladesh, plus another 1,500 or so Pakistani officers and men in the custody of India (including two leading figures: Major-General Rao Farman Ali and Lieutenant-General Abdullah Khan Niazi).[49] Draft Article 2 stated that the government would appoint five judges – it was intended, though not stated within, that two would be from Bangladesh, and three from elsewhere.[50] Thereafter, the Order followed the template set down at Nuremberg, by, for example, denying state immunity and superior orders as defences, encompassing organisations as well as individuals, and allowing for trials *in absentia* and the death penalty. The charges set out in Article 6 of the Nuremberg Charter – namely, crimes against peace, war crimes, crimes against humanity and 'common plan or conspiracy' – were transferred wholesale into draft Article 10, with a few tweaks to bring them in line with the Bangladesh situation. Additional paragraphs were inserted into the draft Article after 'crimes against humanity', which read, verbatim:

> (d) Genocide namely, offences committed in violation of the provisions of the Convention on the Prevention and punishment of the Crime of Genocide (1948) and also in violation of the United Nations Human Rights, 1946.[51]
>
> (e) Wilful destruction of public and private property, wanton destruction of cities, towns, and villages, and any other acts of destruction and devastation aimed at crippling the economy of Bangladesh.[52]

In May 1972, the Bangladeshi barrister M.S. Ali gave a copy of the draft charter to Gerald Draper, a British specialist in humanitarian law, who had previously advised the independence movement on Mujibur Rahman's imprisonment in Pakistan. While Draper was willing to comment on legal questions arising from the draft, he was prepared to offer

48 Sutherland, 'Bangladesh war crimes' (29 March 1972): FCO 37/1056, TNA.

49 The 1,500 figure, later much reduced, appears in Garvey (Delhi) (30 March 1972): FCO 37/1056, TNA.

50 Draft 'Order for constitution of war crimes tribunal' (c. May 1972): FO 37/1056, TNA; Doble (16 June 1972): FO 37/1056, TNA.

51 This may refer to the 1948 Universal Declaration of Human Rights.

52 Draft 'Order for constitution of war crimes tribunal' (c. May 1972): FO 37/1056, TNA.

strategic advice to Bangladesh only in so far as it accorded with Foreign Office policy. (Because of its own role at Nuremberg, the United Kingdom could not publicly oppose a tribunal, but was privately opposed to Bangladesh's convening one because it would impose more strain on relations with Pakistan.)[53] Draper thus advised Ali that convening a tribunal would be 'unwise'.[54] On legal questions, he cautioned that the cases must be watertight, and that, given that the war was not of an international character, charges of international crimes might not be sustained.[55] Another relevant question was whether the crimes of genocide and crimes against humanity, which would be heard before a hybrid court rather than a domestic one, had acquired the status of customary international law by the time the alleged offences were committed in 1971. (As we have seen, this question continues to exercise legal minds at the ECCC, which addresses crimes committed a few years later.)

While this discussion was in progress the other trial programme, dealing with collaborators, was being put into place. These trials played an important role in establishing the credentials of the provisional government led by the Awami League, but they also attracted international criticism on legal grounds. Seventy-three 'special tribunals' were set up to try those who had collaborated with the old regime or had, in support of it, perpetrated crimes such as murder, rape and arson. Their operation was governed by the 'Bangladesh Collaborators (Special Tribunal) Order, 1972' (decreed by the President on 24 January 1972, but backdated to 26 March 1971). The Collaborators Order, like the aforementioned 'War Crimes Tribunal Order, 1972', seemed to be inspired by the Nuremberg Charter. The Preamble made explicit reference to international crimes, including crimes against humanity and the crime of 'waging war' (a component of the 'crimes against peace' charge), as well as to the accused's liability as an individual or as a member of an organisation:

> Whereas certain persons, *individually or as members of organisations* directly or indirectly, have been collaborators of the Pakistan Armed forces . . . and have aided or abetted the Pakistan Armed forces of occupation *in committing genocide and crimes against humanity and in committing atrocities* . . . and have otherwise aided or co-operated with or acted in the interest of the Pakistan Armed forces of occupation or contributed by any act, word or sign towards maintaining, sustaining, strengthening,

[53] 'War crimes in Bangladesh' (20 June 1972): FCO 37/1056, TNA.

[54] Draper to Ellison (29 May 1972): FCO 37/1056, TNA.

[55] Draper to Ali, 'Bangladesh war crimes trials' (c. May 1972), pp. 2, 3: FCO 37/1056, TNA.

> supporting or furthering the illegal occupation of Bangladesh by the Pakistan Armed forces or have *waged war or aided or abetted in waging war* against the People's Republic of Bangladesh.[56]

While the figures differ, an authoritative source, Justice F.K.M. Abdul Munim, indicated that from 24 January to 13 December 1972, forty thousand people were investigated, twenty thousand were charged and taken into custody and less than a thousand people were convicted (with the right of appeal).[57] As a British diplomat reported on 7 December, 'The sentences so far hav[e] not been savage. Not one execution has yet taken place.'[58] Some trials involved very senior figures. On 20 November, for example, Abdul Motaleb Malik, the former civilian Governor of East Pakistan, and his Minister of Law, Jasmuddin Ahmed, were both sentenced to 'transportation' for life. Malik was indicted for waging war against Bangladesh, collaborating with the Pakistan Army and 'creating hatred and disaffection'.[59] The Judge, Abdul Hannan Chowdhury, was persuaded neither by his claim that, like other officials, he had been operating under compelling circumstances, nor by his argument that he had resigned his post and fled to the 'neutral' Hotel Continental, and was thus protected by the Geneva Conventions.[60] Malik was found guilty on all charges, but he was spared the death penalty on grounds of advanced age and his past service. As he was convicted under Article 2(b)(iii) of the amended Collaborators Order, criminalising those who 'waged war or abetted in waging war against the People's Republic of Bangladesh',[61] his case provides a rare post-Tokyo example of someone sentenced for what was in effect a 'crime against peace'.

Most of the other defendants were (according to Justice Munim) members of paramilitary groups such as the Razakars, Al-Badr or Al-Shams – which the acting British Ambassador James Davidson described as 'the local equivalent to SS auxiliaries'.[62] This appeared to be borne out by the first 'collaborator' case to be heard. On 8 June 1972, Chikon Ali was accused of enlisting as a Razakar and was sentenced to death for his part in murder, looting, arson and rape.[63] As this case demonstrates,

[56] Bangladesh Collaborators (Special Tribunal) Order, 1972, p. 1: FCO 37/1058, TNA.

[57] Golds (Dhaka) (13 December 1972): FCO 37/1057, TNA.

[58] Golds (Dhaka) (7 December 1972): FCO 37/1057, TNA.

[59] For slightly differing accounts, see 'Time of trials', *Economist* (25 November 1972), p. 51; and Cumming to Millington (21 November 1972): FO 37/1057, TNA.

[60] Cumming to Millington (21 November 1972): FO 37/1057, TNA.

[61] Bangladesh Collaborators (Special Tribunal) Order, 1972, p. 2: FCO 37/1058, TNA.

[62] Davidson to Sutherland (11 December 1972): FO 370/1058, TNA.

[63] Golds (Dhaka) (12 June 1972): FCO 37/1056, TNA.

these special tribunals played an anomalous role: on the one hand, the 'collaborator' label did not fully convey the magnitude of the crimes committed by those on trial; but on the other hand, without the 'collaborator' label, it was not clear why the accused were not simply charged in ordinary criminal courts under the Bangladesh Penal Code.

At the time, the Awami League provisional government was reluctant to allow the defendants to be represented by foreign counsel, on the ostensible grounds that membership of the Bar in Bangladesh was restricted to nationals. On 17 November 1972, the British MP Dingle Foot, apparently instructed by a Pakistani organisation to defend Malik, arrived in Dhaka without a visa, and instead of being admitted (as he clearly expected), was sent on his way.[64] Foot's junior, Robert Maclennan MP, was admitted, but not allowed to represent Malik. It was Maclennan who sounded an early warning about the legal status of the proceedings, reporting to the British Foreign Office that there was 'little law in these trials' and that the local Bar was 'rightly agitated about them'.[65] Of the Collaborators Order, Maclennan declared

> a) that it was retrospective; b) that the burden of proof in many cases was on the accused; c) that rules of evidence were very sketchy; d) that it was all-embracing, eg: even a speech in support of the Pakistan government constituted an offence leading to a minimum of three years imprisonment.[66]

The following year, the government passed the 'International Crimes (Tribunals) Act, 1973'. This too bore the hallmarks of the Nuremberg Charter: it covered crimes against peace, war crimes and crimes against humanity (as well as genocide and the all-embracing 'any other crimes under international law').[67] This law is the basis upon which the current tribunals have been constituted – the purest modern manifestation of the Nuremberg project. As Rafiqul Islam points out in his chapter, in 2008 the Awami League campaigned on and later won an election on the promise to convene trials against prominent Bangladeshis implicated in the 1971 bloodbath. While acknowledging that delayed justice is better than no justice at all, the League is nevertheless clearly attempting to use the trials to enhance its own legitimacy. Domestic critics point out that many of the present-day defendants are prominent members of

[64] 'War crimes in Bangladesh' (c. November 1972): FCO 37/1057, TNA.

[65] Maclennnan to Douglas-Home (23 November 1972): FCO 37/1057, TNA.

[66] Green to Stuart (17 October 1972), p. 2: FCO 37/1057, TNA.

[67] The International Crimes (Tribunals) Act, 1973: bdlaws.minlaw.gov.bd.

conservative Islamist parties, which suggests that the government might be motivated as much by a desire to silence its political opponents as by concern to right previous wrongs.

The Bangladesh trials have also attracted international criticism on legal grounds from both foreign governments and non-governmental organisations. Embellishing themes raised earlier by Robert Maclennan, these critics point out the shortcomings of the 1973 Act, the procedural inadequacies of the courts, and the detrimental effect on the rights of the accused. In his chapter, Abdur Razzaq, the senior defence counsel for some of the defendants, describes some of the other twists and turns, touching on issues such as 'effective control' in command responsibility doctrine, 'significant' contribution to joint criminal enterprise, and the relationship between customary international law and local statutes.

For better or worse, the trials in Asia have operated as laboratories for international law. Under their auspices, legal cultures – both local and imported – have cross-fertilised and mutated. Some, such as Tokyo's charge of 'murder', immediately expired. Others, such as 'conspiracy' and 'being concerned with', evolved into new forms. And a few, such as 'command responsibility', grew and prospered. Although most Asian states remain unenthusiastic about international, hybrid or regional tribunals, they look set to carry on convening their own trials on their own terms. In the process, new legal ideas will emerge and enter the bloodstream of international criminal law.

1

Treasonable conspiracies at Paris, Moscow and Delhi

The legal hinterland of the Tokyo Tribunal

KIRSTEN SELLARS

It is widely held that the idea of transplanting 'conspiracy' from domestic law into international criminal law was first conceived by an American working in the US War Department in the final year of the Second World War. It is true that in September 1944, Lt-Colonel Murray Bernays began to construct the framework for a case against the Nazi Party's top echelons, encompassing the orchestration of crimes against both Allied nationals and Axis civilians. It is also true that Bernays, inspired by a Californian bootlegging case, *Marino* v. *United States*, found a unifying concept in the common law doctrine of criminal conspiracy. He suggested that the proposed tribunal should try, first, the Nazi leaders and, second, Nazi Party organisations for participating in a vast conspiracy to 'commit murder, terrorism and the destruction of peaceful populations'.[1] Even though it required a leap of the imagination to equate Californian bootlegging with German extermination policies, and even though jurists would later criticise Bernays' approach for trivialising Nazism by equating it with gangsterism, the idea was transported to the London Conference and incorporated into the Nuremberg Charter.

Yet this account is not the whole truth. It is merely a part – and an atypical part at that – of a much bigger story that had begun a full quarter of a century earlier. Discussion about internationalised modes of liability had first arisen during the closing phase of the First World War, when French lawyers had grappled with the problem of prosecuting Wilhelm II and his circle; and it developed further during the

[1] Bernays (15 September 1944), reprinted in B.F. Smith, *The American road to Nuremberg: the documentary record 1944–1945* (Stanford: Hoover Institution Press, 1982), p. 36.

Second World War, when Soviet lawyers contemplated similar actions with respect to Hitler and his minsters. Both groups nursed the idea of applying the concept of complicity to international crimes, and drew their ideas from domestic security law (not the revenue law that had inspired Bernays): the French borrowing concepts from the 1918 treason trials of the '*Bonnet Rouge* gang' and Louis Malvy, and the Soviets from the Moscow trials of the 'old Bolsheviks' in 1936–1938. In their view, international criminal law was simply a projection of criminal law into the international arena, with the attendant theories of liability being transmitted from one to another. This civil law approach made more sense than the Americans' conceptual leap from *Marino* to the Nuremberg Charter, and more accurately reflected the climate of realism that gave rise to international criminal law.

Why did they look to security law in particular? Domestic security law and international criminal law both arose out of a singular preoccupation with security – the former with the punishment of offences against the state, and the latter with the punishment of offences against the international order. For this reason, in the formative years of international criminal law, the prosecuting powers almost instinctively created a hierarchy of international crimes, with the crime of aggression at the top (because this crime most directly threatened the global order), and the crimes purportedly devolving from aggression – namely, war crimes and crimes against humanity – in a supporting role. In addition, domestic security law offered enticing models for potential international modes of liability, such as complicity and conspiracy, which enabled prosecutors to tie civilian and military leaders into crimes planned by groups of people or carried out by subordinates. What can be seen, then, is the transposition of the law governing crimes against the security of the state – *treason* – into international criminal law, and the emergence of the idea that international crimes represented *international treason* against the global order.

Trying the ex-Kaiser

The threads of domestic and international security were first drawn together in the closing months of the First World War. In November 1918, David Lloyd George and Georges Clemenceau publicly launched the idea of trying the just-abdicated Kaiser for aggression and war crimes. Thus, a few weeks after the Armistice on 11 November, Lloyd George, electioneering for his coalition government, declared,

> The Kaiser must be prosecuted. The war was a crime. Who doubts that? It was a frightful, a terrible crime. It was a crime in the way in which it was planned, in the deliberate wantonness with which it was provoked. It was also a crime in its action ... Surely the war was a crime![2]

This was a radical departure from the more traditional approach to the conduct of war embodied in the Geneva and Hague Conventions, and contained within it the innovative idea that embarking upon an aggressive war was a crime, for which a head of state could be held personally responsible. And yet this innovation was advanced entirely in the service of orthodoxy: the underwriting of the new post-war (and Prussian-free) *status quo* in Europe. As the author of a British Foreign Office telegram stated: 'justice requires that the Kaiser and his principal accomplices who designed and caused the War with its malignant purpose or who were responsible for the incalculable sufferings inflicted upon the human race during the war should be brought to trial and punished for their crimes.'[3] Moreover, 'it will be impossible to bring to justice lesser criminals ... if the arch-criminal, who for thirty years has proclaimed himself the sole arbiter of German policy, and has been so in fact, escapes condign punishment'.[4] The final and most important reason for prosecution derived from the entente's concern about the future security of Europe: 'the certainty of inevitable personal punishment for crimes against humanity and international right shall be a very important security against future attempts to make war wrongfully or to violate international law, and is a necessary stage in the development of the authority of a League of Nations.'[5]

When coming to this decision, the entente leaders were furnished with one of the first officially sanctioned legal reports making the case for the ex-Kaiser's indictment: Ferdinand Larnaude and Albert Geouffre de Lapradelle's *Examen de la responsibilité pénale de l'empereur Guillaume II*, produced under the auspices of the French War Ministry in November 1918. In it, the authors argued that Wilhelm II, who had exercised constitutional power until his abdication that same month, was criminally responsible for crimes committed over the course of the war. But under what jurisdiction could he be prosecuted? Believing domestic avenues to be closed to them, they turned to the international sphere. It was apparent to them that the old approaches to crimes of war – which

[2] 'Coalition policy defined, Mr. Lloyd George's pledges', *The Times* (6 December 1918), 9.

[3] Foreign Office to Washington and New York (2 December 1918): FO 608/247, The National Archives, United Kingdom (TNA).

[4] Ibid. [5] Ibid.

had emerged in response to the old conception of war 'as simply a means of political coercion'[6] – were no longer adequate. New legal instruments had to be created, and in the process, they declared, 'A new international law is born.'[7]

New law to meet changed circumstances

Of the proposed charges, the greatest departure from previous practice was the attempt to hold the ex-Kaiser responsible for embarking on a 'premeditated and unjust war'. Here, Larnaude and de Lapradelle made an intriguing link between existing domestic law and the proposed international law:

> Given that *the violation of the public peace of a state gives rise to the gravest of penalties*, it would not be understandable that an attack on the peace of the world might go unpunished. The corporeal responsibility of the emperor, if one might call it that, presents itself first and foremost, and we must seize upon it – as we emerge from war – lest we should fail to bring about from this new international law its most necessary consequences.[8]

This equating of 'the violation of the public peace of a state' with 'an attack on the peace of the world' is one of the first clear attempts to connect treason against the state with treason against the global order. At the time, the authors' reference to 'public peace' would have immediately called to mind a series of French court cases dealing with allegedly treasonable conspiracies with Germany during the war. These trials, instigated by Clemenceau and Léon Daudet, the royalist editor of *Action Française*, against leading Radical-Socialist politicians and the 'defeatist' anti-militarist movement, had already produced convictions. Paul Bolo and Émile-Joseph Duval, who had handled German funds, had been court-martialled and shot in mid-1918 for subsidising anti-war propaganda within France. And three people involved with the anarchist paper *Le Bonnet Rouge* had been sentenced to hard labour for complicity in treasonable attempts to undermine the war effort.

Larnaude and de Lapradelle would have been particularly interested in the trial of Louis Malvy, the once-powerful Radical-Socialist Minister of

[6] F. Larnaude and A. de Lapradelle, *Examen de la responsibilité pénale de l'empereur Guillaume II* (Paris: Ministère de la Guerre, November 1918), p. 12: data.decalog.net/enap1/liens/fonds/F8G90.pdf. Thanks to Julien Anglade for translating the report.

[7] Ibid. [8] Ibid., pp. 16–17. Emphasis added.

the Interior. After being publicly denounced, first by Clemenceau (who accused him of failing to stop the spread of 'abominable' left-wing propaganda among the troops[9]) and then by Daudet (who accused him of high treason and complicity in high treason), Malvy demanded that his parliamentary immunity be lifted so he might stand trial before his political peers – the Senate sitting as a high court – rather than a court martial.

At the Senate hearing, which began on 16 July 1918, the public prosecutor presented evidence that focused less on Malvy's personal activities and more on the Interior Ministry's financial support for *Le Bonnet Rouge*, his subordinates' refusal to arrest leading militants and pacifists, and their obstruction of others' efforts to curb their activities. All this, the prosecution claimed, had undermined public morale and army discipline, and had led to the mutinies of summer 1917. In the event, Malvy was convicted not of treason, but for actions that 'ignored, violated and betrayed his duty' as minister, amounting to the crime of 'forfeiture' – defined in Article 166 of the Penal Code as being 'any crime committed by a public functionary in the exercise of his functions'.[10] As a result, he was banished from France for five years, and lost his seat in the Chamber of Deputies. This sentence raised several intriguing possibilities that were later explored in international criminal law: first, that an official could be stripped of his immunity and held personally responsible for crimes committed in the name of the state; and second, that he could be found guilty not only for his own actions but also for those of subordinates whom he had failed to control.

Complicity in treason

Many of the treason charges brought at these trials alleged *complicity* between the defendants or between the defendants and the Germans, and this caught the attention of Larnaude and de Lapradelle, who contemplated charging the ex-Kaiser for complicity in plans to embark on war and orchestrate war crimes. They wrote,

> Criminologists might ask themselves if complicity – which . . . must entail *an abuse of power* constituting an incitement to commit a *special act* – can still be applied in regard to the German emperor who, manifestly, was only giving a general order. To which they will no doubt reply that, for

[9] 'German propaganda in France', *The Times* (24 July 1917), 6.

[10] 'Paris relieved by Malvy verdict', *New York Times* (8 August 1918), 8.

> complicity, the necessary and sufficient condition is the *relation between cause and effect* between the accomplice and the principal perpetrator, a relation that clearly exists between the order or directives emanating from the German emperor and the charges made against such-and-such officer or soldier within his troops: the leader of a band of brigands is their accomplice as soon as he gives the general order to commit theft, murders, set light or pillage, even if he hasn't specifically ordered this or that murder or arson.[11]

All the same, they admitted that there were difficulties in bringing complicity charges against groups of people for acts committed in the course of the war. Even if the entente powers managed to capture both the ex-Kaiser who had given the general orders and the military personnel who had carried them out, this might prove to be counterproductive, because 'we would only manage, and not without difficulty, to restrict the scope of [Wilhelm II's] personal responsibility by limiting it to a few specific cases, where in fact these cases are countless, and make him appear to be an accessory when in fact he holds a principal role'.[12]

There was one final lesson to be learned from Louis Malvy's trial. His case had been heard by the Senate, convened as a high court under the terms of Article 12 of the Constitutional Act, 16 July 1875, which states: 'Le Sénat peut être constitué en cour de justice par un décret du président de la République, rendu en conseil des ministres, pour juger toute personne prévenue d'attentat contre la sûreté de l'État.'[13] In other words, this was a special court constituted to deal with special 'political' crimes – those committed against the security of the state. Questions were raised during the Malvy proceedings about its status and jurisdiction. Did the Senate, convened as a court, have the status of a sovereign court? And if so, was it able to dispense justice without adhering strictly to the Penal Code? The answer was affirmative, because it deployed what *The Times* called the 'elastic procedure of French justice' by choosing not to deliver a verdict on Léon Daudet's initial charges of treason.[14] Instead, a verdict was delivered on the public prosecutor's charge (submitted after the trial had begun) of 'culpable negligence and criminal disregard of the duties of the Minster of the Interior'.[15] The wide jurisdictional latitude that the Senate granted itself did not go unnoticed. Larnaude and de Lapradelle, while contemplating a special international court to consider

[11] Larnaude and de Lapradelle, *Examen*, p. 9. Original emphases. [12] Ibid., p.10.
[13] Constitution de la IIIe République.
[14] 'The Malvy verdict', *The Times* (8 August 1918), 5.
[15] 'Malvy charges modified', *New York Times* (18 July 1918), 9.

special 'political' international crimes, drew the parallels between their enterprise and the handling of the Malvy 'affair':

> As to the sentence, we have to be sure that the rule of *nulla poena sine lege* only completely applies to internal criminal law as applicable to a common law crime. This rule bends to adapt itself to exceptional circumstances in public law, for instance, in its application to political issues. So it is that in France, in a recent affair, the Court of Justice was able to proclaim its sovereignty and draw from this sovereignty the discretionary powers to determine and choose the applicable sentence. This example is not unique ... Thus, if the various High Courts hold this right in the instance of important political issues, surely all the more reason for it to be recognised at an international level in the prosecution of important international trials.[16]

A few months after Malvy's exile, Clemenceau's and Daudet's campaign against 'defeatism' netted the biggest catch of all. On 29 October 1918, the French Senate went through the preliminaries of charging the former Radical Party Prime Minister Joseph Caillaux, along with another Deputy, Louis Loustalot, and his alleged accomplice, Paul Comby, with having conspired against the security of France. While these dramatic events, which eventually led to the prosecution and conviction of a former head of government, were taking place in Paris, Larnaude and de Lapradelle grappled with the unsettling implications of going even further and placing a *foreign* head of state on trial before an *international* court. This is perhaps why the two authors went only halfway to making the case for stripping him of his sovereign rights. On the one hand, they reasoned, the German emperor enjoyed the international rights of legal immunity, honours and precedence. On the other, he bore international responsibilities – '*Ubi emolumentum, ibi onus esse debet.*'[17] They did not proceed any further with this argument, instead leaving the reader to draw the logical conclusion: that in renouncing his responsibilities he thereby lost his privileges and could thus be compelled to account for himself in a court of law.

The creation of Article 227

When the entente powers convened at the Paris Peace Conference in January 1919 to deliberate over the peace terms with Germany, the members of the Council of Four – David Lloyd George, Georges

[16] Larnaude and de Lapradelle, *Examen*, pp. 22–23. [17] Ibid., p. 17.

Clemenceau, Woodrow Wilson and Vittorio Orlando – quarrelled over how to deal with the ex-Kaiser. Lloyd George and Clemenceau saw his disposal through the mechanism of a trial as being an essential component of the post-war settlement, while Wilson feared a trial would ignite a revolution in Germany (thereby necessitating his nation's further engagement in Europe) as well as establishing an unwelcome international precedent. Yet both desired European stability and a strictly ad hoc trial, and they were able to agree a statement on penalties, which provided the basis for Article 227 of the Versailles Treaty. This announced the formation of a 'special tribunal' to try the ex-Kaiser once the Netherlands had surrendered him for 'a supreme offence against international morality and the sanctity of treaties'.[18]

This Article summoned a gaseous cloud of morality and politics – 'international morality', 'international policy' and 'international undertakings'[19] – while carefully avoiding any reference to 'international law'. The modes of liability that might have linked the ex-Kaiser to the alleged crimes were of course left to the discretion of the prosecutors, while his punishment was left to the discretion of the judges. The legal basis on which they were expected to adjudicate remained an open question, for as the American Secretary of State Robert Lansing observed, 'Manifestly the tribunal . . . is not a court of legal justice, but rather an instrument of political power which is to consider the case from the viewpoint of high policy and to fix the penalty accordingly.'[20] But although this 'special tribunal' was never convened, the French trials of former politicians and their associates for treason at the end of the war had already proved what Lansing had tried to deny: that tribunals could be both courts of legal justice *and* instruments of political power. It was this beguiling combination that most attracted jurists when, in the depths of the Second World War, they returned to the idea of trying enemy leaders for international crimes.

[18] 'Outline suggested with regard to responsibility and punishment', signed by Clemenceau, Lloyd George, Orlando, Wilson and Saionji, undated, with cover note, Hankey to Dutasta (10 April 1919): FO 608/247, TNA. Emphasis added.

[19] Treaty of Peace between the Allied and Associated Powers and Germany (signed 28 June 1919, entered into force 10 January 1920), *Consolidated Treaty Series*, C. Parry (ed.) (Dobbs Ferry: Oceana Publications, 1969–1981), vol. 225, p. 285.

[20] R. Lansing, 'Some legal questions of the Peace Conference', *American Journal of International Law* 13 (1919), 647.

The renewed search for security

When the 'Big Three' Allied powers – the United States, Soviet Union and Britain – began to develop policies for dealing with the German and Japanese leaders after the conflict was over, their approach, as always, was governed by an overriding concern for security. This was most clearly illustrated by the Soviets, who during the war years gravitated towards the idea of a trial as a means of removing future threats to the Soviet Union. In the process, they proposed German criminal responsibility for aggression and war crimes, and also suggested the modes of liability through which they might be prosecuted.

The Soviets had first begun to consider the protections that international criminal law might afford them when they had been compelled to respond to the growing threats posed by Germany and Japan in the 1930s. Evgenii Pashukanis, director of the Institute of Soviet Construction and Law, along with his many followers, had hitherto advanced a 'negationist' approach to law. But Pashukanis' influence was waning, and, after his disgrace and execution in 1937, Andrei Vyshinskii (one of the architects of his downfall) assumed Pashukanis' post at the Institute. Vyshinskii was highly mindful of external security risks to the Soviet Union, and moved towards the idea of convening an international tribunal to try leaders of hostile powers, modelled on the 1936–1938 Moscow trials at which he had prosecuted Zinov'iev, Kamenev, Bukharin and scores of other 'old Bolsheviks' for treasonable conspiracies against the Soviet state. The modes of liability used at the Moscow trials for dealing with 'counter-revolutionary' crimes would later be transplanted into Nuremberg and Tokyo law to deal with German and Japanese 'crimes against peace'.

In July 1938, Vyshinskii set out his vision for the future of Soviet legal doctrine – both domestic and international – in a *Pravda* article entitled, 'About tasks of the Soviet socialist law science'.[21] He stated that his aim was to eliminate 'the consequences of the wrecking activities that were carried out by the despicable Trotskyite-Bukharin gang' in the field of the Soviet legal science.[22] This gang, Vyshinskii wrote, included Evgenii Pashukanis and Nikolai Krylenko, whose efforts 'were directed to prove

[21] A.I. Vyshinskii, 'O zadachakh nauki sovetskogo sotsialisticheskogo prava', *Pravda* (26 July 1938), 3. Thanks to Valentyna Polunina of the 'Asia-Europe' Cluster of Excellence, Heidelberg University, for her translation of, and assistance with, Vyshinskii's *Pravda* article and Trainin's book on complicity.

[22] Ibid.

that Soviet theory of law cannot and should not exist', and who was therefore responsible for 'the most shameless falsification of Marxism'.[23] He continued, 'Wreckers ranted that our law is not only moribund but also bourgeois. They implanted an idea of bourgeois law as the culminating point in the development of law.'[24]

This, he maintained, was wholly wrong. Whereas bourgeois legality brought stagnation and conservatism, socialist legality was 'a creative force promoting social development, helping toilers in their advance forward'.[25] So law not only continued to play an essential role in Soviet society, but it assumed its most developed form within it:

> [The] law gets its solid ground and its genuine development not in the heyday of bourgeois-capitalist relations but in the heyday of socialist relations. The era of socialism is the time of the greatest development of law and the greatest development of the rule of law; it is the triumph of law and legality.[26]

This ascendency of socialist law brought with it many benefits, including the legal instruments necessary for rooting out internal threats to Soviet society. The doctrine of complicity, in particular, had proved to be an extremely useful legal tool in the struggle against the alleged Trotskii-led conspiracies. Vyshinskii argued that this doctrine was neither, as some argued, merely a combination of criminal activities nor, as others claimed, a legal theory of only academic interest. Rather, he wrote,

> [It] plays a huge role in our circumstances, when the enemies of the Soviet people, vile agents of foreign intelligence services, are resorting to conspiratorial activities, organising the stinking criminal anti-Soviet underground. The vulgar understanding of complicity as a combination of criminal activities in the narrow sense of the term has outlived its time. Complicity has assumed a new and extremely urgent character as a form of political struggle.[27]

Vyshinskii stated that the forces hostile to socialism did not attempt to carry out their criminal activities in isolation, but instead tried to leverage their criminal efforts by joining forces with others through conspiracies. By the same token, the forces defending socialism did not just rely on the criminal law applicable to individuals, but were developing tools for

[23] Ibid. [24] Ibid.

[25] S. Kucherov, *The organs of Soviet administration of justice: their history and operation*, quoting from A.I. Vyshinskii, 'Revolutionary legality in the present period of socialist construction' (1932), p. 661.

[26] Vyshinskii, 'O zadachakh', 3. [27] Ibid., 4.

dealing with collective criminal enterprises – tools that could be applied in a practising lawyer's everyday work. So the doctrine was not just of theoretical interest but also of practical importance, 'arming practicing lawyers with a theoretical weapon needed in their judicial, prosecutorial and investigative activities'.[28]

Addressing the problem of *external* threats to the Soviet Union, Vyshinskii encouraged the development of a Soviet doctrine of international law, which should proceed from the 'leading role of the Leninist-Stalinist foreign policy in the struggle for peace, for collective security ... against the forces of reactionism, fascism and war'.[29] He argued that particular attention should be paid to the problem of international aggression, a definition of which, Vyshinskii reminded readers, had first been advanced by 'Soviet diplomacy'.[30] He also called for the formation of institutions to further the international struggle 'against terrorism, against international provocations, and against attempts to adapt international law to the needs and interests of fascist aggressors'.[31]

This approach, broadcast through *Pravda* from Vyshinskii's position as Procurator General, had been constructed over the previous five to six years. Originally a Menshevik, Vyshinskii spent the post-revolutionary period working his way up the Soviet judicial hierarchy, never wholly endorsing the negationist approach to the law espoused by other Soviet jurists during the upheavals of the late 1920s and early 1930s. Instead, he kept his powder dry, anticipating that sooner or later the regime would look to the law once again when it wished to consolidate its gains. It was not until 1932–1933, when the shockwaves caused by forced collectivisation had begun to diminish, that his moment finally arrived. By this time, Stalin was keen to limit the upheavals in the countryside and silence the many critics of his collectivisation policies. He was therefore particularly receptive to Vyshinskii's suggestions that the law – long derided by colleagues as the residue of bourgeois society – could play an important role as an instrument of social control. For the first time in years, the law mattered, and Vyshinskii set himself the task of using it to first sideline and then destroy more powerful figures on the judicial scene (including Evgenii Pashukanis and Nikolai Krylenko), thereby positioning himself as Stalin's oracle on the Soviet legal system.

From 1934 onwards, having softened the ground with a few speeches and articles about socialist legality, Stalin and Vyshinskii turned to the courts to destroy the political opposition. At the time, the 'old Bolshevik'

[28] Ibid. [29] Ibid. [30] Ibid. [31] Ibid.

critics of Stalin's regime had much to object to. As well as the chaos of the collectivisation period, the Communist Party's leadership was now openly sloughing off its Leninist legacy by entering alliances with capitalist powers, advocating 'socialism in one country', abandoning the bread-card system, accepting post-Stakhanov wage differentials, and resurrecting campaigns against abortion and divorce. But the pretext for the regime's judicial assault on the opposition ostensibly had nothing to do with these issues: instead it was the murder of Sergei Kirov, the Leningrad politician (who, had he lived, might have replaced Stalin), in December 1934, that opened the floodgates for the full-scale purge of all Stalin's foes, real or imagined.

The three Moscow 'purge' trials – conducted in 1936, 1937 and 1938 respectively – were by no means the first to convict people for political crimes against the Soviet state, but they were distinct from earlier trials in a number of ways. First, the regime used these trials to target people who were (or once had been) at the very pinnacle of the Party hierarchy; second, precisely *because* they were such senior figures it could be claimed that they posed uniquely grave threats to the Soviet state; and third, the regime broadcast the proceedings and verdicts widely in order to justify further repression and deter future dissent.

The first trial, of the 'Trotskyite-Zinovievite Terrorist Centre', opened on 19 August 1936 to try sixteen oppositionists. Two of the defendants, Grigorii Zinov'iev and Lev Kamenev, were former Politburo members who, after forming the 'New Opposition', had been expelled from the Party in 1927. Allegedly inspired by the exiled Leon Trotskii, all were accused of conspiring to commit treason and terrorism – namely, plotting to assassinate Stalin and his ministers (Kirov purportedly being the first) in order to seize power for themselves. The second, more ambitious and wide-ranging trial, of the 'Anti-Soviet Trotsky Centre', opened on 23 January 1937 to try seventeen recanted oppositionists, including economic leaders such as Y.L. Pyatakov and Y.A. Livshitz, Commissar of heavy industry and Deputy Commissar of the railways. As well as being charged with conspiring to commit treason and terrorism, they were also accused of espionage, wrecking and diversion, with the aim of restoring capitalism in the Soviet Union. The final, most expansive trial of all, of the 'Anti-Soviet Bloc of Rights and Trotskyites', opened on 2 March 1938 to try twenty-one defendants, including surviving critics from the 'Right Opposition', such as Lenin's deputy Aleksei Rykov and *Pravda* editor Nikolai Bukharin. At this last trial, all were tried for conspiring to commit treason, terrorism, espionage, wrecking and diversion, as well as for undermining the Soviet Union's military power and prompting foreign states – namely, Germany, Japan, Britain and Poland – to attack it.[32]

The transcripts of the proceedings, translated into a number of foreign languages, chronicle how the defendants confessed to extraordinary and outrageous crimes, denounced former colleagues and fellow defendants, and begged for hard labour instead of the bullet. But behind these stormy spectacles, methodical, even pedantic, didactic forces were at work. The educational function of the trial was never in doubt, for as the jurist Max Radin pointed out at the time, almost all of the defendants had admitted their guilt at the outset so there was really no need to go through a trial process simply to establish their guilt all over again.[33]

At each successive trial, the prosecution, led by Vyshinskii, alleged ever-widening circles of conspiracy directed against the Soviet Union, which demanded a response from the regime. There was, of course, some truth in this – Germany and Japan were indeed conspiring against the Soviet Union – but this truth was refracted through the prism of the trials, which were designed to eviscerate domestic opponents as well. So it was alleged at the first trial that Leon Trotskii (by then in exile) and a handful of the defendants had contacts with Gestapo agents; by the second, that more defendants had taken instructions from the German and Japanese intelligence agencies; and by the third, that almost all of the defendants were working hand in glove with the German, Japanese, Polish and British intelligence services.

The doctrine of complicity played a central role at each trial. At the first two, the prosecution relied on the 1926 Russian Criminal Code (amended in 1930). Article 17 outlined the basic concept of complicity, which identified three types of participant: 'instigators', 'accomplices' and 'perpetrators':

> Measures of social protection of a juridical-reformatory character are applied not only to persons who have committed the crime (the perpetrators), but also to persons who have participated in it (instigators and accomplices).
>
> Those persons are considered instigators who have induced the perpetrator to commit the crime.
>
> Those persons are considered accomplices who have contributed toward the commission of the crime by advice, directions, making

[32] See also, W. Chase, 'Stalin as producer: the Moscow show trials and the construction of mortal threats', in S. Davies and J. Harris (eds.), *Stalin: a new history* (Cambridge University Press, 2005), pp. 40, 43.

[33] M. Radin, 'The Moscow trials – a legal view', *Foreign Affairs* (October 1937), 66.

> means available, or elimination of obstacles, or by concealing the culprit or the traces of the crime.[34]

And yet Article 17, with its three categories of participant – 'instigator', 'accomplice' and 'perpetrator' – did not quite capture the magnitude of the alleged crimes. Leon Trotskii, for example, had to be more than a mere 'instigator'; he was surely the *arch*-conspirator. After the second trial, in March 1937, the journal *Sotsialisticheskaia Zakonnost'* (Socialist Legality) reported the drafting of a new draft criminal code which showed a new line of thinking about the complicity doctrine.[35] A fourth category of conspirator would be added to the list – 'organiser' – who would be punished more harshly than a 'perpetrator', even if the crime was not carried out.[36] This was a refinement of the premise, apparent throughout the trials, that planning a crime was just as serious as perpetrating one, which is why most of the defendants were sentenced to death, even though the Soviet leadership had not been assassinated and the Soviet Union had not been broken up and returned to capitalism.

At the 1938 trial, Vyshinskii expounded more fully on the question of complicity. He began by asking to what extent the accused would be held answerable for the crimes committed by the conspiracy, and answered: 'Fully. Why? Each of the accused must be held answerable for the sum total of the crimes as a member of a conspiratorial organization whose criminal objects and aims, and whose criminal methods of carrying out these aims, were known to, approved of and accepted by each of the accused.'[37] Then he addressed the problem of intent. Although the aforementioned draft code of 1937 had specified that intent or negligence was a necessary component of a crime, thereby readmitting the concept of fault into Russian jurisprudence, Vyshinskii was having none of it. He wrote,

> There is an opinion current among criminologists that in order to establish complicity it is necessary to establish common agreement and an intent on the part of each of the criminals, of the accomplices, for each of the crimes. This viewpoint is wrong. ... Life is broader than this

34 'Russian Criminal Code ...', p. 8: State Department, Judicial Branch of Government, 861.04: www.fold3.com.

35 For a summary of this article, see 'Recent tendencies in Soviet law' (14 September 1937), p. 27: State Department, Judicial Branch of Government, 861.04: www.fold3.com.

36 Ibid.

37 *Report of court proceedings in the case of the anti-Soviet 'bloc of rights and Trotskyites': heard before the Military Collegium of the Supreme Court of the U.S.S.R., Moscow, March 2–13, 1938* (Moscow: People's Commissariat of Justice of the U.S.S.R, 1938), p. 694.

> viewpoint. Life knows of examples when the results of joint criminal activity are brought about through the independent participation in such activity by individual accomplices, who are united only by a single criminal object common to all of them.[38]

To prove complicity, then, one was not required to prove intent, but only a common purpose – a united will to commit a crime – among the conspirators.

> To establish complicity, we must establish that there is a common line uniting the accomplices in a given crime, that there is a common criminal design. . . . If, say, a gang of robbers . . . set fire to houses, violate women, murder and so on, in one place, while another part of the gang will do the same in another place, then even if neither the one nor the other knew of the crimes committed separately by any section of the common gang, they will be held answerable to the full for the sum total of the crimes, if only it is proved that they had agreed to participate in this gang for the purpose of committing the various crimes.[39]

It was this framing of the idea that would be taken up by the Soviet criminologist Aron N. Trainin and transmitted to the Nuremberg and Tokyo trials.

Trainin on complicity

Inspired directly by Vyshinskii's aforementioned *Pravda* article, Trainin began work on the first book on the Soviet theory of complicity, *Uchenie o souchastii* (Doctrine of complicity), published three years later in 1941.[40] Trainin's academic career had begun during the tsarist era, but after the revolution he established himself as one of the leading commentators on Soviet criminal law. After being appointed Chair of Criminal Law at Moscow University in 1920, he published a series of articles, entitled 'Etiudy po ugolovnomu pravu' ('Studies on criminal law'), in which he set out the new state's approach to punishment. This, he argued, served not as 'revenge for a crime committed' but as 'a means of protecting society from criminal infringements'.[41] In 1925, he published the first textbook on the 'special part' of the Russian Criminal Code

[38] Ibid., pp. 694–695. [39] Ibid., p. 695.

[40] A.N. Trainin, 'Uchenie o souchastii' in N.F. Kuznetsova (comp.), *Trainin, Izbrannye proizvedeniia* (St. Petersburg: Iuridicheskii tsentr Press, 2004).

[41] The studies appeared in the journal *Pravo i zhyzn'* in 1923 (no. 9–10) and 1925 (no. 7–8); M. Traynina, 'A.N. Traynin: a legal scholar under the Tsar and Soviets', *Soviet Jewish Affairs* 13 (1938), 48.

dealing with offences against the state, entitled *Ugolovnoe pravo RSFSR. Chast' osobennaia: Prestupleniia protiv gosudarstva i sotsialnogo poriadka* (Criminal law of the RSFSR. Special part: Crimes against the state and social order).[42]

Taking up the threads of Vyshinskii's *Pravda* piece, Trainin focused on the role that the complicity doctrine might play in the management of internal threats. He defined complicity as 'a joint participation of several persons in committing the same crime, provided each has both guilt and connection to the criminal result'.[43] It only exists, he explained, when two conditions are met: first, that two or more people are involved in the commission of a crime; and second, that these people have entered into a subjective relationship with each other in order to carry it out. '[C]omplicity is not an isolated criminal activity of several individuals,' he wrote, 'liability for complicity requires a certain subjective link between conspirators.'[44] This subjective link, he suggested, was that conspirators were 'serving one goal'.[45]

Hitherto, he argued, legal theorists had misinterpreted the scope of the doctrine. On the one hand, there were those who wrongly claimed that a 'simple fact of intentional participation of several persons in commission of a crime [was] sufficient to be regarded as complicity'.[46] He cited as an example the pre-revolutionary jurist Pyotr Pustoroslev, who in 1912 had addressed 'intentional complicity in a criminal offence without any agreement between the parties, without one participant's knowledge about the participation of another'.[47] Pustoroslev's approach, Trainin argued, would 'turn complicity from an organic unity to a simple *combination of several persons* guilty of committing the same crime'.[48]

On the other hand, Trainin did not believe that complicity necessarily required prior agreement, or indeed *any* agreement, between the conspirators, provided they were all acting to achieve a common purpose. He stated that 'the *overestimation* of subjective connection as an element of complicity' was a common fault in tsarist-era literature,[49] and had even found its way into the works of Soviet legal scholars such as A. Laptev, who had written in 1938: 'Complicity in Soviet criminal law can be

[42] A.N. Trainin, *Ugolovnoe pravo RSFSR. Chast osobennaya: Prestupleniya protiv gosudarstva I sozialnogo poryadka* (Leningrad: Gosudarstvennoe izdatel'stvo, 1925).

[43] Trainin, 'Uchenie o souchastii', p. 265. [44] Ibid., p. 364. [45] Ibid., p. 286.

[46] Ibid., p. 256.

[47] Ibid., p. 255. Trainin quotes from P. Pustoroslev, *Russkoe ugolovnoe pravo: obshchaia chast'* (1912), pp. 431–432.

[48] Ibid., p. 256. Original emphasis. [49] Ibid., p. 257. Original emphasis.

defined as participation of several persons, *based on agreement*, in committing one or several offences.'[50] Trainin responded,

> One cannot deny that quite often conspirators are bound by a prior agreement. Nevertheless, this frequent *actual* combination of a prior agreement and complicity cannot be equated to the legal *principle*: complicity is imaginable also without a prior agreement between conspirators and even without *any* agreement between them.[51]

He therefore criticised what he saw as two 'extreme' theories of complicity:[52] on the one hand, the denial of the need for *any* agreement between the conspirators, and on the other, the requirement for at least a preliminary agreement between them. Both these approaches, he argued, distorted the nature of complicity by either excessively expanding or narrowing its scope.[53] But while Trainin presented himself as occupying the middle ground, this middle ground is exceedingly broad, denying Laptev's contention that prior agreement is necessary, while admitting most of Pustoroslev's position that aggression required no agreement (provided, Trainin stressed, the participants had a common goal).

Finally, when dealing with the existing literature, Trainin stated that he was not of the view that complicity covered only acts of commission. He opposed the opinion expressed by the jurist Georgii Kolokolov, for example, that 'complicity can only take place in the form of an affirmative action, and not in the form of a simple abstention from action'.[54] In his view, the conspirator could contribute to the crime through inaction as well as through action. He wrote,

> It is well known that inaction may also cause criminal result . . . In practice, these cases are quite possible and often take place. For example, a switchman in agreement with robbers does not switch the rail points so as to cause a crash and to facilitate a robbery; a watchman in agreement with a thief does not lock a storehouse, and so on. The switchman and the watchman both are responsible as conspirators.[55]

In Trainin's view, there were three types of complicity, distinguished by the level of danger they posed to society: simple complicity, complicity with a prior agreement between accomplices, and 'special complicity *sui generis*'.[56] Of these, simple complicity was the least dangerous.[57] 'In this case,' he wrote, 'the connection between the conspirators does not exceed

[50] Ibid., p. 259. Trainin quotes from A. Laptev, 'Souchastie po sovetskomu ugolovnomu pravu', *Sovetskaia Iustitsiia* (23–24, 1938), 13. Original emphasis.
[51] Ibid. Original emphasis. [52] Ibid., p. 259. [53] Ibid., p. 260. [54] Ibid., p. 264. [55] Ibid.
[56] Ibid., p. 267. [57] Ibid.

the minimum necessary for complicity' – the actors were aware that other people were participating in the commission of a crime, 'but there is no prior conspiracy to commit an offence, no prior agreement between individual actors'.[58] Such situation might arise if people joined a riot on the spur of the moment. 'Of course,' he explained, 'among the participants may be and are people who previously agreed to arrange a "riot" – people whom the law identifies with good reason as being organisers.'[59] But simple complicity pertained not to the organisers, but to those who joined the criminal activity spontaneously, without prior agreement with the others, even though they shared with the organisers the common goal of engaging in a riot.[60]

The second and more common type of complicity – complicity with the prior agreement between conspirators – was, in Trainin's view, a greater danger to society. He observed that this more dangerous form was recognised by the Russian Criminal Code,[61] which penalised, among other things: failure to pay taxes and compulsory insurance on time and despite ability to pay, especially if 'committed by a number of persons according to a previous agreement or (even without previous agreement) by persons who are connected with ... agricultural operations' (Article 60);[62] failure to pay the special military tax on time and despite ability to pay, especially 'by a number of persons according to previous agreement' (Article 60 again);[63] refusal to perform public duties (such as work on behalf of the state) 'if committed by a number of persons in accordance with previous agreement' (Article 61);[64] and the theft of personal property, or state property from warehouses or storage places, involving 'planning with other persons' (Article 162).[65] Throughout the Code, crimes carried out by groups of people attracted higher tariffs than those carried out by individuals. Article 62(1), dealing with attempts to hoodwink the taxman, made a clear distinction between 'leaders and organisers' (who attracted a higher punishment) and 'other persons' party to the common agreement:

> Systematic concealment of or false statements concerning amounts of articles subject to taxation or inventory, in accordance with common agreement, involves: for the organizers and leaders, imprisonment for not more than two years[,] or compulsory labour for not more than one year, with or without partial confiscation of property[;] for the other

[58] Ibid. [59] Ibid., p. 268. [60] Ibid. [61] Ibid., p. 269.

[62] 'Russian Criminal Code ...', p. 44: State Department, Judicial Branch of Government, 861.04: www.fold3.com.

[63] Ibid., p. 45. [64] Ibid. [65] Ibid., p. 84.

persons involved, a fine of not more than five times the amount of the payments due.[66]

But the most dangerous and complex type of all was 'special complicity *sui generis*' – namely, participation in an organisation or gang created for the purpose of committing crimes.[67] Here Trainin mentioned the 'Right-Trotskyite bloc' and other anti-revolutionary movements and organisations purportedly operating against the Soviet state and the Soviet people. The very existence of such gangs, he believed, represented a substantial threat to society, which is why their actions were considered 'the highest level of a joint criminal activity'.[68] How so? In a case of special complicity, the conspirators were connected not just by a simple or fleeting agreement but by a compact that had assumed a definite organisational form. This form of complicity – a '*readymade human machine* for committing crimes' – was more durable and cohesive than the other types, which is why he argued that 'a criminal organisation represents a socially dangerous phenomenon already by the fact of its existence'.[69]

Consequently under socialist law, liability for *being a member of a criminal organisation* is equal to liability for *committing crimes at the organisation's behest* – each being seen as equally socially dangerous. The fact that an individual member of a criminal organisation may not know all the other members, and may not be aware of the acts committed by them, is of no moment: 'Members of a criminal community are united not by reciprocal knowledge of each other and not by reciprocal awareness of each other's actions but by serving one goal.'[70] All that was required was 'knowledge of the association's goals' – which was the 'substance of the conspirator's criminal intent' *and* the 'subjective basis of liability for the activities of the whole association'.[71] The member was responsible not just for his or her own criminal actions but also, by dint of being a member of a criminal organisation, for the actions of the organisation as a whole.

Complicity internationalised

In his book on complicity, Trainin was primarily interested in the doctrine's deployment against internal threats to the Soviet state. But no sooner was it published than the Germans invaded the Soviet Union, and he began to consider the potential uses of the doctrine against such

[66] Ibid., pp. 45–46. [67] Trainin, 'Uchenie o souchastii', p. 269. [68] Ibid., p. 270.
[69] Ibid. Original emphasis. [70] Ibid., p. 286. [71] Ibid.

external threats. On 26 August 1943, the Soviets broadcast a radio piece entitled 'The responsibility for Nazi crimes', based on an article Trainin had written for the journal *War and the Working Class*; the following day, the Soviet foreign press agency Tass distributed an English-language transcript through its Soviet embassies abroad.[72] The Soviets were clearly sending up a trial balloon to the Allies about some of the legal concepts that might be deployed in the future handling of the German leaders.

Trainin argued that although material and political responsibility for waging aggressive wars resided with the state, *criminal* responsibility must necessarily rest with the leading individuals vested with its authority. Hitler, his cabinet and the heads of the German government were the 'most dangerous and most vicious body of international offenders'[73] because, he wrote, they 'took the lead in preparing, organising and perpetrating the most heinous crime in the history of the human race, the perfidious attack on the Soviet Union'.[74] In other words, Trainin grasped the essential point that waging war was a crime necessarily committed by *leaders*.

Moreover, in addition to the politicians and ministers, Trainin also listed the financial and industrial magnates who had used their economic clout to underwrite the Nazi regime, and it was in relation to them that he broached the doctrine of complicity. Using the same formula that had been advanced at the Moscow trials and reiterated in his book on complicity, he argued that irrespective of whether the magnates had direct personal connections with the Nazi leadership, the 'individual members of a gang or group may not be known to one another and may yet be responsible for all the crimes the gang or group commits'.[75] Trainin's amalgam of ideas, which highlighted both the criminality of aggressive war and the German elite's conspiracy to commit it, was highly significant. By fusing together the charge of aggression with an internationalised mode of liability, he laid the groundwork for the trial of *groups of national leaders* for embarking on aggressive war. It was precisely these two linked concepts that were later instituted at the Nuremberg and Tokyo tribunals as 'crimes against peace' and 'common plan or conspiracy'.

A year after the broadcast, the Soviets relaunched Trainin's proposals, this time as a book, *Ugolovnaia otvetstvennost' gitlerovtsev*, published in

[72] A. Farrin [Trainin], 'The responsibility for Nazi crimes', *Soviet Monitor* (27 August 1943): FO 371/34377, TNA. See also on this broadcast, K. Sellars, *'Crimes against peace' and international law* (Cambridge University Press, 2013), pp. 51–52.

[73] Ibid., pp. 2–3. [74] Ibid., p. 3. [75] Ibid.

Moscow in July 1944 (and translated into English the following year as *Hitlerite responsibility under criminal law*). With the end of the war in sight, Western officials were beginning to consider the problem of how to deal with the German leaders, and started to focus on Trainin's work. What especially caught their interest was the prominence he gave to the offence he now called 'crimes of the Hitlerites against peace'.[76] He reiterated his point that these were crimes for which the Germans were individually responsible and added that those who planned and carried out aggression were committing 'the most dangerous international crime' of them all.[77]

He admitted that existing international criminal law provided little guidance for handling crimes such as aggression, ascribing the 'extreme meagreness' of this area of law to the 'aggressive imperialist rulers who had the cause of peace under constant menace'.[78] But if international law were to be used in conjunction with national criminal law, then there would be sufficient legal basis for the punishment of the 'Hitlerite clique' for their international crimes of aggression and war crimes. Soviet criminal law, for example, provided a useful model for prosecuting groups of people. He observed that the complicity doctrine had been used successfully against 'the anti-Soviet bloc of Right Wing and Trotskyites' at the Moscow purge trials of 1936–1938,[79] and even quoted Vyshinskii's aforementioned comments about the theory at the trial of Bukarin, Rykov and others in 1938.[80] Soon enough, the doctrine of complicity – used against those accused of committing treason against the Soviet state – was put to work against the German and Japanese leaders accused of committing treason against the society of states.

'Waging war against the King'

As has been shown, powerful states preoccupied by the problem of international security took inspiration from domestic security law. Treason trials provided a template for international tribunals, and in the process, the latter spawned new charges of international treason. Interaction between the different bodies of law created the potential for ideas to travel both ways, and this is exactly what happened at the British-run treason trials convened at the Red Fort in Delhi in 1945–1946 to deal

[76] A.N. Trainin and A.Y. Vishinski (ed.), *Hitlerite responsibility under criminal law*, A. Rothstein (tr.) (London: Hutchinson, 1945), p. 42. See also, Sellars, *'Crimes against peace'*, pp. 55–57.

[77] Ibid., p. 37. [78] Ibid., pp. 10, 11. [79] Ibid., p. 84. [80] Ibid.

with senior figures in the Indian National Army, which had fought alongside the Japanese. After the war, the British authorities, concerned about instability in their most important colony, convened these courts martial in order to maintain morale and discipline among the 'loyal' Indian troops under their command. This strategy backfired, and the trials instead became a lightning rod for the Indian independence movement.

The events addressed by the Red Fort trials had begun some four years earlier, on 16 February 1942, the day after Yamashita's Twenty-Fifth Army broke through the British lines and compelled Percival to surrender Singapore to the Japanese. While the British and Australian prisoners of war were marched off to prisons and internment camps, some 40,000 Indian troops from the defeated British Army were gathered together at Farrer Park in south-central Singapore. There, the Japanese gave them a stark choice: either take their chances as prisoners of war or switch their allegiance to the Indian National Army, which would fight on the same side as the Japanese. According to testimony given at the trial, around half of them chose the latter option.

Thereafter, the Indian National Army went through two incarnations. The first was under Mohan Singh, a career officer who was elevated to commander-in-chief in April 1942 and then, after disagreeing with the Japanese over the Army's status and independence, was relieved of his command and imprisoned by the Japanese. The second was under Subhas Chandras Bose, a former Congress politician who, after arriving in Singapore and assuming the leadership of the Army in July 1943, proclaimed the Ārzī Hukūmat-e-Āzād Hind (the Provisional Government of Free India), and then declared war on Britain and the United States. Bose was killed in an air crash at Formosa in the final weeks of the war.

After the conclusion of the war, the British, compelled to settle accounts with the Indian National Army, convened a series of trials of some of its former officers in late 1945 and early 1946. The first and most important of these commenced on 5 November 1945 in a British Army barracks inside Delhi's Red Fort. The British had chosen the three defendants – Shah Nawaz Khan, Prem Saghal and Gurbakhsh Singh Dhillon – from among second-tier commanders who, as well as switching their allegiance from the British Indian Army to the Indian National Army, were also alleged to have been involved in the commission of crimes against their subordinates. All three were charged with 'waging war against the King' – the equivalent of treason, set out in Section 121 of the Indian Penal Code. In addition, Dhillon was charged with murder, and Khan and Saghal with 'abetment of murder'.

At first, this appeared to be a straightforward domestic case of treason. As Advocate General Sir Naushirwan Engineer, the chief prosecuting counsel, informed the court:

> The prosecution will submit that any plea that they [the accused] were bound or justified by law in doing what they did cannot avail them. Joining with rebels in an act of rebellion or with enemies in acts of hostility makes a man a traitor. An act of treason cannot give any sort of rights nor can it exempt a person from criminal responsibility for the subsequent acts. Even if an act is done under a command where the command is traitorous, obedience to that command is also traitorous.[81]

But Engineer faced a significant tactical problem. In order to establish his case for treason, he had to present evidence of the existence of the Indian National Army – news of which the British wartime censors had done their utmost to suppress. So in the process of presenting battle reports, operation orders, command structures, reorganisation policies, intelligence summaries, situation reports, disciplinary notes, supply manifests, staff allotments, security passwords, diary entries and witness statements, Engineer also managed to conjure up victories and defeats, retreats under fire, captures of arms and casualties in battle.[82] In short, he transformed what had been a ghost army, a chimera, into the real thing.

This, of course, had an electrifying effect on Indian public opinion. The evidence laid out by the prosecution showed that Indians, under the nose of the embattled imperial authorities, had formed their own tens-of-thousands-strong army, commanded by their own nationals, which had fought, and sometimes beaten, the British in Burma. This was a thrilling message. The trial of the three accused – who, fortuitously, happened to be Hindu, Moslem and Sikh – not only became a rallying cry for the already aroused independence movement but also managed to temporarily unite this movement across political and religious lines. As Jawaharlal Nehru wrote the following year,

> The legal issues were important enough, involving as they did questions of that rather vague and flexible body of doctrine known as International Law. But behind the law, there was something deeper and more vital . . .

[81] M. Ram (ed.), *Two historic trials in Red Fort: an authentic account of the trial* (New Delhi: Moti Ram, 1946), p. 19.

[82] For a fuller account, see P.W. Fay, *The forgotten army: India's armed struggle for independence, 1942–1945* (New Delhi: Rupa & Co, 1994), pp. 476–477.

> Those three officers and the Indian National Army became symbols of India fighting for her independence. ... The trial dramatised and gave visible form to the old contest: England *versus* India.[83]

In other words, the proceedings, conceived by the British to convey a strong condemnatory message, had precisely the opposite effect.

It was in this febrile atmosphere that the chief defence counsel Bhulabhai Desai took the floor. Over the course of two days he delivered a speech, without notes, which effectively turned the case on its head. His argument was that the issues at hand were matters for public international law, not British Indian municipal law. He argued, first, that the Indian National Army was a properly constituted and self-governing army, run by Indian officers, with its own disciplinary code, ranks, uniforms and regalia, just like the British-run Indian Army, on which it was closely modelled. It had two aims: the liberation of India from British rule, and the protection of Indian populations in Burma and Malaya, especially during the war. So contrary to the prosecution's claims, it was not just a Japanese-run fifth column.

Furthermore, Desai argued, the Provisional Government of Free India, which Bose had proclaimed in 1943, was a properly constituted government, with command over resources and territories, including the Andaman and Nicobar islands, which had been ceded to it by Japan. These features amounted to statehood – and this statehood was recognised by Japan and a number of its allies, such as Burma, Croatia, Manchukuo and Siam. This government had then declared war on Britain and the United States, and thereafter assumed the rights of a belligerent, including the right to impose military discipline within its own army. In summary, the Indian National Army and the Provisional Government of Free India were operating within the bounds of public international law, the sitting court had no jurisdiction over relations between belligerent states, and the defendants, having acquired the rights and immunities endowed on them by the laws of war, had no case to answer.

In the course of making these arguments, Desai returned repeatedly to the question of *allegiance* that was at the heart of the trial. Both the accused and witnesses had stated that the fall of Singapore had convinced them that Britain was incapable of protecting Indian interests and had therefore forfeited its claim to their allegiance: 'I felt like one deserted by the British,' Gurbakhsh Singh Dhillon told the court.[84] The decisive moment, as the defence pointed out, was the gathering at Farrer Park,

[83] J. Nehru, Foreword, in Ram (ed.), *Two historic trials*, iii. [84] Ibid., p. 118.

when the surrendered Indian troops were presented with a choice between loyalty to Britain and loyalty to India. Shah Nawaz Khan testified that when forced to choose between King and Country, 'I decided to be loyal to my country'.[85] The value of the loyalty so peremptorily commanded by the Raj, and so summarily punished if abandoned, was first questioned, and then denied.

It was precisely this issue of loyalty that had defined Bulabhai Desai's own career. In 1928, when an advocate in Bombay, he appeared before the Broomfield Committee on behalf of Gujarati farmers involved in the civil disobedience campaign, Bardoli Satyagraha. Two years later, he spoke at a meeting protesting the conviction of its leader, Vallabhbhai Patel, where – rehearsing points he would make again fifteen years later at the Red Fort – he proclaimed, '[I]f it is patriotic to lay down one[']s life that Germany may not govern England, how can it be less patriotic if any one of us may lay down his life that another may not govern India (prolonged cheers)!'[86] After joining the Indian National Congress, he took part in civil disobedience activities and was imprisoned in 1932. After his release, he rose through the ranks of Congress, eventually serving as majority leader in the Central Assembly. His political career faltered badly earlier in 1945, when he brokered a secret power-sharing deal with the Muslim League, known as the Desai-Liaquat Ali Pact, and it was only his commanding performance at the trial that silenced some of the critics in his own party.

The arguments Desai put forward were remarkable for being so unlike the usual defences presented against treason charges. These normally accepted that national security was paramount, and insisted that the accused had acted in good faith or in ignorance – the sort of line put forward in the Malvy and Caillaux cases. Desai took a completely different tack. He challenged the very premise of treason, by arguing that during a war of liberation the justice of the challenger eclipsed the security of the challenged. Under these circumstances, formal allegiances could be renounced. He did this by calling on international law to support his claims. Before the twentieth century, international law permitted only sovereign and independent – in other words, not colonised – states to legitimately declare or wage war: 'Of course that created a vicious circle, that a subject race will remain in perpetuity a subject race. It can

[85] Ibid., p. 110.

[86] 'Speech of Mr. B.J. Desai, Advocate' (1930), p. 3: Bulabhai Desai papers, 1st and 2nd part, Nehru Memorial Library.

never be made a legitimate war for the purpose of liberating itself.'[87] But, he argued, modern international law had moved on, and now accepted the legitimacy of wars of national liberation:

> The position now is that international law has reached this stage that if liberty and democracy are to have any meaning all over the world, and not merely just for a part of it, and this is not politics, it is law – any war made for the purpose of liberating oneself from foreign yoke is completely justified by modern international law. And it will be travesty of justice if we were to be told as a result of any decision arrived at here or otherwise, that the Indian may go as solider and fight for the freedom of England against Germany, for England against Italy, for England against Japan, and yet a stage may not be reached when a free Indian State may not wish to free itself from any country, including England itself.[88]

Turning the charges back against the prosecution, Desai thus argued that the case was not really about treason at all: 'What is now on trial before the Court is the right to wage war with immunity on the part of the subject race for their liberation.'[89] Thus, from within a treason trial itself emerged a legal critique of the supremacy of domestic security law.

Needless to say, the defence arguments failed to persuade the court. On 31 December 1945, it found all three men guilty of 'waging war against the King' and one guilty of 'abetment to murder', and sentenced them all to transportation – subsequently reduced to cashiering and forfeiture of arrears of pay and allowances. Yet Desai's speech nonetheless had a profound impact on the Indian struggle for independence, and strongly influenced Indian advocates and judges, one of whom, Radhabinod Pal, would take these arguments about security and justice to the International Military Tribunal for the Far East, which was established in Tokyo a few weeks later.

The grand conspiracy

The Tokyo Tribunal was designed, first and foremost, to meet concerns about international security. As the Potsdam Declaration on Japan stated, 'a new order of peace, security and justice will be impossible until irresponsible militarism is driven from the world'.[90] The Charter and Indictment thus laid heavy emphasis on the linked charges of 'crimes against peace' and 'common plan or conspiracy'. Indeed, the lack of

[87] Ram (ed.), *Two historic trials*, p. 153. [88] Ibid. [89] Ibid., p. 141.

[90] Potsdam Declaration, *FRUS* 1945 *The Conferences of Berlin (The Potsdam Conference)* (Washington, DC: Government Printing Office, 1960), vol. 2, p. 1475.

evidence connecting the defendants to the alleged 'crimes against peace' compelled the prosecutors to rely more heavily on 'common plan or conspiracy' than had their Nuremberg counterparts. Aiming to shift the burden of proof away from personal responsibility and towards participation in a criminal conspiracy, they tried to establish guilt by indirect means: first, alleging the existence of a conspiracy; second, establishing an individual's connection to the conspiracy; and finally, using membership of the conspiracy to indicate personal responsibility for substantive crimes. As the Australian Court President William Webb (who was himself troubled by the scope of 'common plan or conspiracy') explained to a defence lawyer, 'Conspirators need not know each other, they need not know of each other's existence, let alone exchange words.'[91] Webb was probably not aware of it, but he was echoing the very idea crafted by Trainin in Moscow.

When Radhabinod Pal, a former judge at the Calcutta High Court, arrived in Tokyo in May 1946, a month or so after the other judges, he immediately questioned the validity of the 'crimes against peace' charge.[92] This altered the dynamic between the other judges, and in time three of them – William Webb, Bernard Röling of the Netherlands and Henri Bernard of France – also began to express reservations about the 'crimes against peace' and 'common plan or conspiracy' charges. The prospect of a unanimous judgment began to dwindle.[93] Those judges who were committed to endorsing the Nuremberg line (led by William Patrick of Britain, Stuart McDougall of Canada and Erima Harvey Northcroft of New Zealand) observed this process with alarm. They believed that the crimes set out in the Tokyo Charter were not open for debate. The sole reason for setting up what Patrick called 'this portentous institution' was to declare that war was a crime and that individuals could be held responsible for it.[94]

William Patrick was particularly nettled by Pal's approach. 'He has made his position quite clear since first he was appointed,' he wrote, 'so why the Government of India ever nominated him . . . is difficult to see.'[95] The simple truth was that the government in question had sought Indian takers for the Tokyo job, and, having already had a few refusals,

[91] IMTFE, vol. 59, p. 28279. Webb addressed 'common plan or conspiracy' in his Separate Opinion at end of the trial.

[92] Patrick to Normand (c. January 1947), p. 5: LCO 2/2992, TNA.

[93] B.V.A. Röling and A. Cassese (ed.), *The Tokyo trial and beyond: reflections of a peace-monger* (Cambridge: Polity Press, 1993), pp. 28–29.

[94] Patrick to Normand (c. January 1947), p. 1: LCO 2/2992, TNA. [95] Ibid.

was evidently relieved when someone suitable finally accepted the appointment.[96] That person was Pal, and even though his stance may have been more radical than many at Tokyo might have wished, it was wholly in accord with Indian, and especially Bengali, sentiment in the late 1940s.

Pal, like Desai, took as his starting point the differing interests of the powerful states and their colonies. He argued that the criminalisation of aggression was premature because it presupposed the existence of a genuine international community united by common interests and capable of offering alternatives to war as a method of resolving disputes.[97] In the absence of this community, states would continue to pursue their partisan national interests by force of arms. He was of the view that the Allies' motives for creating the new charge of 'crimes against peace' were therefore highly suspect, especially considering their own history of violence towards the non-Western nations.[98] Instead of promoting universal values, these nations were perhaps merely serving their own narrow interests, such as maintaining the *status quo* – 'the very *status quo*', he noted, 'which might have been organized and hitherto maintained only by force by pure opportunist "Have and Holders"'.[99]

If this was the case, then there was good reason to be concerned about the implications of the 'crimes against peace' charge for the 'dominated' nations. Pal drew particular attention to the American chief prosecutor Robert Jackson's statement at the Nuremberg Tribunal that 'whatever grievances a nation may have, however objectionable it finds the *status quo*, aggressive warfare is an illegal means for settling those grievances or for altering those conditions'.[100] In other words, aggressive wars were treasonable acts against the international order. This, as Pal recognised, was effectively a call for the paralysis of international affairs, and by implication the criminalisation of the struggle against colonialism. He considered this too high a price to pay for mere security, because, he wrote, the dominated nations 'cannot be made to submit to eternal

[96] Duke (9 October 1946): 306-FEA (1946), National Archives of India (NAI).

[97] IMTFE, Pal Dissent, vol. 105, p. 103. For a more detailed appraisal of Pal's position, see Sellars, *'Crimes against peace'*, pp. 236–238, 250–251.

[98] Ibid., p. 70. [99] Ibid., p. 239.

[100] International Military Tribunal, *Trial of the major war criminals before the International Military Tribunal*, 'The Blue Series', 42 vols. (Nuremberg: IMT, 1947–1949), vol. 2, p. 149.

domination only in the name of peace'.[101] This, of course, was precisely Desai's point.

When it came to issuing judgment, Pal, following the logic of his rejection of 'crimes against peace' charges and the 'common plan or conspiracy' idea, rejected the authority of the Tribunal *in toto*, stating that all the charges brought against the accused were illegitimate, and that '*each and every one of the accused must be found not guilty of each and every one of the charges*'.[102] At the Tribunal, the Canadian judge Stuart McDougall complained that Pal had come to Tokyo with the express aim of 'torpedoing' any judgment against the defendants.[103]

Back in India, Jawaharlal Nehru's government, which had recently won power from the British, was dismayed and embarrassed by Pal's stance. Senior ministers were aghast when he sent a copy of his opinion back to New Delhi (four months *before* the Majority Judgment was read out in court). They knew that he intended to dissent – he had told them so[104] – but they had not expected him to dissent on such all-encompassing grounds. Nehru said outright, 'In this judgment wild and sweeping statements have been made with many of which we do not agree at all.'[105] K.P.S. Menon counselled that Pal's views were his own, not the government's, but that 'however extreme the view . . . and however unfortunate the language in which he has couched his views, it would not be expedient for the Government of India to interfere with his judgment'.[106] Krishna Menon telegrammed to say that nonetheless 'it is most desirable that we take some steps to disassociate ourselves from the views of Justice Pal which [are] not shared by us and may well put us in the wrong' with the other prosecuting powers at Tokyo.[107] And P.A. Menon indicated that 'if the reactions in the U.S.A. and other countries proved to be bitter' the Department would issue a statement 'making it clear that Mr. Justice Pal's views were not those of the Government'.[108] As it turned out, the other powers chose to ignore Pal's dissent, and this took the pressure off the government in New Delhi. There the matter rested.

101 IMTFE, Pal Dissent, vol. 105, p. 239.
102 IMTFE, Pal Dissent, vol. 108, p. 1226. Original emphasis.
103 Gascoigne to Dening (25 November 1948): DO 35/2938, TNA.
104 Pal to K.P.S Menon (4 May 1948): 489-CJK/49 (1948), NAI.
105 Nehru to West Bengal Governor-General (29 November 1948): 489-CJK/49 (1948), NAI.
106 K.P.S. Menon (20 July 1948): 489-CJK/49 (1948), NAI.
107 V.K.K. Menon to K.P.S. Menon (4 August 1948): 489-CJK/49 (1948), NAI.
108 P.A. Menon (6 December 1948): 489-CJK/49, NAI.

Conclusion

The concept of treasonable conspiracies entered the vocabulary of international criminal law at the instigation of the French, the Soviets and, finally, the Americans. It made its international debut in Asia at the Tokyo Tribunal. But Indian jurists questioned the very premise of treason – in both domestic and international forms – asserting the right of the colonised to wage war against the coloniser. As it turned out, it was Bulabhai Desai, not the British authorities, who framed the argument about allegiance in the dying days of the Raj. And it was Radhabinod Pal, not his many detractors, who was vindicated over the soon-to-be-abandoned 'crimes against peace' charge. Their argument that 'treason' was a justified response to unjust circumstances would be both popularised and acted upon. They heralded a new non-aligned perspective that demanded a radical reordering of global priorities, with justice taking precedence over security, rather than security taking precedence over justice.

2

Then and now

Command responsibility, the Tokyo Tribunal and modern international criminal law

ROBERT CRYER[1]

One of international criminal lawyers' clichés is to cite George Santayana's aphorism that 'those who cannot remember the past are condemned to repeat it'.[2] One of the reasons for this is that, like many clichés, it contains more than a modicum of truth. That said, it may also be true, in the international criminal law context, that when the ad hoc tribunals, namely, the International Criminal Tribunal for former Yugoslavia (ICTY) and International Criminal Tribunal for Rwanda (ICTR), revived international criminal law in the early 1990s, it was neither possible nor desirable 'simply to dust off the Nuremberg and Tokyo Judgments, the United Nations War Crimes Commission series of *Law Reports of Trials of War Criminals*, and the U.S. government's *Trials of War Criminals Before the Nuremberg Military Tribunals Under Control Council Law No. 10* and presume that one has a readily available source of answers for all legal problems'.[3] All the same, that is no excuse for not looking backwards for where guidance can be given. It is the purpose of this chapter to look at what can be (and could have been) learned from the Far East trials, and in particular the Tokyo International Military

[1] This chapter builds upon work previously published as R. Cryer, 'The ad hoc tribunals and the law of command responsibility: a quiet earthquake', in S. Darcy and J. Powderly (eds.), *Judicial creativity at the international criminal tribunals* (Oxford University Press, 2010), pp. 159–183; and N. Boister and R. Cryer, *The Tokyo International Military Tribunal: a reappraisal* (Oxford University Press, 2008).

[2] G. Santayana, *The life of reason, or, the phases of human progress*, vol. 1: *Reason in common sense* (New York: Charles Scribner's Sons, 1920), p. 284.

[3] W.J. Fenrick, 'Some international law problems related to prosecutions before the International Criminal Tribunal for former Yugoslavia', *Duke Journal of Comparative and International Law* 6 (1995–1996), 103.

Tribunal, in the context of one of the general principles of liability in international criminal law – command responsibility.[4]

The reasons for choosing general principles of liability, and in particular command responsibility, are various. The first is that in the past, and particularly prior to the creation of the ad hoc tribunals, general principles were on the whole not heavily written about, although there was some literature on command responsibility. This is in spite of the fact that in international criminal law – or more accurately, prosecutions before international criminal courts and tribunals – the normal focus is on those who bear the greatest responsibility,[5] and who thus tend to be somewhat remote from the actual perpetrators on the ground, which renders principles of liability extremely important.[6] The second is that whereas the definitions of war crimes had been the subject of quite a large amount of treaty-based development before the 1990s (which is not to say there was not plenty for the judges to do),[7] the same is less true for command responsibility: consequently, the relatively detailed coverage the principle received in Tokyo and some other courts was actually a significant source (or should have been) for the modern prosecutions. The third reason, and the one that will also be focused on here, is that the nature of command responsibility has been confused from the start, and this is important, not least because the way in which this form of liability is conceptualised is strongly related to the ambit of the principle.

The pre-Tokyo history of command responsibility

The history of command responsibility, or at least the moral ideas that lie behind it, can be traced back for a good few millennia[8] and may also be seen in the military codes that were promulgated in the European Middle Ages.[9]

[4] 'Command responsibility' is used (rather than perhaps the more accurate 'superior responsibility') for its ubiquity rather than for any normative assertion. The two terms are used herein synonymously.

[5] See R. Cryer, 'Prosecuting the leaders: promises, politics and practicalities', *Göttingen Journal of International Law* 1 (2009), 45–75.

[6] W. Schabas, 'Enforcing international humanitarian law: catching the accomplices', *International Review of the Red Cross* 83 (2001), 439–458.

[7] See, for example, S. Darcy, *Judges, law and war: the judicial development of international humanitarian law* (Cambridge University Press, 2014).

[8] See W.H. Parks, 'Command responsibility for war crimes', *Military Law Review* 62 (1973), 2–11.

[9] See, for example, R. Cryer, H. Friman, D. Robinson and E. Wilmshurst, *Introduction to international criminal law and procedure* (Cambridge University Press, 3rd edn., 2014), p. 384.

The post-Vattelian international legal order is not quite the same, and so, as a matter of international law, whilst there are considerable issues that remain the same, this does not necessarily mean that the positive law as we see it today can rely directly on 'precedents' which are not based on sources that are now considered authoritative.[10] Whatever their historical interest, as a matter of positive international law, they cannot be taken to be normative, or sources of international law. Hence, it is best, for the purposes of both brevity and method, to begin at the first major twentieth-century attempt to discuss the responsibility of superiors in a manner that can be seen to relate to international criminal law as we now see it.

This was the 1919 Commission on the Responsibility of the Authors of the War, appointed at the Paris Peace Conference by the victorious allies in the First World War.[11] In addition to its conclusion that the losing powers were responsible for the war, it took the view that the responsibility for war crimes was limited to those who were responsible as principals, orderers and, most importantly for our purposes, those who

> with knowledge thereof and with power to intervene, abstained from preventing or taking measures to prevent, putting an end to or repressing, violations of the laws or customs of war (it being understood that no such abstention should constitute a defence for the actual perpetrators).[12]

In addition to the fairly clear modern form of command responsibility – albeit with a higher mental element (knowledge) than is required today – what is perhaps most notable is that this part of the report was the subject of a dissent by the Japanese delegation, who disagreed with the idea of anything approaching command responsibility. As they wrote,

> In any event, it seems to us important to consider the consequences which would be created in the history of international law by the prosecution for breaches of the laws and customs of war of enemy heads of states before a tribunal constituted by the opposite party. Our scruples become still greater when it is a question of indicting before a tribunal thus constituted

[10] See, for example, R. Cryer, *Prosecuting international crimes: selectivity and the international criminal law regime* (Cambridge University Press, 2005), chap. 1.

[11] For general comment, see M.C. Bassiouni, 'World War I, "the war to end all wars" and the birth of a handicapped international criminal justice system', *Denver Journal of International Law and Policy* 30 (2002), 253–265. On its position in international criminal law, see G. Simpson, 'International criminal justice and the past', in G. Boas, W. Schabas and M. Scharf (eds.), *International criminal justice: legitimacy and coherence* (Cheltenham: Edward Elgar, 2012), pp. 123–124, 132–134.

[12] 'Commission on the Responsibility of the Authors of the War and on Enforcement of Penalties', *American Journal of International Law* 14 (1920), 121.

> highly placed enemies on the sole ground that they abstained from preventing, putting an end to, or repressing acts in violation of the laws and customs of war . . . It is to be observed that to satisfy public opinion of the justice of the decision of the appropriate tribunal, it would be better to rely upon a strict interpretation of the principles of penal liability, and consequently not to make cases of abstention the basis of such responsibility.[13]

The United States delegates on the Commission also expressed reservations on command responsibility.[14] It is no little irony, then, that the first modern case on command responsibility was heard against a Japanese general, Yamashita Tomoyuki, before an American military commission.[15]

If international criminal law was brought to life at the post-war trials, then, in Guénaël Mettraux's memorable phrase, the command responsibility doctrine was 'born in sin' in *Yamashita*.[16] This case is controversial for various reasons, not least the mental element it contained (which is itself not always clear, but was probably along the lines of the idea that the commander knew, or should have known, of the crimes committed by subordinates). What is most relevant here, though, is the disagreement about whether command responsibility was a principle of liability, making someone responsible for the crimes committed by those who were being commanded, or whether it was some form of serious dereliction of duty charge. The charge Yamashita faced was that he 'unlawfully disregarded and failed to discharge his duty as commander to control the operations of the members of his command, permitting them to commit brutal atrocities . . . [and] thereby violated the laws of war'.[17] The US Supreme Court also appeared at times to conceive of it as such, opining at one point that 'the gist of the charge is an unlawful breach of duty by petitioner as an army commander to control the operations of the members of his command'.[18] This interpretation of *Yamashita* can be supported by the review of the case by the Staff Judge Advocate, in which the charge was considered to be 'criminal dereliction of duty'.[19]

[13] Ibid., 152. [14] Ibid., 143.

[15] For general accounts, see, for example, A.-M. Prevost, 'Race and war crimes: the 1945 war crimes trial of General Tomoyuki Yamashita', *Human Rights Quarterly* 14 (1992), 303–338; R.L. Lael, *The Yamashita precedent: war crimes and command responsibility* (Wilmington: Scholarly Resources Inc., 1982); A.F. Reel, *The case of General Yamashita* (University of Chicago Press, 1949); L. Taylor, *A trial of generals: Homma, Yamashita, MacArthur* (South Bend: Icarus, 1981).

[16] G. Mettraux, *The law of command responsibility* (Oxford University Press, 2009), p. 5.

[17] United Nations War Crimes Commission, *Law reports of trials of war criminals*, 15 vols. (London: HMSO, 1947–1949), vol. 4, pp. 3–4.

[18] *In re Yamashita*, 327 US 1 (1946), 14. [19] Parks, 'Command responsibility', 32.

This, however, does not quite explain the nature of the responsibility of the breach of duty – in that, although not without any ambiguity, it is unclear whether the responsibility is based upon the breach of duty, or if it is a form of responsibility for the offences that occurred. The case is not expressly on point, and contains much, in fact, that contradicts the idea that it was setting out a form of dereliction of duty. For example, the military commission convicting Yamashita averred that even though it would be 'absurd ... to consider a commander a murderer or rapist because one of his soldiers commits a murder or a rape', nevertheless, where crimes are widespread and the commander does nothing, 'such a commander may be held responsible, even criminally liable, for the lawless acts of his troops'.[20] As such, although the bulk of post-war cases treat command responsibility as a principle of liability which rendered the superior responsible for the acts of the subordinate, there was still some confusion.[21] This ambiguity manifested itself again in the treatment of command responsibility by the Tokyo Tribunal.

The arguments at Tokyo

The Tokyo Tribunal operated against the background of the *Yamashita* case. The US Supreme Court decided his appeal on 4 February 1946, while the Tokyo Charter was promulgated on 19 January 1946 and amended on 26 April (in part at the behest of the prosecution, to provide succour to some of the charges included in the Indictment).[22] Given this, it is perhaps a little surprising that the Charter was not detailed on the general principles of liability. In fact, it was almost entirely silent on them. Article 5, in relevant part, read:

> The Tribunal shall have the power to try and punish Far Eastern war criminals who as individuals or as members of organizations are charged with offenses which include Crimes against Peace. ...
>
> (a) Crimes against Peace: ... [or] participation in a common plan or conspiracy for the accomplishment of any of the foregoing; ...
>
> (c) Crimes against Humanity: ... Leaders, organizers, instigators and accomplices participating in the formulation or execution of a

20 UNWCC, *Law reports*, vol. 4, p. 35.

21 C. Meloni, 'Command responsibility: mode of liability for the crimes of subordinates or separate offence of the superior?', *Journal of International Criminal Justice* 5 (2007), 621–623.

22 See N. Boister and R. Cryer, 'Introduction', in N. Boister and R. Cryer (eds.), *Documents on the Tokyo International Military Tribunal: Charter, Indictment and Judgments* (Oxford University Press, 2008), p. l.

> common plan or conspiracy to commit any of the foregoing crimes are responsible for all acts performed by any person in execution of such plan.[23]

The Charter had nothing directly on command responsibility, and thus provided little assistance on the nature of the doctrine, or its relationship to other principles of liability. This raised a particular difficulty in Tokyo. Whereas in Nuremberg the evidence clearly established express orders to commit international crimes, in Tokyo, for the most part, this was not the case. As a result, the charges relating to war crimes were not solely based on ordering: Count 54 charged that various defendants had 'ordered, authorised and permitted' war crimes, whilst Count 55 charged the same defendants with 'being by virtue of their respective offices responsible for securing the observance of the said Conventions and assurances and the Laws and Customs of War in respect of the armed forces . . . deliberately and recklessly disregarded their legal duty to take adequate steps to secure the observance and prevent breaches thereof, and thereby violated the laws of war'.[24]

The prosecutors therefore proceeded in two ways. The first was to argue, *pace* Count 54, that the evidence showed that the defendants knew about the offences and either allowed them to occur or had ordered them (even if, for the most part, they could not find documentary evidence of those orders). The second way, *pace* Count 55, was to claim that whether or not the offences were permitted or ordered, they ought to have been prevented by the relevant defendants, since they should have known of the offences, and it was their job to do so.

They thus argued at trial that

> The fact that a Government knows that its nationals have committed and are committing war crimes, coupled with the fact that it makes no real attempt to prevent their continuance, is very cogent evidence of the fact that such crimes were and are being committed as part of the Government's policy or that the Government is quite indifferent as to whether they are committed or not.[25]

The prosecutors also had to deal with the problem that the civilian defendants had tried to pass the responsibility for this on to their military counterparts.[26] They argued that members of the government were

[23] Ibid., Amended Charter, p. 8. [24] Ibid., Indictment, pp. 32, 33.

[25] International Military Tribunal for the Far East, *The Tokyo major war crimes trial*, R.J. Pritchard (ed.), 124 vols. (Lewiston: Edwin Mellen Press, 1998), vol. 83, p. 40079.

[26] IMTFE, vol. 84, p. 40108.

(criminally) responsible for certain actions of their forces in the field, relying on provisions of the Hague and Geneva Conventions which stated that governments were responsible for prisoners of war.[27] On the basis of these provisions (none of which referred to individuals rather than states), they claimed that

> It is . . . clear that it is the Government as a whole which is primarily responsible for the prevention of breaches of these Laws of War. This casts in the first place a duty upon every member of the cabinet and their advisers, and every high officer in the chain of command directly concerned in these matters to satisfy himself that the Laws are being obeyed. Ordinarily no doubt this duty could be discharged by satisfying himself that proper machinery had been established for the purpose. But when information reaches him which raises a doubt as to whether they are being flagrantly disregarded, or shows plainly that they are, then a much higher duty devolved upon him. . . . As regards a Cabinet Minister it is clearly his duty, upon learning of the commission of these crimes, to bring the facts to the notice of his colleagues in the cabinet, and to resign unless effective steps are taken to prevent their commission.[28]

The defence, needless to say, had something of a different point of view. They made much of the fact that the references to governments in the relevant conventions were simply references to the liability of the (abstract) state.[29] They further argued that there was nothing in the conventions that suggested that civilian members of the government had a duty to supervise forces in the field.[30] Where mistreatment could be referred to training or the mentality of a profession, the defence argued that 'it is not the business of the government to supervise the details of military training'.[31] They also made much of the fact that there were differences in the treatment of prisoners of war in different camps, to argue that this demonstrated that there was no planned or systematic

[27] Ibid., pp. 40109–40110, referring to Article 3 of the fourth Hague Convention and Articles 4, 7 and 10–12 of the Hague Regulations. They also referred similarly to Articles 2, 4 and 77 of the 1929 Geneva Convention.

[28] Ibid., pp. 40111–40112.

[29] Ibid., vol. 88, pp. 42258–42259. Although, of course, it is difficult not to quote at this point two famous statements in the Nuremberg Judgment: 'Crimes against international law are committed by men, not by abstract entities, and only by punishing individuals who commit such crimes can the provisions of international law be enforced', and 'individuals have international duties which transcend the national obligations of obedience imposed by the individual state'. (International Military Tribunal, *Trial of the major war criminals before the International Military Tribunal*, 'The Blue Series', 42 vols. (Nuremberg: IMT, 1947–1949), vol. 1, p. 233).

[30] Ibid., vol. 88, pp. 42259–42260. [31] Ibid., vol. 88, p. 42265.

policy of mistreatment, nor a failure to live up to a general duty to prevent crimes against prisoners.[32]

The various judgments at Tokyo

The Majority Judgment had little truck with this, and followed the prosecution line, finding on the evidence that the 'atrocities [were] committed in all theaters of war on a scale so vast, yet following so common a pattern in all theaters, that only one conclusion is possible – the atrocities were either secretly ordered or wilfully permitted by the Japanese Government or individual members thereof and by the leaders of the armed forces'.[33] This is in tune with the way in which they dealt with the evidence in relation to conspiracy, inducting policy in the absence of direct evidence. Like the decisions about conspiracy, the Majority's conclusions were the subject of complete disagreement by Judge Pal, who said that 'there is absolutely no evidence of any order, authorization or permission as alleged in Count 54 . . . In this respect the case before us stands on a footing entirely different from what was found established by the evidence' at Nuremberg.[34] Discussing Japanese actions in the Philippines before October 1944, for example, he took the view that where there were crimes, these were 'stray cases' from which no conclusions could be drawn about government policy.[35]

The precise interrelationship of the charges is not always clear in the Majority Judgment, in particular as 'permitting' in Count 54 could be close to disregard of duty charged in Count 55, a similarity that can be seen in relation to the charge brought against Yamashita Tomoyuki, that he 'unlawfully disregarded and failed to discharge his duty as commander to control the operations of the members of his command, permitting them to commit brutal atrocities'.[36] Matters are not helped by the Majority failing to clearly elaborate what the difference was. The distinction was alluded to by Judge Röling, however: 'If there should be a difference between the "permission" charged in count 54 and the neglect of duty, charged in count 55, "permission" has to be taken in its sense of intentional granting of freedom to commit crimes. Such permission to violate the laws of war is an activity which is closely related to "authorizing", and is without doubt in itself a criminal violation of the laws of

[32] Ibid., vol. 88, pp. 42260–42264, 42267–42268.
[33] Boister and Cryer, *Documents*, Majority Judgment, p. 49592.
[34] Ibid., Pal Dissent, p. 1090. [35] Ibid., p. 1107. [36] UNWCC, *Law reports*, vol. 4, p. 3.

war.'[37] Where the Majority found evidence of guilt under Count 54, they tended not to enter a conviction for Count 55 for the same facts,[38] but their treatment of Count 54 was not based on clear legal reasoning separating out the various crimes.

Of course, the judges also had to deal with the question of Count 55, which alleged that defendants 'deliberately and recklessly disregarded their legal duty to take adequate steps to secure the observance and prevent breaches thereof, and thereby violated the laws of war'.[39] This charge is, in essence, one of the most important for our purposes, in that it relates most closely to one of command responsibility, although there are overlaps with conspiracy. The Majority determined that through both custom and treaty, governments were responsible for prisoners of war.[40] As a result, they said that responsibility fell upon

> (1) Members of the government;
> (2) Military or naval officers in command of formations having prisoners in their possession;
> (3) Officials in these departments which were concerned with the well-being of prisoners;
> (4) Officials, whether civilian, military, or naval, having direct and immediate control of prisoners.[41]

Their view was that this required those responsible for prisoners of war to ensure a system to secure proper treatment, and they became responsible for ill treatment of prisoners if

> (1) They fail to establish such a system.
> (2) If having established such a system, they fail to secure its continued and efficient working.[42]

To elaborate upon this, they explained that it would not be enough just to issue orders to comply with the law of war and then not seek to ensure that they were enforced: 'An Army Commander or a Minister of War, for example, must be at the same pains to ensure obedience to his orders in

37 Boister and Cryer, *Documents*, Röling Dissent, p. 56.
38 See, for example, ibid., Majority Judgment on Dohihara, p. 49779.
39 Ibid., Indictment, p. 33.
40 Ibid., Majority Judgment, p. 48442. Bernard did not believe that Article 4 of Hague Convention IV could found the responsibility (ibid., Bernard Dissent, pp. 12–13).
41 Ibid., pp. 48443–48444.
42 Ibid., p. 48444. It is not always clear what level of authority the Majority thought necessary, so Mutō was convicted as Chief-of-Staff to Yamashita in the Philippines as he was 'in a position to influence policy' (ibid., p. 49820).

this respect as he would in respect of other orders he has issued on matters of the first importance.'[43] This was one of the bases upon which Kimura was convicted; he had issued orders, but not ensured that they were carried out.[44] The same applies to orders issued by Matsui in relation to the conduct of troops in Nanking, and Hata in China.[45]

The Majority accepted that if a system was set up and running properly, even if crimes were committed no criminal liability would accrue to commanders, unless defendants 'had knowledge that such crimes were being committed, and having such knowledge they failed to take such steps as were within their power to prevent the commission of such crimes in the future, or ... [were] at fault in having failed to acquire such knowledge'.[46] They set the standard for this at negligence. If a person was negligent in failing to obtain knowledge, or in taking action to prevent future crimes, then they could be responsible.[47] This included where a person

> accepted assurances from others ... if having regard to the position of those others, to the frequency of reports of such crimes, or to any other circumstances he should have been put upon further enquiry as to whether those assurances were true or untrue. That crimes are notorious, numerous or widespread as to time and place are matters to be considered in imputing knowledge.[48]

Judge Pal, on the other hand, took a quite sanguine view of how much oversight high-level officials had to undertake of a system to ensure proper treatment of prisoners of war, claiming that

> commanders were legally bound to maintain discipline in the army and to restrain the soldiers under their command from perpetrating these

[43] Ibid. Interestingly, Mutō was acquitted with respect to the 'Rape of Nanking' despite being a staff officer, because his superior, Matsui, had done nothing to stop the atrocities. It seems they thought Mutō had no authority to change things (ibid., p. 49820). A similar decision was taken in relation to Sato (ibid., p. 49827), against which Röling dissented (ibid., p. 178).

[44] Ibid., p. 49809. [45] Ibid., pp. 49816 and 49784.

[46] Ibid., p. 48445. They also specifically said that for Army and Navy commanders, and their respective ministers, they were responsible for crimes they should have known of (ibid., p. 48446), adopting similar views in relation to officials in departments having responsibility for prisoners of war (ibid., p. 48447). Hata was considered responsible in part because he either knew or was indifferent about crimes (ibid., p. 49784). Röling dissented on this, on the basis that there was not enough evidence that he could, and should, have known of atrocities (ibid., p. 189).

[47] Ibid., p. 48445. [48] Ibid.

> atrocities . . . [but] . . . We must not forget the actual area of operation of the army and the normal machinery provided wherewith the commander or the commander-in-chief is expected to exercise this control and on the proper functioning of which he is entitled to rely in this respect.[49]

Pal did agree that responsibility for omissions could arise,[50] but said that since there was nothing in the Tokyo Charter that granted them jurisdiction over recklessness, then any part of Count 55 that relied on such a concept was *ultra vires*.[51] This is a rather narrow argument, given that Pal was willing to accept that the relevant law behind the Tribunal had to be international law, and the allegation was, like that in *Yamashita*, that there had been a violation of the law of war by virtue of a failure to prevent atrocities, a point noted by Röling.[52] Judge Röling also thought the ambit of responsibility for omissions was too broad,[53] although he accepted that criminal negligence in failing to obtain knowledge sufficed.[54] He stated that three things were needed to ground command responsibility: that the defendant knew, or should have known, of the crimes; that he had the power to prevent them; and that he had the duty to prevent them.[55]

Judge Bernard was also concerned about the Majority's approach, essentially on the basis that they seemed to treat negligence as being as serious as intentional commission of crimes when '[t]he truth, however, is that the responsibility involved is of an entirely different nature from that of the immediate author and that the seriousness of the anticipated sentence cannot be determined, unless the nature of this responsibility is specified'.[56] This comment, and the difference between the Majority and Bernard on the theory, precedes by about half a century the current difficult debate about the nature of command responsibility as either a form of liability or a separate offence.[57] It is difficult to deny that Bernard had a point.

He was willing to accept that responsibility could arise for negligence by commanders, but only if certain criteria were met. A person was 'guilty of passive complicity of violation of laws of war' only when 'one who, able to prevent that violation from being committed, did not do so', and when the crimes 'could only have been committed because of this negligence,

49 Ibid., Pal Dissent, pp. 1111–1112. 50 Ibid., p. 1111. 51 Ibid., pp. 1051–1052.
52 Ibid., Röling Dissent, p. 58. 53 Ibid., pp. 54–56. 54 Ibid., p. 59. 55 Ibid., pp. 59–60.
56 Ibid., Bernard Dissent, p. 15.
57 See, for example, Meloni, 'Command responsibility', 619–637; V. Nerlich, 'Superior responsibility under Article 28 ICC Statute: for what exactly is the superior held responsible?' *Journal of International Criminal Justice* 5 (2007), 665–682.

imprudence or omission'.[58] He then separated off a slightly different offence, of 'failing in their duties towards the prisoners of war', in which defendants 'who by imprudence, negligence, voluntary disregard of orders or regulations, created a state of fact suited to the multiplication of violations of the laws of war'.[59] He argued that this could be aggravated in:

> a. The circumstance whereby the defendant, having anticipated or had a duty to anticipate because of his office the consequences of his imprudence, negligence or non-observance of orders or regulations, committed it nevertheless;
> b. The circumstances whereby violations of the laws of war of the same nature as those occasioned by imprudence, negligence or voluntary non-observation of orders or regulations, took place.[60]

He stated that he would have sentenced to death those guilty of passive violation of the law of war, and those guilty of failing in duties to imprisonment for life if the failure was an aggravated one.[61] This early approach, irrespective of the view taken of the levels of sentencing (including the death penalty), has the merit of separating off clearly, and consistently with the principle of fair labelling,[62] different levels of culpability. Bernard thus avoided a problem with command responsibility: that it treats intentional and reckless (or perhaps negligent) failures together. We will return to this later. There are also legitimate critiques of the overbreadth of cabinet liability in the Tokyo Tribunal, but the primary point here is that there was considerable discussion (and disagreement) in the Tokyo Tribunal that ought to have informed later discussion on command responsibility. Sadly, as we will see, it did not.

The post-post-war pattern

Even though the issues raised by command responsibility got a thorough airing in Tokyo, the drafters of subsequent protocols and statues have been surprisingly reluctant to investigate this important source and to raise their own game in the process.

After a lacuna in international criminal law developments, it was not until the 1970s, with the drafting of the Additional Protocol I to the Geneva Conventions, that command responsibility returned to the debate. This

58 Boister and Cryer, *Documents*, Bernard Dissent, pp. 16, 17. 59 Ibid., p. 17. 60 Ibid.
61 Ibid.
62 On which, see A.P. Simester and G.R. Sullivan, *Criminal law: theory and doctrine* (Oxford: Hart, 3rd edn., 2007), pp. 30–31.

dealt with the issue in two provisions, Articles 86 and 87, which do not really address the issue of the nature of liability (other than speaking of penal or disciplinary responsibility).[63] What is interesting for our purposes here is to observe that neither of the major commentaries on the Protocol – the ICRC Official Commentary[64] and that of Bothe, Partsch and Solf[65] – made any mention whatsoever of the Tokyo Tribunal, despite the fact that both made clear that the provisions were meant to be based on the post-war position. Instead, these commentaries, as well as the Protocol's drafts, seemed to be limited to the *Yamashita* case and the *High Command* decisions,[66] and suffered as a result: the discussion of the nature of command responsibility did not approach the level of the Tokyo opinions.

It is difficult to explain why the negotiators ignored Tokyo's contribution at this juncture. If anything, the Tribunal should have made a greater claim to their attention than the *Yamashita* case, which in the 1970s was still the go-to 'precedent' for command responsibility. Tokyo was, after all, an international court, unlike the domestic military commission that presided over *Yamashita* (or the domestic court, the US Supreme Court, that reviewed the *Yamashita* decision). Perhaps the Protocol negotiators were deterred by criticisms of Tokyo for its ethnocentrism and failure to observe fair trial rights. If so, the *Yamashita* case was just as flawed. In short, there was no reason to bypass material from Tokyo in the 1970s, and no reason for doing so again in the 1990s.

The ad hocs' statutes and practice

It is fair to say that the ICTY Statute was drafted at a dizzying pace, at least by the usual standards of the United Nations. The ICTR Statute that followed was on most issues (and for our purposes) a *mutatis mutandis* re-tread of the ICTY's. When dealing with command responsibility, Article 7(3) of the former – to which Article 6(3) of the latter is, in all material regards, identical – reads:

63 Protocol Additional to the Geneva Conventions of 12 August 1949, and Relating to the Protection of Victims of International Armed Conflicts: www.icrc.org.

64 Y. Sandoz, C. Swinarski and B. Zimmermann (eds.), *Commentary on the Additional Protocols of 8 June 1977 to the Geneva Conventions of 12 August 1949* (Geneva: ICRC, 1987), pp. 1005–1023.

65 M. Bothe, K.J. Partsch and W.A. Solf, *New rules for victims of armed conflicts: commentary on the two 1977 Protocols additional to the Geneva Conventions of 1949* (The Hague: Martinus Nijhoff, 1982), pp. 523–529.

66 Ibid., p. 525; Sandoz *et al.*, *Commentary*, p. 1013, fn. 29.

> The fact that ... [crimes were] committed by a subordinate does not relieve his superior of criminal responsibility if he knew or had reason to know that the subordinate was about to commit such acts or had done so and the superior failed to take the necessary and reasonable measures to prevent such acts or to punish the perpetrators thereof.[67]

This was almost all the guidance the ICTY was given when it came to determine the ambit of command responsibility. The Secretary-General's Report that accompanied the court's Statute made no reference to the Tokyo Tribunal, or to the difficulties that were raised, discussed and not settled there. That does not mean that the issues had gone away. The ICTY (and to a lesser extent the ICTR) had to approach them as if they had not been aired before. Even though they had.

On the tribunals' practice, the *locus classicus*, at least in the early jurisprudence of the ICTY, is the *Čelebići* Appeal. There they looked at the Trial Chamber's analysis of the Second World War jurisprudence and agreed with its conclusion that command responsibility was a form of liability for the underlying acts.

> Based on an analysis of World War II jurisprudence, the Trial Chamber also concluded that the principle of superior responsibility reflected in Article 7(3) of the Statute encompasses political leaders and other civilian superiors in positions of authority. The Appeals Chamber finds no reason to disagree with the Trial Chamber's analysis of this jurisprudence. The principle that military and other superiors may be held criminally responsible for the acts of their subordinates is well-established in conventional and customary law.[68]

What is interesting is that there was no in-depth discussion of the relationship of the various forms of liability that were at issue in the Tokyo Tribunal, or the question of how they may interact with the ambit of liability that can be seen as falling within command responsibility.

The early practice of the ICTY on this has, seemingly, been subject to internal disagreement. The dispute began in earnest in the *Hadžihasanović* case. Here, the Majority treated command responsibility as a form of complicity or liability for the underlying offences.[69] They

[67] Updated Statute of the International Criminal Tribunal for the Former Yugoslavia, September 2009 (originally adopted by Security Council Resolution 827 on 25 May 1993).

[68] *Prosecutor* v. *Delalić, Mucić, Delić and Landžo* (*Čelebići* Case), IT-96-21-A, Appeals Chamber Judgment (20 February 2001), par. 195.

[69] It is at least implicit in *Prosecutor* v. *Hadžihasanović and Kubura*, IT-01-47-T, Majority Judgment (15 March 2006), pars. 42–43, 46 and 51. Judge Shahabuddeen certainly sees them as having taken that view, although he refers to a non-existent paragraph, in *Prosecutor* v. *Hadžihasanović and Kubura*, IT-01-47-AR72, Appeal Chamber, Partial Dissenting Opinion of Judge Shahabuddeen (16 July 2003) (Shahabuddeen Dissent), par. 32.

tacitly took the view that it was a step too far to hold a person responsible for the crimes committed by another person if they took control after the offences were committed. The minority took a different view. Judge Shahabuddeen challenged the idea that command responsibility is a form of complicity, opining, 'Command responsibility imposes responsibility on a commander for failure to take corrective action in respect of a crime committed by another; it does not make the commander party to the crime committed by that other.'[70] As he accepted, the ambit of superior responsibility is intrinsically linked to its conceptualisation.[71] Judge Hunt essentially agreed.[72] Shahabuddeen relied on a questionable interpretation of Article 7(3) and an admission that his position was essentially one of preference.[73] Judge Hunt, on the other hand, relied on three main cases: *Yamashita*, *Čelebići* and the *Bagilishema* Appeal, alongside some doctrinal views (most notably those of Kai Ambos).[74] What is astonishing is that there was no discussion of the Tokyo Tribunal's decision, still less that of the separate and dissenting opinions it contained, which dealt with the difficult issues that command responsibility entails.

However, the *Hadžihasanović* decision was not the end of the matter. Soon after that case, in *Krnojelac*, the Appeals Chamber, in an extraordinary comment, appeared to engage in a complete *volte face*, opining, without reference to any authority at all, that: 'It cannot be overemphasised that, where superior responsibility is concerned, an accused is not charged with the crimes of his subordinates but with his failure to carry out his duty as a superior to exercise control.'[75] This was followed by a number of Trial Chamber opinions which sought to separate off command responsibility from the underlying crimes. The first of these was the Trial Chamber in *Halilović*, who, partly relying on Shahabuddeen's dissent, attempted to square the circle, by asserting that

[70] Shahabuddeen Dissent, par. 33. [71] Ibid.

[72] *Prosecutor* v. *Hadžihasanović and Kubura*, IT-01-47-AR72, Appeal Chamber, Separate and Partial Dissenting Opinion of Judge David Hunt (16 July 2003) (Hunt Dissent), par. 9.

[73] Shahabuddeen Dissent, pars. 32–33. This jars a little with his disavowal of 'policy-oriented law' in the tribunals: see M. Shahabuddeen, 'Policy-oriented law in the International Criminal Tribunal for the former Yugoslavia', in L.C. Vohrah *et al.* (eds.), *Man's inhumanity to man: essays on international law in honour of Antonio Cassese* (Kluwer: Dordrecht, 2003), pp. 889–898.

[74] Hunt Dissent, fn. 23.

[75] *Prosecutor* v. *Krnojelac*, IT-97-25-A, Appeals Chamber Judgment (17 September 2003), par. 171.

> command responsibility is responsibility for an omission. The commander is responsible for the failure to perform an act required by international law. This omission is culpable because international law imposes an affirmative duty on superiors to prevent and punish crimes committed by their subordinates. Thus 'for the acts of his subordinates' as generally referred to in the jurisprudence of the Tribunal does not mean that the commander shares the same responsibility as the subordinates who committed the crimes, but rather that because of the crimes committed by his subordinates, the commander should bear responsibility for his failure to act. The imposition of responsibility upon a commander for breach of his duty is to be weighed against the crimes of his subordinates; a commander is responsible not as though he had committed the crime himself, but his responsibility is considered in proportion to the gravity of the offences committed.[76]

This is elegant, but the support they give is a brief review of the post-war jurisprudence and the documents that followed it, which, again, did not involve serious discussion of the Tokyo Tribunal's opinions.[77]

The same can be said of the last major case that falls for discussion, that of *Orić*. Here, the Trial Chamber purported to rely on *Halilović* and *Hadžihasanović* cases, but considered the Article 7(3) charges not to be for the offences themselves, but for '[f]ailure to discharge his duty as a superior to take necessary and reasonable measures' to prevent the offences.[78] The prosecutor was unimpressed and appealed this characterisation of the charges.[79] Given that the Appeals Chamber acquitted Orić on the relevant counts, the Majority decided that it was not necessary to pronounce on this directly. Three of the judges on this appeal had something to say on the matter, however. To begin with the dissents, Judge Liu essentially asserted that he agreed with Judges Shahabuddeen and Hunt in *Hadžihasanović*, that custom supported liability for failure to punish pre-command offences,[80] and commented only that owing to the nature of command responsibility, causation is not a necessary aspect of liability.[81] Judge Schomburg, in a typically forthright and thoughtful

[76] *Prosecutor* v. *Halilović*, IT-01-48-T, Trial Chamber I Judgment (16 November 2005), par. 54.

[77] Ibid., pars. 42–52. See also, *Prosecutor* v. *Orić*, IT-03-68-A, Prosecution's Appeal Brief (16 October 2006) (*Orić* Appeal Brief), pars. 200–203, which, on point, is accurate.

[78] *Prosecutor* v. *Orić*, IT-03-68-T, Trial Chamber II Judgment (30 June 2006), par. 782.

[79] *Orić* Appeal Brief, pars. 159–204.

[80] *Prosecutor* v. *Orić*, IT-03-68-T, Appeals Chamber, Partially Dissenting Opinion and Declaration of Judge Liu (3 July 2008), par. 27.

[81] Ibid., par. 32.

opinion, expressly supported Judge Shahabuddeen's opinion on the nature of command responsibility in the case.[82]

Still on *Orić*, Judge Shahabuddeen, in spite of his decision not to revisit the *Hadžihasanović* opinion, gave further comments on the nature of command responsibility. These deserve some discussion, not least because they illustrate an important point in relation to international criminal law and interpretation. He began by claiming that even though perhaps the majority of commentators took the view that it was a form of participation in the underlying offence, the matter had already been dealt with authoritatively by the Appeals Chamber in *Krnojelac*, and thus was not really an issue.[83] This is not really satisfying; the Appeals Chamber had, in the past, prior to *Krnojelac*, repeatedly expressed the view that this was not the case. *Krnojelac*, if it were to be authoritative, needed to deal with all the other Appeals Chamber jurisprudence, and reject it. Judge Shahabuddeen nonetheless added to what he had said before about the nature of command responsibility, even though he thought that the issue was now moot.[84] He referred to *Yamashita*, alongside the Trial Chambers in *Halilović* and *Hadžihasanović*,[85] but again, not to Tokyo.

What can be drawn from this is a high level of confusion. As Elies van Sliedregt has said, after three generations of jurisprudence from the ICTY, there is still ambiguity on fundamental issues of command responsibility.[86] What is also glaring (at least to those who have spent time on the Tokyo Tribunal) is that there is very little discussion of the opinions on the nature of command responsibility that it contained. It is not the contention of this chapter that such consideration would have necessarily settled the debate or that the various opinions in Tokyo Tribunal are

[82] Ibid., Separate and Partially Dissenting Opinion of Judge Schomburg, par. 12.

[83] Ibid., Declaration of Judge Shahabuddeen (Shahabuddeen Declaration), pars. 18–19. It ought to be said that this is not quite the issue – it's about whether the liability is for the underlying crime, rather than for participation in it. In such issues, uses of terms such as 'participation' are unhelpful in so far as they seek to analogise command responsibility and participation.

[84] A pedant might note that the Appeals Chamber had pronounced on the matter a number of times before *Krnojelac*, which did not deal with the previous decisions.

[85] Shahabuddeen Declaration, pars. 22–23. He does note that the holding in *Hadžihasanović* was not dealt with on appeal, but that does not prove that it was agreed with. *Orić* was the first time that the question was expressly dealt with on appeal since the *Hadžihasanović* Interlocutory Appeal.

[86] E. van Sliedregt, 'Command responsibility at the ICTY: three generations of case-law and still ambiguity', in B. Swart, A. Zahar and G. Sluiter (eds.), *The legacy of the International Criminal Tribunal for the former Yugoslavia* (Oxford University Press, 2011), p. 377.

unimpeachable. What is notable, though, is the absence of engagement with those opinions, which, although perhaps framed in the idiom of their time, show the inchoate development of the doctrine of command responsibility. This is unfortunate, in that the authority of the Tokyo Tribunal is at least as strong as the other examples of post-war jurisprudence relied on by the ICTY, and, in many regards, probably stronger. If nothing else the opinions could have been used to bring out the fact that there are different aspects to command responsibility, which are not easily reducible to one simple formula. Judge Bernard's opinion made this very clear. Not, it seems, that anyone was listening.

The Rome Statute: history repeats itself

Sadly, this ignorance of history is not confined to the ICTY. During the negotiations for the Rome Statute, in spite of the fact that there was significant discussion about the jurisprudence of the ad hoc tribunals (especially the *Tadić* case), there was, in the context of command responsibility, essentially no significant reference to the Tokyo Tribunal, even though it is at least arguable that it was the first example of the application of command responsibility to civilian officials. The Rome Statute contains a detailed provision on command responsibility: Article 28, which, in relevant part, reads that both military and non-military superiors (albeit under slightly different conditions) 'shall be criminally responsible for crimes within the jurisdiction of the Court committed by' those under their effective command, authority and control 'as the case may be, as a result of his or her failure to exercise control properly over such forces'.[87]

This provision has been the subject of intense academic commentary,[88] but from our perspective the issue is the extent to which its drafting was influenced by reference to the Tokyo Tribunal, with particular regard to the nature(s) of command responsibility. There is a short answer to this: there was no reference to it at all. In something of a reflection of this, the language of Article 28, despite valiant attempts by

[87] Article 28, Rome Statute of the International Criminal Court: treaties.un.org.

[88] See, for example, G.R. Vetter, 'Command responsibility of non-military superiors in the International Criminal Court (ICC)', *Yale Journal of International Law* 25 (2000) 89–143; E. van Sliedregt, *Individual criminal responsibility in international law* (Oxford University Press, 2012), chap. 8; C. Meloni, *Command responsibility in international criminal law* (The Hague: T.M.C. Asser Press, 2010); K. Ambos, *Treatise on international criminal law*, vol. 1: *Foundations and general part* (Oxford University Press, 2013), pp. 197–232.

some scholars to read it as creating a *sui generis* form of liability,[89] makes fairly clear that it is a form of liability for the underlying offences.[90] Tempting though it is to engage in the minutiae of this debate, the main point is that it falls into the trap identified – by Judge Bernard if no one else – in Tokyo. This trap is to see command responsibility as a monolithic, single form of responsibility, whereas in actuality it encompasses different types of liability, with different levels of culpability.[91] It covers, in omnibus fashion, deliberate failures by commanders to intervene to prevent offences they knew were likely to happen, despite a duty to do so (which falls close to traditional complicity), but it also applies to conduct which is akin to if not the same as negligent dereliction of duty, whilst not clearly separating off the very different levels of culpability that they reflect. These variations were expressed in the interplay of Counts 54 and 55 in the Tokyo Indictment, as noted by Judge Röling, and discussed by Judge Bernard. The drafters of the Rome Statute could have usefully looked back to Tokyo, not necessarily for answers, but at least as a frame of reference.

Although some domestic implementation of the Rome Statute treats command responsibility, in its various forms, as one type of liability,[92] it is worthwhile noting that this has not always been the case. So, for example, the German *Völkerstrafgesetzbuch* (Code of Crimes against International Law) deals separately with failure to know of offences in dereliction of duty, failure to report an offence, and knowing tolerance of an offence when there is a duty and ability to intervene to prevent it.[93] In doing so, German law reflects, to some extent, the different levels of culpability that are covered by command responsibility and implied by Judge Bernard's dissent. However, there is no evidence that those

[89] See, for example, K. Ambos, 'Superior responsibility', in A. Cassese, P. Gaeta and J.R.W.D. Jones (eds.), *The Rome Statute of the International Criminal Court: a commentary*, 3 vols. (Oxford University Press, 2002), vol. 1, pp. 850–855.

[90] Although for an attempt to square the circle, see G. Werle, F. Jessberger *et al.* (eds.), *Principles of international criminal law* (Oxford University Press, 3rd edn., 2014), pars. 583–586.

[91] See, for example, R. Cryer, 'General principles of liability in international criminal law', in D. McGoldrick, P. Rowe and E. Donnelly (eds.), *The Permanent International Criminal Court: legal and policy issues* (Oxford: Hart, 2004), pp. 257–261.

[92] See in English law, for example, International Criminal Court Act 2001, s65. For comment, see R. Cryer, 'Implementation of the International Criminal Court Statute in England and Wales', *International and Comparative Law Quarterly* 51 (2002), 733–743.

[93] Code of Crimes against International Law, ss. 13, 14. Canadian law also treats different types of command responsibility differently (see van Sliedregt, 'Command responsibility', p. 394).

drafting the German law on point did so by reference to the Tokyo Tribunal's views on that issue. It is, in the end, more likely that the reasons for doing so were related to the sophisticated approach to the doctrine of criminal law in that jurisdiction rather than a systematic approach to the historical precedents that at least implied such differentials.

Conclusion

It has not been the purpose of this chapter to give any great answers to the difficult issues raised by command responsibility. The point is more to show that the debate has proceeded to its own detriment in an ahistorical manner. Command responsibility is a complex doctrine that is not easily reducible to one form of culpable responsibility. But these difficulties are far from new: they were clearly present in the Tokyo Tribunal, especially in the separate and dissenting opinions. Had a greater degree of interest been shown in them after the event, the discussion could have started further ahead than it did when the ICTY and Rome statutes were being drafted. It might gently be suggested that a little more historical understanding could have saved international criminal lawyers from the proverbial need to perpetually reinvent the wheel.

3

Colonial justice in the Netherlands Indies war crimes trials

LISETTE SCHOUTEN[1]

Convinced of their racial, cultural and military superiority over the Japanese, the Netherlands and its colony, the Netherlands Indies, were taken by surprise by Japan's attack on Pearl Harbor and its swift southward advance through Southeast Asia. The Royal Netherlands Indies Army was soon compelled to bow to Japan's *force majeure*. The Japanese first landed on Dutch Borneo and Sulawesi on 11 January 1942, then on Java on 1 March 1942. The Dutch colonial regime crumbled, and Governor General Jhr. Alidius W.L. Tjarda van Starkenborgh Stachouwer and Lieutenant General Hein ter Poorten were forced to capitulate on 8 March 1942. This was, of course, a huge blow not only to the Dutch presence and prestige in Asia but also to the mystique of white supremacy and the system of colonial order.

Soon after their arrival, the Japanese interned around 93,000 Dutch and Indonesian prisoners of war.[2] During the ensuing months, the rest of the European population and a significant part of the Eurasian population disappeared behind *kawat* (barbed wire) or into *bilik* (bamboo-screened enclosures).[3] A fifth of prisoners of war – many of whom were used by the Japanese as forced labour elsewhere – perished on the Siam-Burma Railway and in Japan's mines and shipyards, while some thirteen per cent of civilian internees would die in the camps.[4] The Indonesians outside

[1] The author is the translator of the Dutch archival materials unless otherwise stated.

[2] K. Maekawa, 'The *heiho* during the Japanese occupation of Indonesia', in P.H. Kratoska (ed.), *Asian labor in the wartime Japanese Empire: unknown histories* (Armonk, NY: Sharpe, 2005), p. 183.

[3] E. Touwen-Bouwsma, 'Japanese minority policy: the Eurasians on Java and the dilemma of ethnic loyalty', *Bijdragen tot de Taal-, Land-en Volkenkunde* 152 (1996), 560.

[4] L. de Jong, *Het Koninkrijk der Nederlanden in de Tweede Wereldoorlog, 1939–1945*, 14 vols. (Leiden: Martinus Nijhoff, 1988), vol. 11B, pt. 2, pp. 625, 753.

the camps suffered even worse. The Japanese compelled as many as 4.1 million Indonesian labourers to work as so-called *rōmusha* or labour soldiers.[5] From Java alone, around 300,000 Indonesians were sent to work elsewhere; it is thought that around three quarters of this group died from exhaustion, starvation and disease.[6] The Japanese Army and Navy also recruited some 80,000 local auxiliary soldiers, the so-called *heiho*, from the ranks of the disbanded Royal Netherlands Indies Army (KNIL) and from among Indonesian youth,[7] and coerced some 20,000 Indonesian women into serving as so-called 'comfort women'.[8]

While the Second World War was still in progress, the Allies began to establish schemes for the prosecution and punishment of war criminals. Representatives of the Allied governments gathered in the London International Assembly, the International Commission for Penal Reform and Development, and the United Nations War Crimes Commission (UNWCC) to discuss legal methods for dealing with atrocities. Though Germany occupied the Netherlands itself, and Japan its Asian colony, the Netherlands' government-in-exile in London played an active and determined role, through their representatives, Dr J.M. de Moor and Dr M.W. Mouton, in the early international efforts to promote legal approaches to international crimes after the war.[9]

At the war's conclusion, the Dutch convened war crimes trials in both the Netherlands and in the Netherlands Indies. These were, however, mounted in very different circumstances and drew on different bodies of law. While peace had been re-established in the Netherlands, the Netherlands Indies was in a state of great turmoil, as the colonial authorities struggled to contain the Indonesian independence movement. Despite the complex circumstances surrounding the Dutch return to Indonesia, the Netherlands Indies administration was most eager to try those Europeans, Chinese and Indonesians who had collaborated with the Japanese. Investigations were conducted and evidence collected, and the first cases to be brought before the *Temporaire Krijgsraden* (temporary courts martial) were those of suspected collaborators.

5 P.H. Kratoska, 'Labour mobilization in Japan and the Japanese Empire', in Kratoska (ed.), *Asian labor*, p. 20.

6 H. Hovinga, 'End of a forgotten drama: the reception and repatriation of rōmusha after the Japanese capitulation', in Kratoska (ed.), *Asian labor*, pp. 213–215.

7 Maekawa, 'The *heiho*', pp. 189–191.

8 Y. Tanaka, *Japan's comfort women: sexual slavery and prostitution during World War II and the US occupation* (London: Routledge, 2002), p. 82.

9 L. van den Herik, 'The Dutch engagement with the project of international criminal justice', *Netherlands International Law Review* 57 (2010), 303–322.

The Dutch colonial authorities also turned their attention to the Japanese accused of war crimes. Between August 1946 and early 1949 they convened around 450 trials before the *Temporaire Krijgsraden* to hear the cases of 1,055 Japanese and affiliated defendants.[10] Ninety-three per cent were of Japanese nationality, while the remainder came from Japan's colonies of Formosa and Korea. About 400 of the defendants were members of *Kempeitai*, the Army's military police, or *Tokkeitai*, its naval equivalent.[11] There were 1,017 convictions, and nearly a quarter of those convicted received the death sentence. Fourteen were sentenced twice (for different crimes).[12] Forty-two defendants were acquitted. As well as the high conviction rates and heavy sentences, the Dutch war crimes programme was notable for convicting Indonesian independence fighters before the same courts as the Japanese defendants.

The Dutch attempt to reclaim Indonesia

When Japan surrendered on 15 August 1945 the larger part of the Netherlands Indies was still in Japanese hands. The Allied forces reoccupied Hollandia, Biak, Morotai, Tarakan and Balikpapan, but not the rest of the archipelago; instead, they concentrated on recapturing the Philippines, Burma and Malaysia.[13] On the day of Japan's capitulation, the responsibility for Allied operations in the Netherlands Indies was transferred from General Douglas MacArthur's South West Pacific Area command to Lord Admiral Louis Mountbatten's South East Asia Command. Thereafter, the British assumed responsibility for the disarmament and evacuation of Japanese forces, the rescue and repatriation of Allied prisoners of war and internees, and the maintenance of law and order.[14] The first British-led forces arrived in Indonesia in September

10 The figures stated here have been extracted from the database at the International Research and Documentation Centre for War Crimes Trials (Marburg); and from materials at the NIOD Institute for War, Holocaust and Genocide Studies (Amsterdam); the Dutch National Archives (The Hague); and the US National Archives and Records Administration (Maryland). Research is still in progress and the numbers may be greater.

11 L. de Jong, *Koninkrijk*, vol. 12, pt. 2, p. 896.

12 Nakata Fusao, for example, was tried in two different cases, and sentenced to ten and five years, respectively, totalling fifteen years imprisonment.

13 E. Touwen-Bouwsma and P. Groen, 'Van Banzai tot Bersiap', in E. Touwen-Bouwsma and P. Groen (eds.), *Tussen Banzai en Bersiap: de afwikkeling van de Tweede Wereldoorlog in Nederlands-Indië* (Den Haag: Sdu Uitgevers, 1996), pp. 10–11.

14 R. McMillan, *The British occupation of Indonesia 1945–1946: Britain, the Netherlands and the Indonesian revolution* (London: Routledge, 2005), pp. 2–3.

1945. In the meantime, though, Sukarno and Mohammad Hatta had taken advantage of the power vacuum and proclaimed the Republik Indonesia on 17 August 1945.

The British lacked adequate forces to conduct full-scale operations against the Indonesians, and so confined themselves to the occupation of several important areas.[15] The Dutch, weakened by the economic stress of the German occupation of the Netherlands, did not return to their former colonial holdings until mid-September 1945. On arrival, they were confronted by the Indonesian forces and discovered that there were only a few places where they could safely hoist the Dutch flag. Over the following year the Dutch would gradually take over from the British, until formal colonial authority over the Netherlands Indies reverted to the Dutch in November 1946. Over the next three years, the Dutch embarked on a brutal military campaign to prevent the consolidation of the Indonesian Republic. Despite this, they were not able to re-establish their former authority over large parts of the archipelago, and hence were compelled to withdraw by 27 December 1949.

Preparations for the trials

The investigation of Japanese war crimes in the Netherlands Indies was initially a combined Allied effort. During the war the only Dutch body collecting data concerning Japanese war crimes was the Netherlands Forces Intelligence Service. In September 1945, however, the Dutch set up a *Regeringsbureau tot Nasporing van Oorlogsmisdadigers* (Government Office for the Investigation of War Criminals) in Batavia, while a second *Regeringsbureau* was later set up in the Netherlands to interview witnesses who, after their release from Japanese control, had been repatriated back to Europe. At the same time, the Dutch profited from the efforts of British and Australian war crime investigation teams who from 1945 to 1946 had collated information on war crimes and the identity and location of suspected war criminals.[16] This was one reason

[15] Ibid., p. 4.

[16] Four of the seventeen SEAC war crime investigations teams (WCIT) were stationed in the Netherlands Indies: WCIT 1, 2 and 3 were stationed on Java and WCIT 4 on Sumatra. When the British withdrew from the Netherlands Indies in November 1946, their tasks were transferred to the military prosecutors. (J. Ph. Mullemeister, 'Verslag van de werkzaamheden der Nederlandse Liaison Sectie voor oorlogsmisdaden te Singapore over het tijdvak December 1945 tot December 1947' (Singapore, December 1947), pp. 11–12: inventarisnummer (inv. no.) 4526, Collection 400, NIOD.)

why so many Japanese operating on the archipelago were eventually swept into the Dutch net.[17]

In the latter stages of the war, it had been agreed among the Allies that they would follow standardised procedures for the investigation and adjudication of war crimes in Asia, with UNWCC as the coordinating body. But events were moving fast, and shortly after Japan's surrender the British started setting up courts and arresting suspects in their operational area, South East Asia Command, while still waiting for the final Allied decision on arrangements for dealing with war criminals. As a result, UNWCC decided to step away from the Asian scene, and in October 1945, the Commander-in-Chief of Allied Land Forces South East Asia (ALFSEA) assumed responsibility for the investigation, preparation and trial of 'minor' Japanese war crimes in Southeast Asia.[18]

The Dutch (along with the Australians, Americans and French) set up a liaison section with ALFSEA headquarters in Singapore.[19] Initially, this was staffed by two officers, but the volume of cases being proposed was so high that the Dutch set up another research team in Singapore in January 1946: the Netherlands War Crimes Investigation Team, led by Captain J.G. Benders.[20] This body examined war crimes committed by the Japanese, Koreans and Formosans within the Netherlands Indies, and those committed against Dutch nationals elsewhere in the Asia-Pacific theatre. By February 1946, their investigations had been extended to cover Indonesian independence fighters who had committed war crimes, people who had collaborated with either the Japanese or the Indonesian independence movement, and Europeans who had been affiliated with proscribed organisations during and after the war.[21]

In the meantime, in December 1945, ALFSEA headquarters and the Attorney General of the Netherlands Indies had together decided that the cases of greatest interest to the Dutch would be allocated to the Netherlands Indies authorities without interference from Singapore. The Attorney General would assign each case to one of the *Temporaire Krijgsraden*, of which there were eventually twenty-three, twelve of them

[17] L. van Poelgeest, *Japanse Besognes: Nederland en Japan 1945–1975* (Den Haag: SDU uitgevers, 1999), pp. 90–91.

[18] 'Voorlopige informatie van het Departement van Justitie te Batavia over de berechting van oorlogsmisdadigers', 20 February 1946, p. 15: inv. no. 1926, collection 400, NIOD.

[19] Ibid., p. 16.

[20] 'Rapport uitgebracht ingevolge mondelinge opdracht van den heer Procureur-Generaal . . . Professor Mr. Jonkers', 8 March 1946, p. 1: inv. no. 442, collection 400, NIOD.

[21] Ibid.

dealing with war crimes cases. The courts were convened to hear not only cases against the Japanese accused of war crimes but also cases dealing with European, Eurasian and Indonesian collaborators; Indonesian independence fighters; and KNIL soldiers who had committed 'excessen' during the struggle for independence.[22]

The fact that the war crimes trials of the Japanese were being established and conducted in the midst of an independence struggle brought particular problems of legitimacy in its wake. The Dutch were motivated, among other things, by the desire to use the trials to build more cordial relationships between themselves and the Indonesian and other Asian communities (or at least those not immediately in thrall to the independence movement), by positively contrasting their 'benign' colonial rule to that of the 'criminal' colonial rule of the outgoing Japanese. The trials, if nothing else, demonstrated that all parties – Dutch, Indonesian, Chinese, Eurasian and Indian – had suffered at the hands of the Japanese during the occupation, and that everyone (or so the Dutch believed) had a mutual interest in constructing a stable society based on justice, the rule of law, and a modernised, developmental model of colonial control. Yet the Dutch attempts to use the trials to talk up their role as the liberators of Indonesia from 'criminal' Japanese domination ignored a salient point: that most Indonesians and many from other Asian communities did not want liberation *by* the Dutch, but *from* the Dutch. That the Dutch and KNIL forces in the course of their 'politionele acties' (police actions) against Indonesian independence fighters committed atrocities not dissimilar to those ascribed to the Japanese defendants further undermined the credibility of the trial process.[23]

The trials also failed to convey a straightforward message to the Dutch, in both the Netherlands Indies and the Netherlands, that by trying and punishing Japanese war criminals, they had effectively settled the wartime account with Japan. This was because many Dutch, especially in the colony, erroneously ascribed the consolidation of the Indonesian Republic to the *ongoing* machinations of the Japanese.[24] The fact that

[22] J. Bank (Introduction), *De excessen nota: Nota betreffende het archievenonderzoek naar gegevens omtrent excessen in Indonesië begaan door Nederlandse militairen in de periode 1945–1950* (The Hague: Sdu Uitgeverij Konninginnegracht, 1995), Annex 8, p. 2.

[23] See L. van den Herik, 'Addressing "colonial crimes" through reparations? Adjudicating Dutch atrocities committed in Indonesia', *Journal of International Criminal Justice* 10 (2012), 693–705.

[24] R. Cribb, 'Avoiding clemency: the trial and transfer of Japanese war criminals in Indonesia, 1946–1949', *Japanese Studies* 31 (2011), 158–159.

after the surrender some 1,500 Japanese troops had joined the Indonesian forces, and that many other Japanese, despite Allied regulations, had handed over their weapons to the Indonesians, only encouraged this belief.[25] The purported linkage between the Japanese and the Indonesians was reinforced by Dutch propaganda, which presented the Indonesian Republic as a 'Japanese puppet-government of the Quisling type'.[26] This was underlined by the prosecution policy pursued by the *Temporaire Krijgsraden*, which convicted not only the Japanese from the former occupation forces but also the Indonesians nationalists and those who had thrown in their lot with them. It is small wonder that the war crimes trials failed to persuade either the Dutch or the Indonesians that justice had been done and that it was time to move on.

The law for trying war criminals

The Dutch established two sets of war crimes trials, regulated by different bodies of law: one governing the trials held in the Netherlands (dealing with Germans and local collaborators), and the other governing the trials in the Netherlands Indies (dealing with the Japanese, Koreans and Formosans).

In the Netherlands, the authorities suspended Article 1 of the Dutch Penal Code – which prohibited retroactive enactments on the principle of *nullum crimen, nulla poena sine lege* – thus freeing themselves to introduce extraordinary legislation to deal with alleged German war criminals.[27] This took the form of the Extraordinary Penal Law Decree of 22 December 1943, enacted by the government-in-exile in London, which was designed to supplement ordinary penal law, and which, in the interest of 'the security of the State', made possible 'the trial of certain acts committed during the time of the present war, which . . . were gravely deserving of punishment'.[28] An amendment to the Decree, Article 27(a), enacted in July 1947, added new crimes to Dutch courts'

[25] Van Poelgeest, *Japanse Besognes*, pp. 35, 84.

[26] 'Memorandum on the situation in Java' (to E. Bevin) (29 September 1945), in S.L. van der Wal (ed.), *Officiële Bescheiden betreffende de Nederlands-Indonesische Betrekkingen 1945–1950*, 20 vols. (The Hague, Martinus Nijhoff, 1971), vol. 1, no. 116.

[27] United Nations War Crimes Commission, *Law reports of trials of war criminals*, 15 vols. (London: HMSO, 1947–1949), vol. 11, p. 86. Article 1 reads: 'No act is punishable except in virtue of a legal penal provision which preceded such act. Should there be a change in the legislation after the date on which the crime was committed the provision most favourable to the accused shall then be applied' (ibid.).

[28] Ibid.

jurisdiction.[29] This ensured that those accused of crimes against humanity and war crimes not already covered in Dutch law – as set out in Articles 6(b) and 6(c) of the Nuremberg Charter – could be tried. The punishment of these new crimes would proceed by way of analogy, for as the second part of the Article states, 'If such crime does not at the same time contain the elements of a punishable act according to the Netherlands law, the perpetrator shall receive the punishment laid down by Netherlands law for the act with which it shows the greatest similarity.'[30] In short, the crimes were derived from the Nuremberg Charter, while the punishments were derived from Dutch municipal law.

Following the Netherlands' lead, the Netherlands Indies authorities, on 22 September 1945, issued an ordinance – *Staatsblad* 1945 no. 135 – that introduced extraordinary legislation in the Netherlands Indies through changes of and additional provisions to the Netherlands Indies Penal Code.[31] The ordinance suspended Article 1 of this Code, which, as in the Netherlands, embodied the injunction *nullum crimen, nulla poena sine lege*, thus enabling the government to introduce a wider array of war crime charges.[32] Yet the approach taken by the Netherlands Indies with regard to the definition of war crimes was different from that taken by the Netherlands in several important respects. For a start, it drew on different international law sources. The colony's 'Definition of War Crimes Decree' laid down in *Staatsblad* 1946 no. 44 stated that these were 'acts which constitute a violation of the laws and usages of war committed in time of war by subjects of an enemy power or by foreigners in the service of the enemy'.[33] The definition was followed by an *exempli causa* list of offences drawn from the Paris Peace Conference's Commission of Responsibilities of 1919, and amplified by UNWCC in 1944.[34] In other

[29] UNWCC, 'Information concerning human rights arising from trials of war criminals' (1948), pp. 144–145: www.unwcc.org/documents.

[30] Ibid., p. 145.

[31] 'No. 15031. Rechtswezen. Oorlogsmisdrijven. Toelichting op de ontworpen wetgeving inzake oorlogsmisdrijven' (also known as *Bijblad op het Staatsblad van Nederlandsch-Indië* 15031), p. 36: inv. no. 8, 2.21.281.31, collection 584, L.F. de Groot, 1946–1991, Nationaal Archief, Den Haag (NL-HaNA).

[32] Ibid. See also: J.E. Jonkers, *De weg van het strafrecht. Rede uitgesproken bij de aanvaarding van het ambt van hoogleeraar in het Nederlandsch-Indisch strafrecht en procesrecht aan de Rijksuniversiteit Leiden op vrijdag 14 juni 1946* (Leiden: Brill, 1946), pp. 12–14.

[33] UNWCC, *Law reports*, vol. 11, p. 3.

[34] Article 1, *Staatsblad* 1946 no. 44. For a reference to the Commission of Responsibilities and UNWCC being sources, see: 'No. 15031. Rechtswezen', pp. 28–30.

words, the list borrowed from the Hague and Geneva Conventions, rather than from the Nuremberg Charter. After some revealing internal discussions about sources,[35] the Netherlands Indies government opted to add five additional crimes to the existing Penal Code. Four of these crimes – 'Ill treatment of interned civilians or prisoners', 'Carrying out of or causing execution to be carried out in an inhuman way', 'Refusal of aid or prevention of aid being given to shipwrecked persons' and 'Intentional withholding of medical supplies from civilians'[36] – were primarily designed to address offences that had been committed by the Japanese during the war. The fifth offence – commission contrary to the conditions of a truce, of hostile acts or the incitement thereto, and the furnishing of others with information, the opportunity or the means for that purpose[37] – was clearly intended to deal with actions taken after the end of the war (at least four Japanese defendants who had later joined the Indonesians in their fight against the Netherlands were convicted under this provision).[38]

The Netherlands Indies government decided to apply this mix of colonial law and international law because the colony's existing criminal law and the extraordinary legislation did not make sufficient provision for the sort of war crimes committed during the Asia-Pacific war.[39] It was therefore necessary to supplement the Netherlands Indies Penal Code with international law governing the laws and customs of war, in order to give prosecutors and judges greater flexibility when raising charges and making determinations. It was emphasised, however, that the international provisions were not intended to supplant the Code's existing war crimes provisions, but to coexist with them.

> In spite of the reference to the laws and customs of war in the definition of war crimes and except when a deviation from the general Netherlands East Indies Penal Code has been established by decree expressly for war

[35] One report from a Dutch meeting of departmental heads states, 'Some doubt was expressed on whether one should consider the crimes [enumerated] to be war crimes, as the Allies have also committed such acts. However, since UNWCC has laid down this list of war crimes, it seemed better to maintain them.' 'Kort verslag van de vergadering van den Raad van Departements hoofden, gehouden op Woensdag 29 Mei 1946 ten Paleize Koningsplein', p. 3: inv. no. 2289, 2.10.14, Algemene Secretarie van de Nederlands-Indische Regering en de daarbij gedeponeerde Archieven, NL-HaNA.

[36] UNWCC, *Law reports*, vol. 11, p. 94. [37] Ibid.

[38] De Jong, *Koninkrijk*, vol. 12, pt. 2, p. 893. For one of these cases, see: Sentence, *Mizuo Katsuno* (28 May 1947), p. 1 (original translation): www.legal-tools.org.

[39] 'No. 15031. Rechtswezen', pp. 36–38.

> crimes, the Netherlands East Indies existing penal laws ... remain in principle applicable to war crimes.[40]

It should be added at this point that unlike in the Netherlands, the Netherlands Indies government decided not to add crimes against humanity to the courts' jurisdiction, arguing that the provisions on war crimes would be sufficient to cover the crimes committed by the Japanese.[41] It was further argued that the charge of crimes against humanity was designed to punish a state's crimes against its own citizens, and that the Dutch had no particular interest in holding the Japanese to account for the crimes committed against their own people.[42] It might be added that in all likelihood the colonial authorities decided not to adopt the charge because they feared that Dutch and KNIL soldiers might be accused of committing crimes against humanity during the course of their war against their own colonial subjects agitating for independence.

The 'War Crimes Penal Law Decree' (*Staatsblad* 1946 no. 45) introduced Article 4, so that those guilty of a war crime 'will be punished with the death penalty, or imprisonment for life, or imprisonment for not less than one day, and not more than twenty years'.[43] Another Decree, the 'War Crimes Penal Procedure Decree' (*Staatsblad* 1946 no. 47), set out rules of procedure, rules of evidence and other procedural matters, to supplement Article 154 of the Revised Judicial Procedures of the Army (*Herziene Rechtspleging bij de Landmacht*).[44] The amended rules of evidence were especially pertinent to the war crimes trials. They stated that the judge might recognise as evidence 'all documents produced at the sitting and all statements wherever made', ascribing to them 'such conclusive strength as he thinks they may possess, if, in his opinion, the particular circumstances under which the war crime was committed or in which a piece of evidence would have to be furnished, would form an obstacle to the further production of evidence or would result in an inadmissible delay in the termination of the case, should this further evidence have to be produced'.[45]

[40] UNWCC, *Law reports*, vol. 11, p. 91. See also, 'No. 15031. Rechtswezen', p. 42.

[41] 'No. 15031. Rechtswezen', pp. 38–40. [42] Ibid.

[43] 'Strafrecht Oorlogsmisdrijven', *Staatsblad van Nederlandsch-Indië* 1946, no. 45, p. 2.

[44] Revised Judicial Procedures of the Army of 29 August 1945, laid down in *Staatsblad* 1945 no. 112, and revised by *Staatsblad* 1945 no. 126.

[45] 'Rechtspleging Oorlogsmisdrijven', *Staatsblad van Nederlandsch-Indië* 1946, no. 47, pp. 5–6; and UNWCC, *Law reports*, vol. 11, p. 108.

The temporary courts martial

Each *Temporaire Krijgsraad* consisted of a President and two Members, almost invariably Dutch or Eurasian, assisted by a legal secretary, who were either serving officers or civilians who had been given a military rank under the state of emergency that had been in place since 1940. Qualified legal personnel were extremely scarce at the time, and many of the judges worked at both the courts martial and in the civilian courts. The Judge Advocates (prosecutors), also almost invariably Dutch or Eurasian, were usually civilians, and, like the judges, they often served in several capacities – for example, some of the war crime investigators and interrogators were later employed as Judge Advocates. The defence counsel were mostly Japanese lawyers who had travelled from Japan to the Netherlands Indies to represent the defendants (the latter had the right to choose counsel; otherwise, one was assigned to them by the court). If the accused believed that the President or the Members might not be suitable judges in the case, they were allowed to challenge them on grounds of lack of impartiality.

It should be noted that the conditions under which the court officials had to work were far from ideal: sittings often took place in makeshift courthouses, and sometimes amidst fighting between the Dutch and Indonesian troops. As a clerk at one of the civilian *Landgerecht* courts recalled,

> We held our first meeting in February 1946, in the former Supreme Court building at the Waterlooplein ... There we sat around a table with some chairs, all the carpets still dripping with the blood of the murders that had happened just before. Indonesians had killed some Dutchmen. It was a real battle. Well, at that time there was no other building, we had just liberated that building and we did not have the opportunity to clean everything, so we just picked out the best room.[46]

One noted commentator on the trial programme was Levinus Franciscus de Groot, a Dutch judge who presided over many war crimes trials in Batavia, and whose private papers offer a candid commentary on the issues arising from the proceedings. De Groot's experience was in many ways typical of those who were involved in the Netherlands Indies trials. Born in Santpoort and university-educated at Leiden in the Netherlands, he moved to Batavia, where he started his career at the colony's

[46] Statement by Van Rijckevorsel, a clerk at the *Landgerecht*, 'De Nederlandse Rechtspraak in Indonesië', the sixth broadcast of the ten-part series, 'Afscheid van Indië', *Het spoor terug*, VPRO, 5 August 1988.

Department of Justice and the Magistracy. When the Netherlands declared war on Japan in December 1941, he was mobilised as a reserve captain; after the capitulation, he spent the duration of the war imprisoned in Japanese internment camps on Java. After the war, De Groot was appointed as *landrechter* (civilian judge) in Bandung, then as a member at the *Temporaire Krijgsraden* in Batavia, later serving as substitute President and President. The court in Batavia, now Jakarta, was one of the most important military courts in the Netherlands Indies because it dealt with the greatest number of defendants, and some of the highest-profile cases.

While De Groot was generally satisfied with the work of his own court, he also recognised some of the flaws in the administration of justice against the Japanese. He was aware that some of the suspects had not been treated according to the established rules during their interrogations.[47] He recognised that when it came to judgment, some of the judges found it hard to separate their own wartime experiences, as prisoners of war or civilian detainees, from the legal process.[48] And he acknowledged that the judges were frequently presented with unreliable witnesses and unsafe evidence, writing that

> People were only too happy to testify against the Japanese, and they were not overly concerned about the truthfulness of the evidence they gave. Their testimonies were for various reasons often grossly exaggerated. Their identification of people from photos, or [denunciations arising from] face-to-face confrontations with those who had mistreated them or with whom they otherwise had been in contact, were performed with stunning ease and appalling indifference. The people who were involved in the investigation (both trained and untrained staff) often displayed a complete lack of objectivity and responsibility when interrogating witnesses or when collecting other data, which should form the basis of the case. As a result, the suppression of favourable details about the Japanese accused was an understandable but nevertheless reprehensible phenomenon.[49]

[47] L.F. de Groot, *Berechting Japanse oorlogsmisdadigers in Nederlands-Indië 1946–1949: Temporaire Krijgsraad Batavia*, 2 vols. (Den Bosch: Art & Research, 1990), vol. 2, p. 376.

[48] Draft of an untitled article by P. Schumacher on L.F. de Groot (September 1989), annexed to letter from P. Schumacher to De Groot (19 September 1989), p. 4: inv. no. 2, 2.21.281.31, collection 584, L.F. de Groot, 1946–1991, NL-HaNA. Charles van der Sloot, a former investigation officer in Morotai and substitute Judge Advocate at the *Temporaire Krijgsraden* in Makassar, acknowledged that hatred for the Japanese influenced the legal decision making of the court. (Interview of 13 November 2014 on file with the author.)

[49] L.F. de Groot, 'De rechtspraak inzake oorlogsmisdrijven in Nederlands-Indië (1947–1949)', *Militair Rechtelijk Tijdschrift* 78 (1985), 86.

As a consequence, De Groot concluded elsewhere, 'It was therefore extraordinarily difficult for the judge to separate "the wheat from the chaff" and to determine, on the basis thereof, which – if any – evidential value should be granted' to testimonies presented to the court.[50]

Trying criminal groups

Many of the Allies made use of theories of collective responsibility during the trials in Asia. In the Dutch cases, the authorities were inclined to rely on concepts of conspiracy and membership of a criminal organisation rather than on personal liability when they encountered problems in the collection of evidence against individual members of the *Kempeitai* or the *Tokkeitai*. As some observed, it was sometimes difficult to marshal sufficient evidence against individual officers because the victims either did not know the name of their tormentors or may not have been able to recognise them during a later face-to-face confrontation.[51] The case of *Motomura Shigeki et al.* shows how the concept of 'criminal groups' was used to secure the conviction of a group of Japanese *Tokkeitai* members for crimes committed in the area under their control.

This case, heard at Makassar in July 1947, involved sixteen members of the Makassar *Tokkeitai* operating in southwest Sulawesi from March 1942 to August 1945. According to the Indictment, they had carried out a campaign of 'systematic terrorism' against the Indonesian population, which had included

> repeated, regular and lengthy torture, and/or ill-treatment [of those arrested] ... repeatedly striking them with the hand and with sticks during their interrogation, kicking them with the shod foot, hanging them up by the arm or leg, burning them with glowing cigarettes and bicycle bells, wrenching their knee-joints apart, stripping women and exposing them in this condition to the public view, withholding food from arrestees[52]

They were charged collectively under Article 10 of the Netherlands Indies *Staatsblad* 1946 no. 45, which stated that:

[50] De Groot, 'Enkele notities naar aanleiding van het vonnis in de zaak Duursma', annexed to letter, De Groot to De Jong (6 February 1986), p. 4: inv. no. 29, 2.21.281.31, collection 584, L.F. de Groot, 1946–1991, NL-HaNA.

[51] De Jong, *Koninkrijk*, vol. 12, pt. 2, p. 892.

[52] Sentence, *Motomura Shigeki and fifteen others* (18 July 1947), p. 2 (original translation): www.legal-tools.org.

1. If a war crime is committed within the framework of the activities of a group of persons in such a way that the crime can be ascribed to that group as a whole, the crime shall be considered to have been committed by that group, and criminal proceedings taken against and sentence passed on all members of that group.
2. No penalty shall be imposed on the member for whom it is proved that he had taken no part in the commission of the war crime.[53]

This approach was distinct from the approach taken by Articles 9 to 11 of the Nuremberg Charter on criminal groups or 'criminal organizations'.[54] Under the Nuremberg procedure, if the Indictment alleged that certain organisations were criminal, the Tribunal's function was to decide whether they *were* criminal organisations, and if so, whether associated individuals were members of the criminal organisation or not. It did not weigh the individual's guilt or pass sentence on them (this would be done by other courts once their membership had been established). Individuals could exempt themselves by demonstrating that they were not members, or had been coerced into membership or did not play a meaningful part in the organisation's criminal actions. In the Netherlands Indies, however, if the Indictment claimed that a group of people had committed a crime collectively, the court's function was to determine the existence of the crime and the collective nature of its perpetration, and then – provided more than one person could be proved to have committed the crime – pass sentence on them all while also assessing degrees of guilt of each individual.[55] Individuals could exempt themselves by showing that they were not part of the group or had not meaningfully contributed to the group's criminal action. The Decree did not define 'group'; this was left for the court to determine.

[53] UNWCC, *Law reports*, vol. 11, p. 101. See also, 'No. 15031. Rechtswezen', pp. 48–49. It has been argued that the Netherlands Indies authorities introduced it to deal specifically with the crimes committed by the *Kempeitai* (De Jong, *Koninkrijk*, vol. 12, pt. 2, p. 894). L.F. de Groot disagreed: 'The statement that *article 10* related especially to the *Kenpeitai* is *incorrect*. This provision, *in general*, was applied to groups who committed criminal acts and has repeatedly been applied to other cases. It is however true that the prosecution of *all Kempei-units* occurred on the basis of this article.' ('Nadere opmerkingen naar aanleiding van de tweede versie van het concept voor de paragraaf "Berechting der Japanners"' (February 1988), p. 5: inv. no. 29, 2.21.281.31, collection 584, L.F. de Groot, 1946–1991, NL-HaNA. Original emphases.)

[54] International Military Tribunal, *Trial of the major war criminals before the International Military Tribunal*, 'The Blue Series', 42 vols. (Nuremberg: IMT, 1947–1949), Charter, vol. 1, p. 12.

[55] UNWCC, *Law reports*, vol. 11, pp. 101–102.

The Indictment for *Motomura Shigeki et al.* charged that 'these *Tokkeitai* being ... a group in the sense of Art. 10 ... committed war crimes within the framework of its activities, the said unit having by means of its members ... carried out unlawful mass arrests and/or exercised systematic terrorism against persons suspected by the Japanese of punishable acts'.[56] Of the indicted group, four in commanding positions – Sub-Lieutenant Motomura Shigeki (the second-in-command), Senior Petty Officer Sakai Chobei (Motomura's deputy), Warrant Officer Minami Tooru (head of the detachment at Malili Posso and/or Masamba) and Warrant Officer Ono Yoshio (head of the detachment in Mamoedjoe) – were charged with having 'ordered, encouraged or allowed' their subordinates to commit crimes.[57] These officers were also charged alongside the other defendants with personally carrying out crimes. Most of the defendants were charged with mass arrests, torture or the ill treatment of local inhabitants; two of them, the aforementioned Minami Tooru and Masuda Tametsu, were also indicted for rape.

Motomura, the chief defendant, made a partial admission of guilt, declaring himself responsible for the deeds of his deputy and his other subordinates when they were under his control in Macassar, but he denied responsibility for their actions when they were on detachment to other places.[58] He also denied the other charges of ill-treating three American airmen and withholding food from a political prisoner.[59] Sakai also made a partial admission of guilt, admitting that he had conducted and supervised mass arrests, but only accepting responsibility for orders when Motomura was absent, and he was standing in for him.[60] He admitted striking people with the flat of his hand, but denied ill-treating them.[61] The remaining thirteen (another accused, Ono Yoshio, had committed suicide before the trial) all pleaded not guilty to the charges.

During the President's investigation, much attention was paid to the *Tokkeitai*'s command structure and the defendants' presumed knowledge of the provisions governing its operations.[62] Although the prosecution presented 114 witness statements, none of the witnesses testified in court, which made it impossible for the defence counsel to examine them.[63] The court nevertheless decided that sufficient evidence had been produced to conclude that not only the individual defendants but

[56] Sentence, *Motomura Shigeki et al.*, p. 2. [57] Ibid., pp. 2, 3, 4. [58] Ibid., p. 7.
[59] Ibid., pp. 3, 9. [60] Ibid. [61] Ibid., p. 9.
[62] See, for example, Trial transcript, *Motomura Shigeki et al.* (8 May 1947), pp. 4–10: inv. no 389, collection 400, NIOD.
[63] Ibid. (9 May 1947), pp. 1–17; and (13 May 1947), pp. 1–12.

also the *Tokkeitai* 'taken as a group' were guilty of the war crimes.[64] The Judgment emphasised the systematic and standardised nature of the *Tokkeitai*'s ill treatment and torture of their victims to extract confessions.[65] It further observed that their methods were 'also in vogue with the *Kempeitai* . . . and even with the Japanese civil police' as well as being among 'the well-tried method of the German Gestapo and Russian G.P.U.'.[66] Weighing the personal responsibility of the individual members, it found all the accused guilty except for one defendant, Terayama Soichi, who was acquitted.[67] Of those convicted, nine, including Motomura, Sakai and Minami, were sentenced to death; two were sentenced to twenty years' imprisonment; one to fifteen years; one to five years; and one to a year's imprisonment.[68]

The plea of superior orders at Morotai

The trial of Ogihara Goro, conducted in August 1947 at Morotai, focused on defences of superior orders and duress. According to the Indictment, First Lieutenant Ogihara of the *Kempeitai* had proposed to Captain Sougahara of the Japanese Army the execution of some thirty people, among them many people suffering from leprosy, who were living in or near Medi on the island of Halmaheira in the eastern reaches of the archipelago.[69] The Indictment further claimed that Sougahara had acceded to the request, and Ogihara had ordered his subordinate, Kimura Chogoro, to arrange the executions. As well as the crimes committed against Medi's inhabitants, the Indictment contained eight more accusations against Ogihara of inciting war crimes, which had resulted in the execution of a further forty-four Indonesian and Chinese people on the island.[70]

To put Ogihara's trial into context, the same court had a few weeks earlier sentenced Captain Sougahara to death for his part in the executions of the inhabitants of Medi. During Sougahara's trial the court had been unable to establish who had been initially responsible for coming up with the plan because Ogihara and Sougahara had blamed each other.[71] Returning to Ogihara's trial, the accused claimed that Sougahara had wielded more authority then he had, and that it was therefore Sougahara who was ultimately responsible for the executions. If this was really the

[64] Sentence, *Motomura Shigeki et al.*, p. 13. [65] Ibid. [66] Ibid. [67] Ibid., p. 17.
[68] Ibid., pp. 17–19.
[69] Sentence, *Ogihara Goro* (29 August 1947), p. 1 (original translation): www.legal-tools.org.
[70] Ibid., pp. 1–3. [71] Ibid., p. 4.

superior–subordinate relationship between them, it was a strange (and, the court thought, 'improbable') one, Sougahara being an Army captain and Ogihara being a *Kempeitai* first lieutenant.[72] Nevertheless, having claimed that Sougahara was his superior, Ogihara advanced a plea of obedience to superior orders carried out under duress, because, he claimed, disobeying an order was impossible – if he had disobeyed, Sougahara could and would have had him shot.[73] He further argued that even if confronted with an illegal order, his only option other than disobeying would have been to kill himself.[74]

Interestingly, the American-run *Einsatzgruppen* case, which opened in Nuremberg just a few weeks after Ogihara's, in September 1947, raised a similar issue. Once again, the issue of superior orders and duress was discussed. The court noted that the defendants had hardly been compelled to act with a loaded pistol held to their heads; instead, they were in basic agreement with their superiors about the principles and intent of the crime.[75] It concluded that when the will of the subordinate and the will of the superior were 'pooled in the planning and execution' of a crime, the subordinate could not then plead duress under superior orders.[76] Even more to the point, the Tribunal considering the *Einsatzgruppen* case untangled the complications that might arise about the definition of 'superior', stating that

> Superior means superior in capacity and power to force a certain act. It does not mean superiority only in rank. It could easily happen in an illegal enterprise that the captain guides the major, in which case the captain could not be heard to plead superior orders in defense of his crime.[77]

As it turned out, Ogihara's argument that he was simply obeying Souagahara's orders failed to persuade the court. On the one hand, it did not find it proven that Ogihara had proposed and Sougahara had consented to the executions, but on the other, it declared itself satisfied that Ogihara had agreed to the plan.[78] It observed that 'the accused after consultation with *Sougahara* – for there very certainly must have been a

[72] Ibid.

[73] Trial transcript, *Ogihara Goro* (27–28 August 1947), p. 3: inv. no. 399, collection 400, NIOD.

[74] Ibid.

[75] *Trials of war criminals before the Nuernberg Military Tribunals under Control Council Law No. 10*, 'The Green Series', 15 vols. (Nuremberg: US Government Printing Office, October 1946–April 1949), vol. 4, p. 480.

[76] Ibid. [77] Ibid.

[78] Sentence, *Ogihara Goro* (29 August 1947), p. 4 (original translation): www.legal-tools.org.

consultation between the two over the carrying out of the execution – gave his subordinate *Kimura* orders to have the lepers from *Medi* executed', and that his defence amounted to 'a plea of superior orders, casu quo, of duress'.[79] The court rejected this plea for several reasons: first, the *Kempeitai* played a 'special' role within the Japanese command structure – meaning (although the court did not spell it out) that its officers were largely beholden only unto themselves – and second, that Ogihara had at no point been compelled to collaborate in the organisation of the executions.[80] Indeed, Ogihara had attempted to justify the executions as a 'fully justified military measure', rather than acknowledging that the mass murder of civilians was a crime. The only objections to the executions elicited from him in court were that they 'might perhaps have an unfavourable influence on the feelings of the population', and that 'he found it a very disgusting job to kill these lepers'.[81]

After considering all the evidence, the court found Ogihara guilty of 'incitement to murder' and 'incitement to mass murder' and sentenced him to death. In the Judgment, it noted that 'even the severest punishment appears too light a retribution for all the misery and suffering which, partly or chiefly, by the accused's doing were sown upon *Halmaheira* and for the streams of innocent blood with which he drenched the soil of that island'.[82]

When considering how to approach the 'superior orders' plea, the Netherlands Indies authorities were faced with an impediment to the prosecution of the Japanese in the form of Article 51 of the Penal Code, which stipulated that a subordinate was not punishable for a crime committed in the course of carrying out an official order issued by a 'competent authority'.[83] They were aware of the approach taken by Article 8 of the Nuremberg Charter – which removed the superior orders plea as an absolute defence, but allowed its consideration in mitigation of punishment[84] – but expressly decided against following this line.[85] Instead of amending Article 51 so as to narrow the basis on which a superior order plea could be advanced, the legislature, by Article 1(3) of *Staatsblad* 1946 no. 45, cut the knot and suspended the Article from the Code. By doing this, it left the issue of superior orders entirely to the discretion of the judge to either remove a defendant's liability for punishment or establish the subordinate's degree of responsibility.[86]

[79] Ibid. [80] Ibid. [81] Ibid. [82] Ibid., p. 16. [83] UNWCC, *Law reports*, vol. 11, p. 99.
[84] IMT, vol. 1, p. 12. [85] 'No. 15031. Rechtswezen', pp. 46–47. [86] Ibid.

As might be expected, the debate about the expectations placed on subordinates faced with an unlawful order had a knock-on effect on Dutch military operations during the 'police actions'. In January 1948, the Dutch military court-martialled three marines for refusing to obey their platoon commander's order to burn down part of a *kampong* (hamlet).[87] One of the defendants, Sergeant 'S.M.T.', pleaded that he did not see any strategic need for arson and that he had objected to meting out reprisals against apparently innocent civilians. The Judge decided that under the rules of military discipline, a marine did not have the right to make obedience to a military order dependent on his own judgment of its purpose and effectiveness. He declared the sergeant guilty of 'wilful disobedience committed in time of war, in which the guilty also turns another combatant to the crime' and sentenced him to three years' imprisonment, while two marines received three years' and eighteen months' imprisonment respectively.[88] On appeal, the High Military Court reduced the sergeant's sentence by six months and the first marine's sentence by a year.[89] Despite the reductions, these sentences still caused indignation back in the Netherlands.[90] If the authorities were going to lock up Japanese soldiers for obeying unlawful orders, they could not very well lock up Dutch soldiers for *not* obeying what they believed to be the same. The war crimes trials had produced new assumptions about the conduct of military personnel, and this cut both ways.

The question of command responsibility

The last case to be tried before the *Temporaire Krijgsraad* in Batavia was that of General Imamura Hitoshi and Lieutenant General Okazaki Seisaburo in March 1949, which raised the issue of command responsibility. Imamura was the Commander of the Sixteenth Army, which had

87 See 'Sentence court martial, *S.M.T.* (5 January 1948)'; 'Sentence High Military Court, *S.M. T.* (24 March 1948)'; and 'Naschrift', *Militair Rechtelijk Tijdschrift* 41 (1948), 327–340.

88 Ibid., 335. 89 Bank (Introduction), *De excessen nota*, Annex 5, pp. 15–17.

90 Bernard V.A. Röling, the Dutch judge at the International Military Tribunal for the Far East, attempted to simultaneously explain the response to the sentences while also trying to justify the order as military necessity, when he wrote: 'Outrage over the arson verdict is widely felt. This is understandable. Due to the frequently disseminated propaganda on the atrocities committed by the Axis, the public has lost sight of the fact that a war waged according to the laws of war is also inhumane, and that the Dutch, by standards of its civilian society, need to commit inhumane acts.' Röling, 'Noot' on Case 147, *Nederlandse Jurisprudentie* (Zwolle: N.V. Uitgevers-Maatschappij W.E.J. Tjeenk Willink, 1949), p. 279.

invaded the Netherlands Indies in early 1942, while Okazaki had been his Chief-of-Staff. Imamura stayed in this position until 9 November 1942, after which he assumed command of the Eight Area Army, while Okazaki stayed in the Netherlands Indies until June 1943. Both the defendants were charged with war crimes for having allowed their troops to commit murder, mass murder, torture of civilians, rape, mistreatment of prisoners and ill treatment of prisoners of war in Java and Borneo.[91] The Indictment, based on a combination of Article 9 (toleration of subordinates' crimes) and Article 10 (crimes committed by a group) of the 'War Crimes Penal Law Decree',[92] addressed their respective functions both as Commander and Chief-of-Staff, and as members of the Sixteenth Army HQ Group.

The responsibility of superiors appeared as a component of Article 55 of the Netherlands Indies Penal Code:

> As perpetrators of a punishable act (the following) shall be punished:
>
> (1) those who commit the act, cause it to be committed, or are accessories to it.[93]

The phrase 'cause it to be committed' covered the case of a superior officer ordering subordinates to commit a crime. It was thought advisable, however, to introduce specific rules for cases in which superiors had failed to prevent or had tolerated the commission of crimes rather than specifically ordering them. Thus Article 9 of *Staatsblad* 1946 no. 45 declared, 'He whose subordinate has committed a war crime shall be equally punishable for that war crime, if he has tolerated its commission by his subordinate whilst knowing, or at least must have reasonably supposed, that it was being or would be committed.'[94] A memorandum explained that it was up to the court to decide if a superior had taken general measures to prevent the perpetration of war crimes by his subordinates, or had taken specific measures to prevent a particular war crime being committed by a subordinate.[95] If the court found that the superior had done so, the superior should be acquitted.[96]

[91] Sentence, *Imamura Hitoshi and Okazaki Seisaburo* (16 March 1949), pp. 1–6: inv. no. 378, collection 400, NIOD.

[92] De Groot, *Berechting Japanse oorlogsmisdadigers*, vol. 1, p. 46.

[93] UNWCC, *Law reports*, vol. 11, p. 100.

[94] Ibid. *Staatsblad* 1947 no. 16 added an additional paragraph to Article 9 extending the rule to subordinates 'not being subjects of a hostile power or foreigners in the service of the enemy'.

[95] 'No. 15031. Rechtswezen', p. 48. [96] Ibid.

Both Imamura and Okazaki pleaded not guilty to the charges, on the grounds that they could not have known, or have reasonably supposed, that their subordinates were committing war crimes.[97] In addition, Imamura, in a written statement, explained that he firmly believed that he had tried his best to guide and control his subordinates and had taken the necessary precautionary measures.[98]

The Batavian *Temporaire Krijgsraad*, presided over by the aforementioned L.F. de Groot, carried out a detailed study of the command structures of and military operations by the Sixteenth Army, and, after an examination of the defendants, concluded that none of the charges laid against the accused could be proven. It decided that even though it had been established that the majority of the atrocities had actually taken place and the defendants might have known or suspected the war crimes, they could not be held personally responsible because they had actively tried to prevent atrocities during their period of command.[99] Moreover, the Sixteenth Army Headquarters could not, as was charged, be regarded as a 'criminal organisation'. The Judgment stated, 'Given that in this case, the defendants – being the main characters of that group – are the only ones brought before this court and given that no war crimes have come to light as committed by the headquarter, this question should be answered in the negative.'[100] The court acquitted Imamura and Okazaki of all charges on 16 March 1949.

The reasoning in the Judgment and the personal papers of De Groot, including correspondence with Imamura himself, indicate that the court had misgivings about levelling unsubstantiated accusations against the two defendants.[101] The judges seemed to have been guided by several factors beyond the straightforward appraisal of evidence. First, they took into consideration what they believed to be Imamura's unusually lenient policy towards the local population of the Netherlands Indies during the Japanese occupation, which they thought had exercised a moderating influence on 'Tokyo's ruthless war-spirit'.[102] Second, they seemed to have been swayed by the defendants' professional background and demeanour

[97] Trial transcript, *Imamura Hitoshi and Okazaki Seisaburo* (8 March 1949), p. 2: inv. no. 378, collection 400, NIOD.

[98] De Groot, *Berechting Japanse oorlogsmisdadigers*, vol. 1, p. 57.

[99] Sentence, *Imamura Hitoshi and Okazaki Seisaburo*, pp. 21–30. [100] Ibid., p. 30.

[101] De Groot to Imamura (8 September 1950), inv. no. 3, 2.21.281.31, collection 584, L.F. de Groot, 1946–1991, NL-HaNA.

[102] Sentence, *Imamura Hitoshi and Okazaki Seisaburo*, p. 30.

during the trial.[103] In the Judgment, it was noted that the defendants had served in London and Geneva during the interwar years, which, it was strongly implied, had contributed to a more sophisticated sensibility. It stated:

> The court martial during this trial is firmly convinced that both the first and second defendant by their extended and repeated stays abroad … have acquired international views and insights. These go far beyond the level of development and civilisation of the average Japanese 'war lords' of the genre of Harada and Kokubu and many others who, as notorious representatives of the 'unscrupulous' Japanese war spirit, have been tried as war criminals … For this reason and because the defendants did not shun the responsibilities associated with their high positions, more value may be attached to their statements than to those of other Japanese defendants, even though they are not entirely confirmed by legal evidence.[104]

In addition to these considerations, the judges were well aware that the court was operating in a highly fraught political situation. Many Asians (not just Indonesians) believed that Dutch justice was tainted by racial prejudice against the Japanese, who had so brusquely ejected them from their former colony. And many Dutch believed that Imamura and Okazaki were guilty, trial or no trial, and should be sentenced to death. The latter sentiment was borne out by the reaction to the court's decision to acquit, which met with some very strong Dutch objections in the colony and back in the Netherlands, where Imamura was dubbed the 'Seyss-Inquart van Java'.[105] It would take nine months for the Judgment to be executed because Raden A. Hilman Djajadiningrat, the Governor of Batavia, whose official function was to confirm the sentence, persisted with demands for the death sentence.[106] Eventually, as De Groot later

[103] In a letter to Imamura, De Groot later wrote, 'I personally, during the investigation of your case[,] appreciated your attitude as well as the attitude of your Chief of Staff' (8 September 1950), p. 1: inv. no. 3, 2.21.281.31, collection 584, L.F. de Groot, 1946–1991, NL-HaNA.

[104] Sentence, *Imamura Hitoshi and Okazaki Seisaburo*, p. 23.

[105] 'Boek van Haarlemmer over Japanse oorlogsmisdadigers', *Haarlems Dagblad* (30 November 1990), p. 18. See also, De Groot to Imamura (8 September 1950), p. 2: inv. no. 3, 2.21.281.31, collection 584, L.F. de Groot, 1946–1991, NL-HaNA.

[106] According to Matsuura Kojiro (former interpreter at the court) and De Groot himself, Djajadiningrat had tried to refuse to give his confirmation because he had been in close contact with Okazaki during the Japanese occupation and was afraid that the Dutch would discover this relationship. (Notes of L.F. de Groot on translation of Matsuura Kojiro, *Indoneshia 30 Nen* (Tokyo: Jitsugyo na Nihonsha, 1976), p. 6: inv. no. 3, 2.21.281.31, collection 584, L.F. de Groot, 1946–1991, NL-HaNA.)

told Imamura, the Dutch High Representative of the Crown Antonius H.J. Lovink stepped in and ordered the Governor to give his 'fiat executie' to the court's decision.[107]

Conclusion

It proved to be one of the final actions of the colonial authorities. Three days after the Judgment was confirmed, on 27 December 1949, Dutch colonial rule in the Netherlands Indies came to an end.[108] One day before the transfer of sovereignty, Imamura and Okazaki – along with around 700 Japanese prisoners, translators and defence counsel – left Java on board the M.S. *Tjisadane*. After their arrival in Yokohama on 23 January 1950, the convicted Japanese were sent to Sugamo prison in Tokyo to serve the remaining part of their sentences. Imamura was handed over to the Australian authorities and taken to Manus Island, where he, along with his subordinates, served a ten-year sentence that had been issued earlier by an Australian court martial convened in Rabaul in May 1947.[109]

While travelling back to Japan, Imamura wrote to De Groot, thanking him in English for having withstood the antipathy towards him for his occupation of the Netherlands Indies:

> I am much gratitude that you investigated me all the time with your gentle attitude (except so-called pig-basket case), and I could answer to your questions with my good will. Moreover, what I want to express my greatest gratitude which observed the dignity of law against the bad feeling for me that were the national feeling of not only in Java, but also in Holland, I suppose.[110]

De Groot replied to Imamura, again in English, and explained that he was trying to avoid 'the possibility of criticism of the jurisdiction of our Court in judging over ex-enemies as war-criminals'.[111] He added that he had wanted, 'as far as possible – to keep up the standards of Dutch justice, while at the same time – as far as possible – keeping out the bad influence of ill-feelings towards the Japanese as a nation'.[112]

107 De Groot to Imamura (8 September 1950), p. 2: inv. no. 3, 2.21.281.31, collection 584, L.F. de Groot, 1946–1991, NL-HaNA.

108 De Groot, *Berechting Japanse oorlogsmisdadigers*, vol. 1, p. 60. 109 Ibid., p. 362.

110 Imamura to De Groot (13 January 1950): inv. no. 3, 2.21.281.31, collection 584, L.F. de Groot, 1946–1991, NL-HaNA.

111 De Groot to Imamura (8 September 1950), p. 1: inv. no. 3, 2.21.281.31, collection 584, L.F. de Groot, 1946–1991, NL-HaNA.

112 Ibid.

By now, De Groot had left the Netherlands Indies. After his departure in early December 1949, he had resettled back in the Netherlands – a decision he later said he regretted, because he felt that the archipelago was his 'second fatherland', and that he was 'abandoning the (Indonesian) people'.[113] After weathering some criticism over his acquittal of Imamura and Okazaki, he found employment in the Dutch Military Judicial Service.[114] He returned to the archipelago and served as the President of the Court of Justice of Dutch New Guinea from 1960 to 1962. Throughout this period, his involvement with the post-war trials continued to play an important part in his life. Media interest in the trials was limited, both in Indonesia and back in Europe, but he did his best to highlight them, occasionally lecturing and publishing in the *De Telegraaf*. In the later stages of his life he started working on a book about his experiences, *Berechting Japanse oorlogsmisdadigers in Nederlands-Indië, 1946–1949: Temporaire Krijgsraad Batavia*, which was published in 1990. It is clear from this and his private papers that De Groot was unperturbed by – and even proud of – the judgments made by 'his' court.[115] In correspondence with the court's interpreter, Matsuura Kojiro, he wrote:

> As a whole I now am feeling quite satisfied about the results of my – of our! – work. Indeed, the work of investigating and trying war-criminals was far from my ideal of the work for a judge. Nevertheless, the fact that I now can say without too much exaggeration that I helped, according to my best knowledge and capacity, to further justice in such a way that even the condemned received their punishment with the knowledge that we, the Court, had given them the full opportunity to defend themselves, and that we had *listened* to their defence, this fact is something worthwhile![116]

Unlike his colleague Hugo Pos, a Judge Advocate at another court who lost faith in the Netherlands Indies justice system and accepted the legitimacy of the Indonesian independence struggle, De Groot remained a staunch and lifelong supporter of the Dutch trial programme and colonial policies. If he was critical of the Dutch government, it was for releasing the Japanese held in Sugamo Prison for war crimes before they had completed their sentences.[117] He lamented the fact that many war criminals and collaborators escaped prosecution or

[113] De Groot to De Jong (17 January 1986), p. 3: inv. no. 29, 2.21.281.31, collection 584, L.F. de Groot, 1946–1991, NL-HaNA.
[114] 'Boek van Haarlemmer', p. 18.
[115] De Groot to Matsuura Kojiro (4 February 1950), p. 1: inv. no. 406, collection 400, NIOD.
[116] Ibid. [117] De Groot, *Berechting Japanse oorlogsmisdadigers*, vol. 2, p. 437.

received amnesty.[118] When in 1985 a Dutch newspaper editorial criticised colonial justice for not acknowledging the many Indonesian victims of the Japanese occupation, he brushed it aside as being 'too anticolonial'.[119] Just a few months before his death in 1991, he equated Saddam Hussein's atrocities in Iraq with Japanese atrocities in the Netherlands Indies nearly half a century earlier.[120] Memories of that occupation stayed with him to the end.

[118] He wrote in 1985 that, 'It is quite correct that the purge (of collaborators) in the post-war period in Indonesia has been mediocre – poor! –. A matter of prosecution policy.' (De Groot to Schumacher (31 August 1985), p. 1: inv. no. 24, 2.21.281.31, collection 584, L.F. de Groot, 1946–1991, NL-HaNA.) De Groot was especially critical of the fact that many Korean camp guards had escaped justice, as they had been 'worse than their Japanese bosses': 'Te zware straf Japanse oorlogmisdadigers', *Het Nieuwsblad* (1 December 1990), p. 37.

[119] A. Djoehana, 'Duizenden anonieme moorden', *NRC Handelsblad* Culture Supplement (6 August 1985), p. 3; De Groot to Schumacher (31 August 1985), p. 2: inv. no. 24, 2.21.281.31, collection 584, L.F. de Groot, 1946–1991, NL-HaNA.

[120] De Groot to Rinzema-Admiraal (10 March 1991), pp. 1–2: inv. no. 35, 2.21.281.31, collection 584, L.F. de Groot, 1946–1991, NL-HaNA.

4

The superior orders defence at the post-war trials in Singapore

CHEAH WUI LING

At the end of the Second World War, the British military authorities tried over four hundred Japanese defendants at 131 war crimes trials held in Singapore between 1946 and 1948. These trials dealt with Japanese military personnel and their auxiliaries accused of committing crimes against civilians and prisoners of war from Southeast Asian communities and from the various Allied states.

The British established the Singapore trials under the terms of the Royal Warrant, signed on 14 June and promulgated on 18 June 1945, which provided for the trial and punishment of 'violations of the laws and usages of war' committed during any war in which the nation 'ha[d] been or may be engaged' since 2 September 1939.[1] Appended to the Royal Warrant were the 'Regulations for the Trial of War Criminals' covering criminal process and evidential matters. These also specified that the trials should adhere to the military law on courts martial set out in the Army Act of 1881 and Rules of Procedure of 1926.[2] Refinements to this legal framework were added by amendments to the Royal Warrant's regulations and to Allied Land Forces South East Asia 'War Crimes Instruction Number 1'.[3]

In the earlier trials conducted by the British military in Singapore, the accused were defended by British military personnel; subsequently, they were defended by Japanese defence counsel. British advisory officers were generally assigned to provide advice to the defence in such cases. Death

1 War Office, Royal Warrant: Regulations for the Trial of War Criminals (Army Order 81/1945) (London: HMSO, signed 14 June 1945, promulgated 18 June 1945): LCO 53/102, National Archives, United Kingdom (TNA). The opening date, 2 September 1939, fell the day after Germany's invasion of Poland and the day before Britain's declaration of war on Germany; the closing date was not specified.

2 Ibid., Regulation 3.

3 'Allied Land Forces, South East Asia, War Crimes Instruction No. 1' (December 1945): WO 203/2080, TNA.

sentences could only be passed with the concurrence of all judges if the court comprised not more than three judges, or by at least two-thirds if the court comprised more than three judges.[4] The findings of guilt and sentences of these courts were 'subject to confirmation', but acquittals did not require confirmation.[5] The accused could submit petitions to the confirming officer against a court's finding or sentence within fourteen days of the trial's conclusion.[6] For the Singapore trials, advisory opinions were issued by the Office of the Judge Advocate General (JAG) to assist the confirming officer in the review of a court's finding and sentence.

This chapter describes the various strands of the superior order arguments put forward by the defendants and their counsel, and the response to these from the prosecutors and the JAG officials, with the aim of delineating then-prevailing ideas about responsibilities of military personnel during armed conflict.

Shifts in policy

Although the superior orders defence is seldom invoked before contemporary international tribunals,[7] it is recognised and addressed in the International Criminal Court's Statute (the Rome Statute), which sets out the conditions that need to be met before the accused is relieved of responsibility. Article 33 begins:

> 1. The fact that a crime within the jurisdiction of the Court has been committed by a person pursuant to an order of a Government or of a superior, whether military or civilian, shall not relieve that person of criminal responsibility unless:
>   (a) The person was under a legal obligation to obey orders of the Government or the superior in question;
>   (b) The person did not know that the order was unlawful; and
>   (c) The order was not manifestly unlawful.
> 2. For the purposes of this article, orders to commit genocide or crimes against humanity are manifestly unlawful.[8]

Even so, the question of whether superior orders should be recognised as a separate and independent defence was subject to much discussion

[4] Royal Warrant, Regulation 9. [5] Ibid., Regulation 8(iv). [6] Ibid., Regulation 10.
[7] W.A. Schabas, *The International Criminal Court: a commentary on the Rome Statute* (Oxford University Press, 2010), p. 482.
[8] Rome Statute of the International Criminal Court: treaties.un.org.

during the negotiations leading up to the adoption of the Rome Statute, with some arguing that superior orders that were not manifestly unlawful should relieve a subordinate of criminal responsibility, and others arguing that the question of whether superior orders could be a mitigating circumstance should be left to the court's discretion.[9]

These recent debates echoed some of those that took place during the final years of the Second World War, when a number of countries, including Britain and the United States, amended their guidelines on superior orders, primarily to avoid the exoneration of those accused of war crimes committed in the course of the conflict.[10] In April 1944, the British revised Paragraph 443 of the *Manual of military law 1929*, which had previously stated that those who violated the laws of war under superior orders would not be punished.[11] This was amended to read: 'The fact that a rule of warfare has been violated in pursuance of an order of a belligerent Government or of an individual belligerent commander does not deprive the act in question of its character as a war crime; neither does it, in principle, confer upon the perpetrator immunity from punishment by the injured belligerent.'[12] Although the *Manual* had no statutory force, it nonetheless offered authoritative guidance on military discipline and was often cited during the Singapore trials.

As well as being reconsidered at a national level, the superior orders issue was also being discussed in international bodies. When the United Nations War Crimes Commission (UNWCC) addressed it in 1944, some members proposed that the Commission issue a rule to ensure a uniform approach to superior orders in courts dealing with war crimes, while others cautioned that the situation was too diverse to impose an absolute standard on all jurisdictions.[13] The Chinese representative Liang Yuen-Li thought that a rule would offer a 'beacon-light' to nations 'groping for certainty in the field of conflicting practices and doctrines', but doubted whether national courts would give effect to

[9] O. Triffterer, 'Superior orders and prescription of law', in O. Triffterer (ed.) *Commentary on the Rome Statute of the International Criminal Court: observers' notes, article by article* (Munich: CH Beck, Hart, Nomos, 2008), p. 919.

[10] United Nations War Crimes Commission, *History of the United Nations War Crimes Commission and the development of the laws of war* (London: HMSO, 1948), pp. 281–282.

[11] Ibid., p. 281.

[12] War Office, *Manual of military law 1929* (London: HMSO, 7th edn., reprinted December 1939, published 1940), amended by Amendment No. 12 of 1936 and Amendment No. 34 of 1944.

[13] UNWCC, *History*, p. 278.

it.[14] The Commission eventually decided against formulating one, but emphasised that its members had 'unanimously' agreed that obedience to superior orders did not automatically exonerate anyone who had committed a war crime.[15]

In contrast to the Commission, the Allied drafters of the Nuremberg Charter took a firm line on the superior orders defence. Article 8 states, 'The fact that the defendant acted pursuant to order of his Government or of a superior shall not free him from responsibility, but may be considered in mitigation of punishment if the Tribunal determine that justice so requires.'[16] Following the Charter's lead, the Nuremberg Judgment refused to consider the superior orders argument with respect to the high-ranking German defendants, although it tacitly readmitted the idea of a defence by declaring a test for determining culpability – 'whether moral choice was in fact possible'.[17]

The Tokyo Tribunal's Charter was worded differently from Nuremberg's, stating in Article 6 that 'Neither the official position, at any time, of an accused, nor the fact that an accused acted pursuant to order of his government or of a superior shall, of itself, be sufficient to free such accused from responsibility for any crime with which he is charged, but such circumstances may be considered in mitigation of punishment if the Tribunal determines that justice so requires.'[18] The words 'of itself' seem to open the door to consideration of superior orders along with other relevant factors, although not superior orders alone, in deciding the degree of guilt, as well as the possible consideration of superior orders to mitigate punishment. As one commentator noted, the latter was 'a more flexible, and a more logical rule' because what prevailed was 'not the doctrine of absolute liability, but rather the principle which permits all the circumstances of the case to play their parts'.[19] The Tokyo Tribunal did not explore this opening in its Judgment, but instead followed the Nuremberg Judgment in excluding

[14] Liang Y.-L., 'Report on the plea of obedience to superior orders', *Committee III*, UNWCC (28 August 1944), p. 4: www.legal-tools.org.

[15] UNWCC, *History*, p. 280.

[16] International Military Tribunal, *Trial of the major war criminals before the International Military Tribunal*, 'The Blue Series', 42 vols. (Nuremberg: IMT, 1947–1949), vol. 1, p. 12.

[17] IMT, Judgment, vol. 1, p. 224.

[18] International Military Tribunal for the Far East, *The Tokyo major war crimes trial*, R.J. Pritchard (ed.), 124 vols. (Lewiston: Edwin Mellen Press, 1998), Amended Charter, vol. 2, p. 3.

[19] Y. Dinstein, *The defence of 'obedience to superior orders' in international law* (Oxford University Press, 2012) p. 157.

any consideration of superior orders when determining the guilt or innocence of the defendants.[20]

Types of superior orders claims

At Singapore, most defendants held mid-level or low-ranking positions in the Japanese Army and Navy. Consequently, the defence raised superior orders at almost every trial. In some cases, the superior had either directly instructed an accused to commit a specific crime or had issued such instructions to the accused through an intermediary down the chain of command. In other cases, orders had been communicated to the accused in a less direct fashion. These orders were results-oriented or assumed the form of general rules, although their issuance still resulted in a crime being committed. In these latter instances, it may be said that the superiors concerned had given their subordinates some discretion on how to achieve the particular result or on whether and how to apply the rule in question.

Examples of the more straightforward cases involved orders given by a superior to the accused to perform a specific act, which made up the substance of the war crimes charge. In *Miyawaki Fumio*, for example, the accused was charged for his supervision, under orders, of the beheading of Allied prisoners of war at the Seletar Naval Base in Singapore.[21] The prosecution noted the 'barbarous' beheading of the victims by sword, while also conceding that the accused was merely the 'tool of other heartless men'.[22] Another example of a straightforward order arose in the case of *Tamura Shinji*, where the accused, who was commanding a firing squad, was ordered to execute 152 civilians including women and children at Port Blair in the Andaman Islands.[23]

Some cases involved defendants who were not directly involved in carrying out a crime, but who had passed a superior's order down a chain of command to those who had committed it. In *Masaki Nobuyoshi and Honda Akisuke*, for example, Masaki, a military governor in North Sumatra, had ordered Honda to execute five British prisoners of war

[20] IMTFE, Majority Judgment, vol. 101, pp. 48438–48439.

[21] 'Form for assembly and proceedings of a military court . . .', *Miyawaki Fumio* (30 March 1948): WO 235/1100, TNA.

[22] Prosecution, 'Opening address', *Miyawaki Fumio* (1 March 1948), p. 1: WO 235/1100, TNA.

[23] 'Form for assembly and proceedings of a military court . . .', *Tamura Shinji* (2 April 1946): WO235/816, TNA.

near Sinabang.[24] Masaki argued that he had been asked to pass on this order to Honda by the *Kempeitai*, the Japanese military police, though he personally did not approve of the order.[25] In another case, *Harada Kensei*, the accused faced three charges of being concerned with the killing of civilians in British Borneo.[26] Harada admitted that he had ordered the killings but had done so on the basis of his superiors' orders and a blacklist that had been issued by them. The defence argued that the accused 'did nothing but convey to the chiefs of the [*Kempeitai*] detachments under his control' the orders of his superiors.[27]

Some cases dealt with less direct superior orders. In a number of these, a superior officer had instructed his subordinate to achieve a particular outcome, but had given them some discretion over how to achieve it. The subordinate had then committed the crime in the course of obeying the order. In *Mizuno Keiji*, for example, the accused was charged with killing at least 177 Chinese civilians in Singapore when commanding a *Kempeitai* unit,[28] pursuant to the orders of General Yamashita Tomoyuki, who upon occupying Singapore had ordered that 'undesirable elements' of the Chinese population be eliminated.[29] The prosecution argued that although this plan had 'originated' from Yamashita, it was carried out by the sector commanders 'within whose scope and under whose initiative fell the responsibility, the time, place and method of killing these Chinese'.[30] The powers of the sector commanders were thus 'discretionary rather than obligatory'.[31] Emphasis was placed on how the victims had been selected haphazardly – some were chosen because they were 'well dressed', or 'looked fierce' or were 'the odd person in three' – and how none of them had been tried before execution.[32] Furthermore, the prosecution argued that though the accused had committed the crime 'under stress of superior orders', the selection and

24 'Form for assembly and proceedings of a military court', *Masaki Nobuyoshi and Honda Akisuke* (12 January 1948): WO 235/1083, TNA.

25 JAG, 'War crimes trial', *Masaki Nobuyoshi and Honda Akisuke* (4 December 1947), p. 1: WO 235/1083, TNA.

26 'Form for assembly and proceedings of a military court . . .', *Harada Kensei* (9 September 1946): WO 235/884, TNA.

27 'Closing address in defence of the accused', *Harada Kensei* (11 July 1946), p. 6: WO 235/884, TNA.

28 'Form for assembly and proceedings of military court . . .', *Mizuno Keiji* (6 May 1948): WO 235/1110, TNA.

29 'Opening address for the prosecution', *Mizuno Keiji* (8 March 1948), p. 1: WO 235/1110, TNA.

30 Ibid. 31 Ibid. 32 Ibid.

killing of victims had not been 'kept within the defined limits as laid down'.[33]

In other cases, the defence depicted general rules, as opposed to particular orders, as superior orders. In the trial of *Ishida Eiguma et al.*, two of the accused, Ishii Tamie and Yanagita Shoichi, were charged among other things with ordering the killing of Allied prisoners of war in camps along the Burma-Siam Railway.[34] The two accused argued that they had done so in furtherance of then-prevailing general Japanese laws as well as their superior's order authorising the shooting of prisoners for attempting to escape.[35] The defence counsel argued that the 'very essence of sovereignty as existing in . . . modern states is that the State has got the power to make all laws'.[36] Applying this rationale to the case, the defence contended that the Japanese government had invested those in charge of prisoners of war with 'powers to make rules on disciplinary matters'.[37] As the Japanese government's rule-making powers were 'unlimited', so too were the rule-making powers of those through whom it dispensed its authority, such as the prisoner-of-war directors.[38] The accused could not challenge their orders, even if they were illegal orders conflicting with Japan's obligations to other states, because as far as the accused were concerned, 'they were ostensibly legal and lawful orders'.[39]

Superior orders were usually raised to explain *why* the accused had committed the crime, but in the trial of *Ishida Eiguma et al.* the defence used superior orders to contest *how* the crime was committed. In this case, charges were laid against a group of Japanese soldiers, holding different ranks, for the ill treatment of prisoners of war in camps located along the Burma-Siam Railway. The defence protested against the joint charging of the accused under Regulation 8(ii) of the 1945 Royal Warrant, which covered 'concerted action' and enabled evidence to be 'jointly and severally admissible against each and everyone of the accused'.[40] It argued that in order for this provision to apply, the uniformity of conduct of the accused may have been less the result of a planned conspiracy leading to 'concerted action' and more the result of 'imitation' or 'identical orders or some orders from a common

[33] Ibid., p. 3.

[34] 'Charge sheet', *Ishida Eiguma (a.k.a. Ishida Hidekuma), Nakamura Shigeo, Ishii Tamie, Yanagita Shoichi and Chida Sotomasu* (24 September 1946), pp. 1–3: WO 235/963, TNA.

[35] 'Opening address for the defence', *Ishida Eiguma, Nakamura Shigeo, Ishii Tamie, Yanagita Shoichi and Chida Sotomasu* (c. late 1947), p. 13: WO 235/963, TNA.

[36] Ibid. [37] Ibid. [38] Ibid. [39] Ibid. [40] Ibid., p. 2.

superior'.[41] So here, superior orders were raised to suggest the mode by which the crime was committed rather than the reason for its commission.

Claims of necessity and self-defence were also used to justify superior orders. In the trial of *Furukawa Ichiji and Matsushita Koichi*, for instance, the defendants were accused of killing a civilian for stealing food in Port Blair in the Andaman Islands.[42] The defence argued that Furukawa and Matsushita had been acting in accordance with a proclamation warning that those caught stealing food would be executed.[43] It sought to justify the passing of this proclamation and the actions of the accused by pointing to a number of then-existing circumstances: the siege by Allied forces on the Japanese, the severe food shortage in the Andamans, and the deteriorating law-and-order situation caused by numerous robberies of food.[44] Under these circumstances, the defence argued, the proclamation was an exercise of 'the right of self defence' as well as 'an act of necessity'.[45] The passing of this order should, therefore, be viewed as 'an emergency measure'.[46]

Arguments for exculpation

The question of whether superior orders should be considered when determining the guilt of an individual was subject to much discussion in the Singapore trials. According to Paragraph 443 of the *Manual of military law 1929*, superior orders could not 'in principle' confer immunity upon an accused or deprive the act of its criminality.[47] But it did not absolutely prohibit the consideration of superior orders alongside other factors in determining whether an accused should be convicted. Indeed, the Paragraph went on to state that 'undoubtedly, a court confronted with the pleas of superior orders adduced in justification of a war crime is bound to take into consideration the fact that obedience to military orders, not obviously unlawful, is the duty of every member of the armed forces, and that the latter cannot in conditions of war discipline be expected to weigh scrupulously the legal merits of the order received'.[48] A court was thus

41 Ibid., p. 4.

42 'Form for assembly and proceedings of a military court', *Furukawa Ichiji and Matsushita Koichi* (24 June 1946): WO 235/852, TNA.

43 'Closing address' for the defence, *Furukawa Ichiji and Matsushita Koichi* (c. 22 April 1946), pp. 4–5: WO 235/852, TNA.

44 Ibid., p. 4. 45 Ibid., pp. 6–7. 46 Ibid., p. 5. 47 Par. 443, *Manual of military law 1929*.

48 Ibid.

'bound' to consider superior orders – an obligation obviously exploited by the defence counsel – although Paragraph 443 did not clarify exactly *how* such orders were to be considered.

The defence put forth a range of arguments as to why the existence of superior orders should exculpate the accused. In one approach, it referred to the special characteristics of the Japanese military system, arguing that superior orders should excuse the accused because Japanese soldiers were trained to absolutely and unquestioningly obey orders. In *Shimizu Kiyogi et al.*, for example, it pointed to various Japanese laws regulating the Army, such as the Imperial Message issued by the Emperor Shōwa, which required Japanese soldiers to consider their superiors as 'representatives of the Imperial orders', and the Internal Service Code of the Army, which prohibited soldiers from arguing 'the causes or reasons of an order'.[49] After the trial of *Harada Kensei*, the defence submitted a petition on Harada's behalf which elaborated on the connection between the Emperor and the dissemination of military authority:

> Men in the Japanese Army ... look upon their superiors' orders as representative of those given directly from the Emperor Himself, and do not harbour a ghost of doubt that their superiors [are] sometimes likely to give orders of an unlawful nature. Their firm belief in their superiors is further strengthened by the august words of His Majesty in the Imperial Message to the Army and Navy which state that orders from superiors should be considered as orders from His Majest[y]. The Emperor is sacred and inviolable in Japan. The Japanese Constitution has an explicit description of the supreme sovereignty of the Emperor in Act 3. Hence it follows that subordinates regard it as a violation of . . . sovereign[ ]ty to argue and discuss the appropriateness of their seniors' orders.[50]

It was further claimed in *Nagaosa Hirio et al.*, a case involving the beating and torture of civilians in Port Blair, that the dissemination of the Emperor's authority through military orders was bolstered by the Japanese legal system, under which it was 'common practice' for the superior who gave the orders, rather than the subordinate who executed them, to be held responsible for any ensuing illegal actions.[51] The prosecution rejected attempts by the defence to cite Japanese law, stating in *Harada Kensei*, for example, that the accused was not being

[49] 'The humble petition of . . .', *Shimizu Kiyoji, Uchiyama Chokichi and Mukai Heihachi* (10 August 1946), p. 5: WO 235/882, TNA.

[50] 'The humble petition of . . .', *Harada Kensei* (c. 12 July 1946), p. 2: WO235/884, TNA.

[51] 'The humble petition of . . .', *Nagaosa Hirio et al.* (20 May 1946), p. 10: WO235/844, TNA.

tried under Japanese law, but for contravening 'the International laws and usages of war'.[52]

The defence also claimed that religious and cultural mores reinforced the tendency of Japanese military personnel to unquestioningly obey superior orders. In *Tamura Shinji*, for example, the defence claimed that absolute obedience was 'the religious belief of every Japanese soldier'.[53] And in *Sato Tamenori et al.*, involving the ill treatment and death of Burmese civilians on the Andaman Islands, the defence, in an allusion to the Japanese deference to elders, suggested that non-obedience was impossible because two of the defendants, Baba Ikuo and Ishida Tadashi, were 'young enough to be children' of the superior issuing the illegal order.[54]

The subordinate as automaton

The defence and prosecution represented the accused in different ways when arguing for the latter's guilt or innocence in the Singapore trials. In a number of cases, the defence argued that the accused carried out his superior's orders mechanically or like an automaton, denying that he exercised any willpower or active decision-making capacity. This argument was commonly made on behalf of mid-rankers who were charged with passing orders down the chain of command. In *Miyawaki Fumio*, for example, the accused was charged with transmitting his superior's order to his subordinates to execute a number of Allied prisoners of war: although he did not carry out the executions, he gave the order for them to start and was present when they were carried out.[55] The defence argued that the accused had 'only mechanically obeyed the imperative superior order',[56] and that 'he did not participate in the execution voluntarily or from his own accord'.[57]

[52] 'Prosecutor's closing address', *Harada Kensei* (11 July 1946), p. 41 (transcript): WO235/884, TNA.

[53] 'Closing address in defence ...', *Tamura Shinji* (c. 11 March 1946), p. 1: WO 235/816, TNA.

[54] 'Closing address in defence ...', *Sato Tamenori, Kiyomoto Takuichi, Tazawa Keizo, Ishida Tadashi, Baba Ikuo* (7 March 1946), p. 6: WO 235/814, TNA.

[55] JAG, 'To:- G.O.C. Singapore District', *Miyawaki Fumio* (17 March 1948), p. 1: WO 235/1100, TNA.

[56] Defence, 'Opening address', *Miyawaki Fumio* (1 March 1948), p. 1: WO 235/1100, TNA.

[57] Defence, 'Closing address', *Miyawaki Fumio* (2 March 1948), p. 2: WO 235/1100, TNA. The defence counsel also argued that the accused mistakenly believed that the executions had been ordered after legitimate judicial proceedings had taken place.

In the trial of *Okamoto Toshio et al.*, one of the charges faced by the three accused concerned the killing of eight prisoners of war in Singapore under superior orders.[58] One of the accused, Okamoto Toshio, stood accused of having directed the second accused, Kobayashi Keiichiro, to execute the prisoners. Kobayashi had organised the execution, which was in turn carried out by the third accused, Too Shizuo. Okamoto argued that he had been instructed by his superiors to order the prisoners' execution. In line with this, the defence portrayed Okamoto as being 'a mere carrier of his superiors' orders' for he was 'neither the performer not the person who decided the plan of execution'.[59] With respect to Kobayashi, the defence claimed that he was 'nothing but a cat's paw' of those who had decided on the execution because he did not perform the beheading, and because he had acted under compulsion rather than 'his free and voluntary intention' – in other words, he had not acted on his own behalf.[60]

In *Kuwahata Tsugio and Murakami Isao*, Kuwahata was accused of having received and transmitted his superior's order to Murakami for the execution of two American prisoners of war in Indo-China.[61] The defence argued that the accused had 'simply acted mechanically as tools of execution'.[62] In support of this, reference was made, among other things, to Chapter 7, Paragraph 15, of the *Manual of military law 1929*, which stated that 'where a person commits an offence through the medium of an innocent agent, he is criminally responsible even though absent when the offence is committed'.[63] It highlighted the two examples set out in the *Manual*: first, that of a soldier who knowing a note to be forged 'induces' a fellow soldier to get it changed;[64] and second, that of a soldier who, claiming some boots belonged to him, 'induces' a fellow soldier to steal them.[65] The defence drew a parallel between these examples and the position of the accused, arguing that he was an 'innocent agent' and that his superior was the one responsible.[66] Even so, the *Manual* was referring to perpetrators who were unaware they were

[58] 'Charge sheet', *Okamoto Toshio, Kobayashi Keiichiro and Too Shizuo* (a.k.a Noboruo Shizuo) (16 December 1947): WO235/1103, TNA.

[59] Defence, 'Closing address', *Okamoto Toshio, Kobayashi Keiichiro and Too Shizuo* (c. 29 December 1947), p. 2: WO235/1103, TNA.

[60] Ibid., pp. 3, 4.

[61] 'Form for assembly and proceedings of a military court . . .', *Kuwahata Tsugio and Murakami Isao* (29 July 1946): WO 235/865, TNA.

[62] 'Closing address by the defence counsel', *Kuwahata Tsugio and Murakami Isao* (c. 5 June 1946), p. 1: WO 235/865, TNA.

[63] Ibid., p. 2. [64] Ibid. [65] Ibid. [66] Ibid.

committing a crime: if it could be shown that they were aware, the argument would collapse (as happened in this case, when the prosecution pointed out that Kuwahata had protested against the order, and then had implemented it secretively).[67]

The defence justified their representation of the accused as mere instruments in the hands of their superiors on other grounds as well. In *Kuwahata Tsugio and Murakami Isao*, for example, reference was made to the 'irrevocable and absolute' nature of superior orders in the Japanese Army,[68] and to Army regulations which stated that: 'Under no circumstances is it permitted to argue [an order's] justice or question its reasons or purposes', and that 'individuals should be habituated to obey their superiors faithfully and to carry out their orders unconditionally.'[69] The defence went on to explain that there was 'absolutely no scope for inserting personal free will as far as [an] order is concerned'.[70] In the case of *Shimizu Kiyogi et al.*, the accused faced various charges of forcibly removing, ill-treating and killing civilian residents in British Borneo. In their petition against the court's findings, the defence referred to various Japanese edicts and codes regulating Army conduct, such as the Emperor's Imperial Message and the Army's Internal Service Code, prohibiting soldiers from challenging an order.[71] Based on this legal regime, Japanese soldiers were to be 'habituated to follow with their superiors' orders through fire and water'.[72]

In the 'Double Tenth' case of *Sumida Haruzo et al.*, the accused were charged with having contrived the arrest, confinement, ill treatment, beating and torture of civilians in Singapore. The defence ascribed their conduct to the nature of the war in which they found themselves, suggesting that it 'was a crime accruing from war itself, rather than the responsibility of any particular individual',[73] and that the accused 'had only played a sad role of dancing to the tunes of a great hand called war, and had not acted according to their own likings'.[74]

67 'Closing address for the prosecution', *Kuwahata Tsugio and Murakami Isao* (c. 5 June 1946), p. 2: WO 235/865, TNA.

68 'Closing address by the defence counsel', *Kuwahata Tsugio and Murakami Isao* (c. 5 June 1946), p. 2: WO 235/865, TNA.

69 Ibid., p. 1. 70 Ibid., p. 2.

71 'The humble petition of . . .', *Shimizu Kiyoji, Uchiyama Chokichi and Mukai Heihachi* (10 August 1946), p. 5: WO 235/882, TNA.

72 Ibid.

73 'The humble petition on behalf of . . .', *Sumida Haruzo and six others* (27 April 1946) p. 5: WO 235/891 Part 1, TNA.

74 Ibid.

The mistaken subordinate

Another recurrent argument raised by the defence was that the accused had mistakenly believed that the orders given by their superiors were legal – a mistake potentially relieving them of criminal responsibility. The 1945 Royal Warrant makes no reference to the relevance of such mistakes in relation to superior orders. It should be recalled, however, that Paragraph 443 of *Manual of military law 1929*, after noting that the existence of superior orders does not provide immunity in principle, went on to state that a court faced with claims of superior orders was bound to consider that 'obedience to military orders, not obviously unlawful, is the duty of every member of the armed forces'.[75] Based on this, it could be argued that 'not obviously unlawful' orders were relevant and were to be taken into consideration by British military courts.

At the trial of *Tokumaru Daizo et al.* in April 1947,[76] in which the accused were charged with ill-treating civilians in the *Kempeitai* headquarters at Oxley Rise, Singapore, the defence advanced a detailed legal argument about why the Nuremberg Charter's position on superior orders did not exclude consideration of the defence of mistake. It was argued that Article 8 of the Charter was 'based on the same principle' as Paragraph 443 of the *Manual of military law 1929*,[77] and that British case law and other sources recognised that a military subordinate might be excused for making a reasonable mistake of law.[78] The defence then drew attention to the position in Japanese military law, where there was 'an absolute duty to obey orders lawful or otherwise'.[79]

The prosecutors and JAG officials frequently raised the issue of an order's obvious illegality and the defendant's knowledge of such illegality. In *Kasai Tsuguo et al.*, for example, the ten defendants were accused of being involved in the arrest and execution of twenty-eight civilian residents in Miri, Sarawak, following an order issued by their superior.[80] The JAG advisory opinion issued in this case noted that an order to execute civilians without trial was 'wholly and obviously illegal'.[81] It also pointed

[75] Par. 443, *Manual of military law 1929*.

[76] 'Form for assembly and proceedings of a military court . . .', *Tokumaru Daizo, Taki Tadayoshi, Josef Kutron* (22 April 1947): WO 235/976, TNA.

[77] 'Closing address of defence of the accused by Kurise Shozaburo', *Tokumaru Daizo, Taki Tadayoshi, Josef Kutron* (c. 24 February 1947), p. 7: WO 235/976, TNA.

[78] Ibid., pp. 6–8. [79] Ibid., p. 8.

[80] 'Form for assembly and proceedings of a military court . . .', *Kasai Tsuguo* and nine others (8 January 1947): WO 235/941, TNA.

[81] JAG, 'War crimes trial', *Kasai Tsuguo et al.* (15 November 1946), p. 2: WO 235/941, TNA.

out that given the small size of the *Kempeitai* detachment, the accused must have known if a trial of the victims had taken place, and that some of the accused had specifically raised doubts about the legality of the execution.[82] In short, these discussions focused on the defendants' knowledge that the order in question was unlawful.

Emphasis was also placed on the steps that an accused might have taken to ascertain whether the order received was legal or not. In the case of *Harada Kensei*, the defendant was charged with ordering and having being involved in the execution of a number of civilians in British Borneo.[83] The prosecution criticised Harada for not making any effort to check whether his superiors had conducted a trial prior to executing them, noting that although the accused held a relatively senior rank, he made no effort to use his authority to check whether 'elementary principles' of international law had been complied with.[84] It was further argued that the accused had acted 'callously and indifferently, as no reasonable man would have acted'.[85]

A further point arises from Paragraph 443 of the *Manual of military law 1929* – namely, that members of the armed forces 'cannot, in conditions of war discipline, be expected to weigh scrupulously the legal merits of the order received'.[86] This is important because it suggests, first, that soldiers could be expected to assess the legality of an order themselves, but, second, they were not required to weigh the order scrupulously. The prosecution alluded to the issue of a soldier's capacity to judge the legality of orders in some cases at Singapore. By showing that the accused had not bothered to ascertain whether an order was illegal, it aimed to show that the accused had not cared about its criminality – hence their depiction, in the *Harada Kensei* trial, of the accused as acting 'callously and indifferently'.[87] This portrayal suggested that the defendant might have been favourably inclined towards the illegal order received, thereby undermining the defence's claim that he would not have proceeded had he known the order was illegal.

In a number of cases, the defence put forward a different conception of legality, arguing that the accused had genuinely tried to ascertain whether

82 Ibid.

83 'Form for assembly and proceedings of a military court . . .', *Harada Kensei* (9 September 1946): WO 235/884, TNA.

84 'Prosecutor's closing address', *Harada Kensei* (11 July 1946), p. 41 (transcript): WO235/884, TNA.

85 Ibid. 86 Par. 443, *Manual of military law 1929*.

87 'Prosecutor's closing address', *Harada Kensei* (11 July 1946), p. 41 (transcript): WO235/884, TNA.

the order was legal or not. In *Okamura Hideo*, for example, the accused was charged, among other things, with shooting an Indian prisoner of war under superior orders at a camp on Palau Island.[88] The defence referred to the trial testimony given by witnesses on Japanese law, which stated that the test of whether an order had to be obeyed was whether or not it had been issued by the Japanese Emperor.[89] The essential question, it was explained, was whether it was 'possible (not certain but possible) that the command received could have been given by the Emperor'.[90] This expands the grounds of 'legal' orders to cover illegal orders that might *possibly* have been issued by the Emperor.

There were occasions, though, when even the defence counsel admitted the limitations of a defence on grounds of mistake. In *Nagaosa Hirio et al.*, for example, the accused were charged with the ill treatment, torture and killing of civilians suspected of espionage in the Andaman Islands.[91] Although the defence argued (among other things) that the accused had acted on the orders of their superiors, it also acknowledged that some had had prior police experience in Japan, and therefore 'knew full well that the use of torture was wrong'.[92] Trying another tack, it argued that the accused, while being 'fully aware that their own actions were not in accordance with regulations', still tortured civilians during interrogation because they believed the extraction of information was militarily necessary and because they were under 'constant pressure' from their superiors to complete their investigations.[93]

The fearful subordinate

A number of defendants explained that they had obeyed their superior's orders because they were afraid of the consequences had they not. This implied that they would have resisted the illegal order had they not been so afraid of the consequences.[94] The defence argued that the accused were

88 'Charge sheet', *Okamura Hideo* (22 January 1946): WO 235/820, TNA.

89 'Defence counsel's address', *Okamura Hideo* (8 February 1946), p. 4: WO 235/820, TNA.

90 Ibid.

91 'Form for assembly and proceedings of a military court . . .', *Nagaosa Hirio* and seven others (22 June 1946): WO235/844, TNA.

92 'Closing address by defence counsels', *Nagaosa Hirio et al.* (c. 7 May 1946), p. 4: WO235/844, TNA.

93 Ibid., p. 5.

94 The modern international criminal law doctrine of duress, set out in Article 31(1)(d) of the Rome Statute, requires the accused to be under 'a threat of imminent death or of continuing or imminent serious bodily harm'.

justifiably fearful because disobedience was severely punished in the Japanese Army. In the aforementioned case of *Kasai Tsuguo et al.*, in which the defendants followed orders to execute twenty-eight civilians in Sarawak, the defence pointed to evidence suggesting Kasai, the organiser of the executions, would have faced 'death or life imprisonment' under the Japanese military code had he refused to do so.[95] It further contended that under these circumstances, it would be 'cruel' to hold him responsible, because it would be tantamount to asking him 'why he did not face the death sentence'.[96]

It should be noted that in these cases, the feared consequences were not immediate or pressing. The prosecution raised this in the aforementioned case of *Furukawa Ichiji and Matsushita Koichi* in the Andamans, where Furukawa had ordered Matsushita to shoot the victim. With respect to Matsushita's culpability, the prosecution in the closing address noted that his act 'may be excused' if committed 'in subjection to the power of others', but that it must be shown that the accused was compelled to commit it under threat of death or serious injury.[97] It argued,

> Matshushita has pleaded in his defence, that he shot Shazad Mir on the orders of his superior officer Furakawa. That alone, gentlemen, is no defence. It is a rule of law that a person is responsible for the natural consequences of his acts. That act may be excused, however, if committed by a person acting in subjection to the power of others, provided that he is compelled to act as he does by threats of death or serious physical injury . . . Those threats . . . must be continued during the whole time that he so acts, and the part taken by him in the act throughout must be strictly a subordinate part. Matshushita's is no such case!! Matshushita was in no fear or death or physical injury, nor was his part a subordinate one. Furakawa merely ordered Matshushita to shoot Shazad Mir and he did so without question.[98]

Contesting the defence's claim that the defendant's fear of subsequent punishment would be sufficient to exculpate them, the prosecution here stated that this was not enough because the action of the accused was 'perfectly voluntary' and he was 'completely free from any form of duress'.[99]

[95] 'Closing address in defence', *Kasai Tsuguo et al.* (17 October 1946), p. 5: WO 235/941, TNA.

[96] Ibid.

[97] 'Mr President and members . . .', *Furukawa Ichiji and Matsushita Koichi* (22 April 1946), p. 5: WO 235/852, TNA.

[98] Ibid. [99] Ibid., p. 6.

In other cases, the defence also pointed to Japan's harsh military training to explain the low-ranking defendants' failure to resist illegal orders. In *Takasaki Shinji and Kaneshiro Takeshi*, for example, the two defendants were charged for being involved in the ill treatment and killing of prisoners of war in camps located in Siam.[100] It argued that Takasaki was 'a low classed commissioned officer' who had been trained to carry out orders with absolute obedience, and who was 'perfectly aware' that insubordination 'would be a matter of strict punishment, followed by deprivation of rank and honour'.[101] It was thus contended that only 'a very brave and extremely clever person' would have opposed an order in a similar situation.[102] The law, the defence argued, should not require a soldier to act in a 'super-humanly clever manner' but should reflect 'the standard of action of the ordinary mem[ ]bers of the community'.[103] In other words, the law could not expect soldiers with similar training and operating under similar circumstances to disobey orders.

There was much discussion at the Singapore trials about the extent to which the accused had resisted illegal orders. A number of defendants stressed how they had protested to their superiors. In the petition submitted by the defence in the aforementioned *Takasaki Shinji and Kaneshiro Takeshi* case, the defence emphasised how Takasaki, when ordered to execute prisoners of war, had entertained doubts: he had therefore asked whether the prisoners could be sent to the military police instead of being executed immediately.[104] When his superior instructed him again to execute the prisoners, he thought it was his responsibility as a subordinate to simply obey the order.[105] When sentencing the accused, the court stated that while obedience to orders 'not obviously unlawful' was the duty of all members of the military forces, the accused could not escape liability if they committed acts 'which both violate unchallenged rules of warfare and outrage the sentiments of humanity'.[106] The court's position appeared to be that it was not enough for the accused to have offered only limited resistance before going on to carry out their superiors' orders.

[100] 'Charge sheet', *Takasaki Shinji and Kaneshiro Takeshi* (2 May 1946): WO 235/862, TNA.
[101] 'Mr. President and members . . .' (defence closing statement), *Takasaki Shinji and Kaneshiro Takeshi* (c. 6 May 1946), p. 1: WO 235/862, TNA.
[102] Ibid. [103] Ibid., p. 2.
[104] 'The humble petition of . . .', *Takasaki Shinji and Kaneshiro Takeshi* (20 May 1946), p. 2: WO 235/862, TNA.
[105] Ibid., p. 3.
[106] 'Sentence', *Takasaki Shinji and Kaneshiro Takeshi* (6 May 1946), p. 4: WO 235/862, TNA.

Those who held positions of special responsibility were deemed to have had a higher duty to resist superior orders. In *Mabuchi Setsuo et al.*, three of the accused were medical officers who faced charges for intentionally killing a captured American aviator at Saigon as ordered by the *Kempeitai*.[107] The victim had been admitted to hospital and later killed by a fatal injection administered by two of the defendants, Nakamura Kinji and Wakamatsu Hitoshi. Regarding these accused, the defence argued that their 'state of mind was that of a person obsessed by the fear of having his life taken' and in a 'terror-stricken state'.[108] Addressing the responsibility of Nakamura, the prosecution argued that 'as a medical officer with a human life at stake' he 'should have fought like a tiger, but he did not', and that his conduct 'registered an all[-]time low in weakness'.[109] This criticism was repeated in the JAG's advisory report, which noted that their membership of the medical profession 'imposed on them a far higher degree of ethical and moral responsibility towards a patient in their care than that normally required of a captor towards a prisoner of war'.[110] Because of this, it noted that the crime was 'all the more revolting', and that 'nothing can excuse these two doctors who took advantage of surgical methods to commit a cold-blooded murder'.[111]

While the prosecution acknowledged that a fear of serious and immediate consequences could exculpate a person, it also outlined the limits to this defence. In the case of *Kasai Tsuguo et al.*, which involved the killing of twenty-eight civilians under superior orders, the defence argued that one of the accused, Kasai, had obeyed his superior's orders that the civilians be executed because of the drastic consequences of disobeying them.[112] The prosecution noted that 'it would appear that the case for the Defence substantially revolves around the proposition that, under special circumstances, the innocent may be slain to save your

107 'Form for assembly and proceedings of a military court', *Mabuchi Setsuo, Nakamura Kinji, Wakamatsu Hitoshi and Hisakawa Shigehiro* (14 August 1946): WO 235/869, TNA.

108 'Closing address by the defence counsel', *Mabuchi Setsuo, Nakamura Kinji, Wakamatsu Hitoshi and Hisakawa Shigehiro* (c. 12 June 1946), pp. 3, 4: WO 235/869, TNA.

109 'Closing address by the prosecution', *Mabuchi Setsuo, Nakamura Kinji, Wakamatsu Hitoshi and Hisakawa Shigehiro* (c. 12 June 1946), p. 2: WO 235/869, TNA.

110 'War crimes courts' (JAG advisory opinion), *Mabuchi Setsuo, Nakamura Kinji, Wakamatsu Hitoshi and Hisakawa Shigehiro* (23 July 1946), p. 2: WO 235/869, TNA.

111 Ibid.

112 'Closing address in defence', *Kasai Tsuguo et al.* (17 October 1946), p. 5: WO 235/941, TNA.

own life – but International Law says otherwise'.[113] It is important to note, however, that while the prosecution sought to base its claims on international law, this point had not yet been resolved at the international level. Instead, its case appeared to track the English common law on duress, which requires a feared threat to be of a certain level and nature, and denies its relevance when the crime committed involves the taking of life.[114] The implicit (though unacknowledged) reference to English domestic law further complicated matters for the Japanese defence counsel in the Singapore trials, who already faced difficulties in using English law and procedures to support their case.

The subordinate not just following orders

As has been seen, the trial lawyers presented different conceptions of what was expected of military personnel when faced with illegal superior orders. On one hand, the defence categorised the Japanese soldier as being subject to, or overwhelmed by, an all-powerful military system backed by the power of the Emperor and the Japanese state. On the other, the prosecution and the JAG officers presented the soldier as being an active moral agent who was able exercise a certain amount of judgment and determination when faced with illegal superior orders, and who should be held accountable if he carried them out.

In some cases, the prosecution argued that the accused could not raise a superior orders defence because they had gone beyond the scope of the order and thus assumed responsibility for it themselves. In the aforementioned case of *Nagaosa Hirio et al.*, for example, the accused were charged with both beating and torturing civilians in Port Blair while investigating suspected spying activities. The defence argued that they had done so pursuant to superior orders and that obedience to such orders was 'absolute'.[115] The prosecution countered that the accused had 'by their own evidence' admitted that they had permission only 'to beat their victims'.[116] They were thus to be denied the superior order defence because they had gone beyond the order's scope.

[113] 'Closing address of the prosecution', *Kasai Tsuguo et al.* (17 October 1946), p. 44 (transcript): WO 235/941, TNA.

[114] For an overview of the common law stance, see A. Ashworth, *Principles of criminal law* (Oxford University Press, 2009), pp. 212–213.

[115] 'Closing address by defence counsels', *Nagaosa Hirio et al.* (c. 7 May 1946), p. 4: WO235/844, TNA.

[116] Ibid., p. 3.

In discussions about superior orders, much emphasis was placed on the accused's attitude towards the crime. In *Okayama Hikoji*, for example, the defendant was accused of involvement in the notorious 'Double Tenth' incident in which Japanese personnel tortured prisoners during interrogations in Changi Gaol in Singapore.[117] The prosecution stressed that the accused could only invoke superior orders as a defence if he remained 'within those orders'.[118] It proceeded to highlight how Okayama had used 'full force' when administering beatings, which he would not have used had he 'not got his heart in his work'.[119] The use of full force suggested enthusiastic and willing participation in criminal activity, rather than reluctant or involuntary obedience to superior orders. The defence countered that the use of full force was not a demonstration of willingness or enthusiasm but of obedience to Japanese Army discipline, and added that 'if the accused were to use any force less than that which would satisfy his superiors he himself would definitely be in the soup'.[120]

The prosecution sometimes tried to present the absence of any manifest disapproval of superior orders as a positive endorsement of them. In the aforementioned case of *Miyawaki Fumio*, for example, in which the accused had killed Allied prisoners of war under orders from his superior, the prosecution observed that while the defendant had argued that it was 'death to disobey an order', he had neither made any protest ('open or tacit') nor expressed 'any sort of disapproval of such blatantly wicked orders'.[121] The prosecution extrapolated from the defendant's failure to express disapproval 'at least tacit approval' of the orders received and implemented.[122] In other words, the accused was portrayed as endorsing superior orders rather than simply following them.

Conclusion

When discussing whether superior orders should exculpate the accused or mitigate the sentence, trial participants drew on a range of moral and

[117] 'Form for assembly and proceedings of a military court . . .', *Okayama Hikoji* (18 November 1946): WO 235/907, TNA.

[118] 'The prosecuting officer makes his closing address', *Okayama Hikoji* (26 June 1946), p. 21 (transcript): WO 235/907, TNA.

[119] Ibid. [120] Ibid.

[121] Prosecution, 'Closing address', *Miyawaki Fumio* (2 March 1948), p. 2: WO 235/1100, TNA.

[122] Ibid.

cultural arguments. These reflected different ideas about what could be expected of soldiers in their relations with their superiors. The Japanese defence counsel argued that it was normal for soldiers to prioritise their military duty to obey orders over other considerations. But the British prosecutors and JAG advisers, by elaborating on the conduct expected of soldiers faced with illegal orders, and denying that they might be freed from blame for following them, aimed to promote a different model of soldiering.

This model was most clearly articulated in the trial of *Kasai Tsuguo et al.*, where the British prosecutor described soldiering as a 'profession of honour',[123] and advanced the idea that soldiers should act beyond mere obedience to orders. He conceded that the position of the accused faced with illegal orders was 'unenviable', but that it was 'part of the misfortunes and added burdens suffered and borne by those men all nationalities who have the distinguished honour of belonging to the profession of arms'.[124] In essence it was being argued that in the face of error, soldiers were to exercise caution; in the face of fear, they were to offer resistance; in the face of dishonour, they were to do the honourable thing. It encapsulated the growing sentiment that orders were orders but crimes were crimes, even in wartime.

[123] 'Closing address of the prosecution', *Kasai Tsuguo et al.* (17 October 1946), p. 44 (transcript): WO 235/941, TNA.

[124] Ibid.

5

The Khabarovsk trial

The Soviet riposte to the Tokyo Tribunal

VALENTYNA POLUNINA[1]

The Soviet authorities opened the trial of twelve Japanese military personnel, who were accused of planning biological war and experimenting on human beings, on 25 December 1949 in the far eastern city of Khabarovsk, close to the Manchurian border. While earlier Soviet-sponsored military courts dealing with crimes committed in Europe were seen as an extension of the Nuremberg Tribunal,[2] the Khabarovsk trial dealing with crimes committed in Asia was conceived as a *corrective* to the Tokyo Tribunal. Ultimately, the Soviets were trying to prove that Tokyo – with its equivocal determination on 'crimes against peace' against the Soviet Union, and its failure to address Japan's biological weapons programme – was inadequate. The Khabarovsk trial was set up to address the crimes *not* properly considered at Tokyo: the defendants were thus charged with aggressively 'manufacturing and employing bacteriological weapons' against the Soviet Union and China.[3]

Tokyo's many flaws

Two Soviet prosecutors involved with the Tokyo Tribunal, Solomon Rosenblit and Marc Raginskii, produced a number of officially sanctioned

[1] The author is the translator of the Russian materials unless stated otherwise.

[2] According to Andreas Hilger, there were 38 Soviet trials of Germans in 1945, 245 in 1946, 841 in 1947, 2432 in 1948, 15145 in 1949, and 1416 in 1950. 'Die Gerechtigkeit nehme ihren Lauf?': Die Bestrafung deutscher Kriegs- und Gewaltverbrecher in der Sowjetunion und der SBZ/DDR', in N. Frei (ed.) *Transnationale Vergangenheitspolitik. Der Umgang mit deutschen Kriegsverbrechern in Europa nach dem Zweiten Weltkrieg* (Göttingen: Wallstein Verlag, 2006), p. 182.

[3] *Materials on the trial of former servicemen of the Japanese Army charged with manufacturing and employing bacteriological weapons* (Moscow: Foreign Languages Publishing House, 1950) (*Materials*), p. 7.

commentaries about the trial: in 1948, they published a substantial piece about it in *Pravda*; in 1950, they wrote one of the first books about the Tribunal in any language; then in 1985, Raginskii alone wrote another book about it when studies of it were still rare outside Japan. These showed, first of all, that the Soviets were not *wholly* critical of the Tokyo trial: they had, after all, agreed to participate in it alongside the other Allied powers and had endorsed both its aims and its outcome. The Soviet prosecution team, led by Sergei Golunskii, played a central role in the proceedings dealing with Soviet–Japanese relations, and the Soviet judge Ivan Zarianov actively concurred with the Majority Judgment.

The two authors argued that the Tribunal's most important achievement was that it 'condemned aggression as an international crime' and found that 'imperialist Japan was closely associated with Hitlerite Germany, with which it had sought to conquer . . . and enslave entire nations'.[4] Expanding on this theme, they stated that the Majority Judgment had confirmed that, 'Japan for many years had been preparing an aggressive war against the U.S.S.R., that in 1938–1939 it had launched attacks on the Soviet Union, and that aggression against the U.S.S.R. was one of the main components of Japanese policies.'[5] They praised the 'just and harsh sentence' dispensed by the majority of the judges[6] and acknowledged that Tokyo, along with Nuremberg, had laid the basis in international law for bringing war criminals to justice, regardless of their rank or official position.

Having commended these features of the Tokyo trial, Raginskii and Rosenblit then proceeded with the criticisms. They began by pointing out that the Tribunal was not established on an equal footing – the United States predominated. In contrast to Nuremberg, where the judges elected their own Court President, Tokyo's Court President, William Webb, an Australian, was appointed by General Douglas MacArthur, the American Supreme Commander for the Allied Powers. Not only that, but in contrast to Nuremberg, where the participating Allies nominated their own chief prosecutors, Tokyo's sole Chief Prosecutor, Joseph Keenan, an American, was appointed by US President Harry Truman. They also pointed out that the court's Charter was written by American legal scholars, and the trial was conducted along 'Anglo-American' lines[7] – indeed, 'the most complicated and most conservative' character

[4] M.I. Raginskii and S.I. Rosenblit, *Mezhdunarodnii protsess glavnikh iaponskikh voennikh prestupnikov* (Moskva-Leningrad, Izdatel'stvo akademii nauk SSSR, 1950), p. 9.
[5] Ibid. [6] Ibid. [7] Ibid., p. 79.

of the common law proceedings made it possible for the defence to 'deliberately protract' the trial.[8]

Still on the subject of inequality, the authors expressed their displeasure at the absence of representatives from the Soviet satellite, the Mongolian People's Republic, from among the prosecutors and judges. Mongolia had been the site of a Soviet and Mongolian clash with the Japanese Kwantung Army near the Khalkhin-gol River (or Nomonhan) in 1939, and so it had a justifiable claim to membership of the court. (The British and Americans had decided to accept the membership of *their* satellite Asian states, India and the Philippines, on the grounds that the Indians had fought in the Allied forces and the Filipinos had suffered occupation by the Japanese.) But when the Soviets pushed Mongolia's claim, they met 'fierce resistance from the Anglo-American reactionary bloc', on the grounds that Mongolia was not a member of the Allies' wartime alliance.[9] The authors also expressed dissatisfaction that only English and Japanese (but not Russian and French, as at Nuremberg) were designated the working languages of the court. Although the Soviet prosecutors had reserved in advance their right to disclose evidence in Russian, the predominance of English and other unequal arrangements 'secured American influence on the preparations and progress of the trial'.[10]

The Soviets' other major criticism of the trial was that it failed to prosecute *all* the major Japanese war criminals. Although they did not raise the prospect of trying the Emperor Shōwa before or during the proceedings, they took issue with the Allies' failure to try leading members of the *zaibatsu*, Japan's huge financial and industrial conglomerates, which, Raginskii and Rosenblit wrote, 'the American imperialists count on to implement the plans for the revival of Japan's military potential for war against the USSR and democratic China'.[11] They indicated that during the trial preparations, Golunskii had proposed indicting the Japanese industrialists whose companies had produced the armaments and investments necessary to prosecute the war – such as Nakajima Chikuhei, the aircraft industry tycoon; Iwasaki Koyata, the president of Mitsubishi; and Aikawa Yoshisuke, the founder of Nissan[12]– but that 'the chief prosecutor Keenan, supported by other prosecutors, did not accept this proposal'.[13]

[8] Ibid., p. 78.

[9] M.I. Raginskii, *Militaristy na skam'e podsudimykh: po materialam Tokiiskogo I Khabarovskogo protsessov* (Moskva: Iuridicheskaia literatura, 1985), p. 42.

[10] Raginskii and Rosenblit, *Mezhdunarodnyi protsess*, p. 49. [11] Ibid., p. 67.

[12] Ibid., p. 66. [13] Ibid., p. 67.

Raginskii and Rosenblit (and others) reserved their strongest criticisms for those who challenged the Soviet attempts to prove Japan's aggression against the Soviet Union. Anatoly Nikolaev, a member of the Soviet delegation's Secretariat at Tokyo, was at pains to point out that the Japanese counsel shared their clients' outlook and beliefs.[14] Raginskii singled out for special mention Kiyose Ichiro, a former member of parliament, who, he said, was 'better known as a reactionary bourgeois politician than as a scientist', and Ikeda Shunkichi, a former Deputy Chief-of-Staff of the Kwantung Army, who had defended his wartime superior, General Umezu Yoshijirō.[15]

Raginskii claimed that the accused were being protected not only by the defence counsel but also by 'many high officials from the USA and England who . . . did not shun dirty slanders against the USSR and other nations'.[16] While this was not universally true – if it had been, the accused would not have been in court – it *was* nevertheless true that Western officials sought to undermine the Soviet case against Japan. To this end, senior American figures provided testimony to the defence showing that, contrary to the Soviets' arguments, the Japanese had avoided rather than provoked conflict with the Soviet Union, and that it was the Soviets, not the Japanese, who had violated their Neutrality Pact by attacking Manchuria in August 1945.[17] The former American general George C. Marshall inflicted the greatest damage on the Soviet case with an affidavit, read out by a defence lawyer in court, which overturned their justification for breaching the Neutrality Pact.[18] The two authors, responding in *Pravda*, complained that 'the judges could be guided by the intrigues and machinations of all sorts of political speculators instead of by law and conscience while determining guilt'.[19]

Even without Marshall's intervention, the Soviet prosecutors faced an uphill struggle trying to sustain the argument that the Soviet Union was a victim of Japanese aggression. It was therefore particularly important that the captured Japanese servicemen who were coerced or persuaded to speak on the Soviets' behalf at Tokyo produced credible and consistent

[14] A.N. Nikolaev, *Tokio: sud narodov. Po vospominaniiam uchastnika protsessa* (Moskva: Iuridicheskaia literatura, 1990), p. 61.

[15] Raginskii, *Militaristy*, p. 44. [16] Ibid.

[17] K. Sellars, *'Crimes against peace' and international law* (Cambridge University Press, 2013), pp. 229–230.

[18] Ibid., pp. 232–233.

[19] M.I. Raginskii and S.I. Rosenblit, 'Chto narody zhdut ot mezhdurarodnogo voennogo tribunala v Tokio', *Pravda* (2 June 1948), 3.

testimony. The prosecutors put forward a preliminary list of seventy-seven of these witnesses and submitted various affidavits, but in the end, they chose to produce only three people in court: Colonel Sejima Ryudzo, a staff officer in the Kwantung Army (who the Soviets later tried as a counter-revolutionary and spy); Lieutenant-General Kusaba Tatsumi, Commander of the Fourth Army in Manchuria (who committed suicide shortly after his arrival in Tokyo); and Major-General Matsumura Tojekazu, Deputy Chief-of-Staff of the Kwantung Army (who put on such a lacklustre performance that the Soviets sentenced him to a long spell in a labour camp).[20] The prosecutors did not produce the other seventy-four witnesses – despite the defence insistence that they appear so that they could be cross-examined over the contents of their affidavits.[21] Presumably it was felt that the Japanese witnesses might be tempted to make statements undermining the Soviet case in court.[22]

Finally, the Majority Judgment itself was rather more equivocal on the question of Japanese aggression than the Soviets had hoped. 'The Tribunal is of the opinion' – it read – 'that a war of aggression against the U.S.S.R. was contemplated and planned throughout the period under consideration, that it was one of the principal elements of Japan's national policy, and that its object was the seizure of territories of the U.S.S.R. in the Far East.'[23] Yet except for the sections on two border clashes, at Lake Khasan in 1938 and Khalkin-gol in 1939, it was silent on both the subject of Japanese attacks on the Soviet Union and the Soviets' justifications for breaching the Neutrality Pact.

When voicing their criticisms of the Tokyo trial, the Soviets focused on the more politicised issues, such as the Americans' selective approach to the defendants and their unequal, if not actively hostile, treatment of the USSR. They were less interested in the Tribunal's many *legal* flaws, which set them apart from the dissenting judges from India, the Netherlands and France, who concentrated on the retrospective creation of the charges, the unsatisfactory interpretation of the facts, and the misapplication of the law. From the Soviet perspective, the Khabarovsk trial – where they could control the framing of the charges, the progress of the proceedings, the conduct of defendants and witnesses, and most importantly, the account of the Soviet Union's conduct during the war – was a necessary corrective to the perceived problems of the Tokyo Tribunal.

[20] S.I. Kuznetsov, *Problema voennoplennykh v rossiisko-iaponskikh otnosheniiakh posle Vtoroi mirovoi voiny* (Irkutskii universitet, 1994), pp. 127, 128, 130.

[21] Sellars, '*Crimes against peace*', pp. 228–229.

[22] Kuznetsov, *Problema voennoplennykh*, p. 127.

[23] *Materials*, p. 406.

Ishii's 'offensive research'

The Japanese government-sponsored biological warfare research programme was created and led by Lieutenant-General Ishii Shiro, an ultranationalist with strong connections with imperial, political and military circles. He believed that biological weaponry was the weapon of the future,[24] and that forced experimentation on humans – though it might cause researchers 'some anguish as doctors'[25] – was a necessary stage in their development, stating,

> There are two types of bacteriological warfare research, A and B. A is offensive . . . research, and B is defensive research. Vaccine research is of the B type, and this can be done in Japan. However, A type research can only be done abroad.[26]

By 'abroad' Ishii meant China, especially Manchuria, which the Japanese Kwantung Army had occupied in 1931–1932. Manchuria was a particularly suitable territory for the construction of secret biological warfare facilities because it provided sufficient 'experimental material' (in other words, people), while also sharing a border with the Soviet Union and Mongolia – a matter of strategic significance in the event of a future war against the Soviets.[27]

Although Ishii's subordinates began experiments in Manchuria in 1932, Japan's biological warfare programme was formally brought into existence by a secret Imperial Decree issued by the Emperor Shōwa on 1 August 1936.[28] By the end of the war, this programme included facilities in Singapore, Rangoon and Bangkok[29] and various facilities located across China,[30] including the largest and best equipped of them all: Unit 731. This facility, established in 1939 in the vicinity of Pingfan Station, about twenty kilometres outside of Harbin, and misleadingly entitled the 'Water Supply and Prophylaxis Administration of the Kwantung Army',[31] covered six square kilometres. It consisted of more than 150 buildings, including two prisons, barracks, laboratories, a refrigerated chamber for studying

[24] S.H. Harris, 'Japanese biomedical experimentation during the World-War-II era', *Military Medical Ethics* 2 (2003), 476.

[25] Nie J.B., 'The West's dismissal of the Khabarovsk trial as "communist propaganda": ideology, evidence and international bioethics', *Journal of Bioethical Inquiry* 1 (2004), 32.

[26] S.H. Harris, 'Japanese biological warfare research on humans: a case study of microbiology and ethics', *Annals of the New York Academy of Sciences* 666 (1992), 21–52. The microbiologist and biological defence research: ethics, politics and international security, 24.

[27] *Materials*, pp. 262–263. [28] Harris, 'Japanese biomedical experimentation', 478.

[29] Ibid., 477, 482. [30] Ibid. [31] *Materials*, p. 526.

frostbite, three crematoria, buildings to house thousands of small research animals, stables, schools for the children of personnel, a vast administrative building, and buildings for recreational purposes, including a library and two brothels.[32] The Unit also had at its disposal a proving ground near Anta Station for outdoor experiments, and an aircraft unit, which included heavy bombers and transport planes.[33]

Unit 731 personnel conducted human experiments at Pingfan on a systematic and large-scale basis. According to testimony given at the Khabarovsk trial, between four hundred and six hundred captives were sent to Unit 731 every year. At least three thousand captives were killed between 1940 and 1945 – a number that does not include victims at other medical experimentation sites or those who died before 1940.[34] Although mostly Chinese, they also hailed from Korea, Mongolia and the Soviet Union, and of these, many were nationalists or communists who had fallen foul of the Japanese authorities. Although most were males, there were also some women.[35] The Japanese referred to them all equally as *maruta*, or 'logs'.[36]

In some experiments, people were deliberately infected with diseases such as anthrax, plague, typhoid, cholera, glanders and 'songo' fever (haemorrhagic fever). But not all experiments involved pathogens: other people were subjected to physiological studies of the body's reaction to artificially caused conditions such as an extremely low temperatures, low pressure, or overdoses of heroin and Korean bindweed. Others still were subjected to vivisection to find out about the progress of physiological symptoms.[37]

In August 1945, when the Soviet Union declared war on Japan and advanced into Manchuria, Ishii's network suddenly collapsed. The Japanese Army decided to destroy evidence of these medical atrocities, and surviving prisoners were killed to prevent them from testifying later. The most senior figures – including Unit 371's chief Ishii Shiro, his successor Kitano Masaji, and Unit 100 head Wakamatsu Yujiro – were evacuated back to Japan and promptly arrested by the incoming American occupation forces. Unlike the German concentration camp doctors tried by the Americans at the 1947 'Doctors' trial', none of the senior Japanese officials most responsible for the experiments was held to account for these crimes, and quite a number of their subordinates

32 Harris, 'Japanese biomedical experimentation', 478–479. 33 *Materials*, p. 252.
34 Ibid., pp. 257, 430. 35 Ibid., pp. 15–22, 257–258. 36 Ibid., pp. 67, 437.
37 Nie, 'The West's dismissal', 35.

went on to enjoy successful careers as scientists and public officials in Japan after the war.[38]

Why the Khabarovsk trial?

The immediate Soviet motive for convening the Khabarovsk trial in December 1949, four years after the end of the Second World War, was governed by two factors: the collapse of their relations with the United States at the start of the Cold War, and, not unconnected with this, their desire to consolidate relations with the months-old People's Republic of China.

Previously, however, the Soviets had kept completely silent about Japan's biological weapons programme, even though they had almost certainly known about the Harbin facility soon after its establishment.[39] After the surrender of the Kwantung Army in Manchuria in August 1945, the Soviets had combed through the 60,000 prisoners of war searching for the programme's leaders,[40] only to discover that they had all escaped back to Japan, where the Americans had picked them up. So while the Tokyo Tribunal was in session, the Soviets made repeated requests to Washington for permission to interrogate Ishii and other senior figures about their research. The Americans stalled, telling them that their requests were being considered.[41] There was a modicum of truth in this: they did discuss among themselves the possibility of granting the Soviets access to the Japanese, first, on the grounds that they would not gain 'any positive technical intelligence in the BW field',[42] and second, because the Americans' own monitoring of the general thrust of Soviet

[38] Harris, 'Japanese biomedical experimentation', 494.

[39] A KGB report on Japanese agents in Harbin stated that one of their roles was to prepare 'special sabotage groups for the wartime which have the means of bacteriological sabotage [so as] to contaminate water supplies, grain, and fodder as well as food depots with the bacteria of epidemic diseases'. (Letter to GUGB NKVD, 'On terrorist, subversive and espionage activities of Japanese agents among the Harbin inhabitants' (20 September 1937), p. 23: 60268A, State Archive of the Security Service of Ukraine.)

[40] B.G. Yudin, 'Research on humans at the Khabarovsk war crimes trial. A historical and ethical examination', in Nie J.-B. *et al.* (eds.), *Japan's wartime medical atrocities: comparative inquiries in science, history, and ethics* (London: Routledge, 2010), p. 62.

[41] P. Williams and D. Wallace, *Unit 731: Japan's secret biological warfare in World War II* (New York: Free Press, 1989), p. 187.

[42] State-War-Navy Coordinating Subcommittee for the Far East, 'Request of Russian prosecutor for permission to interrogate certain Japanese' (26 February 1947), p. 1: Box 4, RG 9999, IWG, Select Documents on Japanese War Crimes and Japanese Biological Warfare, 1934–2006, National Archives and Records Administration, Maryland (NARA).

questioning 'might serve as a key to Soviet knowledge and activity in the BW field'.[43] Eventually Washington decided against allowing them access, but its officials continued to string them along, knowing that as long as the Soviets thought they *might* be granted access to Ishii and the others, they had a strong motive for keeping silent about the Americans' amnesty-for-information deal, and for acceding to the exclusion of Japanese medical crimes from the Tokyo Tribunal's proceedings.

Moscow had its own secrets to protect. Like the Japanese, it had set up a biological weapons programme in the 1930s,[44] and, like the Japanese, it may have involved experiments on human beings. Recent literature suggests, for example, that highly infectious pathogens may have been tested on prisoners at a former monastery in the small town of Suzdal in Vladimir *oblast* during this period.[45] At the end of the war, Stalin, having seen Japanese documents captured in Manchuria, ordered the establishment of a more modern Soviet biological weapons facility at Sverdlovsk (now Ekaterinburg).[46] According to an American report written in March 1946, the Soviet Union was 'unquestionably fully capable of carrying out extensive research and development in biological warfare' and 'would require only a few years' preparation (at the most 5) to wage open, large-scale biological warfare'.[47]

Back at Tokyo, meanwhile, the Soviets were eventually disabused of the notion that the Americans were going to permit them to interrogate the Japanese leaders of the programme. But they waited until the Tokyo Majority Judgment had confirmed the Japanese leaders' criminality before breaking their silence on Japan's medical crimes and the Americans' amnesty-for-information deal with the chief protagonists. Thereafter, from late 1948 onwards, the Soviets' decision to transform an intelligence secret into a propaganda opportunity was driven by two entwined international factors. The first was the escalation of the Cold War. The second

43 Ibid.

44 M. Leitenberg and R.A. Zilinskas (eds.), *The Soviet biological weapons program: a history* (Harvard University Press, 2012), p. 18.

45 Ibid. The Russian scientist Lev Fedorov states that in summer 1941, the Soviets continued the experiments on political prisoners and Japanese prisoners in Mongolia, infecting them with anthrax, glanders and the plague – one of these prisoners apparently escaped, causing a plague epidemic there. (Williams and Wallace, *Unit 731*, pp. 231–232.)

46 K. Alibek, *Biohazard* (New York: Random House, 1999), p. 37.

47 'Biological warfare. Activities & capabilities of foreign nations', Military Intelligence Division, War Department (30 March 1946), pp. 19–20: Box 2, RG 9999, IWG, Select Documents on Japanese War Crimes and Japanese Biological Warfare, 1934–2006, NARA.

was the Soviets' awareness that they had fallen behind the United States in the arms race – especially the atomic arms race. The Soviets' defensive response – at least until such time as they acquired the Bomb themselves – was to cast themselves as the defenders of global peace, holding the line against imperialist warmongers. Lev Smirnov, the Soviet State Prosecutor at Khabarovsk, referred to this when he told the court:

> Since the first days of its existence, the Soviet Union has been fighting undeviatingly and consistently for lasting, democratic peace. Being a genuine bulwark of peace and herald of the ideas of socialist humanism, the Soviet Union, marching at the head of the democratic forces of the world emphatically repudiates the employment of inhuman means of mass extermination. This is exactly why, despite all the efforts of the instigators of a new war in the Anglo-American bloc, the Soviet Union has been for a number of years striving in the United Nations organization to secure the absolute prohibition of atomic weapons.[48]

A trial of Japanese defendants, unmasking Japan's plans for a biological war – a form of warfare that was potentially just as lethal and indiscriminate as any nuclear war – was a promising embellishment of this theme. Judicial proceedings would, moreover, be the perfect rejoinder to the flawed American-run Tokyo Tribunal, enabling the Soviets to present their own version of the events of the Asia-Pacific War, blame the Western Allies for hushing up the Japanese biological weapons programme, and embarrass the Americans for shielding Ishii and Hirohito from prosecution. Finally, the Soviets could bring, and be seen to be bringing, justice not just to Soviet citizens (the victims of Japan's aggressive plans), but also to 'Chinese patriots' who had borne the brunt of Japan's biological crimes[49] – thereby establishing stronger relations with the new-born People's Republic of China.

The planning stages

The decision to start the trial proceedings in Khabarovsk was made at the highest level. Under Stalin's chairmanship, the Soviet of the Ministers of the USSR passed a Resolution on 8 October 1949 entitled, 'About the Organisation in Khabarovsk of a Trial of the So-called Japanese "Anti-epidemic Unit Number 731" . . .'.[50] A working group consisting of Sergei

[48] *Materials*, pp. 409–410. [49] Ibid., p. 15.

[50] Kruglov, Safonov and Gorshenin to Stalin, Molotov, Malenkov, Beria, Kaganovich and Bulganin (22 November 1949), 5270/k, p. 13: D 596, Op 1a, R 9492, State Archive of the Russian Federation (GARF). Unfortunately, the text of the Resolution is not available to researchers, although it is mentioned in other archival documents.

Kruglov, the Minister of Internal Affairs; Grigori Safonov, the Procurator General; and Konstantin Gorshenin, the Minister of Justice, immediately started organising the Khabarovsk trial. These preparations were made in a hurry. Four days after the Resolution was passed, this group, along with senior ministers from the Ministry of Internal Affairs, decided that the investigative activities – including the interrogation of the defendants, the training of prosecution witnesses, and the preparation of documentation and experts' reports – should be finished within a few weeks, by 1 November 1949.[51] The first drafts of the Indictment and the prosecutor's opening speech were ready on 21 November. These were prepared by the aforementioned Solomon Rosenblit, who by then was working at the USSR's Office of Public Procurator, and was able to draw on his previous experience as a member of Roman Rudenko's investigation team at the Nuremberg Tribunal and as Sergei Golunskii's assistant at Tokyo.[52]

Kruglov, Safonov and Gorshenin were keen to engage judges, prosecutors and defence counsel with experience in war crimes trials, and ideally with experience of the international trials – if the Khabarovsk trial could be raised to meet certain international standards, the Soviets would be better able to present it as a credible alternative to the Tokyo trial. In a letter to Molotov, they indicated that Dmitri Chertkov, the future President of the court, had participated in a Soviet-run war crimes trial of Germans in Poltava in the Ukrainian SSR in 1947.[53] Even better, Lev Smirnov, the future prosecutor, had international experience, having taken part not only in the Soviet-run war crimes trial of Germans in Smolensk in the Russian SSR in 1945 but also in the international military tribunals at Nuremberg and Tokyo.[54] Smirnov's experience was also relevant for another reason: in January 1947, while at the Tokyo Tribunal, he had been directly involved in negotiations with the Americans about a possible exchange of information about the Japanese biological warfare programme.[55]

The investigation – which had concluded that 'Detachment 731 . . . had the aim of waging a bacteriological attack during the war against the Soviet

[51] 'Protocol 1 of the meeting dedicated to the organisation of an open trial of senior officials from the so-called Japanese "anti-epidemic Detachment 731" in Khabarovsk' (October 12, 1949), p. 5: D 596, Op 1a, R 9492, GARF.

[52] Raginskii to Dorman (21 November 1949), p. 18: D 596, Op 1a, R 9492, GARF.

[53] Gorshenin, Kruglov and Safonov to Molotov (26 November 1949), 11: D 596, Op 1a, R 9492, GARF.

[54] Ibid. [55] See, for example, Williams and Wallace, *Unit 731*, pp. 186–187.

Union'[56] – took longer than planned. Consequently, Kruglov, Safonov and Gorshenin submitted the first working group report to Stalin and the Soviet of the Ministers a month late, on 22 November. In this, they made three important suggestions, all of which were accepted. First, they proposed pressing charges against the Japanese defendants according to Paragraph 1 of the Decree of the Presidium of the Supreme Soviet of the USSR of 19 April 1943, which had originally recommended 'death by hanging' for 'German-fascist villains' and the Soviet 'spies and traitors'.[57] But because the death penalty had been abolished by another Decree of 1947, they recommended instead a maximum prison sentence of twenty-five years.[58] Second, they suggested convening a short trial, beginning on 7 December and ending no later than 14 December. And finally, they proposed handpicking the observers to the trial, issuing special tickets to soldiers and workers within Khabarovsk, while also broadcasting outside the courthouse.[59]

Because the initial timetable had not been adhered to, Stalin signed another Resolution – 'On the Organisation of a Trial on Japanese War Criminals in Khabarovsk' – on 1 December 1949, stating that the trial would open on 17 December and close not later than 25 December 1949.[60] This also set out a scale of punishments for those convicted: ten to twenty-five years in forced labour camps for the more senior Unit 731 personnel, and one to three years for subordinate technical staff.[61]

Another Presidium Resolution – 'On the Case of 12 Former Servicemen of the Japanese Army' – of 17 December, dealt with the charges laid against the defendants.[62] This specified that the Indictment was to be issued to the accused on 22 December 1949, three days before the actual commencement of the trial.[63] (If this seemed exceptionally late

[56] Kruglov, Safonov and Gorshenin to Stalin, Molotov, Malenkov, Beria, Kaganovich and Bulganin (22 November 1949), 5270/k, 13: D 596, Op 1a, R 9492, GARF. The Soviets later broadened charges to include members of Unit 100 as well.

[57] Decree of the Presidium of the Supreme Soviet of the USSR, 'O merakh nakazaniia dlia nemetsko-fashistskikh zlodeev, vinovnykh v ubiistvakh i istiazaniih sovetskogo grazhdanskogo naseleniia i plennykh krasnoarmeitsev, dlia shpionov, izmennikov rodiny iz chisla sovetskikh grazhdan i ikh posobnikov' (19 April 1943).

[58] Ibid.

[59] Kruglov, Safonov and Gorshenin to Stalin, Molotov, Malenkov, Beria, Kaganovich and Bulganin (22 November 1949), 5270/k, 16: D 596, Op 1a, R 9492, GARF.

[60] Resolution of the Presidium of the Supreme Soviet of the USSR (1 December 1949), 5484-2098ss: D 596, Op 1a, R 9492, GARF.

[61] Ibid.

[62] Resolution of the Presidium of the Supreme Soviet of the USSR (17 December 1949), 5627-2146cc, 3: D 596, Op 1a, R 9492, GARF.

[63] Ibid.

in the day, it was an advance on previous Soviet-convened war crimes trials, when the accused often received the Indictment at the opening of the trial, and sometimes not until after the verdict had been reached.)[64] It also ordered the central press to publish the full text of the Indictment and the local press to publish shorter versions.[65]

The framing of the Indictment

Although the Soviets did not manage to catch Ishii and the other most senior figures in the biological warfare programme, they were able to round up a heterogeneous group of others connected one way or another with the Kwantung Army's Unit 731 and Unit 100. They included one very high-ranking figure, Yamada Otozō, former Commander-in-Chief of the Kwantung Army; three senior administrators; various mid-ranking managers, bacteriologists, physicians and veterinarians who were involved in the day-to-day running of the biological warfare sections; and two low-ranking soldiers, Corporal Kikuchi Norimitsu and Private Kurushima Yuji, who had cultivated pathogens. Making a virtue of necessity, the Soviets intimated that the range of defendants was intended to demonstrate both the broad scope of Japan's biological weapons programme and the deep penetration of 'militarism' into every layer of Japanese society.

The Khabarovsk Indictment made clear where Soviet preoccupations lay. If the Tokyo Tribunal had neither sufficiently emphasised that Japan had committed 'crimes against peace' against the Soviet Union nor attempted to exonerate the Soviet Union from breaching the Neutrality Pact, then the Indictment made up this shortfall, declaring:

> Aggression against the Soviet Union figured as the principle undertaking in the criminal plans of the Japanese imperialists. In the Japanese militarists' strategical plans for aggression, the U.S.S.R. was usually referred to as 'Target No. 1.' . . . Japanese aggression ended only with the surrender of Japan to the United Nations, following on the decisive defeat inflicted by the Soviet Army on Japan's main striking force – the Kwantung Army, which was concentrated in Manchuria.[66]

64 F.-C. Schoeder, 'Das Sowjetrecht als Grundlage der Prozesse gegen deutsche Kriegsgefangene', in A. Hilger, U. Schmidt and G. Wagenlehner (eds.), *Sowjetische Militärtribunale, Band 1: Die Verurteilung deutscher Kriegsgefangener 1941–1953* (Köln: Böhlau, 2001), p. 89.

65 Resolution of the Presidium of the Supreme Soviet of the USSR (17 December 1949), 5627-2146cc, 3: D 596, Op 1a, R 9492, GARF.

66 *Materials*, pp. 8, 9.

In this version of events, the Soviet Union was acting in defence against the aggressive Kwantung Army, which, armed with bullets and bacteria, was laying waste to China and threatening to do the same to the Soviet Union. If the Soviet Union had broken the Neutrality Pact and crushed the Japanese, it did so to avert a bacteriological holocaust.

The defendants were charged on four grounds: 'Formation of special units for the preparation and prosecution of bacteriological warfare', 'Criminal experiments on human beings', 'Employment of the bacteriological weapon in the war against China' and 'Intensification of preparations for bacteriological warfare against the U.S.S.R.'.[67] These charges were derived from the aforementioned 1943 Presidium Decree, 'On Measures of Punishment for German-Fascist Criminals Guilty of the Murder and Torture of Soviet Civilians and Red Army Prisoners of War; also for Spies and Traitors to the Motherland among Soviet Citizens and their Accomplices.'[68] The Preamble targets 'German, Italian, Romanian, Hungarian and Finnish fascist monsters . . . as well as traitors among Soviet citizens', while Article 1 singles out 'German-fascist villains' and the Soviet 'spies and traitors'.[69] In other words, this Decree was thus originally designed to facilitate the trial and punishment of *European* war criminals and their local collaborators – not Japanese defendants. Moreover, because it was drafted several years prior to the Nuremberg and Tokyo charters, it contained no specific reference to the substantive charges of crimes against peace, crimes against humanity or war crimes, but instead relied on different formulations such as 'murder and torture of civilians and Red Army prisoners of war', 'brutality', and 'atrocities'.[70]

The importance of this Decree should not be underestimated: no fewer than 81,780 people accused of crimes committed during the war – of whom at least 25,209 were non-Soviets – were sentenced under its terms between 1943 and 1952.[71] But the full text was not publicly released during this period. Neither the accused nor their defence counsel knew what it contained, nor were sections of it quoted either in indictments or in sentences. This raises the question, why did they use the Decree as the basis for the Khabarovsk trial, when they might have used the Tokyo Charter? After all, the latter had the patina of international credibility, and may have seemed more appropriate for prosecuting Japanese

[67] Ibid., pp. 9, 15, 22, 25. [68] Presidium Decree (19 April 1943). [69] Ibid. [70] Ibid.

[71] A.E. Epifanov, 'Otvetstvennost' za voennye prestupleniia, sovershennye na teritorii SSSR v period Velikoi Otechestvennoi Voiny (istoriko-pravovoi aspekt)', unpublished PhD thesis, Akademiia upravleniia MVD Rossii (2001), p. 4.

defendants. It is possible that the Soviets rejected the Tokyo Charter because it was directed at 'major war criminals in the Far East'[72] – in other words, the wartime leaders of Japan's government and armed forces – 'charged with offenses which include Crimes against Peace'.[73] The Khabarovsk defendants, with the exception of Yamada Otozō, former Kwantung Army Commander-in-Chief, were either not senior enough or had not committed offences encompassed by 'crimes against peace'. Furthermore, the incorporation of the Tokyo Charter into domestic law would have been a cumbersome process, whereas the Decree, which was already to hand, could provide a quick fix.

Having made this decision, the question was how to apply to Japanese defendants a Decree which targeted just European fascists from Germany, Italy, Romania, Hungary and Finland, as well as local Soviet collaborators.[74] The solution was to proceed by way of analogy: the Japanese had committed similar crimes and were thus similarly liable under its terms. As Kruglov, Safonov and Gorshenin stated in their working party report to Stalin on 22 November 1949, 'although Japanese military are not mentioned in this Decree, their criminal activities are analogous to the crimes of the fascist German army'.[75] The concept of analogy was, of course, already well known in the Soviet legal system: Article 16 of the 1926 Russian Criminal Code, which was widely replicated in the other republics, stated that if a socially dangerous action was not foreseen by the Code, liability would be determined by the sections of it dealing with the most closely related crimes.[76]

In order to sustain the claim to analogy, the prosecution had to prove that Japanese crimes were similar to German crimes. The prosecutor Lev Smirnov thus compared Japanese biological warfare experiments with the human experiments conducted by the German doctors in the extermination camps: 'One's attention cannot help being drawn to the similarity in the methods of destroying human beings on a mass scale employed by the Hitlerite war criminals and by the Japanese

[72] International Military Tribunal for the Far East, *The Tokyo major war crimes trial*, R.J. Pritchard (ed.), 124 vols. (Lewiston: Edwin Mellen Press, 1998), Amended Charter, vol. 2, p. 1.

[73] Ibid., p. 2. [74] Presidium Decree (19 April 1943).

[75] 'Results of the investigation into criminal activities of nine persons among accused Japanese generals and officers serving in the anti-epidemic Detachment 731' (22 November 1949), 5270/k, p. 16: D 596, Op 1a, R 9492, GARF. The Decree was also applied by analogy to Austrian, Dutch and Belgian citizens (Epifanov, 'Otvetstvennost' za voennye prestupleniia', p. 53.)

[76] Article 16, RSFSR Criminal Code (1926).

imperialists.'[77] Smirnov invoked the legacy of the Nuremberg trial when making his case, arguing that 'the experimenters in the Ishii Detachment performed the same experiments as those performed by that sinister S.S. experimenter Dr. Rascher, which the Nuremberg International Tribunal quite justly classed among the cruelest and most inhuman of the experiments on human beings performed by the vile Hitlerites'.[78]

It might be argued that the Decree could not be used as a legal basis for the Khabarovsk trial because there were no Soviet civilians and Red Army POWs among the victims. It should be noted, however, that while the evidence suggested that Chinese citizens constituted the biggest group among the victims, Soviet citizens (or at any rate, 'Russians') were also killed in the Japanese experiments. As the investigation commission concluded, 'Chinese patriots and Soviet citizens who for various reasons found themselves detained on the territory of Manchuria by authorities of the Kwantung Gendarmerie and Japanese Military Mission were used in order to conduct experiments on the effect of bacteriological means manufactured in Unit 731.'[79]

Finally, the Decree was obviously created with the aim of prosecuting crimes against Soviet citizens committed *on the territory* of the Soviet Union. The prosecution emphasised the planning aspect. It also made a weak stab at presenting evidence that the Japanese had committed crimes on Soviet territory by claiming cases of biological sabotage, such as the contamination of the River Derbul, 'in particular in the Trekhrech'e area', with glanders bacilli.[80]

The arguments in court

At the beginning of the trial, all of the accused pleaded guilty to the charges (except Kajitsuka Ryuiji, former chief of the Kwantung Army's

[77] *Materials*, p. 410.

[78] Ibid., pp. 432–433. The defence lawyers were also keen to establish the equivalence of the Japanese with German crimes. P.Y. Bogachov, speaking on behalf of the Satō Shunji, began his closing speech with the words: 'The evil deeds which have been the objects of your investigation have something in common with the atrocities committed by the German fascists in the territory of the Soviet Union and of other European countries ... They have the same ideological basis. The crimes investigated were the direct result of the alliance between imperialist Japan and fascist Germany' (Ibid., p. 496).

[79] Kruglov, Safonov and Gorshenin to Stalin, Molotov, Malenkov, Beria, Kaganovich and Bulganin (22 November 1949), 5270/k, 13: D 596, Op 1a, R 9492, GARF. 14: D 596, Op 1a, R 9492, GARF.

[80] *Materials*, pp. 26, 315–316, 530.

Medical Administration, who denied participation in plans against the Soviet Union and pleaded guilty in part[81]). The prosecution's purpose was to reveal in all its horrifying detail Japan's preparation and deployment of biological weapons. The testimony elicited from those involved in the activities of Unit 731 and 100 was particularly shocking. Towards the end of the trial, the transcript records the following exchange between Lev Smirnov and witness Karukazu Satoru, Section Chief of the Special Division of the Harbin Gendarmerie Administration:

> QUESTION: What do you know about the fate of the people who got into the detachment's prison?
>
> ANSWER: The people who got into this prison never came out.[82]

So why, the prosecution asked, were these horrendous crimes not examined during the Tokyo proceedings? Smirnov noted that a reference to the biological warfare detachment known as either Tama or Ei, operating around Nanjing, and experimenting on people by injecting them with poisons, was entered into the Tokyo record.[83] He claimed that the Soviets then handed the Chief Prosecutor Joseph Keenan further evidence about the biological programme, but that, 'Certain influential persons' – namely, the Americans – 'were evidently interested in preventing the exposure of the monstrous crimes of the Japanese militarists, for the documents on the activities of the Tama Detachment, and on similar experiments performed by the Ishii Detachment, were not submitted to the Tribunal.'[84]

In other words, Smirnov's prosecutorial aim was not just to reveal the mechanics of the Japanese biological weapons programme but also to take issue with the Allies' conduct of the Tokyo Tribunal and protection of the senior figures. This becomes abundantly clear in Smirnov's concluding speech:

> We know that the secret bacteriological units of the Japanese Army which were commissioned to prepare for and conduct bacteriological warfare were formed by command of the Japanese Emperor Hirohito. We know the names of the criminals in the Japanese General Staff and Ministry of War who backed and directed the clandestine work ... We know the names of the contemptible, morally corrupt servitors of Japanese imperialism, generals of the former Japanese Army – the bacteriological scientists Ishii Shiro, Kitano [Masaji], Wakamatsu Yujiro[85] .... Those miscreants are not in the defendants' box. Outside the borders of our country, they enjoy the protection of those reactionary forces in the

[81] Ibid., p. 30. [82] Ibid., p. 368. [83] Ibid., p. 311. [84] Ibid., p. 433. [85] Ibid., p. 464.

> imperialist camp who are themselves dreaming of the time when they will be able to hurl upon mankind loads of T.N.T., atomic bombs and lethal bacteria.[86]

In the process, the prosecution elicited horrific information about the treatment of the prisoners in the Japanese facilities, taking care, where possible, to confirm the presence of Russians among the victims. Yamada Otozō testified that he 'virtually sanctioned the violent killing of Chinese, Russians and Manchurians, who were sent for experimental purposes'.[87] Kawashima Kiyoshi said that 'we used imprisoned Chinese patriots and Russians whom the Japanese counterespionage service had condemned to extinction'.[88] Furuichi Yoshio stated that 'a group of Russians, Manchurians, Chinese and Mongolians, with their legs in chains' were subjected to frostbite experiments conducted in preparation for a winter campaign against the Soviet Union.[89] And Mitomo Kazuo described how an unnamed Russian prisoner was dosed for weeks with hallucinogenic Korean bindweed, then, when no longer any use as a subject of experimentation, was murdered by cyanide injection, dissected, and buried next to cattle carcasses.[90] (The transcript recorded at this point that, 'There is movement in the courtroom, a low murmur of indignation.')[91]

While the prosecution's approach was predictable enough, the defence lawyers played an equally, if not more, important role in the advancement of the Soviet cause. In line with the common practice in the Soviet Union, they did not attempt to prove the innocence of the accused, but simply tried to mitigate their guilt, emphasising their contrition and willingness to cooperate. It was to this end that the defence counsel D.E. Bolkhovitinov asked his client, Nishi Toshihide, former Lieutenant-Colonel of the Kwantung Army's Medical Service, 'Do you now realize the utter criminality of the ultimate aims of the work of Detachment 731 . . . and do you now repent of your deeds?'[92] There was certainly no attempt to challenge the facts of the case. N.P. Belov, representing Yamada Otozō, thus began his closing speech with the observation:

> The biggest difficulty for the defence . . . lies in that here there is no room for debate concerning the facts and proofs as such. The evidence of the witnesses, the original documents at hand in the case, which were collected during the stage of preliminary investigation, and the detailed explanations given by the accused themselves, have confirmed in their sum total the factual side of the indictment.[93]

[86] Ibid., p. 465. [87] *Materials*, p. 16. [88] Ibid. [89] Ibid., pp. 21–22.
[90] Ibid., pp. 323–324. [91] Ibid., p. 324. [92] Ibid., pp. 291–292. [93] Ibid., pp. 467–468.

Even so, the defence counsel's role at Khabarovsk was hardly decorative or nominal, as some have claimed.[94] Like the prosecution, they had a crucial role to play in advancing the Soviet critique of the Tokyo Tribunal, and in particular, its American sponsors. They did so by making two connected arguments: one being that the defendant was operating under superior orders, and the other deriving from the complicity doctrine, as set out in Article 18 of the RSFSR's Criminal Code.

Taking the superior orders claim first, the defence counsel argued that their clients, who were thoroughly imbued with the spirit of Japanese nationalism, had simply obeyed the orders handed down to them by their superior officers, and that this should be taken into account in mitigation of punishment. Thus, V.P. Lukiantsev said of his client, Onoue Masao, the former chief of Unit 731's Branch 643 involved in breeding rodents: 'Without the slightest reflection, Onoue blindly obeyed the orders of his superiors, he was a living tool in the hands of his rulers, his own ego did not exist.'[95] And Bolkhovitinov, defending Nishi Toshihide, said, 'From his earliest youth he had dinned into his mind . . . implicit obedience to all his commands, the idea of Japan's special mission . . . His superiors gave him orders in the name of the emperor, and Nishi blindly obeyed these criminal orders.'[96]

Lev Smirnov put up some token resistance against the superior orders arguments, stating – in line with Article 8 of the Nuremberg Charter and Article 6 of the Tokyo Charter – that, 'No pleading with reference to orders from superiors or to the status of servicemen can serve as justification for the heinous crimes they committed, and which have been fully proved in Court.'[97] All the same, the superior orders issue raised the loaded question of who, exactly, these superiors were and what role they played within the alleged Japanese conspiracy to wage aggressive biological warfare. The Soviet doctrine of complicity identified four categories of conspirators: instigators, organisers, accessories and perpetrators, with instigators and organisers attracting harsher punishments than accessories and perpetrators. Referring to some of these categories, Bolkhovitinov said,

> [N]either . . . Nishi Toshihide, nor . . . Hirazakura Zensaku, can be classed in the group of organizers and instigators of the crimes. On the contrary, it

[94] See, for example, Yudin, 'Research on humans', p. 71; P.R. Piccigallo, *The Japanese on trial: Allied war crimes operations in the East, 1945–1951* (Austin: University of Texas Press, 1979), p. 153.

[95] *Materials*, p. 514. [96] Ibid., pp. 503–504. [97] Ibid., p. 447.

> has been proved that their role was a secondary one. They belong to the group which obeyed the orders of their superiors; criminal orders it is true, but this is, undoubtedly, a circumstance that mitigates their guilt.[98]

Likewise, Lukiantsev argued that Karasawa Tomio, section head of the Production Division of Unit 731, who took part in experiments on humans, played the role 'of executor [perpetrator], but not of leader and organizer of the crime'.[99] And G.K. Prokopenko contended that Kikuchi Norimutsu, a medical orderly who had cultivated typhoid, TB and dysentery germs, was merely 'an accomplice of his superiors'.[100]

It was clear where these arguments were leading. Having identified their clients as the small fry in the conspiracy, it was but a short step to identifying the big fish: the instigators and organisers. The defence counsel named names, and by no coincidence, some happened to be the very people that the Americans were shielding from prosecution. As Lukiantsev informed the court,

> Karasawa is not the chief and principle criminal. Being only a major in rank and subordinate to others, Karasawa obeyed the orders of ... General Kawashima [tried at Khabarovsk] ... General Ishii ... General Umezu [tried at Tokyo], and lastly, he obeyed the will of the Emperor of Japan, Hirohito, all of whom, it seems to me, ought to be chiefly answerable for the manufacture and employment of bacteriological weapons.[101]

Even the defendants joined this chorus: Takahashi Takaatsu, head of the Kwantung Army's Veterinary Service, regretted that 'the chief criminals, the chief organizers and chief instigators of bacteriological warfare are not in the defendants' box',[102] while Hirazakura Zensaku of the Veterinary Service at Unit 100 hoped that the Emperor, Ishii and Wakamatsu would be 'severely punished'.[103]

Finally, on the theme of complicity, the defence lawyer N.P. Belov, representing the most high-ranking defendant, Yamada, mounted another line of attack on the Tokyo Tribunal and its American sponsors – targeting the heads of the *zaibatsu* and the Emperor, while also managing to catch Joseph Keenan in the backswing:

> Comrade Judges, to the amazement of the peace-loving peoples of all the countries of the world, in the dock at the Tokyo trial there was not a single representative of the 'zaibatsu' – the combines of Japanese monopoly capital. Nor was their head, Emperor Hirohito, there. The reason for this was the ties that bound, and bind, the American monopolists with

[98] Ibid., p. 503. [99] Ibid., p. 511. [100] Ibid., p. 507. [101] Ibid., p. 511.
[102] Ibid., p. 521. [103] Ibid., p. 519.

> their Japanese colleagues are too strong. That is precisely why the American prosecutor could not bring himself to speak before the International Tribunal of the role played by the industrial and financial magnates in planning and organizing the second world war.[104]

The defence had already played a crucial role in the denunciation of the Emperor and those responsible for Japan's biological warfare programme, but they still had one final contribution to make. The Indictment had already specified four crimes relating to preparation for and execution of biological warfare. But the defence team and their clients actually *added* to the roster of crimes set out in the Indictment. Two lawyers, A.V. Zverev and V.P. Lukiantsev, conceded that their respective clients, Takahashi Takaatsu and Karasawa Tomio, had committed crimes against humanity.[105] And two of the accused, Kawashima Kiyoshi and Satō Shunji, themselves admitted that they had committed a crime against humanity.[106] The frequency of the references to this crime, which did not appear on the Khabarovsk charge sheet (and only nominally in the Tokyo Indictment[107]) strongly suggests that the Soviets wished to establish a precedent for crimes against humanity charges because they were contemplating further allegations against senior Japanese figures – a suggestion that was borne out by subsequent events.

During their final pleas, some of the accused expressed their gratitude for their 'humane treatment',[108] for being provided with defence counsel, and for the generosity of the Soviet court. The defendant Kawashima Kiyoshi, the former chief of the Bacteriological Research Division, stated that 'the Soviet Union is a democratic country which cares for the welfare of the people and stands on guard for peace'.[109] And Mitomo Kazuo, who participated in human testing in Unit 100, added that, 'I learned to know the Soviet people, I saw that they are humane and noble.'[110]

The Judgment and sentences

The court, which pronounced the sentences on 30 December 1949, found all twelve defendants guilty. Four of the accused – the most senior figures, Yamada Otozō, Kajitsuka Ryuiji, Takahashi Takaatsu and Kawashima Kiyoshi – were sentenced to twenty-five years in a labour camp. The rest received terms ranging from ten to twenty years, with the exception of the

104 Ibid., p. 478. 105 Ibid., pp. 490, 511. 106 Ibid., pp. 516, 519.
107 Sellars, *'Crimes against peace'*, p. 190. 108 *Materials*, p. 515. 109 Ibid., p. 515.
110 Ibid., p. 520.

lowest-ranking defendants, Kurushima Yuji and Kikuchi Norimitsu, who were given three years and two years respectively.[111]

One notable feature of the sentences was that while the prosecutors had demanded the harshest punishment available – long terms of imprisonment – the judges had the manoeuvrability to hand down marginally lighter sentences than recommended. This was a break from the unstated but almost universally observed practice at the time in the Soviet Union. (At the earlier Kharkov trial, for example, the prosecutors' demand that all four defendants be hanged was followed to the letter.)

The other striking feature was the relative leniency of the sentences compared to the sentences handed down by the Soviets in previous trials and by the Allies at the Nuremberg and Tokyo tribunals, which had freely dispensed the death penalty. Assuming their guilt, why were the Khabarovsk prisoners not similarly sentenced? One reason is that the Soviets had abolished capital punishment in May 1947 by the Presidium, 'On the Abolition of the Death Penalty'.[112] (This explains why Ivan Zarianov was among the judges who voted against the executions at the Tokyo Tribunal.)[113]

If this was the only reason, the accused were among the last to be spared capital punishment, because the Soviet authorities were planning to reinstitute the death penalty for 'grave crimes against the Soviet state' through a new Presidium Decree, 'On the Use of the Death Penalty for Traitors to the Motherland, Spies, and Subversive Saboteurs', which was issued on 12 January 1950, just weeks after the sentences were handed down.[114] The Soviet leaders' rush to get the trial over quickly was likely connected to this: if they had held the trial later, they might have been obliged to execute the senior figures. But it was precisely the senior figures they most wanted to keep alive – they might, after all, divulge more information about the biological warfare programme in exchange for shorter sentences further down the line.

[111] Ibid., pp. 534–535.

[112] Decree of the Presidium of the Supreme Soviet of the USSR, 'Ob otmene smertnoi kazni', 26 May 1947 (Moscow: Gosudarstvennoe Izdatel'stvo iuridicheskoi literatury, 1950), reprinted verbatim in *Ugolovnyi kodeks RSFSR* (Moscow: Ripol Klassik, 2013), pp. 140–141.

[113] Sellars, '*Crimes against peace*', p. 255.

[114] Decree of the Presidium of the Supreme Soviet of the USSR, 'O primenenii smernoi kazni k izmennikam rodiny, shpionam, podryvnikam-diversantam', 12 January 1950 (Moscow: Gosudarstvennoe Izdatel'stvo iuridicheskoi literatury, 1950), reprinted verbatim in *Ugolovnyi kodeks RSFSR*, pp. 141–142.

Another reason for the Soviets' haste in convening the trial was that they wanted to use it to deflect Japanese and American complaints in late 1949 that 375,000 Japanese prisoners of war were being held incommunicado in the Soviet Union.[115] If so, the trial was designed to confirm that some of the Japanese prisoners were far from being innocents abroad, and the Soviets were wholly within their rights to refuse to repatriate them wholesale until the guilty parties had been winnowed out. These two motives for the speedy trial seem to be confirmed by Georgii Permiakov, the interpreter present during the interrogations and at the proceedings, who wrote,

> Moscow forced the investigators to hurry. It was known in high quarters in the Ministry of the Interior that the death penalty would be restored the following year. That is why the people at the top requested the completion of the Khabarovsk bacteriological trial before the end of 1949 – at the time some awkward talks were planned between Moscow and Tokyo on the fate of Japanese POWs.[116]

Conclusion

The Soviets publicised the Khabarovsk trial far and wide. In 1950, they produced volumes made up of materials from the trial – swiftly translated into Chinese, Japanese and English – which included the testimonies of the accused, documentary evidence and the findings of the experts. The Soviet press covered the trial extensively; *Pravda* and *Izvestiia* published the most important documents *in toto*. The sentences in particular were highlighted, so as to convey the message of the humanism and restraint of the Soviet judicial system, and the forbearance of the Soviet people. The People's Republic of China also contributed to the publicity, depicting the Khabarovsk trial as 'an expression of friendship of the Soviet people towards the Chinese people' and 'a warning to Anglo-American warmongers trying to use biological weapons and endanger peace in the Far East and throughout the world'.[117] Needless to say, both the Soviets and the Chinese used the trial to underline the close and cordial relationship

115 Both the Japanese government and the American occupation authorities requested information about the POWs. On 30 December 1949, the same day the Khabarovsk tribunal handed down its Judgment, US Secretary of State Dean Acheson sent a note to Alexander Paniushkin, the Soviet Ambassador in Washington, urging his government to allow an international humanitarian body to investigate their fate.

116 Permiakov quoted in Yudin, 'Research on humans', p. 63.

117 *Renmin Ribao* (People's Daily), quoted in 'Chinese newspaper on the case of former military of the Japanese Army', *Pravda* (1 January 1950), 4.

between the two communist powers in the run-up to the signing of the Sino-Soviet Treaty of Friendship, Alliance and Mutual Assistance in February 1950.

The Khabarovsk trial was greeted with rather less enthusiasm elsewhere, especially in the West, where it was perceived as being yet another Stalinist trial modelled on the infamous Moscow purge trials of the 1930s. The fact that there was no prior announcement of the trial, that the authorities had excluded international observers, and that there was a strong whiff of propaganda about the proceedings, made it easy to dismiss it as a mere show trial. But unlike the purge trials, the evidence presented at Khabarovsk is unlikely to have been fabricated. Some scholars have convincingly argued that the testimonies heard there have subsequently been largely corroborated, either by documents discovered in archives or by testimonies offered by former Japanese servicemen.[118] There appears to have been no need for the Soviets to concoct evidence – the reality was horrendous enough.

It has been seen that the Khabarovsk trial was conceived as a corrective to the Tokyo Tribunal. This was confirmed by another event that took place on 1 February 1950, and which represented the culmination of the Khabarovsk project. That day, the Soviet Ambassador in Washington, Alexander Paniushkin, handed a note to the US Secretary of State, Dean Acheson. This proposed the establishment of an international criminal court to try the Emperor and four senior generals involved with the biological warfare programme – Ishii Shiro, Kitano Masaji, Wakamatsu Yujiro and Kasahara Yukio.[119] These five men were, of course, the same individuals that the Americans continued to shelter from prosecution. The note attracted a flurry of press attention, especially in the Soviet Union, China and Japan. But Acheson, ascribing devious Cold War motives to the Soviet Union, declined to reply.

[118] Yudin, 'Research on humans', pp. 70–72; Nie, 'The West's dismissal', pp. 35, 37; S. Wang, 'Medicine-related war crimes trials and post-war politics and ethics', in Nie J.-B. *et al.* (eds.), *Japan's wartime medical atrocities: comparative inquiries in science, history, and ethics* (London: Routledge, 2010), p. 41; Williams and Wallace, *Unit 731*, p. 230.

[119] See, for example, 'Bring the Japanese war criminals to book!', *Pravda* (4 February 1950), p. 1.

6

The People's Republic of China's 'lenient treatment' policy towards Japanese war criminals

ŌSAWA TAKESHI[1]

In summer 1956, the People's Republic of China tried and convicted forty-five Japanese citizens for war crimes committed during the Asia-Pacific and civil wars, and pardoned and released over a thousand more Japanese accused of similar crimes. Its handling of this issue was at once a demonstration to other countries of the Communist Party's firm grip on the levers of state power, while also being a component of its peace offensive towards Japan, which it hoped to manoeuvre into a 'neutralist' position in the Cold War.[2] At home, the issue was intimately bound up with the treatment of Chinese nationals accused of war crimes and counter-revolutionary activities, as well as its relations with Taiwan – now occupied by another old enemy, the Kuomintang – which it ultimately sought to reintegrate into China.

When it came to those convicted of the most serious war crimes, the Chinese authorities were more lenient than the Allied powers in eschewing capital punishment and life imprisonment as punishments. Instead, they tried to transform these offenders by inculcating in them a sense of remorse, while encouraging them to serve as soldiers of peace on return to their native land. This approach revealed an attitude quite unlike that of a victorious nation seeking revenge upon a defeated people – indeed, it showed remarkable prudence, being designed, at least in part, to ensure that the issue would not poison relations between China and Japan in succeeding generations.

[1] Translated from Japanese by Lucy North and Chinese by Alainna Wrigley.

[2] Ōsawa Takeshi, 'Zaika-hōjin hikiage kōshō o meguru sengo Nitchū-kankei: Nitchū minkan kōshō ni okeru "san-dantai hōshiki" o chūshin to shite', *Ajia kenkyū* 49 (2003), 54–70; Ōsawa, Takeshi, 'Maboroshi no Nihonjin "senpan" shakuhō keikaku to Shū Onrai: Chūka Jinmin Kyōwa-koku gaikōbu tōan o tegakari ni', *Chūgoku kenkyū geppō* 712 (2007), 1–11.

The evolution of this policy was not without problems, however. Powerful though the Chinese Communist Party was by 1956, the sound of the boots of the Japanese Imperial Army still rang loudly in the ears of the nation: China had, after all, only recently gained its independence from the occupying forces. While Mao Zedong, Zhou Enlai and their comrades on the Central Committee eventually managed to implement the 'lenient treatment' policy, they nevertheless faced serious objections from within and outside the Party during the decision-making process, from those who thought it would arouse the 'indignation of the people'.[3] Consequently, the leadership was compelled to counter these arguments and prepare the ground before embarking on the trials or releasing any prisoners.

Considerable research has been done on this extraordinary policy. Most studies trace its origins back to the Chinese Red Army's magnanimous treatment of prisoners captured during the civil war with the Kuomintang, touching not only on its conceptual aspects, which they see as being characterised as 'revolutionary humanitarianism', but also on its strategic aspect, which they argue was aimed at breaking down the opposing military forces while establishing a united front across the lines.[4] Yet because of restrictions on access to the relevant historical documents, almost no substantial research has been conducted on the process by which this policy was decided upon and enacted.

From the outset, most of the work relating to the treatment of Japanese war criminals was handled by the Supreme People's Procuratorate, under the overall direction of Zhou Enlai, who was both Premier of the State Council and Foreign Minister. (Other ministries also played their part in the policy's development.) This chapter, drawing mainly on official documents made available in 2004, and stored at the Archives of the Ministry of Foreign Affairs of the People's Republic of China, reconstructs the development of the government's approach to the Japanese war criminals – tracing the interaction between theory and practice from the initial decision-making period to the policy's eventual realisation.

[3] See, for example, 'Guanyu dui Riben zhanfan de shenpan he liangxing wenti de jidian yijian de baogao' (12 January 1956): 105-00501-05, Archives of the Ministry of Foreign Affairs of the People's Republic of China (MFA).

[4] See, for example, Arai Toshio, 'Sabaku to wa nani ka: chūgoku no senpan seisaku', *Kikan chūgoku* 61 (2000), 31–40; Liu Jiachang and Tie Han, *Ri weijiang zhanfan gaizao jishi* (Shenyang: Chunfeng wenyi chubanshe, 1993); and Ren Haisheng, *Gongheguo teshe zhanfan shimo* (Beijing: Huawen chubanshe, 1995).

The antecedents of the war crimes policy

The origins of the policy towards war criminals can be traced as far back as the early years of the Chinese Red Army and the Autumn Harvest Uprising of 1927, when, for strategic reasons, the Party proposed the adoption of a magnanimous policy towards captured Kuomintang troops. Around this time, Mao's 'Three Rules and Eight Points' – which instructed Red Army soldiers to, for example, pay for goods and return borrowed items to the civilian population – formed the basis of revolutionary laws of war. Over the next few years, when the Party was formulating its policy on how to reform its class opponents, it also began to criticise the old prison system and to consider new penal approaches. Even so, its capacity for carrying out its ideas for improving the criminal justice system – such as abolishing corporal punishment and attempting to reform criminals – was extremely limited, and these ideas remained confined to the theoretical sphere.[5]

By the early 1930s, before the Long March, the Party, aiming to strengthen and consolidate its power base in the areas under its control, began to issue a series of laws governing various areas of social, economic and political life, including 'On Punishments for Corruption and Waste' (December 1933),[6] and 'Statute of the Chinese Soviet Republic on Punishment of Counter-revolutionary Crimes' (April 1934).[7] Addressing the issue of communist criminal justice, Mao prohibited the inhumane treatment of prisoners and championed the adoption of 'moral inculcation' (*ganhua zhuyi*) – a doctrine of educational reform of prisoners based on the communist mentality and the discipline of labour.[8] While practice no doubt occasionally diverged from theory, it nevertheless may be said that this approach already contained the seeds of a system based on the reform and re-education of offenders.

With the outbreak of war with Japan on 7 July 1937, the Party was compelled to develop theories and institute practices for dealing with

[5] Xin Guo'en *et al.*, *Mao Zedong gaizao zuifan lilun yanjiu* (Beijing: Renmin chubanshe, 2006), p. 22.

[6] *Collected works of Mao Tse-tung (1917–1949)*, 9 vols. (Arlington: US Joint Publications Research Service, 1978), vol. 4, p. 88.

[7] For the text, see W.E. Butler (ed.), *The legal system of the Chinese Soviet Republic 1931–1934* (New York: Transnational Publishers Inc., 1983), pp. 204–207.

[8] Mao Zedong, 'Zhonghua suweiai gongheguo zhongyang zhixing weiyuanhui yu renmin weiyuanhui dui di-er ci quanguo suweiai daibiao dahui de baogao', in Zhongguo xiandai shi ziliao bianji weiyuanhui (ed.), *Suwei'ai Zhongguo* (Beijing: Zhongguo xiandai shi ziliao bianji weiyuanhui, 1951), pp. 265–266.

Japanese (as well as Kuomintang) prisoners of war as part of their broader efforts to establish a united front and dissolve their enemies' forces. Mao's famous essays, 'On practice' and 'On contradiction', both published just after the war's start, represent the most detailed articulation of the Party's theoretical approach to that date. 'On practice' discusses the possibility of intellectual reform by first bridging the epistemological gap between the subjective and the objective world and then revolutionising the connection between these two spheres.[9] 'On contradiction' supplies a theoretical basis for the reformation of prisoners of war and war criminals by exploring the possibility under certain conditions of transforming contradictions.[10]

This period also saw significant developments in Mao's thinking on strategy. In the essay 'On policy' (December 1940), for example, he called for the release of all prisoners captured from the Japanese, 'puppet' or Nationalist armies.[11] As for spies, a small minority who had 'incurred the bitter hatred of the masses' would be executed.[12] Others would be tried and punished, he wrote, but under a fairer legal regime: 'Corporal punishment must be abolished ... the stress must be on the weight of evidence and confessions should not be taken on trust.'[13] The priority in treatment of prisoners, he wrote, would be on 'reformative education'.[14] This would entail the deployment of both 'subjugation and leniency' through a 'trifold combination' of 'administration, education, and production'.[15] Stressing the strategic element, Mao argued that the overall policy would be beneficial to the cause, because large numbers of prisoners of war could then be 'won over ... to work for our army'.[16]

Dealing with counter-revolutionaries

In June 1949, just before the establishment of the People's Republic of China, Mao, building on these doctrinal developments, composed the essay, 'On the people's democratic dictatorship', which, among other things, clarified his concept of 'reform through labour'. He wrote,

[9] Mao Zedong, 'On practice', *Selected works of Mao Tse-tung*, 5 vols. (Peking: Foreign Language Press, 1965–1977), vol. 1, pp. 295–309.

[10] Mao, 'On contradiction', *Selected works*, vol. 1, pp. 311–347.

[11] Mao, 'On policy', *Selected works*, vol. 2, pp. 446–447. [12] Ibid., p. 447. [13] Ibid., p. 446.

[14] Xin Guo'en *et al.*, *Mao Zedong gaizao zuifan lilun yanjiu* (Beijing: Renmin chubanshe, 2006), pp. 24–25.

[15] Ibid., p. 25. [16] Mao, 'On policy', *Selected works*, vol. 2, p. 447.

> As for the members of the reactionary classes ... If they are not willing to work, the people's state will compel them to work. Propaganda and educational work will be done among them too and will be done, moreover, with as much care and thoroughness as among the captured army officers in the past. This ... may be called a 'policy of benevolence' if you like, but it is imposed by us on the members of the enemy classes.[17]

There was no shortage of subjects for this new regime. During the early years of the People's Republic, the Party set about suppressing 'counter-revolutionary' tendencies through the campaigns against the 'three evils' (corruption, waste, and bureaucracy) and the 'five evils' (bribery, tax evasion and various thefts against the state). Those accused of these and other crimes were still subjected to severe punishments, although not necessarily to execution, as exemplified by the 'Act of the People's Republic of China for Punishment of Counterrevolutionaries' of February 1951.[18] As Mao explained,

> The number of people killed cannot be too great. If it is, we would lose the people's sympathy, as well as our labour force. In principle, the indignation of the people would not be assuaged if those who have a debt of blood [i.e. commit murder] or commit other major criminal offences are not executed. They should be executed resolutely, to help appease public indignation.[19]

At the same time, Mao's theory of 'reform through labour' was being institutionalised throughout the penal system. Two directives promulgated in September 1954 – 'Act of the People's Republic of China for Reform through Labour '[20] and 'Provisional Measures of the People's Republic of China for Dealing with the Release of Reform-through-Labour Criminals at the Expiration of Their Term of Imprisonment and for Placing Them and Getting Them Employment' – signalled the

[17] Mao, 'On the people's democratic dictatorship', *Selected works*, vol. 4, p. 17.

[18] For the text, see Leng Shao Chuan and Chiu Hungdah (eds.), *Criminal justice in post-Mao China: analysis and documents* (Albany: State University of New York Press, 1985), pp. 177–182.

[19] Mao, 'Guanyu zhenya fangeming' (30 April 1951), in Zhonggong zhongyang wenxian bianji weiyuanhui (ed.), *Mao Zedong wenji*, 8 vols. (Beijing: Renmin chubanshe, 1993–1999), vol. 6, p. 121.

[20] For the text, see *Zhonghua Renmin Gongheguo laodong gaizao tiaoli* (7 September 1954): fgk.chinalaw.gov.cn. For a partial translation, see J.A. Cohen, 'Act of the People's Republic of China for Reform through Labour (1954) (excerpts)', in Leng and Chiu (eds.), *Criminal justice*, pp. 253–267.

entrenchment of the policy.[21] A year and a half later, in April 1956, Mao wrote the essay 'On the ten major relationships', in which he stated:

> [F]rom now on there should be fewer arrests and executions in the suppression of counter-revolutionaries in society at large. They are the mortal and immediate enemies of the people and ... a small number should be executed. But most of them should be handed over to the agricultural co-operatives and made to work under supervision and be reformed through labour.[22]

This did not mean that the regime was not prepared to mount trials or impose harsh punishments against those it perceived to be threats – it did both – but it shows that Mao was prepared to initiate policies ostensibly based on rehabilitation as well as retribution, provided they served useful political ends. These ends, as Mao stated, included avoiding the stigma of killing captives, keeping prisoners alive to extract further information from them, gaining a humane reputation abroad, and being good for the people's cause.[23] He added, 'Counter-revolutionaries are trash, they are vermin, but once in your hands, you can make them perform some kind of service for the people.'[24]

Although driven by different motives, the Party's handling of the 'reactionaries' within China and its management of the 'war criminals' from Japan had overlapping features – both, after all, were counter-revolutionaries, the Japanese simply being the international variety. Both were portrayed as simultaneously inflicting abuses on the Chinese people and assaults against the Chinese state. And both, when appropriate, could be dealt with through a policy of magnanimity and rehabilitation.

The convergence of the two approaches was most apparent in the People's Republic's approach to Taiwan. Having weathered the first Taiwan Strait Crisis of 1954–1955, the Party had begun to lean towards a less confrontational approach when contemplating absorbing Taiwan into the People's Republic of China.[25] The 'lenient treatment' policy was but one strand in this wider objective. When applied to the Japanese prisoners accused of war crimes, it was designed to construct a sense of

[21] For the text, see J.A. Cohen, *The criminal process in the People's Republic of China, 1949–1963: an introduction*, 2 vols. (Boston: Harvard University Press, 1968), vol. 2, pp. 634–635.
[22] Mao, 'On the ten major relationships', *Selected works*, vol. 5, p. 299. [23] Ibid, p. 300.
[24] Ibid.
[25] Liao Xinwen, 'Teshe guonei zhanfan juece de tichu yu shishi', *Dang de wenxian* 44 (1995), 34.

shared national experience, and when applied to the Kuomintang prisoners, who were accused of both war crimes and counter-revolutionary activities, it was calculated to shake up its old political foes in Taipei.[26] The war crimes issue was thus harnessed to the broader goal of communist-led Chinese national unity.

A thaw in Sino-Japanese relations

The Party's approach to Japanese war crimes may have arisen organically out of its experiences in China, but it was also shaped by international factors. During the early years of the People's Republic, it sought to counter the United States' attempted 'containment' and non-recognition of China by trying to drive a wedge between the United States and Japan. At the very least, it hoped to encourage Japanese neutralism in struggles of the Cold War.[27] China's handling of its relations with Japan – and, as part of that, the issue of Japanese war crimes – was driven by these weighty international imperatives.

After the San Francisco Peace Treaty came into force in April 1952, the Chinese instituted an approach to relations with Japan known as 'people's diplomacy' – essentially trade and cultural exchanges – designed ultimately to stimulate more cordial relations higher up. After the conclusion of the Korean War in July 1953, and the signing of the Sino-Soviet Joint Declaration in October 1954 (which called for the restoration of diplomatic relations with Japan), some of the formal impediments to official contacts between China and Japan were removed. Over the ensuing months, exchanges between Japan and China increased, with an agreement between fisheries associations on fishing rights signed in April 1955, and a third civil trade agreement (following agreements in 1952 and 1953) concluded in May 1955. In September 1955, Mao urged the 'normalisation' of relations with Japan,[28] while Zhou extended invitations to Prime Minister Hatoyama Ichirō and Foreign Minister Shigemitsu Mamoru to visit Beijing.

[26] Zhou Enlai, 'Zai er jie zheng-xie changweihui shijiu ci huiyi (kuoda) shang de fayan' (14 March 1956), *Dang de wenxian* 44 (1995), 20–21.

[27] Zhang Xiangshan, 'Xin Zhongguo chengli chuqi zhongyang zhiding de dui Ri zhengce he huodong fangzhen', *Zhong-Ri guanxi guankui yu jianzheng* (Beijing: Dangdai shijie chubanshe, 1998), pp. 225–227.

[28] Mao Zedong, 'Guanyu dui Riben ying mingque tichu waijiao guanxi zhengchanghua wenti de piyu' (14 September 1955), in Zhonggong zhongyang wenxian yanjiushi (ed.), *Jianguo yilai Mao Zedong wengao*, 15 vols. (Beijing: Zhongyang wenxian chubanshe, 1987–1999), vol. 5, p. 384.

At the same time, from the Japanese side, Hatoyama and his conservative Liberal-Democratic Party Cabinet began to encourage 'autonomous diplomacy' – the positioning of Japan between the two power blocs – by maintaining relations with the United States while also signing accords with China and the Soviet Union. The Japanese government, through its diplomatic mission in Geneva, asked the Chinese to consider investigations into the whereabouts of Japanese prisoners of war and other unaccounted-for citizens in the People's Republic. And both Japan and China considered the problem of how to make it easier for nationals resident in the other country – for example, people who had married abroad, and former wartime forced labourers in Japan – to travel back and forth.

Quantitative increases in Japanese–Chinese contacts were beginning to qualitatively transform the nature of their relations. It seemed as though both countries were standing on the threshold of a new era of reconciliation. Indeed, one could say that this was one of the most delicate and critically important periods of Sino-Japanese relations in the post-war period. Expectations were especially high on the Chinese side – and the idea began to grow within the Party leadership that its 'lenient treatment' of Japanese war criminals might, if handled properly, become a trump card in its relations with Japan.

At Fushun and Taiyuan

In 1955, the Chinese held 1,109 Japanese nationals – mostly men, a few women – in two detention centres for war criminals, located in Fushun in Liaoning Province and Taiyuan in Shanxi Province. The majority, 969 individuals, had been arrested by the Soviets in the aftermath of the Asia-Pacific War, and then transferred from the USSR to China in July 1950, after the birth of the People's Republic.[29] They had been held at Fushun, near the China–Korea border, until China entered the Korean War, when they were moved north to Harbin Prison, Hulan Prison in Harbin, and Harbin Daoli Prison in Heilongjiang Province, before being returned to Fushun in 1953.[30] In addition to these prisoners, the Chinese held another 140 Japanese prisoners at Taiyuan, the majority of whom had

[29] Sun Shiqiang, 'Fushun zhanfan guanlisuo lishi yan'ge yu dashi jianji', in Fushunshi zhengxie wenshi weiyuanhui (ed.), *Zhenhan shijie de qiji: gaizao wei Man huangdi Pu Yi ji Riben zhanfan jishi* (Beijing: Zhongguo wenshi chubanshe, 1990), p. 257.

[30] Wu Haoran, 'Riben xiaoji yixia zhanfan gaizao jishi', in Fushunshi zhengxie wenshi weiyuanhui (ed.), *Zhenhan shijie de qiji*, pp. 174–175.

fought in Yan Xishan's army during the Chinese civil war before their capture by the communist forces.

The outlines of the 'lenient treatment' policy towards these prisoners could already be discerned in spring 1952, when, in accordance with Zhou Enlai's instructions, a system aimed at instilling remorse was instituted at the detention centres.[31] This three-step process – consisting of 'education', 'confession' and 'repentance' – was designed to bring about personal transformation.[32] Leaving aside questions of effectiveness, the process was carried out quite exhaustively, from study programmes in which the prisoners were instructed on how to behave as law-abiding citizens, to trips to factories and mines where they could observe the success of the socialist revolution (as well as being exposed to people's resentment about Japanese depredations).[33] On a trip to Nanjing, for example, some of the prisoners reportedly knelt down on the spot to confess each time someone denounced the crimes committed by the Japanese. Even the more recalcitrant prisoners were apparently moved, including Adachi Seitarō, who was quoted as saying,

> The peace-building strength of the Chinese people surges forth like the roaring sea, suddenly increasing by leaps and bounds, like bamboo shoots springing up after a rain shower. The great and flourishing future of the Chinese people illuminates a bright road of the happiness of mankind. I must speed my own transformation, advancing to follow the trend of the times.[34]

From March 1954 onwards, the Supreme People's Procuratorate began dispatching more than 700 members of the 'Team for investigation of Japanese war criminals and Manchukuo traitors' to the Fushun detention centre to conduct full-scale investigations into the prisoners' crimes.[35] This process was overseen by Li Fushan, Director of the General Office of the Supreme People's Procuratorate, who, in 1954, was appointed Director of the 'Northeast China Work Group' to carry out the investigation. The number of prisoners' confessions increased, and the practice of their writing testimonies reached an all-time high. Armed with this information, the Procuratorate, from February 1955 onwards, began to

[31] Jin Yuan, 'Qiji yu qianqu: huiyi dui Ri, wei fanzhan de gaizao gongzuo' in Fushunshi zhengxie wenshi weiyuanhui (ed.), *Zhenhan shijie de qiji*, pp. 6–8.

[32] Ibid., pp. 8–11; Sun Mingzhai, 'Gaizao Riben zhanfan gongzuo de huigu', in Fushunshi zhengxie wenshi weiyuanhui (ed.), *Zhenhan shijie de qiji*, pp. 135–136.

[33] Huang Yao and Zhang Mingzhe (eds.), *Luo Ruiqing zhuan* (Beijing: Dangdai Zhongguo chubanshe, 1st edn., 1996), pp. 327–328.

[34] Ibid., p. 238. [35] Jin, 'Qiji xie qianqiu', pp. 11–12.

prepare the indictments of the prisoners it believed had committed the most serious crimes,[36] and to lay plans to pardon and release those who had committed less serious offences.

On 15 September, it produced the 'Party Report from the People's Supreme Procuratorate' – the first document (so far as is known) to set out concrete assessments of each prisoner's responsibility for war crimes.[37] This report, drawing on research by a team of specialists working under Zhang Dingcheng, the Procurator-General, recommended that: 28 prisoners should be sentenced to execution, imprisonment exceeding fifteen years or long-term imprisonment; 48 prisoners should be sentenced to imprisonment for a period of ten to fourteen years but (having already served time) should be released after serving one to two years of their sentence; 79 prisoners sentenced to imprisonment for a period of eight to nine years should be pardoned and released without serving any more time; and 909 prisoners should be exempted from prosecution and released.[38] It should be noted that while the Procuratorate was prepared to release the majority, it nevertheless pushed for the need to execute the worst offenders.[39]

This report marked the beginning of an intense period of discussion within the Party about the form that the war crimes policy should take, with the Chinese Communist Party's Central Committee, mindful of relations with Japan, pushing for the abandonment of the death penalty and life imprisonment for Japanese war criminals for the sake of rapprochement with Japan, and the People's Supreme Procuratorate, mindful of the reaction of the Chinese public, demanding harsher sentences for the most notorious crimes.

Who to indict?

Spurred by the Procuratorate's recommendations, the Party leadership formed a high-powered interdepartmental body to advise the Central Committee – 'Leaders of investigation and handling of Japanese war criminals' – headed by Liao Chengzhi, Vice Director of the Central Committee's International Liaison Department, and principal advisor

36 'Zuigao renmin jianchayuan dangzu baogao' (19 February 1955): 105-00220-06, MFA.

37 'Guanyu zaiya riben zhanfan yu wei manhanjian de zhenxun jieguo yu chuli yijian de qingshi baogao' (15 September 1955): 105-00501-01, MFA.

38 Ibid.

39 Ibid. The Procuratorate wanted to execute seven people and to impose suspended death sentences on three people.

on Sino-Japanese relations.[40] This team met on 28 October 1955 to begin to compose the 'Petition report (first draft)', which sought to resurrect the ideal of 'lenient treatment'.[41] This document, addressing the issue of punishment, suggested: first, that there should be no death sentences (including death sentences with reprieve for good behaviour); second, that the only form of punishment should be imprisonment, either for a fixed term or indefinitely; and third, that the date of commencement for any sentence of imprisonment should be counted from the day the prisoner was imprisoned in China.[42] These and other proposals directed the discussion away from proposals to impose the death penalty.

At the same time, though, the 'Leaders' team, which included senior figures from the Procuratorate, was divided within itself about who to indict, and how severely they should be punished. While the Party leaders, and senior members of the team, advocated indicting only the worst offenders, others on the team felt that all the prisoners, as war criminals, should be subject to the legal process, even if most of them would eventually be discharged. They pointed out that the great majority of them had already been imprisoned in China without trial for five years or longer[43] (not to mention the five years that many had also spent in captivity in the Soviet Union between 1945 and 1950). They therefore felt that it was necessary to go through the legal process before releasing them as a retrospective justification for the prisoners' long incarceration without trial.

With this problem unresolved, the 'Leaders' team met again on 7 November. The discussion did not move in the direction Liao Chengzhi had hoped, however. The report drafted during this meeting suggested that twenty-nine individuals should be sentenced to death, imprisoned indefinitely or imprisoned for more than fifteen years – thereby resurrecting proposals to impose the death sentence or long sentences on some of the Japanese.[44] At this same meeting, concern

40 Aside from Liao himself, and the aforementioned Li Fushan, the main members of the 'Leaders' team were Li Chuli (Vice Minister, International Department of the Party's Central Committee), Jia Qian (Chief Judge, Criminal Division of the Supreme People's Court), Ling Yun (Director, First Section of the Ministry of Public Security) and Chen Shuliang (Deputy Director, Department of Asian Affairs at the Ministry of Foreign Affairs).

41 'Guanyu chuli zaiya riben zhanfan gongzuozhong jige wenti de qingshi baogao (chugao)' (1 November 1955): 105-00501-02, MFA.

42 Ibid. 43 Ibid.

44 'Guanyu chuli zaiya riben zhanzhen zuifan de qingshi baogao' (7 November 1955): 105-00501-02, MFA.

was also expressed about the lack of evidence to support some of the proposed indictments – a concern intimately related to the question of who ought to be indicted. Thus, while the report arising from this meeting recommended the imprisonment of 120 individuals for eight to nine years (including time already served on Chinese soil), it also acknowledged that the main indicia of these individuals' guilt were personal testimonies, which, as was recognised, were an inadequate basis for prosecution.[45] The paucity of evidence had a crucial bearing on the framing of the war crimes policy.

The jurist Mei Ru'ao provided the most useful advice in relation to this difficult problem. Having served as the Chinese judge at the 1946–1948 International Military Tribunal for the Far East, and then as a legal advisor to the Foreign Ministry, Mei expressed deep interest in the discussions carried out by Liao Chengzhi and his 'Leaders' team. In a memorandum to Liao on 10 December, Mei insisted that the Chinese avoid the slightest suggestion that the prisoners were being released because of lack of evidence or insufficient grounds for prosecution. Instead, they should present the unconditional release of the prisoners of war as a 'grand gesture' of magnanimity:

> We should take the high-sounding, generous way out, and not the casual or careless way out. It must be said that it is based on political and humanitarian considerations … and it must not be said to be due to technicalities or judicial procedure (e.g. not prosecuting because 'the suspected crime was trivial', or there was 'insufficient evidence').[46]

Mei advised:

> We should make a proud and upright declaration that, based on political and humanitarian considerations (e.g. the war has been over for ten years, our sympathy for and friendship with the Japanese people, our policy of leniency and compassion for the prisoners who are worn with age etc.), we have resolved to *'exempt these people from the legal process'* (i.e. *'not being handled by legal proceedings'* or *'not handing them to the judicial organs for processing'*) and shall release and repatriate them.[47]

In other words, he was arguing that the Chinese should state that they were releasing the prisoners *even though they were guilty* as a significant show of goodwill towards Japan.

[45] Ibid.

[46] 'Mei Ru'ao fa liao chengzhi wan "guanyu riben zhanfan de shifang he shenpan"', (10 December 1955), p. 1: 105-00501-03, MFA.

[47] Ibid., p. 2. Original emphasis.

This approach got around the problem of what to do with those prisoners against whom it was more difficult to construct a case. The 'Leaders' team's report dated 20 December, which was drafted just prior to Central Committee's final decision on the matter, struck a firmer and more confident note. On the question of who to put on trial, it stated that the 'practical investigation of truth' had yielded eighty-two individuals who could be indicted for 'heinous crimes' attestable through 'concrete evidence' and leading to sentences of twelve or more years' imprisonment.[48] But given that more than a thousand Japanese prisoners were being held, it added that 'it is problematic that the number indicted is so few, for which reason it was suggested that seventy-three more prisoners be indicted for "relatively less heinous crimes" attestable via "partial evidence"'.[49]

Second, on the issue of punishment, the report advised a maximum sentence of life imprisonment. This seems to suggest a last-minute compromise between, on the one hand, those who supported the Procuratorate's line, who were inclined towards harsher policies including the death penalty, and on the other hand, those within the 'Leaders' team who sought to realise the leadership's desire to adhere to the 'lenient treatment' policy. In the end, the proposal was that, of the suggested indictees: fifteen prisoners to be sentenced to life imprisonment, twenty-one prisoners to twenty years' imprisonment, twenty-four prisoners to eighteen years' imprisonment, twenty-four prisoners to fifteen years' imprisonment, ten prisoners to twelve years' imprisonment and sixty-one prisoners to imprisonment of between six and ten years.[50]

After three months of debate, this proposal was passed to the Party leadership. On 27 December 1955, Zhou Enlai met with Luo Ruiqing, Minister of Public Security, and Li Kenong, Director of the Central Department of Social Affairs. The next day, Zhou chaired a meeting of the Central Committee, where he clearly stated his position:

> Japanese war criminals are to be treated with leniency, and are not to be sentenced to execution or indefinite imprisonment. Only a small number will be sentenced to imprisonment, and this will be for a definite term.[51]

[48] 'Guanyu chuli zaiya Riben zhanzheng zuifan qingshi baogao' (20 December 1955): 105-00501-02, MFA.

[49] Ibid. [50] Ibid.

[51] Zhou Enlai and Zhonggong zhongyang wenxian yanjiushi (ed.), *Zhou Enlai nianpu 1949–1976*, 3 vols. (Beijing: Zhongyang wenxian chubanshe, 1997), vol. 1, p. 531.

This decision was then passed directly to Sun Mingzhai, the Warden of the Fushun detention centre. As Jin Yuan, an employee at the centre, recalled, this policy did not go down at all well.

> After returning to Fushun, Head Procurator Tan Zhengwen[52] and Warden Sun Mingzhai held a meeting with the Procuratorate's Northeast China Work Group and all the workers from the Fushun war criminal administration centre, which more than 900 people attended. During the meeting, they conveyed the Central Committee's decision and the directive from Premier Zhou Enlai. After they announced the Central Committee's decision to not sentence even one of the Japanese war criminals to death, the meeting hall was in uproar. Some immediately stood, demanding that the Central Committee alter the decision. It was not just the average Party cadres who were unable to accept the decision – some leading cadres were also unable to understand the reasoning behind it . . . People were unable to understand why these butchers who killed without batting an eye would not be executed.[53]

Tan took note of these views and returned to Beijing with the suggestion that the Central Committee change its decision.

> After listening to Head Procurator Tan Zhengwen's report Premier Zhou Enlai reflected for a moment. He said, slowly and steadily, 'I understand how the cadres and people feel, but the Central Committee's decision cannot be altered. So long as the leading cadres have considered the decision thoroughly, then the ideological work of the regular cadres and masses beneath them is well done. In the long run, a lenient policy for dealing with the Japanese war criminals is the correct one. Right now there may be a few comrades who cannot understand the policy, but in 20 years' time they will believe that this policy was the correct one to take. Therefore the Central Committee's policy must be firmly implemented. To reiterate, not even one person can be killed, no-one can be sentenced to death, we must limit the number of people sentenced to the utmost.'[54]

On his return to Fushun, Tan held a meeting with all the cadres to convey back to them Zhou's instruction. Many still found the Central Committee's decision unpalatable, but accepted that it had to be carried out unconditionally.[55] This was not the end of the matter, however.

[52] In an earlier paragraph, Jin introduced Tan Zhengwen as head Procurator of the Procuratorate's Northeast China Work Group, a position which he held while Deputy Procurator-General of the Supreme People's Court.

[53] Jin Yuan, *Qiyuan: yige zhanfan guanlisuozhang de huiyi* (Beijing: Jiefangjun chubanshe, 1999), p. 176.

[54] Ibid., pp. 176–177. [55] Ibid., p. 177.

The opposition gathers steam

In the months to come, the Central Committee's 'lenient treatment' policy would give rise to mounting criticism from both the Procuratorate and subordinate agencies working with prisoners and victims. After a general meeting, the Procuratorate produced a revised 'Party report', dated 12 January 1956, which again petitioned for indefinite life sentences. The report offered three examples showing that life sentences had solid precedents in law: first, the two international military trials at Nuremberg and Tokyo, where the maximum penalty was execution; second, the Soviet trial of Japanese war criminals at Khabarovsk in 1949, where the maximum sentence was twenty-five years' imprisonment (because the Soviets had temporarily abolished the death sentence); and third, the Chinese Criminal Code, which listed life sentences among the punishments that could be dispensed by a court.[56]

Legal precedents aside, the Procuratorate seemed to have been most interested in advancing the argument that the policy of lenient treatment might give rise to popular resentment, especially in the provinces occupied by the Japanese. In the course of conducting investigations into the crimes committed by prisoners in the detention centres, Procuratorate officials had also been gathering a huge amount of evidence from the victims of the Japanese. Its report highlighted Mei Ru'ao and others' opinion that a maximum sentence of twenty years was too short, and stated: 'Elimination of the death penalty is lenient enough. If, on top of this, the life sentence is also eliminated, it will be near impossible to quell the *indignation of the people*'.[57] While this indignation of course had many shades and hues, what is significant is that the Procuratorate used this sentiment as a means of stimulating reconsideration of the policy.

While Zhou Enlai was considering the 'Party report', the opposition's appeals on the basis of the 'indignation of the people' did not abate. To stem the rising tide of objections, he set up another team to assess guilt and propose punishment, this time led by Deputy Procurator General Tan Zhengwen. Tan's team, consisting of leaders of political and legal departments as well as legal specialists from outside the Party, aimed to force the differing views on the treatment of war criminals into some sort of alignment and to push for a final decision. This team possessed a higher degree of legal specialisation than Liao Chengzhi's 'Leaders' team,

[56] 'Guanyu dui riben zhanfan de shenpan he liangxing wenti de jidian yijian de baogao' (12 January 1956): 105-00501-05, MFA.

[57] Ibid. Emphasis added.

although there was considerable overlap of membership between the two.[58] When Tan Zhengwen's research team submitted its own report on 20 February,[59] it fully supported the Procuratorate's call in the 'Party report' for life sentences.

The opposition was by now proving to be formidable. The Central Committee recognised that it needed to build a broader support for its policy, and especially to persuade those people who were directly affected by the war crimes of the Japanese, many of whom were proud members of the Party and saw themselves as having been instrumental in the success of the revolution. It decided that it would have to set up public meetings to explain its policy to the Chinese public. This process was carried out in both the cities and in rural areas, starting with the convening of Political Consultative Conferences, which attracted delegates from a wide range of organisations both inside and outside the Party, and continuing with large-scale propaganda campaigns.

The propaganda offensive

The first public discussion, held at the 'Nineteenth Expanded Meeting of the Standing Committee of the Second Chinese People's Political Consultative Conference National Committee', was convened in Beijing on 14 March 1956. Luo Ruiqing, Minister of Public Security, and Tan Zhengwen, Deputy Procurator-General, both delivered reports, while Zhou concluded with a general overview. Luo's report made the case for the 'lenient treatment' policy. He proposed that no war criminal would be sentenced to death, that the fifty or more prisoners accused of the gravest crimes would be charged in accordance with the Chinese Criminal Code and that the majority of the prisoners would be pardoned and released.[60] He offered several reasons for the adoption of the policy: first, it would ensure the success of efforts to suppress counter-revolutionary activity, as

[58] Those who participated in both teams included the aforementioned Tan Zhengwen, Li Fushan, Jia Qian, Ling Yun and Chen Shuliang, as well as Shi Liang (Minister of Justice), the Party members Zhong Hanhua (Vice President, Military Court of the People's Liberation Army), Wang Ruqi (Lawyers' Department Director, Ministry of Justice) and non-Party specialists such as Mei Ru'ao and Zhou Gengsheng (legal advisors to the Ministry of Foreign Affairs), Zhang Zhirang (Vice President, Supreme People's Court), and Pan Zhenya (Vice Minister, Ministry of Supervision).

[59] 'Guanyu riben zhanfan he weiman hanjian de jige wenti xiang zhongyang de qingshi baogao caogao' (20 February 1956): 105-00501-06, MFA.

[60] Luo Ruiqing, 'Luo Ruiqing guanyu zhanzheng zuifan wenti de fayan' (14 March 1956), *Dang de wenxian* 44 (1995), p. 25.

well as safeguarding national security; second, that it would, over time, alleviate the indignation of the people; and third, it would enhance the war criminals' own sense of remorse. Finally, the policy would serve international ends, because it would 'serve as a serious warning to Japanese militarists' and 'promote solidarity between the Chinese and Japanese peoples'.[61] Continuing on this last theme, Luo said,

> This policy will . . . support the Japanese people's struggle for peace and battle for democracy, maintain peace throughout all of Asia, facilitate friendly cooperation between the Japanese and Chinese people, as well as isolate the American aggressors and their stooges.[62]

Summing up the discussion, Zhou effectively called for an end to residual anti-Japanese sentiment and the opening of a new era of reconciliation: 'It has already been ten years. There ought to have been a conclusion. Now we need to settle this quickly.'[63] He explained that fifty-one individuals were scheduled to be sentenced to prison terms of eleven to twenty years; that the release of the majority of war criminals would take place over three separate periods, not all at once; and that after the 'Chinese People's Political Consultative Conference' had concluded, further consideration of the policy would take place.[64] The outcome of this particular conference decided decisively in Zhou's favour: it expressed 'unanimous support' for the policy of lenient treatment for Japanese war criminals.[65]

The strong endorsement of the policy seems to have had a sobering effect on those who still advocated harsher punishments. Immediately after the conference, on 16 March 1956, Tan Zhengwen's team submitted a paper, 'Report on investigating the principal situations of the Japanese war criminals and opinions on their disposal', which contained the following self-critical statement:

> As a result of our lack of understanding in relation to political changes occurring both inside and outside of China, and because of our failure to fully comprehend the principles behind the Central Committee's policy of lenient treatment for Japanese war criminals, our proposed method of treatment was biased insofar as the number of proposed subjects of indictment was too great while the content of their sentences was too severe.[66]

[61] Ibid. [62] Ibid.
[63] Zhou, 'Zai erjie zhengxie changweihui shijiuci huiyi (kuoda) shang de fayan', p. 19.
[64] Ibid, pp. 19–20. [65] Ren Haisheng, *Gongheguo teshe zhanfan shimo*, p. 24.
[66] 'Zhongyang huiyi wenjian: guanyu zhencha riben zhanfan de zhuyao qingkuang he chuli yijian de baogao' (16 March 1956): 105-00501-07, MFA.

The report acknowledged the 'leniency' principle and concurred with Zhou's proposal to indict fifty-one prisoners.[67]

Having succeeded in obtaining consensus, the Central Committee in late March established a new team, the 'Leaders for the treatment of war criminals', which was charged among other things with 'strengthening political leadership as well as bringing about a higher degree of mutual cohesion and overall unity in the various associated departments'.[68] On 2 April, another body, the interdepartmental 'Joint Office for the handling of Japanese war criminals'[69] tabled an 'Implementation plan for the treatment of Japanese war criminals'.[70] This described procedures for mounting prosecutions and stressed the need for systematic propaganda campaigns directed at both national and international audiences.[71]

The Party clearly felt that it was worth making a considerable effort to neutralise anti-Japanese sentiment and to provide explanations for the 'lenient treatment' policy. Their efforts to win the support of the Chinese public intensified. On 11 April, the Central Committee sent out a notice to Party organisations in the metropolis as well as the surrounding rural areas instructing them to hold discussions that would generate suggestions on how best to deal with the Japanese war criminals as 'a means of reaching a final decision'.[72] This shows that it was prepared to go to considerable lengths to secure public support. At the same time it also made clear that it was not prepared to budge from its position: as a note accompanying the notice explained, 'the Central Committee has already decided to release and return to their native home' most of the Japanese prisoners[73] – indicating their unwavering commitment to the policy. The solicitation of suggestions was merely designed to engage people's interest in the issue.

67 Ibid.

68 'Chuli zhanfan zhidaozu fa zhang hanfu waijiaobu fubuzhang wan wenshu' (27 March 1956): 105-00501-06, MFA.

69 The 'Joint Office', led by the jurist Jia Qian, was created by the Procuratorate, the Supreme People's Court, and the Administrative Department in January 1956.

70 'Chuli riben zhanfan gongzuo jihua' (2 April 1956): 105-00502-01, MFA.

71 'Guanyu chuli riben zhanfan de xuanchuan fangzhen he xuanchuan gongzuo jihua' (2 April 1956): 105-00502-01, MFA.

72 Zhongguo gongchandang zhongyang weiyuanhui, 'Zhong-Gong Zhongyang guanyu zhengqiu dui Jiang, Ri, wei zhanfan he qita fangeming zuifan de chuli yijian de tongzhi' (11 April 1956), *Dang de wenxian* 44 (1995), 21–22.

73 Chuli Riben zhanfan lianhe bangongshi, 'Mijian guanyu chuli Riben zhanfan de xuanyun fangzhen he xuanyun gongzuo jihua' (11 April 1956), pp. 17–22: 105-00502-01, MFA.

This was not the only kind of public engagement. The Chinese authorities were also transporting the Japanese prisoners around the countryside on special tours, accompanied by prison wardens, Party officials and a barrage of press coverage. As previously mentioned, these trips were designed, at least in part, to bring about the prisoners' personal transformation by 'opening the door' and bringing them into contact with the Chinese people's 'social influences and support'.[74] But as a document appended to the aforementioned 'Implementation plan' shows, the ultimate aim of these tours was propagandistic – namely, to persuade the Chinese that the war criminals had embarked on emotional (as well as physical) 'journeys of repentance'.[75] Whether or not the Central Committee's explanations actually succeeded in dissolving anti-Japanese sentiment or building support for the 'lenient treatment' policy is, of course, less certain.

Trials and punishments

On 25 April 1956, Zhang Dingcheng, head of the Procuratorate, presented a report to the thirty-fourth meeting of the First Standing Committee of the National People's Congress, setting out the final decision on the leniency policy.[76] This report covered: first, those who would be exonerated from indictment, the lenient sentences to be given to those who were indicted, and consecutive sentences for double crimes; second, the internal structure of the Special Military Tribunal of the Supreme People's Court; third, the language to be used in court; fourth, the system of defence; fifth, the conclusive character of sentences handed down by the Special Military Tribunal; and sixth, the possibility of early release based on good behaviour.[77] This final decision was promptly

74 Ling Yun, 'Jiaoyu gaizao Guomindang zhanfan gongzuo de huigu', *Fanzui yu gaizao yanjiu* 2 (1993), 52.

75 'Guanyu chuli riben zhanfan de xuanchuan fangzhen he xuanchuan gongzuo jihua' (2 April 1956): 105-00502-01, MFA.

76 Zhonghua renmin gonghe guo quanguo renmin daibiao dahui changwu weiyuanhui, 'Guanyu chuli zaiya riben qinlve zhongguo zhanzheng zhong zhanzheng fanzui fenzi de jueding' (25 April 1956), in Wang Zhanping (ed.), *Zhengyi de shenpan: zuigao renmin fayuan tebie junshi fating shenpan riben zhanfan jishi* (Beijing: Renmin fayuan chubanshe, 1st edn., 1991), p. 2.

77 Zhang Dingcheng, 'Zhonghua renmin gongheguo zuigao renmin jianchayuan zhencha zaiya de riben qinrue zhongguo zhanzhengzhong de zhanzheng fanzui fenzi de zhuyao qingkuang he chuli yijian de baogao' (25 April 1956): 105-00501-07, MFA.

formalised by an Order of the President of the People's Republic of China the same day.

In the ensuing months, the majority of prisoners would be pardoned and allowed to return home to Japan – 335 were released on 21 June, 328 on 15 July, and 354 on 18 August 1956. These releases were accompanied by a blizzard of propaganda in support of the policy. Around the time of the first prisoner release, the *Renmin ribao* (People's Daily) published no less than twenty-five reports on the subject, covering every conceivable angle. The culmination was an interview with some of the former prisoners, who reportedly apologised for their crimes, praised the generosity of the Chinese and expressed their desire to embark on a new and reformed life.[78] As the journalist Li Gao wrote,

> Many shed grateful tears when they heard that the Supreme People's Procuratorate had announced the decision to exempt them from prosecution on 21 June, and all raised their hands asking to speak. Eight of them expressed how they felt in succession. One of them, Miyazaki Toshio, said while choking back tears, 'I used to be an electrician in a mine, then I put down my hammer and picked up a gun to join the war of aggression. I killed Chinese people who were like my father, humiliated good and decent women like my mother, and killed babies still nursing in their mothers' embrace. Crimes like these cannot be forgiven. And yet, the Chinese people pardoned me and educated me on how to be a person. From this day forward, I want to oppose war and uphold peace, return to the ranks of the working people in response to the loving kindness of the Chinese people.'

The remaining forty-five prisoners, who had been accused of the gravest crimes, were tried before the Special Military Tribunal, convened in Shenyang and Taiyuan in June and July 1956, respectively. Eight of these prisoners were from the Kantō Army (who had been imprisoned in Fushun), twenty-eight had been operative in Manchukuo (Fushun again), eight were from among the Japanese who stayed behind in Shanxi (imprisoned at Taiyuan) and one was a special service spy (Taiyuan again).

Of these forty-five, four were given the maximum sentence of twenty years' imprisonment: Lieutenant General Suzuki Hiraku, commander of the 117th Division; Saitō Yoshio, the head of the Military Police Training School in Manchukuo; Nagatomi Juntarō, manager of the 'Nagatomi Agency'; and Takebe Rokuzō, Director-General of the Management

[78] Li Gao, 'Huizui he ganen: bei shifang de riben zhanzheng fanzui fenzi fangwenji', in *Renmin ribao* (3 July 1956), 4.

and Coordination Agency of the State Council of Manchukuo (who was granted provisional release immediately after his trial because he was suffering a serious illness). The remaining convicted prisoners were sentenced to between eighteen and eight years imprisonment. Of the forty-four who served their sentences, all but one (Lieutenant General Sasa Shinnosuke, captain of the 39th Division, who died while serving his sentence) were eventually returned to Japan. Twenty-nine were released before serving their full sentences.[79] It is in light of these facts that the Chinese treatment of Japanese war criminals can be described as 'lenient'.

Conclusion

China's policy for the treatment of Japanese war criminals was a crucial element in Mao Zedong's broader project of establishing united fronts at home and abroad. It emerged out of the broad flow of events, national and international, that the People's Republic found itself in at the time. Sino-Japanese relations were considered within the context of the Cold War, while Taiwan was considered within the context of national consolidation. The fact that Zhou Enlai personally reviewed each of the cases of the forty-five Japanese war criminals indicates the importance that the Party leadership ascribed to them in this political context.[80]

Even the domestic policy of absorbing counter-revolutionaries, ordinary criminals and war criminals into the ranks of the common people through the policy of 'reform through labour' had an international dimension, because it reflected the Party's fundamental duty to bring about a global communist revolution. By offering convincing explanations to the masses, the Party was able to contain the Chinese people's understandable sense of indignation towards the Japanese in order to realise their policy of lenient treatment for war criminals – a policy rarely pursued by other nations. It also meant that public indignation was, in a sense, sacrificed for the higher purpose of bringing about a future revolution, as well as being corralled for the sake of normalising Sino-Japanese relations.

This chapter has presented an objective view of the Chinese policy of 'lenient treatment' towards Japanese war criminals, which affected over a thousand people, most of them guilty of serious crimes. Even so, the

[79] '45 ming Riben zhanfan bei panxing qi yu shifang shijian yi lanbiao' in Fushunshi zhengxie wenshi weiyuanhui (ed.), *Zhenhan shijie de qiji*, pp. 263–267.

[80] See Wang Shilin, 'Canyu zhenxun riben zhanfan gongzuo de huigu', in Xu Guiying and Ji Min (eds.) *Gaizao zhanfan jishi*, Zhongguo wenshi chubanshe (2000), p. 191.

picture would not be complete without examining one of the finer points of this policy, which concerns the small minority of Japanese prisoners wrongly accused of being war criminals. As the 'Report on investigating the principal situations of the Japanese war criminals and opinions on their disposal' admits,

> Among the 1,012 prisoners who shall be exempted from prosecution, the treatment of seven prisoners among them as war criminals appears somewhat unjustifiable. . . . Despite the fact that these seven cannot reasonably be treated as war criminals, we have already recorded their names in the list of war criminals, which list has since been passed into the hands of three organisations including the Japanese Red Cross Society. Their names have furthermore been publicised as war criminals in Japanese newspapers and they have already served lengthy sentences of imprisonment. At this point, re-categorising these individuals as prisoners of war or some other such term would merely result in a new series of problems, and it is likely to be dealt with passively. For this reason we conclude that it is best to include these seven among the others who were exempted from prosecution and to allow them to be released together with the latter.[81]

This author's own investigations indicate that the seven individuals referred to are: Nakajima Kyōko, a nurse; Kodama Hanako, a Shanxi Manufacturing employee; Takagi Etsumasa,[82] a dentist; Hamada Ryōzō, the head of a hospital; Uenaka Masataka, an employee of an engineering company; Tetsumura Takeshi, a corporal in a munitions workshop; and Hirano Mineo, a member of the Lieutenant Colonel's section in the Cultural Department of the General Patrol for the Shanxi Railway.

[81] 'Zhongyang huiyi wenjian: Guanyu zhencha riben zhanfan de zhuyao qingkuang he chuli yijian de baogao' (16 March 1956): 105-00501-07, MFA. When this report was written, it was anticipated that 1,012 prisoners would be exempted from prosecution. This number was ultimately increased to 1,017 prisoners.

[82] Transcription of this name is uncertain.

7

Cambodia, 1979

Trying Khmer Rouge leaders for genocide

TARA H. GUTMAN

The People's Revolutionary Tribunal (PRT) was convened on 15 August 1979 to try two Khmer Rouge leaders for the crime of genocide. Its judgment of guilt was handed down five days later. Despite being one of the first courts to invoke the Genocide Convention, it goes unmentioned in most accounts of Cambodia's history and almost all accounts of the development of international criminal law. If, as has been suggested, the Tokyo Tribunal was Nuremberg's 'morally and legally defective twin'[1] then the People's Revolutionary Tribunal, hidden from view and legally compromised, could be said to be Nuremberg's illegitimate child.

Events in Democratic Kampuchea

The PRT was established to try Pol Pot and Ieng Sary, two senior leaders of the government of Democratic Kampuchea, now known colloquially as the Khmer Rouge, for 'acts of genocide'.[2] Pol Pot, or 'Brother No. 1', was Secretary of the Central Committee of the Communist Party of Kampuchea and Prime Minister in the government of Democratic Kampuchea, and his brother-in-law, Ieng Sary, was the Deputy Prime Minister and Minister for Foreign Affairs.

The Communist Party of Kampuchea controlled Cambodia for almost four years, from 17 April 1975 until 7 January 1979, renaming it

1 G. Simpson, 'War crimes: a critical introduction', in T.L.H. McCormack and G.J. Simpson (eds.), *The law of war crimes: national and international approaches* (The Hague: Kluwer, 1997), p. 2.

2 Article 1, Decree Law No. 1, in H.J. De Nike, J. Quigley and K.J. Robinson (eds.), *Genocide in Cambodia: documents from the trial of Pol Pot and Ieng Sary* (*Documents*) (Philadelphia: University of Pennsylvania Press, 2000), p. 45.

'Democratic Kampuchea'. It dismantled the social fabric of the already war-torn society, initially by forcibly evacuating urban populations to rural areas, then by imprisoning them in work camps. Aiming to transform the country into a closed, self-reliant agrarian society, the regime, known as *Angkar*, 'the Organisation (of the Revolution)', prohibited 'bourgeois' medical services, banking, telephony, post, commerce, media and foreign relations. Families were separated and the observance of religious practices was forbidden. Adults were forced to take orders from children, who were anointed 'the pillar of this new society'.[3] Cooking or eating in one's own home was prohibited, and picking fruit from a tree for personal consumption was punished by imprisonment. Having wholly ruptured civil society, the Khmer Rouge executed, starved or fatally neglected around a quarter of Cambodia's population of eight million people.[4]

In January 1979, Vietnam launched an attack against Democratic Kampuchea, ejected the Khmer Rouge from its government seat in Phnom Penh and replaced it with a Hanoi-backed cadre of Cambodian exiles known as the Kampuchean United Front for National Salvation. The 'Salvation Front', which included the current Prime Minister, Hun Sen, made up the Cambodian presence in what was effectively a Vietnamese-sponsored intervention and administration.

In the wake of the Vietnamese victory, the international community, formerly concerned about the welfare of Cambodians under the Khmer Rouge regime, changed its tune. Fresh from its defeat in Vietnam, the United States, which had accepted the Khmer Rouge as a counterweight to Vietnam and the USSR, denounced its ouster and labelled the Vietnamese invasion illegal. No international action against the Khmer Rouge would ensue for another two decades – the discussion shifted from 'What's to be done about the genocidal crimes?' to 'How do we get Vietnam out?' In one of its blackest chapters, the UN General Assembly accepted the credentials of the overthrown government of Democratic Kampuchea, allowing it to take a seat in the General Assembly in August 1979, seven months after it had lost power.

Democratic Kampuchea issued statements denouncing the Salvation Front's newly established government, the Peoples' Revolutionary

[3] 'Report on an investigation into crimes of the Pol-Pot-Ieng Sary clique against the population of Phnom Penh', *Documents*, p. 293.

[4] B. Kiernan's widely accepted estimate is that 1,671,000 of a population of 7,890,000 perished: *The Pol Pot regime: race, power, and genocide in Cambodia under the Khmer Rouge, 1975–79* (New Haven: Yale University Press, 2nd edn., 2002), p. 458.

Council of Kampuchea (PRCK), as a 'puppet' government[5] and the prosecution of the Khmer Rouge leaders as an 'abject farce'.[6] They were soon joined by China and the Western powers, led by the United States, which denounced Vietnam's illegal invasion and considered all PRCK policies to be illegitimate, including the People's Revolutionary Tribunal. (One American official, discussing the realist policy pursued by Washington against the new Cambodian government, admitted, 'The choice for us was between moral principles and international law. The scale weighed in favor of law because it served our security interests.'[7]) When the Vietnamese representative submitted copies of the court's documents – including evidentiary materials and the Judgment – to the UN Secretary-General, they were duly circulated and largely ignored. The foreign media's failure to cover the trial, and Cambodia's lack of press outlets, further deepened the silence on the subject.

The court documents, statements of evidence and the Judgment itself only resurfaced in the English-language scholarly literature much later. In 1990, Helen Jarvis, an Australian librarian, chanced across a volume of selected trial documents from a roadside bookseller in Phnom Penh, and, after gaining permission to access and copy more documents at Cambodia's National Archives, proceeded to catalogue them (this set can be found at the National Library of Australia).[8] A decade later, a single book, *Genocide in Cambodia: documents from the trial of Pol Pot and Ieng Sary*, was published on the initiative of John Quigley, an American legal scholar who had kept the documents issued to him when he had attended the trial at the invitation of the Vietnamese in 1979.[9] The secondary English literature on the PRT is very scant and tends to take the view that it was a show trial.

5 'Vietnam's urgent establishment of the puppet Kampuchean organization is a grave step in expanding its war of aggression against Kampuchea', Peking Domestic Service (7 December, 1978), *Foreign Broadcast Information Service, Asia & Pacific* (7 December 1979), p. A12.

6 'Kampuchean envoy holds press conference on PRK tribunal' (31 July 1979), *Documents*, p. 9.

7 N. Chanda, *Brother enemy: the war after the war* (New York: Harcourt Brace Jovanovich, 1986), p. 377.

8 H. Jarvis, 'A personal view of the documents of the People's Revolutionary Tribunals', *Documents*, p. xiv.

9 Correspondence with John Quigley, on file with the author.

Laying the foundations

The new Cambodian leadership was unlikely to have instigated the Tribunal by itself. Some speculate that Hun Sen's mentor, the Soviet diplomat Igor Rogachev, proposed the trial,[10] and others note that the Soviet Supreme Court judge Valentin Shubin participated in it,[11] but little evidence has come to light of Soviet involvement in its planning. The real impetus came from Vietnamese officials, who, like the Soviets, were well versed in the trajectory of international criminal law, from the Nuremberg and Tokyo tribunals, to the Genocide Convention and to the trial of Eichmann (not to mention the 1967 Russell-Sartre 'people's' tribunal on the Vietnam War). Subsequent Vietnamese involvement was formalised in May 1979, when, after a meeting between PRCK leaders and members of the Central Committee of the Vietnamese Communist Party, it was announced that Vietnam would provide 'an Executive Team' – headed by Tran Huu Duc – 'for a Cambodian court in order to help Cambodia convene a trial to sentence the Pol Pot-Ieng Sary clique'.[12] Thereafter, the Vietnamese and the Cambodians collaborated closely on the project.

Once conceived, both parties had strong political motives for pursuing the project to the end. The Vietnamese government wished to use the trial to internationally legitimise its overthrow of the Khmer Rouge, and thereby marshal assistance from other countries for its attempts to stabilise the country against Pol Pot's still-active forces, dampen down the refugee flows across its own borders and attract the aid and loans necessary to begin the rehabilitation of Cambodia. The Cambodian government shared these motives, but was especially interested in using the trial to personally stigmatise Pol Pot and Ieng Sary, the most intransigent of the Khmer Rouge leaders (while perhaps aiming to split the organisation and co-opt into the government more useful or biddable leaders, such as Khieu Samphan and Nuon Chea).[13] At the same time, on the international scene, it was keen to challenge the UN's retrospective recognition and seating of the Khmer Rouge, and acquire UN representation for itself. A senior official, Ros Samy, expressed his government's

10 Interview with Elizabeth Becker (author of *When the war was over: Cambodia and the Khmer Rouge revolution*), on file with the author.

11 T. Fawthrop and H. Jarvis, *Getting away with genocide? Elusive justice and the Khmer Rouge tribunal* (Sydney: UNSW Press, 2005), p. 50.

12 E. Gottesman, *Cambodia after the Khmer Rouge: inside the politics of nation building* (New Haven: Yale, 2002), p. 62.

13 Fawthrop and Jarvis, *Getting away with genocide?*, p. 42.

indignation at the Chinese and American campaign against it when addressing a reception for foreigners who had been invited to observe the court proceedings:

> [T]he Peking reactionary ruling circles in collusion with the U.S. imperialists and other reactionary forces have frantically sabotaged the revolutionary cause of the Kampuchean people, trying by all means to shield and aid the remnants of the Pol Pot-Ieng Sary clique, with a view to restoring the barbarous regime of genocide in Kampuchea. ... Accordingly, the setting up of the Tribunal ... is an urgent task, and it meets the aspirations of the Kampuchean people and mankind's conscience.[14]

Although the alliance between the United States and China in support of the Khmer Rouge ultimately proved to be an insurmountable obstacle for the PRCK, it proceeded to create the institutional framework for criminal proceedings almost from scratch. As an indication of the magnitude of the task it faced, the government was at the same time setting up ministries and proposing to reintroduce the use of money. Resources were minimal and local legal expertise was almost negligible. Phnom Penh – the intended site of the trial – was a wasteland. Its markets were closed and its houses stood empty, with rusting cars parked in driveways.[15] There was no running water or electricity. The returning residents were living on a subsistence diet of wild fruit, roots and leaves, supplemented by the occasional distribution of rice or flour.[16] It was in this post-traumatic environment, with hostilities continuing in the outer provinces, that the legal foundations were laid.

Observations on the Statute

The PRT drew substantially, but not exclusively, from the civil law system inherited from the French. The Statute governing the Tribunal – 'Decree Law No. 1: Establishment of People's Revolutionary Tribunal at Phnom Penh to Try the Pol Pot–Ieng Sary Clique for the Crime of Genocide' – came into force in July 1979.[17] It suffered from a number of problems, which made it a shaky basis for prosecution. Among these were the absence of the presumption of innocence, the confinement of the subject

[14] 'Speech delivered by Mr. Ros Samy', *Documents*, p. 70.
[15] J. Quigley, 'Introduction', *Documents*, p. 1.
[16] H.C. and J.B. Mehta, *Hun Sen: strongman of Cambodia* (Singapore: Graham Brash, 1999), p. 92.
[17] Decree Law No. 1, *Documents*, pp. 45–47.

matter jurisdiction to the crime of genocide, and the promotion of political goals at the expense of accountability.

Starting with the first of these issues, the title, preamble and first two articles of the Statute demonstrated a presumption against the defendants' innocence. This was premised on a claim made in the earlier declarations[18] and confirmed in the findings of the Tribunal's pretrial investigation, that genocide had occurred at the hands of the Khmer Rouge government ('the Pol Pot–Ieng Sary clique'). Pre-empting the Judgment, the Preamble stated that

> [The] Pol Pot-Ieng Sary clique have massacred millions of persons, forced the entire Kampuchean people to live in genocidal conditions, physically and morally, destroyed all economic, cultural, and social structures, thus bringing them the danger of extermination[19]

While upholding the presumption of innocence may have been an affront to survivors of the regime, it nonetheless remains one of the fundamental principles of a fair trial, and was notable for its absence.

Second, the Statute limited the PRT's jurisdiction to genocide. Although the Khmer Rouge's crimes are still commonly characterised as 'genocide' within Cambodia and internationally, the appropriateness of this term, when applied to the events that occurred in Cambodia, has long been questioned in academic circles. Under the Genocide Convention, the legal definition of genocide is confined to the persecution of groups of people – national, ethnic, racial or religious – on the basis of their belonging to that group and with the intent to destroy the group.[20] For the most part, the crimes of the Khmer Rouge did not fit into this definition since their larger objective appears to have been to eradicate political and social groups: only a small proportion of their crimes, albeit heinous, were specifically perpetrated against religious groups such as Buddhist clergy, the Cham (Muslim) ethnic groups, and local national groups (particularly the Vietnamese and Chinese[21]). The case against Pol

[18] Declaration of 2 December 1978 of the National United Front for the Salvation of Kampuchea, summarised in M. Vickery, *Cambodia, 1975–1982* (Chiang Mai: Silkworm, 1984), pp. 216–217; Declaration of 8 January 1979 of the People's Revolutionary Council of Kampuchea, cited in Preamble, Decree Law No.1, *Documents*, p. 45.

[19] Decree Law No. 1, *Documents*, p. 45.

[20] Article 3, Convention on the Prevention and Punishment of the Crime of Genocide: treaties.un.org.

[21] While the Tribunal's evidence raises examples of Chinese being singled out for worse treatment than others, Kiernan's research suggests that overall the Chinese were not, as a group, systematically subjected to more extreme policies (*The Pol Pot regime*, pp. 295–296).

Pot and Ieng Sary may have been more decisively proven, and the crimes more accurately described, had the court's jurisdiction included crimes against humanity, which, drawing on the postwar jurisprudence, was a broader offence encompassing murder, extermination, enslavement or deportation committed against a civilian population or persecutions on political, racial or religious grounds, and did not carry a requirement to prove the intention to destroy a group.[22]

The PRT's singular focus on genocide may have related to the perceived primacy attributed to that crime over all other international crimes. Alternatively, its drafters may have considered genocide a better choice than crimes against humanity because of its unambiguous standing as treaty law, and because of its applicability 'in time of peace or in time of war'.[23] (The charge of crimes against humanity was potentially more problematic because of the earlier nexus, established by the Nuremberg Charter, with armed conflict.[24])

Third, the Statute revealed a political purpose. It set out a range of penalties, with 'instigators and planners' of genocide attracting either the death sentence, or a life sentence, or imprisonment for fifteen to twenty years; and the perpetrators of 'multiple acts of cruelty and barbarity' attracting five to fifteen years imprisonment, except with 'mitigating circumstances', which might attract less than five years.[25] Even so, a 'policy of leniency' could be extended in a case where the convicted person was 'sincerely repentant'.[26] This suggests that when weighing peace against justice, the PRCK was inclined to prioritise peace by, for example, providing the space in which 'repentant' Khmer Rouge leaders could be co-opted into the government, thereby hastening the end of the ongoing conflict.

The remaining articles of the Statute set out the operational structure of the court. They covered the appointment and powers of the presiding judge and ten lay members, the role of the prosecutor, the defendant's right to representation, a condemned defendant's 'right to ask for mercy', and convictions *in absentia* if the defendant failed to appear.[27]

[22] Article 6(c), Charter, International Military Tribunal, *Trial of the major war criminals before the International Military Tribunal*, 'The Blue Series', 42 vols. (Nuremberg: IMT, 1947–1949), vol. 1, p. 11.

[23] Article 1, Genocide Convention. The question of whether customary international law had evolved by 1975–1979 to exclude the nexus between crimes against humanity to armed conflict recently arose in Case 002 at the ECCC: the Trial Chamber decided that the nexus had been excluded by then.

[24] Article 6(c), Charter, IMT, vol. 1, p. 11. [25] Article 2, Decree Law no. 1, p. 45.

[26] Ibid. [27] Ibid., pp. 46–47.

Staffing the Tribunal proved to be a challenge: only a small percentage of Cambodians who had finished high school had survived the purges of 'intellectuals' pursued by the Khmer Rouge. A former deputy prosecutor tasked with heading the Cambodian side of the collaboration with Vietnam searched the makeshift camps around the capital for survivors with legal qualifications. He located seven people, two of whom agreed to participate.[28] Even prior to the Khmer Rouge era, there were not many Cambodian lawyers with a working knowledge of international law – one of the few examples of engagement with it was Cambodia's 1960–1962 International Court of Justice case against Thailand contesting the ownership of Preah Vihear temple (Cambodia was represented by former US Secretary of State Dean Acheson).[29] Nevertheless, after the proclamation of the Statute, office bearers and Tribunal members were appointed. In a clumsy breach of the separation of executive and judiciary, Keo Chanda, the head of the PRCK's new Information Ministry, was also designated Presiding Judge. Ten citizens from varied backgrounds were installed as lay assessors, a process common to civil law systems.[30]

A unique indictment

The Indictment charged Pol Pot and Ieng Sary with genocide.[31] The twenty-five-page document presents summaries of evidence of mass atrocities drawn from the investigations dossier. The latter comprised 147 evidentiary documents including witness statements, thematic reports, and original Democratic Kampuchea documents such as directives, training materials, speeches and minutes of bilateral meetings between China and Cambodia. The Indictment alleged that the crimes were committed by the Khmer Rouge and amounted to acts of genocide. This evidence itself remains unchallenged in the sense that it is not considered to have been fabricated or exaggerated – indeed, three decades later, the Office of Co-Prosecutors at the Extraordinary Chambers in the Courts of Cambodia (ECCC) considered it to be 'probative', and entered PRT documents into evidence.[32] Yet the legal case, like the process itself, was improvised and imprecise.

[28] Fawthrop and Jarvis, *Getting away with genocide?*, p. 41.

[29] *Temple of Preah Vihear* (*Cambodia* v. *Thailand*), ICJ Reports (1962).

[30] At present, lay assessors, a feature of civil law criminal cases, are still used in France (*cours d'assise*) but no longer in Cambodia.

[31] Indictment, *Documents*, pp. 463–488.

[32] Correspondence with Craig Etcheson (ECCC Office of the Co-Prosecutor, writing in a personal capacity), on file with the author.

Both Pol Pol Pot and Ieng Sary were charged with 'committing' genocide, an act which was criminalised by the Genocide Convention, and also with 'planning' and 'instigating' genocide, which were not. Though these modes of liability have now evolved into sophisticated doctrines at the ad hoc tribunals, they were just as 'rudimentary and fragmentary' in 1979 as they had been in the Nuremberg Charter.[33] Judged by the prevailing norms of the time when the Indictment was drafted, this indicates improvisation rather than bad faith. Moreover, given the absence of both jurisprudence and settled Khmer legal terms, 'planning' and 'instigating' may simply have been rough translations of the words 'conspiracy' and 'incitement' found in the Genocide Convention.[34]

The Indictment catalogued ten criminal acts, each of which is detailed and supported by either witness testimony or investigative reports or both. The thrust of the argument, put forward, among others, by the PRT's Presiding Judge, was that 'the Pol Pot-Ieng Sary clique committed the crime of genocide not only against a particular ethnic group ... but against the Kampuchean people as a whole'.[35] This interpretation of genocide to include 'auto-genocide' (a government exterminating citizens of the same group) is one that has since been advanced by scholars, and considered by advocates and judges (in, for example, Argentina),[36] but does not yet appear in international jurisprudence. While nearly all the acts described would constitute the basis of criminal charges under international law, only two fall readily within the scope of the accepted definition of genocide: first, the envisaging and carrying out of 'a pre-established plan to kill ethnic minorities', including the Ta Puon, Lao, Thai and Vietnamese;[37] and, second, the killing of religious figures, including Buddhist monks and Muslim leaders.[38]

The defendants' individual *prima facie* responsibility rested on their holding high office within the organisation. The Indictment thus

[33] G. Werle, 'General principles of international criminal law', in A. Cassese *et al.* (eds.), *The Oxford companion to international criminal justice* (Oxford University Press, 2009), p. 58.

[34] Articles 3(b), 3(c), Genocide Convention.

[35] 'Press conference of Keo Chanda', *Documents*, p. 48.

[36] For the recent discussion about laying genocide charges against members of the former Argentine junta for destruction of *part* of the national group, see M. Ferriera, 'Genocide, and its definition as the "partial elimination of a national group"', *Genocide Studies and Prevention* 8 (2013), 8–9, 12–13.

[37] Section A 1(b) Indictment, *Documents*, p. 465.

[38] Sections A 5(a) and A 5(b), Indictment, ibid., pp. 472–473.

submitted that Pol Pot in his roles as Party Secretary and Prime Minister personally directed policy and 'organized and directed the implementation of genocide . . . carried out with particular ferocity'.[39] Ieng Sary was held responsible for the same crimes by virtue of his roles as member of the Permanent Bureau and as Deputy Prime Minister in charge of foreign affairs. In this latter capacity he was also charged with luring about a thousand students, intellectuals and officials back to Cambodia ostensibly to rebuild the country, and then ordering their execution.[40] He was further charged with *defending* the crime of genocide in international fora (a hitherto unknown crime) and colluding with China in order to carry out a 'criminal plan'.[41]

The senior leaders' criminal intent was established, *inter alia*, by reference to the 1976 Constitution of Democratic Kampuchea, which they had drafted and publicised. This declared that

> [T]here is only one Kampuchean nation. The Khmer language is the only language . . . the various nationalities . . . no longer exist in Kampuchea . . . The conscience, languages, ethnic characteristics, customs, habits, and religions of the former nation of origin are to be totally abolished.[42]

This, it was argued, demonstrated Democratic Kampuchea's plan to wipe out non-Khmer national groups. According to the evidentiary report, twenty-one ethnic minorities were disproportionally affected in addition to the Vietnamese, Chinese, Khmer of South Vietnamese origin (Khmer Krom) and Chven (Malay).[43] This and other reports described the targeting of and particular hardships and brutality endured by the minority populations: the Cham (Muslims), for example, were forced to cut their hair, eat pork, change their names and wear black trousers rather than their traditional dress. It concluded:

> While investigating the Pol Pot-Ieng Sary genocidal crimes against the Kampuchean people as a whole, one can perceive more clearly the seriousness of their crimes perpetrated against ethnic minorities. In carrying out their criminal acts, the clique . . . either relied on its policy of immediate forcible assimilation as a legal justification or resorted to sheer armed

[39] Section C 3(a), Indictment, ibid., p. 487. [40] Section C 3(b), Indictment, ibid. [41] Ibid.

[42] 'Report on the crimes committed by the Pol Pot-Ieng Sary clique against national minorities in general and the Cham Muslims in particular', *Documents*, p. 313.

[43] Ibid., p. 311. The report did, however, undermine this claim when it noted that in some cases, the brutal treatment described did 'not reflect separate individual instances of racial discrimination' but rather 'were typical of systematic suppression as part of state policy' (ibid., p. 317).

force for extermination purposes, as in the cases of the Thai and the Cu La people, or used both forms as in the case of the Cham people.[44]

On the proceedings and Judgment

The trial of the two defendants began on 15 August 1979 and ran for five days. Civil law systems allow for trials *in absentia*; and, in accordance with the usual practice, the prosecutors publicly presented a previously prepared case to the judges – the argument was over particulars. All sessions, trilingual with simultaneous translation into Khmer, French and English, were held in open court in front of around 500 people; outdoor speakers were also set up in the surrounding grounds for the overflowing audience.[45] Vietnam had provided a three-person legal support team, and an East German prosecutor, Carlos Foth, advised during the investigative phase of the trial.[46] The prosecution presented the Indictment and thematic reports (covering the targeting of minorities and religious groups, mass cremations, medical reports, the destruction of the economy and so on), as well as evidence from twenty-six witnesses.[47] In his closing speech, the Prosecutor, Mat Ly, made special reference to the efforts taken to ensure the legal validity of the proceedings:

> Set up under a Decree Law of the revolutionary government, the tribunal has conducted the trial fairly and impartially. It does not give judgment on the basis of sentimentality with a purpose of vengeance, nor impose a verdict of the victor on the vanquished. On the contrary, it holds public sittings attended by well respected journalists, public figures, and jurists, and uses objective, concrete evidence, observing normal judicial procedures to guarantee justice.[48]

To affirm this, Cambodia invited some sixty-eight international guests – mainly lawyers and journalists – to either participate in or report on the trial.[49] The invitees included lawyers from India, Syria, Algeria, Laos and

44 Ibid., p. 319. Investigators were unable to find any Cu La survivors, who had previously numbered around two thousand in the vicinity of Pailin (ibid., p. 316).

45 Correspondence with John Quigley.

46 H. De Nike, 'East Germany's legal advisor to the 1979 tribunal in Cambodia', *Searching for the Truth* (Phnom Penh: Documentation Center of Cambodia, 2nd quarter, 2008), p. 39.

47 The original list contained fifty-four names ('Names of witnesses', *Documents*, pp. 63–64), although this number was later reduced.

48 'Closing argument of Mat Ly', *Documents*, p. 489.

49 'List of invitees' and 'List of foreign lawyers', *Documents*, pp. 60–63.

the USSR; judges from Japan and Cuba; representatives of church groups and political organisations; and a number of French, Southeast Asian and East European journalists. While the records do not specify who actually attended, participants noted the presence of eight foreign lawyers – from Algeria, Cuba, India, Japan, Syria, the Soviet Union and the United States. Five of them accepted the invitation to offer either verbal or written opinions on the case: an American, Hope R. Stevens, presented a statement in defence of the accused; the Syrian Mohammed Hikmet Tukmanee acted for the plaintiffs in the concurrent civil action; and Ozaki Susumi from Japan, Francisco Varona Duque de Estrada from Cuba and John Quigley from the United States provided statements in support of a finding of genocide. As well as attending the trial, some foreign guests were escorted to the notorious torture centre Tuol Sleng, and given the opportunity to speak to witnesses.[50]

The Tribunal's Judgment on genocide expressed a more nuanced understanding than had the Indictment of the *dolus specialis* and the confinement of the crime to the destruction of groups *as such*. Based on the documentary evidence, including resolutions, official directives, meeting minutes and teaching materials, it found that both Ieng Sary and Pol Pot 'committed these crimes with genocidal intent'.[51] The crimes were 'carried out in a systematic way and by the same methods and procedures throughout the territory of Kampuchea and under the control of the authorities of Angkar at all levels'.[52] Continuing with the notion of 'auto-genocide', but also identifying groups, including certain protected groups, the Tribunal held that the crimes were

> far in excess of what is required for genocide in the December 9, 1948 Convention. The accused not only wiped out the intellectuals, the officers, and civil servants of the former regime, religious believers, and ethnic minorities for the sole reason that they were intellectuals, officers and civil servants, religious believers, and ethnic minorities, they also killed, en masse and in a planned way, innocent people of different social strata. The accused sought to exterminate their own people, their own nation[53]

On being pronounced guilty *in absentia*, the defendants were granted seven days to request a reduction of the death sentence, but neither availed themselves of the opportunity.[54] Pol Pot and Ieng Sary both

[50] Correspondence with John Quigley. [51] Judgment, *Documents*, p. 541. [52] Ibid.
[53] Ibid., p. 547.
[54] Under the civil law system, after a trial *in absentia*, an appeals process is initiated or retrials are convened once the suspect is apprehended. Appeals are run on law and fact, and new evidence is admissible.

continued to play a leading role in the Khmer Rouge, controlling troops and perpetuating the civil war for well over a decade. At the United Nations, the Vietnamese delegates distributed copies of the Judgment to fellow delegates in the General Assembly, but little acknowledgement was made of the crimes it chronicled until member states de-recognised the Khmer Rouge in the wake of the Asian Cold War in 1992.

Criticisms of the trial

The trial has been criticised on numerous grounds: first, that it was an inapposite application of the Genocide Convention; second, that there were substantive procedural defects, particularly in relation to the defence; and finally, that these and other factors made it a show trial. Yet although the trial was deeply flawed, and while some of these criticisms are valid, it was not necessarily wholly devoid of legal merit.

The first argument raised against the Tribunal is that the *definition* of genocide in the Statute did not accord with the international definition.[55] Although the Statute relied on the Genocide Convention as a source of law,[56] it did not incorporate relevant provisions (as in now usual practice in the statutes of international and hybrid tribunals). There was, however, no requirement for domestic legislation to incorporate the terms because under customary international law, the Convention applied automatically. The drafters' awareness of this was evidenced by the Preamble, which noted that 'genocide is … defined in international law'.[57]

Furthermore, the reference to genocide in Article 1 did not purport to define the term. Rather, it set out the nature of the acts to be tried. The Article stated that the PRCK had taken the decision

> To set up a People's Revolutionary Tribunal at Phnom Penh to try the acts of genocide committed by the Pol Pot-Ieng Sary clique, namely, *planned massacres of groups* of innocent people; expulsion of inhabitants of cities and villages in order to concentrate them and force them to do hard labor in conditions leading to their *physical and mental destruction; wiping out*

[55] S. Luftglass, 'Crossroads in Cambodia: the United Nation's responsibility to withdraw involvement from the establishment of a Cambodian tribunal to prosecute the Khmer Rouge', *Virginia Law Review* 90 (2004), 902; S. Starygin, 'Internal rules of the Extraordinary Chambers in the Courts of Cambodia (ECCC): setting an example of the rule of law by breaking the law?' *Journal of Law and Conflict Resolution* 3 (2011), 37 n. i.

[56] Article 8, Decree Law No. 1, *Documents*, p. 47.

[57] Preamble, ibid., p. 45.

> *religion; destroying* political, *cultural and social structures and family and social relations.*[58]

These acts all have approximate counterparts in Article 2 of the Genocide Convention – in particular (a), (b) and (c) – which reads:

> In the present Convention, genocide means any of the following acts committed with intent to destroy, in whole or in part, a national, ethnical, racial or religious group, as such:
>
> (a) Killing members of the group;
> (b) Causing serious bodily or mental harm to members of the group;
> (c) Deliberately inflicting on the group conditions of life calculated to bring about its physical destruction in whole or in part;
> (d) Imposing measures intended to prevent births within the group;
> (e) Forcibly transferring children of the group to another group.[59]

It is quite possible that the discrepancy between the two lists of acts may simply have been the result of inaccurate translation. In particular, the use of 'as such' in the chapeau to Article 2 of the Convention may have been read to mean 'such as', indicating a non-exhaustive list (an error which also occurred in early drafts of the 'Law on the Establishment of Extraordinary Chambers in the Courts of Cambodia for the Prosecution of Crimes Committed during the Period of Democratic Kampuchea').[60] Whether or not this was the case, Article 1 of the Statute was clearly neither intended to be nor treated as a definition. This is evidenced by the plentiful references in the Indictment, prosecution case, evidence and Judgment to the Convention definition's chapeau requirements of special intent and the protection of religious, national and ethnic groups.[61] As the Statute itself is silent on these issues, there can be no doubt that the Convention definition was being applied.

Even so, correction of this point does not restore the Tribunal to rude good health. The application of the Genocide Convention was problematic,

[58] Article 1, ibid. Emphases added. [59] Article 2, Genocide Convention.

[60] The 'such as' error persists in Article 4 of the unofficial translation into English of the Law on the Establishment of Extraordinary Chambers, published on the ECCC website at: www.eccc.gov.kh.

[61] In *Documents*, see Indictment on intent to kill ethnic minorities (p. 465), deprivation of food and forced labour leading to 'physical and moral ruin' (p. 469), abolition of Buddhism and Islam (pp. 472–473), acts indicating an intention to commit genocide (p. 479); see also, 'Religious Issues' documents on persecutions (pp. 144–155); and see also, Judgment on killing of clergy, eradication of religion, systematic killing of ethnic minorities, forced assimilation, extermination of foreign nationals (p. 529), acts committed with genocidal intent (pp. 541, 542).

mainly because the prosecution and judge expanded the notion of genocide from protecting not only groups that differed from the perpetrator's own, but also members of the perpetrators' own group. The charge of genocide against the Cambodian population at large, since described as 'auto-genocide', was not at the time nor is today accepted as being included in the crime of genocide.

The more accurate method of charging, not envisaged by the Statute but nevertheless available in customary international law, would have been to describe the acts as crimes against humanity.[62] However, the fact that the ECCC is currently hearing charges of genocide against defendants in Case 002 suggests that PRT's choice of law was not entirely wrongheaded.

The second criticism is that the Tribunal suffered from procedural defects, such as bias, trial *in absentia* and inadequate defence. The assumption at its heart is that most of those involved with it were themselves victims of the Pol Pot's regime, and consequently were not impartial arbiters. This criticism has some validity: the appointment of affected persons creates a perception bias. But several more factors need to be taken into account: first, that Cambodian and Vietnamese appeals for international assistance to the PRT went largely unheeded outside the communist bloc; second, that the independent foreign legal observers who *did* attend supported the process and concurred with the Judgment;[63] and finally, it was almost impossible to find skilled local lawyers who had not been affected by the events of the Khmer Rouge period.

The trial has also been criticised from a common law perspective for being held *in absentia*, which is seen as precluding an adequate – in the sense of a contested – defence.[64] Individuals' rights to be tried in their own presence, to defend themselves in person or through counsel of their choosing, and to call and confront witnesses are enshrined in Article 14 (d) and (e) of the 1966 International Covenant on Civil and Political Rights.[65] It should be noted that this Covenant entered into force on 23 March 1976, at the height of Khmer Rouge rule, and that Cambodia did not ratify it until 26 August 1992.

62 W. Schabas, 'Cambodia: was it really genocide?', *Human Rights Quarterly* 23 (2001), 472–473.

63 *Documents*, 'Closing argument of Hope R. Stevens', pp. 504–508; 'Closing argument of Mohammed Hikmet Turkmanee', pp. 513–517; 'Statement of John Quigley', pp. 518–519; 'Statement of Susumi Ozaki', pp. 519–521; 'Statement of Francisco Varona Duque de Estrada', pp. 521–522.

64 See, for example, Luftglass, 'Crossroads in Cambodia', 902.

65 International Covenant on Civil and Political Rights: treaties.un.org.

Notwithstanding the near-universal acceptance of these rights, numerous civil law jurisdictions do not consider them to be absolute. They allow *in absentia* trials to be held in certain limited circumstances, provided that the accused is informed of the charges and represented by counsel, and that a retrial is mounted *de novo* if the accused is apprehended. The French legal system, from which both Vietnam and Cambodia derive their civil law systems, upholds the defendant's due process rights to appear, to be represented and to confront evidence, but if, having been served notice of the charges, a defendant elects to abscond, he is considered to have waived these rights.

The Nuremberg Tribunal was the first to allow international crimes to be tried *in absentia.* When drawing up the Nuremberg Charter, both the Americans and British, then mindful that Hitler and Goebbels' deaths were still unverified, agreed to provide for trials without a defendant's presence 'in the interests of justice', despite the inconsistency with their own legal traditions.[66] This provision, set out in Article 12 of the Charter, applied only to the case of Martin Bormann, who was found guilty and sentenced to death. It was later discovered that Bormann had died in May 1945, before it had been drafted.

A qualified version of *in absentia* proceedings is seen in the national courts that follow the principle *semel praesens semper praesens* (once present, ever-present). This essentially allows a trial to continue in the absence of a defendant who, after an initial appearance, fails or refuses to reappear. The United States and Germany uphold this idea,[67] as do or did the hybrid courts in East Timor, the Special Court for Sierra Leone and the Extraordinary Chambers in the Courts of Cambodia. The most far-reaching UN-supported process is taking place at the Special Tribunal for Lebanon, which, drawing on the Lebanese system (which derives from the French), allows entire trials to be conducted *in absentia*, and is presently trying five defendants who have yet to be apprehended.[68]

The reality in Cambodia in 1979 was that trials *in absentia* were consistent with national practice, and that insisting on the defendants' presence in court would have resulted in no trial at all. (Attempts were made to apprehend the defendants, but these were not successful.)[69] While *prima facie* the absence of the accused undermines the primary

[66] Article 12, Charter, IMT, vol. 1, p. 12.

[67] P. Gaeta, 'To be (present) or not to be (present): trials *in absentia* before the Special Tribunal for Lebanon', *Journal of International Criminal Justice* 5 (2007), 1167–1168.

[68] Article 22(1), Statute of the Special Court for Lebanon: www.stl-tsl.org.

[69] 'Decision No. 3', *Documents*, p. 52.

goal of a trial – to establish the individual guilt of the accused – it nevertheless enables other goals to be served, such as the collection of evidence, the establishment of truth and the creation of a forum for victims to publicly present their cases. Further, given the long-standing acceptance of *in absentia* proceedings in civil law jurisdictions, internationalised courts and civil legal systems, it cannot be argued that holding trials without defendants was a serious shortcoming of the PRT's process.

The more serious defect relates to the lack of an adequate defence. Three counsel were appointed by the court: two Cambodians and one *pro bono* American attorney, who were required to mount a defence case in the absence of a client. Although, in fairness, it is unlikely that they any had access to exculpatory evidence, their failure to challenge the prosecution case has nevertheless attracted well-deserved criticism.[70]

In their closing statements, each counsel demonstrated an understanding of various elements of due process, yet none raised a legally recognised defence. The counsel in fact admitted the accused's responsibility for the planning and commission of acts of genocide, as had been already evidenced by the prosecution's documentary evidence and witness testimony:

> In our judicial system, a defense lawyer, in order to guarantee respect for legality and to preserve the interests of the people and the country, must try to shed light on the truth . . . so that the court's decision will be just and will punish a guilty party only as is appropriate under the law . . .[71]
>
> From the defendants' point of view, we find that the tribunal has carried out the necessary procedural formalities to try the defendant in absentia . . .[72]
>
> As defense attorneys, we find no basis for denying the criminal acts charged in the indictment.[73]

Instead, the defence lawyers sought to mitigate the defendants' responsibility by casting China as the architect of a vast criminal plan. They maintained that Pol Pot and Ieng Sary 'were fully aware of their criminal acts and had the deliberate intention of committing them', but that there were also 'unacknowledged forces' at play, namely the Chinese leadership, which had 'incited, encouraged, pressured, and protected' them.[74] The defendants might have been 'criminally insane monsters', but they were monsters who were carrying out a programme 'the script of which

[70] Schabas, 'Cambodia', 470, 476; correspondence with Gregory Stanton, on file with the author.

[71] 'Closing argument of Attorney Yuos Por', *Documents*, p. 508. [72] Ibid., p. 509.

[73] Ibid. [74] Ibid.

was written elsewhere for them'.[75] It was their 'blind, nearly insane, obedience to the dogmas of Maoism' that had compelled them to commit crimes that 'no person with a conscience and normal mental state would ever have committed'.[76]

Because the Chinese had 'supplied . . . the entire ideological base and the entire material base to commit their crimes',[77] and because it had used the defendants 'as an instrument' to carry them out,[78] it was argued that they too should have appeared before the Tribunal to answer for their crimes. By apportioning a share of the blame to China (and to a lesser extent, the West), the defence counsel effectively served to reinforce Vietnamese political ends, but failed to fulfil their duty towards their clients. Both defendants were sentenced to death *in absentia*.

A show trial?

The third and final criticism levelled at the Tribunal was that it bore the hallmarks of a show trial. Because it was convened in the aftermath of the Vietnam War, it was bound to attract highly politicised criticism from those Western, Southeast Asian and East Asian parties aligned against Vietnam, whether or not it met acceptable legal standards. But with that era long gone, it is now possible to assess where the trial really sat on the spectrum of legality. Unsurprisingly, the first to denounce the Tribunal was the Khmer Rouge. Even before it had opened, the Khmer Rouge's representatives described it as a Vietnamese trick 'to shift the responsibility for their widely known and glaringly monumental crimes onto the shoulders of Democratic Kampuchea'.[79]

In the decades that followed, other scholars have also condemned it, by citing its various political purposes and its procedural and substantive defects. In the English-language literature, for example, Gregory Stanton stated that the PRT was 'largely considered a show trial',[80] followed by Kathryn Railsback (quoting Stanton),[81] and Steven Ratner and Jason

[75] 'Closing argument of Hope R. Stevens', *Documents*, p. 507.

[76] 'Closing argument of Attorney Yuos Por', *Documents*, p. 510. [77] Ibid., p. 509.

[78] Ibid., p. 510.

[79] 'What kind of tribunal are the Vietnamese Le Duan-Pham Van Dong criminals trying to set up?', *Documents*, p. 9.

[80] G. Stanton, 'Kampuchean genocide and the world court', *Connecticut Journal of International Law* 2 (1986–1987), 347.

[81] K. Railsback, 'A Genocide Convention action against the Khmer Rouge: preventing a resurgence of the Killing Fields', *Connecticut Journal of International Law* 5 (1989–1990), 460, fn. 15 (quoting a UCLA address in which Stanton called the PRT a 'show trial').

Abrams, who noted the 'highly politicized' nature of the prosecutions and the 'lack of fundamental elements of due process'.[82] Scott Luftglass claimed that it was 'widely regarded as a farcical trial'.[83] William Schabas described it as 'public denunciation'.[84] Evan Gottesman thought its verdict 'part historical truth and part political strategy'.[85] Yet Tom Fawthrop and Helen Jarvis, while noting that the Judgment was 'pre-determined', declined to 'write off the whole affair as a propaganda show'.[86] Howard De Nike disagreed with the show trial 'shibboleth' and advocated further study.[87] And John Quigley cautiously defended the process.[88]

The People's Revolutionary Tribunal may indeed have been, in Stanton's words, 'largely considered a show trial'. But was it really a show trial – an abuse of power and the antithesis of law? George Hodos describes the usual features of such proceedings:

> The show trial is a propaganda arm of political terror. Its aim is to personalize an abstract political enemy, to place it in the dock in flesh and blood and, with the aid of a perverted system of justice, to transform abstract political-ideological differences into easily intelligible common crimes. It both incites the masses against the evil embodied by the defendants and frightens them away from supporting any potential opposition.[89]

Any list of features common to the standard 'show trials' – the Moscow trials of 1936–1938, the Soviets' post-war East European trials, and China's Gang of Four trial of 1981 – would almost certainly include: the deployment of the legal process as a tool of terror or oppression, the retroactive definition of crimes, the fabrication of evidence, the use of physical and psychological torture to force false confessions and the conduct of proceedings before a vetted audience. The PRT did not meet any of these criteria. The trial lacked *mala fides*. In contradistinction with show trials, it did not abuse the legal system so much as try to create one in a vacuum where no law, and barely any form of governance,

[82] S.R. Ratner and J.S. Abrams, *Accountability for human rights atrocities in international law: beyond the Nuremberg legacy* (Oxford University Press, 2nd edn., 2001), p. 168.

[83] Luftglass, 'Crossroads in Cambodia', 902. [84] Schabas, 'Cambodia', 477.

[85] Gottesman, *Cambodia after the Khmer Rouge*, p. 65.

[86] Fawthrop and Jarvis, *Getting away with genocide*, pp. 43, 49.

[87] De Nike, 'Reflections of a legal anthropologist on the trial of Pol Pot and Ieng Sary', *Documents*, p. 20.

[88] Quigley, 'Introduction', *Documents*, pp. 17–18.

[89] G.H. Hodos, *Show trials: Stalinist purges in Eastern Europe, 1948–1954* (New York: Praeger, 1987), p. xiii.

existed. Moreover, in contrast to its predecessors at Nuremberg and Tokyo, it did not retrospectively apply international criminal charges (Cambodia became a party to the Genocide Convention by accession on 14 October 1950).[90] What it did do was to mount a case against leading members of the Khmer Rouge, based on substantial evidence that they had perpetrated international crimes during their rule. This attempt at a legal reckoning is now being replicated – with overlapping defendants, charges and evidence – at the Extraordinary Chambers in the Courts of Cambodia.

Having said that, it is obviously true that the Tribunal had a political agenda. It served a judicial purpose, and also a political one, which was to justify the Vietnamese invasion of Cambodia. After that, the PRCK's agenda was to win both national and international support by differentiating itself from the Khmer Rouge.[91] Once this was achieved, it was hoped that foreign aid would be ushered in to facilitate social restoration. Yet a political motivation hardly distinguishes it from the post-war tribunals, or, in fact, from all international criminal trials. The aim of discrediting the perpetrators of international crimes is common to all, as is the delicate dance between diplomacy and justice, often occluded by *realpolitik*. As one observer noted, 'the separate goals of justice and consolidation of power may not be mutually exclusive or even especially rivalrous'.[92] So in order to determine whether the political dimension is an abuse of power, it is necessary to examine whether the trial is a judicial instrument for political oppression. In the PRT's case, there is no evidence, beyond the aim of disgracing the Khmer Rouge, to suggest that this was so.

Another tribunal in Cambodia

For decades after the conclusion of the PRT, neither Pol Pot nor Ieng Sary, nor any other senior Khmer Rouge leader, was brought to trial. Pol Pot died in the provinces in April 1998, thus thwarting an international plan to apprehend him just days later, and evading justice forever.

[90] There is debate over whether Cambodian domestic law recognised the crime of genocide, which turns on whether Cambodia was a monist or dualist system at the time of the PRT. This study does not canvass this issue, but recognises its significance for the domestic legality of the trial.

[91] See Gottesman, *Cambodia after the Khmer Rouge*, pp. 61–62.

[92] C.A. Smith, *The rise and fall of war crimes trials: from Charles I to Bush II* (New York: Cambridge University Press, 2012), p. 20.

Meanwhile, Chinese support for the Khmer Rouge had been drying up, and differences among its factions had intensified. Ieng Sary, who continued to control Khmer Rouge insurgents in the northwest of the country, was offered a pardon for his conviction for genocide, and an amnesty from prosecution under a law outlawing the Khmer Rouge, in return for his and his troops' defection to the government.[93] Ieng Sary agreed and, after the issue of the Royal Decree on 14 September 1996 granting him these concessions,[94] he returned to Phnom Penh. Thereafter he lived in the city in considerable comfort, and frequently travelled abroad,[95] until 12 November 2007, when he and his wife were arrested and charged to appear before the ECCC.

This hybrid court was established in 2003 as collaboration between the Royal Government of Cambodia and the United Nations to 'bring to trial senior leaders of Democratic Kampuchea and those who were most responsible' for the crimes committed under the regime.[96] Ieng Sary, who died before sentencing, was one of the four accused in Case 002. He was first charged with crimes against humanity and grave breaches of the 1949 Geneva Conventions, and later, in 2009, with genocide against the Muslim Cham and the Vietnamese. The co-investigating judges considered that neither the previous PRT Judgment nor the subsequent Royal Decree prevented his prosecution before the ECCC.[97] Ieng Sary's defence counsel appealed this issue to the Pre-Trial Chamber, arguing that the Court had no jurisdiction over him because he had already been tried and convicted by the PRT in relation to the same conduct, and then had been pardoned and given an amnesty against further prosecution.[98] In other words, had his 1979 conviction been recognised, Ieng Sary may have been immune from prosecution for the crime of genocide on the grounds of *ne bis in idem* – a person should not be tried twice for the same crime.

[93] Fawthrop and Jarvis, *Getting away with genocide?*, p. 137.

[94] For a translation of the Decree, and discussion of the translation, see *Nuon et al.*, 002/19-09-2007-ECCC/TC, Trial Chamber Decision on Ieng Sary's Rule 89 Preliminary Objections (*Ne Bis In Idem* and Amnesty and Pardon), (3 November 2011), (*Nuon* Trial Chamber Decision, *Ne Bis In Idem*), par. 19 and fn. 21.

[95] Ibid.

[96] 'Agreement between the United Nations and the Royal Government of Cambodia Concerning the Prosecution under Cambodian Law of Crimes Committed during the Period of Democratic Kampuchea' (ECCC Agreement): www.eccc.gov.kh.

[97] 002/19-09-2007-ECCC/OCIJ, Co-Investigating Judges' Provisional Detention Order (14 November 2007), pars. 5, 14.

[98] 002/19-09-2007-ECCC/OCIJ(PTC 75), Ieng Sary's Appeal against the Closing Order (25 October 2010), par. 39.

The Pre-Trial Chamber was thus compelled to examine the applicability of the *ne bis in idem* principle. It found that the principle was not enshrined in Cambodia's Criminal Procedure Code, except with respect to those who had been *acquitted* of crimes.[99] Moreover, on examination of Article 14(7) of the International Covenant on Political and Civil Rights, which did enshrine the principle,[100] it found that this was only applicable domestically (whereas the ECCC was 'an internationalised court functioning separately from the Cambodian court structure').[101] The Chamber also examined international procedural rules and found that these allowed a defendant to be retried in limited circumstances, such as when a national court's proceedings were not independent and impartial.[102] The Chamber concluded that because the PRT had failed to separate executive and judicial functions,[103] because no evidence was presented in defence of the accused,[104] and because the trial was conducted so rapidly, suggesting a 'predetermined' guilty verdict,[105] it could not be described as independent and impartial.[106] Consequently, the prosecution, conviction and sentencing of Ieng Sary in 1979 was not a bar to 'the jurisdiction of the ECCC over Ieng Sary, nor any of the charges'.[107] Once it had established that there was no impediment to proceeding to trial, the Chamber took the view that the PRT's merits could be contested in open court, and weighed by the Trial Chamber.

Ieng Sary's defence counsel appealed, submitting that the purpose of the double jeopardy rule is to spare the defendant the hardships ('psychological, emotional, physical and monetary') of being tried twice.[108] The prosecution responded that since Ieng Sary was not tried in person and did not serve any sentence, he was not subjected to any such hardships.[109] In the alternative, it argued that an exception to the rule against double jeopardy applied if the initial trial was manifestly not impartial or

99 *Nuon et al.*, 002/19-09-2007-ECCC/OCIJ (PTC75), Pre-Trial Chamber Decision on Ieng Sary's Appeal against the Closing Order (*Nuon* PTC Decision)(11 April 2011), par. 122.

100 Article 14(7) ICCPR states, 'No one shall be liable to be tried or punished again for an offence for which he has already been finally convicted or acquitted in accordance with the law and penal procedure of each country.'

101 *Nuon* PTC Decision, pars. 128, 131. 102 Ibid., pars. 157, 158. 103 Ibid., par. 168.

104 Ibid., par. 171. 105 Ibid., par. 173. 106 Ibid., par. 175. 107 Ibid.

108 *Nuon et al.*, 002/19-09-2007-ECCC/TC (Document E51/11), Ieng Sary's Supplement to His Rule 89 Preliminary Objection (*Ne Bis In Idem*) (27 May 2011), par. 10.

109 *Nuon et al.*, 002/19-09-2007-ECCC/TC (Document E51/13), Co-Prosecutor's Combined Response to Ieng Sary's Supplements to his Rule 89 Objection (*Ne Bis In Idem* and Royal Pardon and Amnesty) (7 June 2011), pars. 11–12.

independent.[110] In further submissions and in court, the defence acknowledged that the PRT was not 'a model trial',[111] but, given that Ieng Sary had been convicted by it, nor was it a sham trial designed to assist him to escape justice.[112] The Trial Chamber again rejected the defence argument, adding that the *ne bis in idem* principle had to be weighed against the interests of the international community and victims in securing robust prosecutions.[113] The argument was wound up when the Supreme Court Chamber rejected Ieng Sary's final application to appeal the issue.[114]

These debates cast a strong light on the 1979 trial, and whatever the verdict of lawyers and scholars on this enterprise, it left behind one extraordinary and irreplaceable legacy – the evidence collected by the PRT investigators. Set to work just months after the fall of the Khmer Rouge regime, they managed to create a record almost immediately after the events discussed at both the PRT and the ECCC; little had faded with time. The validity of this evidence has not been contested and much has since been independently verified. During the ECCC's preliminary investigations between 2006 and 2008, the Officers of the Co-Prosecutors reviewed the volume of documents from the 1979 trial, and, after concluding that the material was 'both credible and probative', placed the entire volume on the case files for both Case 001 and Case 002.[115] Even the more sensational allegations – of cannibalism and of feeding people alive to crocodiles – have been since lent credence by independent sources.

Conclusion

The international community failed in its obligations to Cambodia under the Genocide Convention. Between April 1975 and January 1979, state parties to it should have acted on the available information and called on the United Nations to take action under Article 8 to prevent and suppress

110 Ibid., par. 4.
111 002/19-09-2007-ECCC/TC, Ieng Sary's Supplement to his Rule 89 Preliminary Objection (*Ne Bis In Idem*) (27 May 2011), par. 29.
112 See Trial Chamber's summary of this argument in *Nuon* Trial Chamber Decision, *Ne Bis In Idem*, pars. 19–20.
113 Ibid., p. 28 and par. 33.
114 *Nuon et al.*, 002/19-09-2007-ECCC/TC/SC(1), Supreme Court Chamber Decision on Ieng Sary's Appeal against Trial Chamber's Decision on Ieng Sary's Rule 89 Preliminary Objections (*Ne Bis In Idem* and Amnesty and Pardon), (20 March 2012), p. 3.
115 Correspondence with Craig Etcheson (in personal capacity).

acts of genocide. But they did not. After the Vietnamese ousted the Khmer Rouge, the UN could have sent investigators, lawyers, observers or monitors to assess the situation and to participate, scrutinise and support the trial process. But it did not. The Cambodians and Vietnamese convened their tribunal all the same – a remarkable feat in itself, given the conditions prevailing in Cambodia in 1979. This court was motivated by political imperatives and marred by substantial defects, and when measured against today's international standards, it fails to measure up. But for its many faults, it was no typical show trial; it was a serious attempt to reckon with the crimes committed by the Khmer Rouge. Victims and witnesses wept with relief when telling their stories. If there was a failure of justice, then the blame lies not only with those who mounted a flawed tribunal but also with the international community, which abdicated its solemn responsibility under the Convention to prevent and punish the crime of genocide.

8

Crimes against humanity in East Timor

The Indonesian ad hoc Human Rights Court hearings

MARK CAMMACK[1]

In 2000 the Indonesian legislature created the Pengadilan Hak Azasi Manusia Ad Hoc, a special ad hoc Human Rights Court with the power to try genocide and crimes against humanity. Based in Jakarta, this domestic court was designed to pre-empt a proposed *international* tribunal to try Indonesian officials for crimes committed around the time of the 1999 independence referendum in East Timor. In 2002 and 2003, the Court tried eighteen defendants from the Indonesian military, police and civil administration. All the indictments alleged crimes against humanity for acts of murder or assault carried out as a part of a widespread or systematic attack directed against a civilian population, and all defendants were charged for acts committed by subordinates based on the doctrine of command responsibility. Six of these defendants were convicted at trial, but all were eventually acquitted on appeal. As some previous accounts of the trials have convincingly shown, the Human Rights Court failed to either identify or punish the perpetrators.[2] Rather than revisit this issue, this study aims to uncover the legal and political dynamics at work during the proceedings, with the aim of casting light on *why* they failed to achieve their purpose.

The inescapable if unstated subtext to all these trials was the abiding power of Tentara Nasional Indonesia (Indonesian National Armed Forces, TNI). Indeed, the establishment of the facts of what happened in East Timor in 1999, and the consideration of the law on crimes against humanity and command responsibility, were of little importance

[1] The author is the translator of the Indonesian materials unless stated otherwise.

[2] See D. Cohen, *Intended to fail: the trials before the ad hoc Human Rights Court in Jakarta* (International Center for Transitional Justice, 2003); *Unfulfilled promises: achieving justice for crimes against humanity in East Timor* (Open Society Justice Initiative and Coalition for International Justice, 2004).

compared to this single overriding issue. The perils of charging still-serving officers with crimes against humanity were obvious. And the TNI itself had made no move to disown those charged before the Court. Instead, the Indonesian Army and the police demonstrated continued support for their colleagues by their conspicuous presence at the trials. The Army mounted a special show of support for defendants who were members of the elite special forces ('Komando Pasukan Khusus', KOPPASUS), filling the courtroom to capacity with the defendants' colleagues, bussed in for the purpose of being seen, and all wearing the unit's signature red beret. The defendants themselves remained on active duty throughout (and after) the trials.

The power of the military within Indonesian society meant that the position of the prosecutors and judges was precarious. If they were going to subject the military to criticism, never mind hold its members to account, they had to proceed with caution.

Many lawyers on both the defence and the prosecution side tried to present Indonesia as the beneficent bearer of 'development' to an ungrateful East Timor and blamed the violence on anyone other than the Indonesian security forces. But the defendants' innocence or guilt was, on occasion, genuinely contested. In particular, some of the judges were committed to delivering justice on behalf of the powerless and now foreign victims of their country's wrongs. They were in a minority, and they gained little support from within Indonesia. But against the odds and contrary to their own best interests, they struggled to bring to light evidence that the TNI had formulated and executed a campaign of violence against East Timorese supporters of independence.

The referendum and aftermath

Violence in East Timor escalated sharply from January 1999 onwards, when B.J. Habibie's Jakarta government announced a plan to hold a referendum offering the citizens of East Timor the choice of either remaining part of Indonesia under a grant of special autonomy or becoming independent. This decision had more to do with Indonesia's economic problems than with anything related to East Timor itself. The currency devaluation that spread across Southeast Asia beginning in mid-1997 had devastated the Indonesian economy. Growing anti-government sentiment resulting from the financial crisis culminated in riots in May 1998, which left more than a thousand dead and forced the resignation of long-time Indonesian President, Suharto. Habibie,

Suharto's successor, decided to offer independence to the East Timorese to gain the support of Western governments in his efforts to rebuild the Indonesian economy.

It is not clear to what extent the TNI was consulted in the decision to hold a referendum, but it was clearly not happy with the decision. Since the forced annexation of East Timor in 1975, the military had expended a large number of lives and considerable resources acquiring and holding the territory. The military also feared that allowing East Timor to secede would fuel separatist tendencies elsewhere in the archipelago. Even though the central government managed to counter the centripetal forces of local ethnic attachments, existing interethnic conflicts and violence in a number of islands lent credence to fears that Indonesia might break apart.

So followed a concerted campaign of violence and terror directed against those who supported East Timorese independence. The principal perpetrators were members of voluntary militias, which the Indonesian authorities described as neighbourhood watch groups. But it was well known that they were recruited and armed by the TNI to terrorise voters into rejecting independence. The partisan nature of the militias was reflected in their names: Mahidi (an acronym for 'Live or Die for Integration'), AHI (an acronym for 'I Live for Integration') and Besi Merah Putih ('Red and White Iron', referencing the colours of the Indonesian flag). Other names conveyed the militia's terror-inducing intent: Aitarak (Thorn), Sakunar (Scorpion) and Halilintar (Lightning).

Militia violence, of which there were hundreds of examples throughout 1999, intensified dramatically after the announcement of the landslide vote in favour of independence on 4 September 1999.[3] Thereafter, more than a thousand people were killed, a quarter of a million people were forcibly removed to Indonesian West Timor, and 70 per cent of East Timor's infrastructure was looted and torched. Under pressure from the international community, the Indonesian government acceded to demands to permit the deployment of peacekeepers, and on 20 January 2000 an Australian-led force entered East Timor under a United Nations mandate to restore order.

[3] Upwards of 90 per cent of the 400,000 registered voters cast ballots, and of those 78 per cent of the voters chose independence against 21 per cent who voted to remain a part of Indonesia.

Reports on crimes in East Timor

The Indonesian authorities understood that crimes committed in East Timor under a UN-supervised referendum would not pass unnoticed, and almost immediately launched efforts to head off international criticism. Jakarta first tried to prevent the UN Commission on Human Rights from convening a special session to discuss the situation in East Timor in September 1999. When the special session went ahead despite Indonesian protests, Indonesia concentrated on ensuring that any prosecutions of crimes committed there would be conducted in Indonesia by Indonesian courts. The difficulty it faced would be persuading the United Nations and the international community that Indonesia could be trusted to do this when the evidence indicated that Indonesian security forces were responsible for the violence. Jakarta recognised that in order to demonstrate its serious intent, it was essential for an Indonesian organisation to complete a credible investigation into the violence. For this the government turned to Komisi Nasional Hak Azasi Manusia, the Indonesian Human Rights Commission known as Komnas HAM.[4]

On 9 October 1999, Komnas HAM established the Komisi Penyelidik Pelanggaran HAM (Human Rights Violations Investigatory Commission, KPP-HAM) to conduct the investigation. KPP-HAM concluded that the Indonesian authorities had orchestrated gross human rights violations in East Timor between January and October 1999, including mass murder, persecution, forced disappearances, gender-based violence and the forced movement of civilian populations.[5] Although the report focused on five incidents – four of the five incidents later addressed by the Court plus one other – it also documented gross human rights violations committed in all of East Timor's thirteen administrative districts. It found evidence that the military, the police and the civil administration were involved in the creation, support, arming and training of the militias responsible for much of the violence.[6] It concluded that the massive and widespread attacks against civilians were not simply the result of the inability of the security forces to protect

[4] See 'Segera dibentuk: komisi penyelidik pelanggaran HAM TimTim' (A commission to investigate human rights violations in East Timor will soon be formed), *Kompas* (23 September 1999).

[5] KPP HAM Komnas HAM, *Laporan penyelidikan pelanggaran hak azasi manusia di Timor Timur* (Report on the investigation into human rights violations in East Timor) (31 January 2000), pars. 61–75.

[6] Ibid., pars. 34–56.

the population, but had resulted from a conscious and planned Indonesian effort to terrorise East Timorese independence supporters.[7]

When the KPP-HAM investigation was announced, some raised concerns that the Indonesian armed forces would prevent it from aggressively investigating the crimes in which they were implicated. The validity of these concerns was borne out by the TNI's efforts to obstruct the investigation and intimidate investigators. That KPP-HAM nevertheless produced a report tracing responsibility for the violence to the most senior ranks of the military is attributable to various factors, the first among them being TNI's weakened position in East Timor. The Australian-led international intervention had deprived the TNI of some of its power to control the situation, and it was clear that they wanted KPP-HAM to conduct a thorough investigation to avoid a worse scenario, which was to pre-empt United Nations action.

The TNI's predicament is illustrated by a public spat between a lawyer representing General Wiranto, the Commander of the armed forces, who criticised the Commission's actions as unpatriotic, and KPP-HAM Chair Albert Hasibuan, who responded that it was patriotism that had induced him to take on the investigation and to prevent Wiranto and other members of the Indonesian military from being tried by an international tribunal.[8] Hasibuan's argument was not an easy one to answer.

At the same time, the UN-mandated five-member International Commission of Inquiry on East Timor (ICOIET), launched on 15 October 1999, conducted its own investigation on behalf of UN Secretary-General Kofi Annan. It too reported that it had found evidence of systematic and widespread intimidation and terror, destruction of property, violence against women and displacement of people, and hence recommended the establishment of an international tribunal to try those responsible.[9] Some within the United Nations were sceptical of Indonesia's ability to prosecute the perpetrators and their commitment to doing so. Be that as it may, the Secretary-General decided to accede when Jakarta insisted that Indonesian national courts be given priority.

[7] Ibid, pars. 152–160.

[8] 'Wiranto diduga tak lakukan pencegahan pembumihangusan Tim-tim' (Wiranto suspected of not taking action to prevent scorched earth in East Timor), *Kompas* (13 September 1999). It was rumoured at the time that Habibie's successor, President Abdurrahman Wahid, used the KPP-HAM report to pave the way to removing Wiranto from his position.

[9] 'Report of the International Commission of Inquiry on East Timor to the Secretary-General', A/54/726, S/2000/59 (31 January 2000), pars. 142, 154.

It is an established principle of international law that international tribunals should complement rather than supplant national legal systems, and that international prosecutions should not be instituted if a state with jurisdiction over the matter is willing and able to investigate and prosecute human rights violations. Accordingly, the Security Council announced that it 'welcome[d]' Indonesia's commitment to bring to justice those responsible and encouraged it 'to institute a swift, comprehensive, effective and transparent legal process, in conformity with international standards of justice and due process of law'.[10]

The Human Rights Court Law

Preparations to try human rights crimes committed in East Timor began even before Komnas HAM and ICOIET had completed their investigations. After a number of missteps, a bill proposing the creation of a human rights court was introduced in the legislature in June 2000; the Human Rights Court Law (Law 26/2000) was approved in November. This established a special tribunal with the power to try human rights crimes. Unlike most other Indonesian courts, which are made up of three judges, the Human Rights Court is comprised of five judges – two career judges and three ad hoc judges. The permanent jurisdiction of the Court is prospective only, but the Statute also authorises retroactive jurisdiction upon issuance of a presidential order and on the recommendation of the legislature, including in the case of East Timor.

In addition to establishing a new court, the Human Rights Court Law also defines the crimes of genocide and crimes against humanity – the only crimes over which the court has jurisdiction. The definition of both crimes is taken nearly word for word from the definition of the same crimes in Articles 6 and 7 of the Rome Statute. Article 9 defines crimes against humanity as the commission of one of ten predicate crimes when the crime is committed as part of a widespread or systematic attack that is directed at civilians. As is typical of Indonesian statutes, the Human Rights Court Law is accompanied by an official elucidation, which stated on Article 9 that the phrase 'attack directed at civilians' means 'a series of actions carried out against civilians in furtherance of the policy of the authorities or an organization'.[11]

[10] 'Letter dated 18 February 2000 from the President of the Security Council to the Secretary General', S/2000/137 (18 February 2000).

[11] *Penjelasan Atas Undang-Undang Nomor 26 Tahun 2000 Tentang Pengadilan Hak Azasi Manusia* (Law No. 26/2000), Article 9.

The Law defines the crimes within the jurisdiction of the Court and specifies the punishments for those crimes, but it does not include provisions on general principles of criminal law. (Article 41, for example, refers to, but does not define, 'attempting, plotting or assisting' the commission of genocide and crimes against humanity.[12]) It must be presumed, then, that the general principles applicable to the prosecution of human rights crimes are derived from those contained in the Indonesian Criminal Code, Kitab Undang-Undang Hukum Pidana. The Law does, however, define the requirements for liability for genocide and crimes against humanity on the basis of command responsibility.

As with the articles defining substantive offences, Article 42 on command responsibility appears to be based on a translation of the corresponding provision, Article 28, of the Rome Statute. Article 42(1) imposes liability on military commanders for crimes committed 'by troops under his or her effective command and control, and for any such criminal action by troops under his or her effective command and control arising from improper control of these troops'.[13] This form of liability also requires proof that the commander knew or had reason to know of a subordinate's commission of crimes but failed to take reasonable measures either to prevent or terminate them or to deliver the subordinate to officials for 'inquiry, investigation, and prosecution'.[14] Article 42(2) defines the requirements for imposing liability on police or civilian commanders. The principal difference between the two provisions is that the *mens rea* requirements are stricter for police and civilian commanders: it must be shown that the commander either knew of the commission of crimes by subordinates or consciously disregarded information clearly indicating their commission.

The investigation and indictments

Although human rights abuses were committed throughout 1999, the Human Rights Court trials focused on just five incidents.[15] The first incident occurred on 6 April in the town of Liquisa when pro-integration forces attacked independence supporters who had taken refuge in the residence of Father Rafael dos Santos inside the Catholic church compound, killing twenty-two people or more. The second incident occurred

[12] Ibid., Article 41. [13] Ibid., Article 42(2). [14] Ibid.

[15] For reasons that have never been explained, the Presidential Order authorising the creation of the Human Rights Court limited its jurisdiction to crimes committed in just two months, April and September 1999.

ten days later in the capital, Dili, when pro-integration forces attacked independence supporters who had sought protection in the house of Manuel Carrascalão, killing twelve people. The other three incidents occurred in September 1999 after the announcement of the vote. On 4 and 5 September, pro-integration forces attacked independence supporters who had taken refuge in the Catholic Diocese in Dili, resulting in forty-six deaths. The following day, on 6 September, pro-integration forces attacked independence supporters who had sought protection in the residence of Bishop Belo in Dili, leading to ten more deaths. And on 6 September, pro-integration forces attacked independence supporters who had sought refuge in the Ave Maria Church in Suai in the district of Covalima, which led to twenty-seven immediately identifiable deaths (although estimates put the figure much higher, at several hundred deaths).

The Human Rights Court Law assigns the initial investigation of human rights crimes to Komnas HAM.[16] Thereafter, the prosecution of crimes is to be carried out by the Attorney General,[17] who may appoint ad hoc prosecutors from outside the government but is not required to do so.[18] All the prosecutors who prepared the dossiers and argued the cases at the Human Rights Court in 2002–2003 were chosen from the ranks of career prosecutors in the office of the Attorney General. There is very little information about their investigation of the five incidents. A team of fifteen prosecutors made a single trip to East Timor on 19–28 July 2000, when they collected physical evidence and many of the witness statements. They also questioned witnesses and suspects in Jakarta, and in the city of Kupang in West Timor. Departmental regulations specify that only those witnesses whose statements are contained in the dossier may be called to testify at trial, so the list of witnesses was predetermined by these prosecutors, even though they did not go on to present the case at trial.

These prosecutors were more inclined to gather statements from Indonesian rather than East Timorese sources. The dossier prepared by the prosecutors dealing with the case of Timbul Silaen, Chief of Police in East Timor in 1999, was typical. This consisted of pre-trial statements from twenty-five witnesses, one expert and the accused himself. Eighteen of the witnesses were Indonesian, and of these, all but three were either members of the national police force (ten) or military officers (four) or government officials (one). Many of them were either named as suspects in the Komnas HAM report or were later charged themselves. The remaining three Indonesians all identified themselves as Aitarak militia

[16] Law No. 26/2000, Article 18(1). [17] Ibid., Article 23(1). [18] Ibid., Article 23(2).

members. Two stated that they were also members of the Pam-Swakarsa, state-sponsored voluntary security organisations used by the TNI and the police as fronts for pro-Indonesia militias. None gave statements directly implicating Aitarak, the Pam-Swakarsa or the Indonesian armed forces in the violence. The seven Timorese witnesses whose statements were included in the dossier were present during the attack either on the church in Liquisa (three) or the Diocese of Dili (four).

After their investigation, prosecutors charged eighteen defendants with crimes under the Human Rights Court Law. Eleven of these defendants were members of the TNI. Starting from the highest rank, charges were raised against a Major-General who was the former Commander of the Udayana Regional Military Command, two Brigadier-Generals who served as military commanders for East Timor, a Colonel who headed a special forces task force in East Timor, four Lieutenant-Colonels who had been district-level military commanders, and two sub-district-level Army officers. Five defendants were from the Indonesian police: a Brigadier-General serving as a provincial chief of police; and four Lieutenant-Colonels who were district-level police chiefs. Three defendants were civilian officials: the former Governor of East Timor; and two Regents, the highest district-level civilian position (one was also a Lieutenant-Colonel in the Army). One defendant did not hold any formal position: he was Eurico Guterres, who was both Commander of the Aitarak militia in Dili, and Deputy Commander of the Forces for Integration Struggle (Pasukan Perjuangan Integrasi, PPI), an umbrella group for the pro-integration militias.

All of the indictments alleged crimes against humanity for acts of murder or assault carried out as a part of a widespread or systematic attack directed against a civilian population. All of the defendants, including Eurico Guterres, were charged for acts committed by subordinates based on the doctrine of command responsibility.

The prosecution's evidence at trial

Almost none of the critical documentary evidence gathered by KPP-HAM establishing Indonesian involvement in the violence in East Timor was either provided to the trial prosecutors or introduced by the prosecutors at trial.[19] On the contrary, most of the testimony presented by the prosecution was favourable to the defence. This was because the prosecutors,

[19] See, for example, A. Nababan, Table 2, 'Annex 1' in Cohen, *Intended to fail*, pp. 103–108.

who found themselves in the unenviable position of charging still-serving military commanders, were inclined to downplay the defendants' contribution to, or find other justifications for, the crimes committed in East Timor. Following the contents of the dossiers, they called witnesses who were for the most part members of the Indonesian security forces or civilian administration. In some trials, they called witnesses who were testifying for the defence in other cases. In every trial, the prosecutors called witnesses who were being *tried* in other cases. They presented very little testimony from East Timorese victims, although they were not wholly responsible for this absence. Many of the East Timorese summoned refused to appear in court.

The prosecution often presented accounts of incidents that were completely at odds with the theory on which the defendants were charged. The testimony of one particularly pro-defence prosecution witness illustrates this process. Mathius Maia, who was the Mayor of Dili in 1999, testified at least twice as a witness for the prosecution, once at the trial of former Governor Abilio Soares and again at the trial of Soedjarwo, the former District Military Commander for Dili.[20] At Soares's trial, Maia's testimony focused on the 17 April attack on Manuel Carrascalão's house, while at Soedjarwo's trial, Maia focused on the 6 September attack on the residence of Bishop Belo. The prosecutors knew exactly what Maia would say when called to testify, since his trial testimony was identical in all significant respects with his pre-trial statement.

At the Abilio Soares trial, the first of two prosecutors began by eliciting that the defendant had appointed Maia as Mayor of Dili. He then asked him about his mayoral duties, specifically his responsibilities in the area of law enforcement and security, and how the office of Mayor related to other local government offices. This entire examination covered two pages of printed transcript and could not have taken more than ten minutes.

The second prosecutor began asking Maia about the events of 17 April in Dili. These had begun at the Governor's lodge, where the PPI had convened a 'grand assembly', attended by some 5,000 pro-integration militiamen, to mark the inauguration of the Pam-Swakarsa. Inflammatory speeches had been made, and the events of the day had culminated with the attack, led by members of the Aitarak militia, on the house of the prominent independence leader

[20] Information about Maia's testimony at both trials is based on unofficial transcripts of the trials prepared by the Indonesian human rights organisation, Lembaga Studi dan Advokasi Masyarakat (Institute for Social Research and Advocacy).

Manuel Carrascalão, during which at least a dozen independence supporters were killed. Maia stated that he had attended the rally, but disclaimed any knowledge of whether Abilio Soares, the Governor, or Eurico Guterres, the PPI Deputy Commander, had given speeches at it. This was a significant point, since the prosecution's case rested in large part on the theory that Guterres had incited the attack against Carrascalão during his speech at the 'grand assembly', which had led to the attack on the latter's house.[21]

Maia then proceeded to impugn Carrascalão himself. He said that the latter had served as a member of the House of Representatives, but had quit after the cancellation of a lucrative government road construction project, and began working with the clandestine independence movement to topple the Indonesian government. He also claimed that after the 6 April incident in Liquisa, Carrascalão had taken agricultural workers who were believed missing or killed there, and held them hostage in his house in Dili. Carrascalão had then portrayed these hostages as refugees, requesting 'dollars' from independence supporters to buy food for them, which he then 'pocketed'. Concluding this version of events, Maia claimed that after the 'grand assembly' on 17 April, Pam-Swakarsa members passing Carrascalão's house heard the hostages cry out for rescue, whereupon the 'clash' had ensued. He added that he had no intention of discrediting or 'marginalizing' Carrascalão, but that he was a man who had once enjoyed benefits from Indonesia, only to betray it later on.

Maia's testimony – note, still for the *prosecution* – continued at the Soedjarwo trial. When discussing the attack on Bishop Carlos Belo's house on 6 September, for which Soedjarwo was charged, Maia stated that there was in fact no attack. He claimed that ballot boxes had been improperly stashed inside Belo's house, that the Catholic East Timorese members of the Aitarak militia would never attack the house of a bishop, and that the fire that burned the house down had been started from inside. Maia also stated that Bishop Belo had been manoeuvring to rid the territory of Indonesian troops, and had concocted the story about an attack on his house in order to persuade the international community to

[21] Eurico Guterres was charged under the same command responsibility statute as police and military commanders, despite the fact that the allegations against him included active incitement to murder (which may have supported charging him as a principal or accomplice). Proving the case against him on the basis of command responsibility made it more difficult to secure a conviction because the Indictment was predicated on his omissions in failing to prevent, repress or punish the acts of others.

send in troops and force a withdrawal of the Indonesian military. When one of the prosecutors asked him if he knew the fate of those inside the house when it burned, resulting in the deaths of ten people, Maia replied that he had heard that they had been rescued by members of Aitarak – the very same militia that had carried out the attack.

The prosecutors' analysis of the law

Some of the actions of the prosecutors during the proceedings indicated an appalling lack of understanding of the most basic legal concepts. One particularly egregious example was contained in the aforementioned dossier filed by the prosecutors in the case of police chief Timbul Silaen. The bulk of it consisted of summaries of the pretrial statements and documentary and physical evidence. At the end of the dossier, the prosecutors addressed the sufficiency of the evidence to support the filing of charges. They examined this evidence in the light of the requirements of Article 42 of the Human Rights Court Law, which defines command responsibility, but made no mention of any article defining a substantive crime. The command responsibility provision is thus treated as the substantive norm defining the acts that serve as the basis for punishment. The prosecutors' analysis failed to recognise that conviction under the command responsibility doctrine requires proof of the commission of crimes by the commander's subordinates. In short, they concluded that the dossier evidence established *prima facie* proof of guilt without ever mentioning the statutory provisions governing crimes against humanity.

Their analysis of the article in the Human Rights Court Law defining command responsibility is also seriously mistaken. Article 42(2) deals with command responsibility liability for the police and civilian officials. Subsection (a) states the *mens rea* requirement – that the superior 'is aware of or deliberately ignores information that clearly indicates his or her subordinates are perpetrating, or have recently perpetrated a gross violation of human rights'. Subsection (b) defines the *actus reus* requirement – that the superior 'fails to act in a proper manner as required by the scope of his or her authority by preventing or terminating such action or delivering the perpetrators of this action to the authorised official for inquiry, investigation, and prosecution'. Although these two subsections are joined by the word 'and', the prosecutors treated them as independent crimes, stating that 'while part of a single article, [the subsections] regulate two distinct acts and constitute alternative bases for liability, each of which can stand alone and be charged separately'.[22] This demonstrates an astonishing (and perhaps wilful) misunderstanding of the command responsibility doctrine, and also of the basic principles of criminal law.

Over the course of the proceedings the prosecutors corrected the most serious misstatements of the law. The Indictment in the *Timbul Silaen* case, for example, cited both the command responsibility provision of the Human Rights Court Law and the articles that define crimes against humanity. It also correctly recognised that guilt under the command responsibility doctrine requires proof of both the *mens rea* element and a failure to prevent or punish the commission of crimes against humanity. But even when the prosecutors stated the law correctly, problems remained. Most notable was the prosecutors' conspicuous determination to argue the case without making the defendants appear blameworthy.

The subtle manner in which the East Timor prosecutors argued the defendants' guilt without making them seem guilty is illustrated by the final plea or 'requisitor' delivered by the prosecutors at Timbul Silaen's trial. As East Timor's Chief of Police in 1999, he held a province-wide jurisdiction and was charged with all five of the incidents that were the subject of the trials. After presenting a summary of the testimony of each of the witnesses who testified at the hearing, the prosecutors presented a summary of the 'indications' from the evidence, which included the following:

> That the security apparatus such as the Army, Mobile Police Brigade, and Police ... under the control of the accused as the Chief of Police for East Timor did not attempt to prevent these attacks and clashes between the pro-integration and pro-independence groups before they occurred; and did not confiscate the weapons of the two groups, whether they be firearms, home-made guns, or sharp instruments such as swords, machetes, and spears;
>
> That when attacks or clashes between pro-integration and pro-independence groups occurred the security forces generally focused their actions on rescuing the victims and the refugees and did not attempt to stop the attack or the clash. As a result of the attacks or clashes there were civilian victims both fatalities and wounded;
>
> [That] ... despite the loss of life through murder and injuries resulting from assault during these attacks or clashes, the accused did not carry out an investigation and did not form a team to carry out an investigation and prosecution of security forces as the subordinates of the accused, but merely ordered or instructed his subordinates to investigate the incident.[23]

[22] Berkas perkara atas nama tersangka Drs. G.M. Timbul Silaen, Jakarta (21 December 2000), p. 48.

[23] Requisitor, No. 01/HAM/TIM TIM/02/2002, p. 135.

This summary is followed by a point-by-point analysis of the elements of the charges. The prosecutors first addressed Count 1 of the Indictment, which alleged failure to prevent or punish widespread or systematic acts of murder by persons under the defendant's command or control. This charge, according to the prosecutors, required proof of ten distinct facts: four elements under the doctrine of command responsibility, three elements of murder under the Indonesian Criminal Code and three elements establishing crimes against humanity.

The analysis begins with the requirements for command responsibility. The first element is found to be satisfied by the fact that, as Chief of Police, Silaen was the commander of all police assigned in the province. The prosecutors argued that he failed to exercise effective control over the police under his authority – element number two – because he rarely travelled to local police commands to provide direct personal guidance, usually gave only written instruction or verbal orders by telephone, and never followed up to make sure that orders had been carried out. They next addressed the requirement that Silaen knew or had reason to know that his subordinates had committed crimes; they thought this element was satisfied because they informed him of each of the attacks after they had taken place. Finally, the prosecutors argued that the defendant failed to take necessary and proper steps to prevent or punish crimes by persons under his command, proven by evidence that although he ordered investigations of the incidents reported to him, he failed to order an inquiry into the possible involvement of his own subordinates.

The prosecutors' argument for imposing liability for crimes against humanity is therefore the defendant's failure to investigate whether members of the police under his authority were involved in the attacks on civilians. While this markedly minimises the level of the defendant's culpability, especially compared to the allegations against him contained in the aforementioned Komnas HAM report, it probably provides an adequate basis for liability as a matter of law. The prosecutors' argument for finding the defendant guilty could hardly be less convincing, though. To begin with, it is highly doubtful that evidence that the defendant ordered an investigation *into the crimes* supports a finding beyond a reasonable doubt that he failed to investigate *whether his own troops were involved* – an order to investigate would, on the face of it, seem to encompass an inquiry into all those involved. In addition, there is limited force, to say the least, to the prosecutors' argument that the defendant should be punished for failing to investigate whether the Indonesian police committed human rights crimes in East Timor when the prosecutors themselves had conducted such an investigation and had not charged the police with wrongdoing (except on the basis of command responsibility).

The prosecutors give a broad interpretation to the scope of a commander's liability under the doctrine of command responsibility. As applied to the facts of the case against Timbul Silaen, this breadth facilitated their arguing his guilt without ever accusing him of significant wrongdoing. A similar strategy is apparent in the prosecutors' interpretation of crimes against humanity, in which they define the requirements of the law in terms so capacious as to virtually drain the crime of blameworthiness.

When dealing with crimes against humanity, the prosecutors devote two paragraphs to the issue of whether the defendant is a 'person' within the meaning of the Indonesian murder statute, and a full five pages to arguing the undisputed fact that the killings alleged in the Indictment constituted murder under the Indonesian Criminal Code. The treatment of the requirement that the attacks be widespread or systematic, however, covers just over one page and is distinctly unenlightening. It quotes from two papers, provided as part of the prosecutors' training prior to the trials, in which the word 'widespread' is defined as 'action directed toward a multiplicity of victims, rather than a single intention and a single victim'[24] and as 'large scale and coordinated action based on a shared motivation and directed at a large number of victims'.[25] On the basis of these two statements, the prosecutors declared that 'widespread' meant: 'Multiple criminal acts committed at the same time or a single criminal act followed by additional occurrences or criminal acts' and/or 'Criminal acts or events resulting in a large number of victims as well as destruction.'[26]

The prosecutors then state that the following facts established at the trial were relevant to the widespread or systematic requirement:

> That on 6 April 1999 at the residence of Father Rafael within the church complex in Liquisa, and 17 April 1999 at the residence of Manuel Carrascalão, and at the Diocese of Dili, the Ave Maria church complex

[24] Ibid., p. 136, quoting Muladi, 'Notes on the Human Rights Court' (Jakarta, 13 February 2002).

[25] Ibid., pp. 136–137, quoting Jean-Jacques Heintz, 'Serious violations of international law: some experience gained from the ICTY and the ICTR practice' (Jakarta, 27 February 2002).

[26] Ibid., p. 137.

> in Suai, and the residence of Bishop Belo, pro-integration masses carried out a coordinated attack on independence supporters who had taken refuge inside these locations, entering with the use of firearms and home-made guns.
>
> That these attacks resulted in approximately 48 deaths as detailed above consisting of old and young, male and female.
>
> That in addition to the attacks referred to above, there was also gunfire and the destruction by fire of homes.[27]

This is the entirety of the discussion of the issue. According to the prosecutors, the requirement that the crimes were committed as part of a widespread or systematic attack is proven by the evidence.

Finally, in their discussion of the requirement that the attacks were directed against a civilian population, the prosecutors stated that Indonesian law on this issue, like the Rome Statute, requires proof that the attack was carried out pursuant to or in furtherance of a state or organisational policy to commit such attack. The prosecutors set the scene:

> As a result of the Indonesian government's announcement of the second option offering an independence vote the existence throughout East Timor of two large groups, both of which were present earlier, became increasingly apparent, one group favouring integration and the other favouring independence;
>
> Beginning in about July, with the establishment of the United Nations Mission to East Timor (UNAMET) ... the pro-independence group became bolder in the commission of acts of terror against the pro-integration group;
>
> That from the beginning of August government offices in East Timor no longer functioned effectively, especially in the districts of Dili, Liquisa, and Covalima. ... [M]any local officials, most of whom were ethnic East Timorese, left their jobs and returned to their hometowns to participate in the vote, which meant that the maintenance of order and security could no longer be managed effectively;
>
> Thus, the government's policy of permitting an independence vote eventuated in the commission of uncontrollable criminal acts by the two sides, in which the army, mobile police brigade, and police were also involved.[28]

The prosecutors' characterisation of the events focused on central government's initial decision to permit an independence referendum, which had encouraged the rival factions to pursue their objectives through violence. By positing a causal relationship between government policy and its unintended consequence (the disintegration of the security

[27] Ibid. [28] Ibid., pp. 139–140.

situation in East Timor), they may conceivably have been trying to satisfy the crimes against humanity requirement that attacks be in furtherance of a state or organisational policy. In the process, though, they also managed to almost entirely absolve the Indonesian security forces and local government officials of any wrongdoing.

As has been seen, the prosecution's remarkable achievement was to bring charges for the commission of crimes against humanity without actually making the defendants appear blameworthy. Instead, their arguments reinforced the central claims of the defence – that the violence had occurred in the context of clashes between opposing political factions, that the international community's involvement had only made things worse, and that it was impossible for the security forces to control the situation. If there was any injustice, it was that honourable Indonesian soldiers and police officers could be prosecuted and punished for failing to maintain order among a population intent on killing each other. Blame lay with the East Timorese, who were responsible for the violence, and the United Nations, which had demanded the trials.

The Court and its judgments

The Human Rights Court has been justly criticised for acquitting a majority of those brought to trial. But considering the total abdication by the prosecutors, it is surprising that there were any convictions at all. Of the eighteen defendants tried, six were convicted and twelve were acquitted. The result is even more surprising if instead of focusing on the verdicts recorded against individual defendants one examines the outcome of the trials. The eighteen defendants were tried in twelve trials. Ten of the trials involved a single defendant. In one trial five defendants were tried together, and three defendants were joined in another trial. The greater number of defendants convicted than defendants acquitted results from the fact that in both trials involving multiple defendants the judges returned verdicts of not guilty against all of the defendants. If one compares 'acquitting panels' against 'convicting panels', the number of convictions and acquittals is exactly equal. In six of the twelve trials the Court returned guilty verdicts and in the six other trials it found the defendant not guilty.

There is no readily apparent explanation for the different outcomes of the trials. The pattern of convictions and acquittals cannot be explained based on the strength of the evidence. There was considerable overlap in the witnesses called at the various trials, and most of the evidence at all of the trials was exculpatory. Nor is the outcome of the trials explainable by other factors. While it might be supposed that Indonesian judges would be more inclined to convict defendants who were ethnic Timorese, that factor alone does not explain the convictions. Two of the six defendants found guilty were Timorese, but the other four were not. A third Timorese was acquitted. Nor is the outcome related to the military status of the defendant. The six defendants who were convicted included three members of the military, one police officer, one civilian official, and Eurico Guterres, who held no formal office. The most plausible explanation is that the different verdicts in the trials, all of which were based on much the same evidence, resulted primarily from the composition of the panels of judges.

This can be tested by examining the voting record of individual judges to see if they voted consistently for conviction or acquittal. The Human Rights Court is comprised of five judges – two career judges and three ad hoc judges.[29] The twelve panels that heard the cases were assembled from a pool of twenty-three judges: twelve members of the career judiciary and eleven ad hoc judges. Assembling twelve panels of five judges each required filling a total of sixty positions. Most of the judges were thus assigned to more than one trial: eight of the judges served on three panels; six judges served on two panels; two judges served in four trials, one judge in five trials, and one judge in six trials.

Of the eighteen judges who served on more than one trial, eleven voted consistently either to acquit or to convict while seven judges had mixed records of convictions and acquittals. This provides some support for the theory that the composition of the panels determined the outcome of the case. Almost all of the inconsistent voting records, moreover, resulted from one of the twelve trials. Five of the seven judges with mixed voting records were on the panel that tried the *Soedjarwo* case. All five of the *Soedjarwo* judges had also served on other trials, and all of those other trials had resulted in an acquittal. In all, these five judges had cast a total of thirteen votes for acquittal in other trials, but they convicted Soedjarwo. If we eliminate the *Soedjarwo* case from the analysis, there are seventeen judges who served on more than one trial. Of those, fifteen voted consistently to convict or acquit while just two had mixed records.

[29] The President appoints the ad hoc judges on the recommendation of the Supreme Court; they are required to have graduated from a law faculty, hold a position in an Indonesian law faculty and possess expertise in and commitment to human rights. They serve for renewable five-year terms.

The analysis of crimes against humanity

In the judgments, the approach to the law was uniformly simplistic and imprecise. When discussing crimes against humanity, they typically recited one or more definitions of the words 'widespread' and 'systematic', and then referred to facts established by the evidence that happened to fit the definition of those terms. The requirement that the attack be widespread, for example, was generally described in terms of the number of victims, repeated acts of violence, the existence of collective action, and the geographical distribution of the violence.[30] Thus, in the *Damiri* Judgment the Court stated that 'widespread' denoted 'massive action, repeatedly performed, on a large scale in the sense of both a broad area and a large number of victims carried out by means of collective action'.[31]

Some of the judgments – acknowledging that the most common definition of the systematic element of crimes against humanity focuses on the existence of a policy or plan – equated the systematic element with the existence of a pattern of similar actions. The *Soedjarwo* Judgment, for example, defined systematic as 'an organized action conforming to a certain pattern, based on a common policy, involving significant resources, carefully engineered and methodically planned'.[32]

The requirement that there be an 'attack', and that the attack be directed against a civilian population, is treated inconsistently in the judgments. A number of them make the point that

> 'an attack targeted on civilians' need not necessarily be launched against the population as a whole. An attack on a group of civilians holding similar political views should fall within the definition of the above term.[33]

A number of judgments discussed whether the evidence described a 'clash' or an 'attack'. The Judgment in the case of Yayat Sudrajat, who was charged with the events occurring on April 6 in the town of Liquisa, expressly rejected the defence argument that the evidence did not prove an attack and that there was only a 'clash' between Besi Merah Putih and pro-independence supporters inside Father Rafael's residence. The Court stated,

[30] The statements of law contained in the judgments draw heavily on materials provided to the judges as a part of training organised by the Supreme Court and the Department of Justice prior to the trials. Some judgments do not cite any authority other than the definition of the crimes under the Human Rights Courts Law and the Indonesian Criminal Code.

[31] Putusan N. 09/PID.HAM/AD.HOC/2002/PN.JKT PST, p. 166. [32] Ibid., p. 36.

[33] Ibid., p. 34.

> That in a situation where one side consists of men, women, the elderly and children who are unarmed inside a house within a church complex seeking protection because they are afraid, and the other side consists of members of Besi Merah Putih entering the church complex armed with traditional weapons and other sharp instruments in a state of high emotion, the resulting violence is not a clash under conditions and circumstances in which the two sides are equals attacking each other, but rather a situation in which one side is passive and seeking protection out of fear, and the other side is actively forcing entry to achieve their objective.
>
> Considering that based on this assessment, the Court believes that the incident ... was an attack by one side consisting of Besi Merah Putih against another side consisting of refugees who were supporters of independence who were afraid and seeking protection.[34]

Finally, while some of the judgments contained no express definition of this aspect of crimes against humanity, all acknowledged the occurrence of collective violence targeting civilians who supported the independence of East Timor.

Judicial approach to command responsibility

The discussion about the requirements for proving liability under the command responsibility doctrine was also confused and unfocused. The judgments carved up the language of the command responsibility statute into a list of three to five separate statements labelled as elements. The division was based principally on the grammatical structure of the statute rather than on the concepts it expresses. There was virtually no attempt to analyse the meaning of the language or understand how the various components of the statute relate to each other. In the Judgment on the case of Endar Priyanto, for example, the Court wrote that conviction requires proof of the following elements:

1. A person effectively acting as Military Commander is responsible for serious human rights violations.
2. Perpetrated by troops under his effective command and control or under his effective power and control.
3. No appropriate control was exerted over the troops.
4. The military commander was aware or should have been aware that his troops were perpetrating or had just perpetrated serious human rights violations.

[34] Putusan N. 11/PID.HAM/AD.HOC/2002/PN.JKT PST, p. 65.

5. The military commander did not take appropriate and necessary measures to prevent or suppress the crimes or to surrender the perpetrators to the authorities.[35]

Some of the problems with this formulation of the requirements of the law are obvious. Element one overlaps with element two, and element three is a more general statement of the requirement contained in element five. Other problems with the analysis become apparent in the application of the law to the facts. None of the judgments assessed how the knowledge requirement in the command responsibility statute related to the elements of crimes against humanity. They addressed the question of whether the accused knew or had reason to know that his subordinates committed murders or assaults, but they did not consider whether the accused had the necessary mental state with respect to the context elements that make murders and assaults crimes against humanity.

Despite the lack of clarity, all of the judgments recognised the critical importance of defining effective command and control under the command responsibility doctrine. The evidence at most of the trials included testimony from experts on the meaning of command responsibility, and some of the judgments relied on expert testimony when defining the concept. The *Timbul Silaen* Judgment, for example, stated that 'for command responsibility [liability] there must be a relation between the commander and the subordinate who commits the violation, and the gross human rights violation committed by the subordinate must have an effective connection between the commander and the subordinate'.[36] Citing the testimony of an expert, P.L.T. Sihombing, the Court gave the following general statement of the principle of command responsibility:

> accountability in a command structure (kesatuan komando) lies in the chain of command, i.e., in the hierarchical line that runs from the highest command to the lowest command, while with respect to a policy or command which originates from above and is passed down hierarchically through the unit of commanders until it reaches the level at which it is to be implemented, the decision to carry it out can only be made by officers who are situated (directly) within the chain of command.[37]

The command responsibility doctrine was addressed most fully in the case of *Herman Sedyono et al.*, in which five district-level military, police and civilian officials were tried together for the attack on the church in

[35] Putusan N. 05/PID.HAM/AD.HOC/2002/PN.JKT PST, pp. 60–61.
[36] Putusan N. 01/PID.HAM/AD.HOC/2002/PN.JKT PST, p. 46. [37] Ibid.

Suai. After having concluded that the evidence established that members of the Laksaur and Mahidi militias committed crimes against humanity, the Court addressed the question of whether any of the defendants could be held liable for their acts. It wrote that command responsibility is predicated on 'a hierarchical relationship of a superior over a subordinate that is based on the authority of a formal position of power as defined by law'.[38] The evidence showed that the Laksaur and Mahidi militias were 'community groups that emerged spontaneously in response to the desires of their members who volunteered in order to promote a pro-integration victory in the popular consultation'[39] – in short, ordinary citizens, not members of the armed forces. The five defendants 'knew of the existence of, were acquainted with, and had a good relationship' with the militias, but, under Indonesian constitutional law governing the relations between the state and society, 'a good relationship and mutual acquaintance between the accused and the community groups of Laksaur and Mahidi does not constitute a commander-subordinate relationship'.[40] Instead, it represented 'the ideal relationship between government, in its role as the guarantor of security and enforcer of the law, and citizens'.[41] The Court thus concluded that 'it cannot be said that whenever a member of the community breaks the law the government must share responsibility as the party with effective command and control'.[42]

This description of command responsibility seemed to limit the doctrine to commanders who are in a formal position of authority over the perpetrators of the crimes. More than that, the discussion seemed intended to delegitimise the doctrine as an alien intrusion on Indonesian law. Rather than address the evidence of links between the defendants and the militias – or simply declare that there was no such evidence – the Court intimated that the allegations of fault were based on nothing more than the defendants' position of authority over the perpetrators of the crimes. By rejecting such liability as contrary to Indonesian constitutional law, it identified the command responsibility doctrine as being foreign and thus illegitimate.

In reality, the judges' interpretation of the requirements of the law was not a significant factor in determining the verdicts. What principally distinguished the judgments returning verdicts of guilty from those finding the defendant not guilty was the judges' evaluation of the credibility of the trial witnesses. In cases where the defendant was convicted,

[38] Putusan N. 03/PID.HAM/AD.HOC/2002/PN.JKT PST, pp. 109–110. [39] Ibid., p. 110.
[40] Ibid. [41] Ibid., pp. 110–111. [42] Ibid., p. 111.

the judges discounted the testimony of witnesses who were members of the security forces or part of the government on the grounds that their testimony was self-serving, and credited the testimony of East Timorese witnesses. The judges who acquitted found ample support for the verdict in the testimony of the witnesses presented by the prosecution. The judgments in the following cases – of Tono Suratman, Soedjarwo and Adam Damiri – illustrate aspects of the decision-making process.

The *Tono Suratman* case

Tono Suratman, the military commander in East Timor, was charged in relation to the attacks carried out in April against independence supporters sheltering inside the church compound in Liquisa and Manuel Carrascalão's house in Dili. He was transferred out of East Timor in August 1999 after the UN mission in East Timor complained that he was sponsoring militia violence. The Court found him not guilty of the charges.

In the Judgment, the Court addressed the question of whether Suratman's subordinates had committed crimes against humanity. One of the incidents it considered was the attack on independence supporters who had sought refuge in Carrascalão's house. On the morning of 17 April, some 5,000 integration supporters from all over East Timor had gathered in the grounds of the Governor's office for a 'grand assembly' to inaugurate the Pam-Swakarsa. According to Eurico Guterres, the ceremony was organised by the regional government, and led by PPI Commander João Da Silva Tavares. According to Tavares, the participants brought generic weapons and blades with them because it is customary for East Timorese to carry blades when travelling. After the 'grand assembly', Guterres and Tavares stated, pro-integration groups were parading around Dili when they saw a woman lying in front of Carrascalão's house. When they attempted to assist her, a confrontation erupted spontaneously between them and the independence supporters, numbering up to two hundred, who were hiding out in Carrascalão's house. This incident, which resulted in twelve deaths, was immediately reported to Suratman by walkie-talkie.

The Court also considered testimony from Alfredo Sanches and Florindo de Jesus, who were sheltering in Carrascalão's house when the attack occurred, and testified that the TNI had taken part in it alongside the militias. It was not persuaded by their account, stating that twenty-six other witnesses contradicted them by testifying that the TNI was present only to quell the violence. Carlos Amaral, a TNI member implicated in the attack, claimed that he was on leave on 17 April (although, the Court noted, his alibi was doubtful, because he only produced documentary proof of his absence after the issue of his involvement was raised). The Court emphasised minor differences in the accounts of Sanches and De Jesus – 'Sanches claimed that (some of) the TNI who joined in the attack were in uniform, whereas De Jesus claimed that (some of) the attackers were TNI in civilian clothes' – and questioned whether the witnesses could clearly see who was involved since they were both squatting behind a wall trying to hide.[43] In any case, according to the Court, seeing attackers in TNI uniforms did not necessarily mean the TNI was involved in the attack: civilians also wore military attire, as evidenced by photographs submitted by the defence showing pro-independence Falintil and CNRT members wearing TNI uniforms.

In the Court's view, even if TNI troops had mingled with pro-integration militias around the walls of Carrascalão's house, it did not necessarily mean that the TNI members had taken part in the attack: if members of the TNI had joined in there would have been a far larger number of casualties; instead, it was the TNI and the police who quelled the violence and rescued those who had taken refuge in the house. It noted, for example, that after Sanches had been shot twice by militiamen with home-made guns, and De Jesus had been slashed several times, members of the mobile police brigade and the Indonesian Red Cross had taken them to a TNI hospital.

The verdict acquitting Tono Suratman is in line with the testimony of the majority of the witnesses, but whether it was the most plausible interpretation of the evidence is another matter. The Court's conclusion that none of Suratman's subordinates were involved in the 17 April attack is particularly questionable. The testimony of Alfredo Sanches and Florindo de Jesus, if believed, was plainly sufficient to prove that TNI members joined in the attack that day. The Court's reasons for rejecting that testimony are not impressive. Its statement that twenty-six witnesses contradicted the testimony of Sanches and De Jesus is misleading, if not outright false – while none of them testified that TNI members were among the attackers, few had any first-hand knowledge about the attack. Inconsistencies in the two witnesses' testimony about who among the TNI attackers was in uniform does not significantly undermine the credibility of their claims that they recognised people who they knew to be TNI. The Court itself intimates that Carlos Amaral, one of the TNI men named as an attacker, concocted a false alibi; this in turn corroborates the other

[43] Putusan N. 10/PID.HAM/AD.HOC/2002/PN.JKT PST, p. 85.

evidence identifying Amaral as one of the attackers. Finally, the Court's suggestion that Sanches and De Jesus could not have seen the attackers clearly enough to identify them is unconvincing, given the detailed nature of their other testimony. In this case, the judges seemed determined to find the defendant not guilty regardless of the evidence.

The trial of Soedjarwo

Lieutenant-Colonel Soedjarwo served as District Military Commander for Dili in September 1999. He was charged with the 5 September attack on the Catholic Diocese and the 6 September attack on the residence of Bishop Belo. The Court found him guilty, but based its conviction on a strained and questionable command responsibility argument while ignoring inferences that would support more robust findings of guilt.

After the 5 September attack on the Diocese, Soedjarwo ordered the deployment of some sixty TNI troops under the leadership of Captain Hartono to prevent an attack on civilians sheltering in Bishop Belo's residence. According to Hartono's testimony, however, on the morning of 6 September Belo requested that the troops be withdrawn from the scene because he was planning to hold a church service. Hartono communicated the Bishop's request to the defendant, who told him to comply. In explanation of his decision to withdraw the troops, Soedjarwo stated that he believed it improbable that supporters of integration would launch an attack against Bishop Belo's residence because he was so highly respected by the East Timorese. Bishop Belo's testimony made no mention of a church service. Rather than requesting that troops be withdrawn, Belo had asked for TNI protection of independence supporters sheltering inside the residence who needed to walk to the beach to relieve themselves. Fifteen minutes after requesting this protection, however, the sixty TNI soldiers left the premises in two trucks. Shortly after that, the Aitarak militia attacked the residence, killing ten people and setting fire to the building.

While the Court did not enter express findings regarding credibility, it apparently considered it implausible that, on the day after a murderous mob assault on independence supporters inside the offices of the Catholic Diocese, and in the face of continuing threats by the same militias against refugees inside the official residence adjacent to the Diocese, Bishop Belo would ask troops protecting the premises to leave the scene because he was planning a church service. Such an interpretation of the facts was hardly bold or unreasonable, and was supported by Belo's testimony that he had asked not for withdrawal of the troops but for protection by them.

The Court concluded that after the violence at the Diocese, Soedjarwo should have prioritised the protection of the residence, and held him liable for failing to prevent or repress the attacks that occurred against it. It also held that, under the Human Rights Courts Law, it was not necessary that the crimes committed should be carried out by troops under his direct military authority. Although the soldiers serving under Soedjarwo's command were not the active perpetrators of the attacks, they were passive perpetrators because the responsibility to prevent, control and repress the violence rested with them. Soedjarwo, as the person with effective control and command over these troops, was obliged to take action to prevent the violence, but had not done so.

The Court found Soedjarwo guilty, but the basis on which he was convicted is open to serious question. It was certainly correct that the command responsibility doctrine is not limited to crimes committed by members of a military command. But it must be proven that the perpetrators of the crimes were subordinates of the accused within a structure of command or control. A perpetrator might not necessarily be an immediate subordinate, but the commander's liability extends only to crimes committed by subordinates over whom he exercises *effective* command or control. This requirement is not satisfied in the *Soedjarwo* Judgment. The Court found him guilty for crimes committed by pro-integration militiamen without referring to any proof that either he or his subordinates had the power to prevent or repress the crimes or punish the perpetrators.

In addition to their being legally flawed, the grounds on which the Court found Soedjarwo guilty largely absolved the TNI of culpability. Neither the defendant nor anyone else under his authority was found to have committed a crime. Rather, it found him guilty for attacks carried out by the militias on the ground that his subordinates failed to prevent those attacks. Soedjarwo's conviction was thus based on his responsibility as a commander for culpable omissions by his subordinates – a failure of the troops under his control to prevent acts of violence carried out by militiamen. By this logic, Soedjarwo was two steps removed from any active wrongdoing.

The fact that the Court stretched the boundaries of the command responsibility doctrine in order to find Soedjarwo guilty might be construed as an effort to find a way to punish a defendant in circumstances where the standard interpretations of the law did not justify a conviction. That is not what happened in the *Soedjarwo* case. Instead, its generous interpretation of commander liability served to minimise the defendant's culpability rather than to extend the doctrine to reach a broader group of offenders. It predicated Soedjarwo's conviction on the fact that he knew or should have known that the residence would be attacked if left unprotected, and that he therefore acted negligently in withdrawing TNI protection. But the facts found by the Court would support a stronger inference of guilt. If Soedjarwo, knowing that the withdrawal of protection would result in an attack, nevertheless ordered the troops to leave the residence, it can reasonably be inferred that he intended the attack to occur. This would justify convicting him as an accomplice, described in the Indonesian Criminal Code as someone who 'intentionally provides assistance at the time the crime is committed' or 'intentionally provides the opportunity, means, or information for the commission of crime'.[44]

It is possible, of course, that the Court chose to predicate Soedjarwo's conviction on the omissions of his subordinates because it believed that this was the only theory of guilt supported by the evidence. Yet a careful review of the record shows that evidence contained in the pre-trial statements of victims of the attacks might also have supported the conviction of Soedjarwo for crimes committed by TNI members directly under his command. A number of East Timorese witnesses were summoned to testify at his trial, but none of them appeared. When it became clear that it would not be possible to receive live testimony from them, the Court first ruled that the pre-trial statements of six witnesses would be admitted in evidence, and then, inexplicably, determined that the testimony of all but one of those witnesses would be excluded from consideration. Only Bishop Belo's pre-trial statement, in which he did not address the identity of the perpetrators of the attacks, was used in the decision. The other five East Timorese victims, however, all implicated the security forces in the attack on the Diocese of Dili on 5 September.

The testimony of Nonato Soares, who had been a member of the TNI since 1977, and who was the village head of Bidau Lecidere Dili in 1999, was especially pertinent.

Soares stated that on the night of 4 September, following the announcement of the results of the vote, TNI members from the Dili District Military Command circled his house on motorcycles firing weapons. The next morning Soares, accompanied by his wife and five children, sought protection at the District Military Command's headquarters, but was told that he would not be safe there: TNI members and militias were hunting for him because of his purported ties with

[44] Article 56, *Kitab Undang-Undang Hukum Pidana* (Criminal Code).

Bishop Belo. He then took his family to the Diocese and was present when it was attacked, resulting in the deaths of nearly fifty people. Among the militiamen who were firing at the Diocese, he stated that he also saw armed and uniformed TNI and mobile police brigade members, although he could not recall any of them actually firing their weapons. Soares's own experience was also telling: a militiaman stabbed him in the stomach at the Diocese compound; then a member of the police rescued him and took him to the nearby port; then a TNI member threatened to kill both Soares and his wife, and hit him on the head with the butt of his pistol; then another militiamen stabbed him. Soares was eventually taken to a hospital and treated for his wounds.

The *Soares* and *Damiri* cases

The two judgments that went the furthest in establishing the institutional responsibility of the Indonesian state for the violence in East Timor were those against Abilio Soares and Adam Damiri. Notably, four of the five judges who decided the case against Soares were also on the panel that decided Damiri's guilt.

Abilio Soares was Governor of East Timor in 1999 and was charged in connection with all five incidents over which the Court exercised jurisdiction. He was convicted under the command responsibility doctrine for crimes by subordinates who held positions in the civilian administration, and also for crimes committed by the pro-integration militias.

Immediately after the referendum, Soares reactivated the Pam-Swakarsa, with money from the provincial budget (which he also controlled), with the ostensible purpose of staunching the bloodshed in East Timor. Yet the Court found that the Pam-Swakarsa were essentially a cover for the militias. They consisted of various pro-integration factions – including the Aitarak and Laksaur militias, operating under the umbrella of the PPI – which were heavily involved in terrorising the civilian population. The Court found that Soares exercised *de facto* authority over the PPI leadership through various forms of direct and indirect assistance; it also noted the 'emotional tie' between Soares and Eurico Guterres, the PPI's Deputy Commander.[45] In a significant move, the Court decided that killings and assaults were part of a planned strategy – orchestrated by the Governor and the regional government, and perpetrated by groups loyal to Indonesia – to ensure that Indonesian interests prevailed.

[45] Putusan N. 02/PID.HAM/AD.HOC/2002/PN.JKT PST, p. 86.

The trial of Adam Damiri, the last of the trials to be completed, went furthest in trying to establish the truth of the events in 1999. Damiri, a Major-General in the TNI, was the highest ranking military official charged with the commission of crimes in East Timor. At the time of the events charged against him, he was serving in the TNI's Territorial Command as Commander of the Udayana region, which included East Timor. The charges against him were read out in July of 2002, but the verdict was not announced until thirteen months later, more than twice the time allowed under the Human Rights Court Law. The delay in the completion of his trial was in part a result of the judges' efforts to obtain the testimony of East Timorese victims of the violence.

When it became clear that the prosecutors either could not or would not secure the attendance of East Timorese witnesses at the trials, the judges began pressing them to present the testimony of Bishop Belo and Father Rafael dos Santos via video-link.[46] The prosecutors – note, *prosecutors* – objected that it was expensive, and that the Indonesian Criminal Procedure Code did not recognise the taking of testimony from a remote location. But the judges prevailed, and Belo and Dos Santos were both finally scheduled to testify in December 2002. For reasons that have never been explained, Belo did not appear for the scheduled testimony. Dos Santos testified from Dili in January 2003. Additional efforts to obtain the testimony of East Timorese witnesses were unsuccessful, and the evidentiary phase of the trial was finally completed in April.

The prosecutors were scheduled to deliver their final plea and sentence recommendation that same month, but on the date of the hearing they announced that they were not prepared and the trial was postponed. Further postponements were ordered because Damiri, who was still an active-duty military officer, was fighting another separatist insurgency in the Indonesian province of Aceh. When the plea was finally delivered on 5 June, the prosecutors unexpectedly recommended that Damiri be acquitted and the charges dropped as guilt had not been proven.

This came as a surprise. Yet the *Damiri* prosecutors' conduct was of a piece with the prosecutors' conduct generally. Throughout the East Timor trials they had gone through the motions of prosecuting the defendants while scrupulously avoiding accusations of serious wrongdoing. Indeed, a visitor to the courtroom might have wondered which side the prosecutors were arguing. At the end of the process, after

46 'Hakim minta jaksa gelar "teleconference"' (Judges demand prosecutors arrange 'teleconference'), *Kompas* (13 November 2002).

international interest had shifted elsewhere, their recommendation of acquittal seemed to be borne of relief that the tiresome pretence of appearing to accuse the Indonesian military of crimes against humanity was no longer necessary. To drive home the point that they disliked being in the position of prosecuting the defendants as much as the defendants disliked being prosecuted, the prosecutors added the following statement at the end of their plea:

> It is hoped that what we have presented in Court as the ad-hoc prosecution team is not felt by the military community, and by the accused, Major General Adam Damiri in particular, as vengeful or as a response to the wishes or pressure from third parties, but merely the implementation of Law No. 16/2000 in furtherance of the mandate of MPR Decree XVII/98 and Presidential Decree No. 96/2001 [establishing the Court].[47]

The prosecutors' recommendation that the defendant be acquitted was almost certainly based on considerations of policy rather than evidence and dictated by senior officials in the office of Attorney General. It did not have the anticipated effect on the judges, however.

The Court finally met to announce the verdict against Damiri on 5 August 2003, and, as is typical of Indonesian criminal trials, the verdict was contained in a lengthy written Judgment that had to be read in its entirety in open court. To get through it, the five-member panel of judges read by turns as fast as they could from morning until afternoon. The Judgment included a detailed summary of the testimony of all the witnesses followed by an analysis of the legal issues. The whole thing was written in wordy and repetitive legalese, and those in attendance paid almost no attention to what the judges were saying until the verdict was due to be announced at the very end of the decision.

Midway through the delivery of the Judgment, just before midday, a car bomb exploded in front of the J.W. Marriott Hotel, five miles south of the courtroom. Twelve people were killed, and around 150 others were injured by the explosion. News of the blast reached the courtroom through journalists who were covering the trial, and some of them packed up their bags and left to report on the bombing. Early speculation that it was carried out by the Jemaah Islamiah, the same group responsible for the much deadlier bombing in Bali ten months earlier, was later shown to be correct.

It is unlikely that those attending the trial paused to consider the connection between what was happening in the courtroom and the

[47] Requisitor, No. 09/HAM/TIM TIM/02/2002, p. 106.

explosion of a bomb five miles away. But if the judges at the Damiri trial had wished to acquit, or simply wished to avoid rendering a conviction, the bombing at the Marriott made it that much easier for them to do so. Without the threat of international prosecutions the East Timor prosecutions would never have happened, but by 2003, the international community's interest in East Timor had evaporated. The Indonesian military, earlier condemned as the terroriser of East Timor, was now being recast as the holder of the 'front line in the war on terror'. After the attack on the Marriott Hotel, the judges could rest easy in the assurance that the United States and other members of the international community would not take a serious interest in their verdict on Adam Damiri.

The reading of the Judgment continued into the late afternoon. Those in attendance, who were mostly family and other supporters of the defendant, were in high spirits. The prosecutors' final plea seemed to guarantee an acquittal. When the diminutive female judge who chaired the panel announced at the end that Damiri had been found guilty and sentenced him to three years' imprisonment, the courtroom erupted with shock and anger. Damiri himself let out a roar of rage. In the commotion, one of the spectators was heard threatening to kill the ad hoc judge Rudy Rizky. There seemed to be the genuine likelihood of violence until one of the defence attorneys took control of the situation and the judges made their escape.

That night, Rudy Rizky checked into a Jakarta hotel rather than return to his home in Bandung. There was nothing in his conduct at the Damiri trial that would explain why the death threat was directed at him rather than one of the other judges, but a careful observer of the trials might have guessed why he was singled out. He had served on a total five trials, all of which returned verdicts of guilty. The only panel that entered a Judgment of conviction and did not include Rizky was the panel that decided the *Soedjarwo* case.

One of the most notable features of the *Damiri* Judgment was a simple and obvious point contained in the Court's evaluation of the credibility of the trial evidence. It observed that of the thirty witnesses who testified at the trial, twenty-four were either themselves defendants before the Human Rights Court or colleagues of the accused in the TNI. As a result, the Court noted, these witnesses gave evidence that tended to cover up or minimise Damiri's guilt. Although the possible bias of witnesses who were members of the Indonesian government or security forces was a matter of obvious significance that should have been addressed in all of the trials, the *Damiri* Judgment was the only one to have even mentioned the issue. In its treatment of other important issues, it also rejected the defence argument that Bishop Belo's statement must be disregarded because he did not testify in person before the Court, and, citing *Prosecutor* v. *Tadić*,[48] it ruled that the principle stated in the Indonesian Criminal Procedure Code that that *unus testis, nullus testis* (one witness is no proof) is not controlling in cases of gross human rights crimes.

Damiri was convicted based on his responsibility as a commander for crimes against humanity committed by members of the TNI. His guilt was based on having failed to investigate and punish crimes *after* they had been committed. (There was no suggestion that Damiri had a role in planning or directing the violence, or could have *prevented* the commission of the incidents charged against him.) The Court found that he either knew or should have known of the crimes committed based on evidence of reports of the incidents provided to him. One particularly damning piece of evidence, which showed that the highest levels of the TNI were not only aware of but also approved the military's support for the militias, was a telegram from Damiri's Chief-of-Staff, Brigadier-General Mahidin Simbolon, to the Army's head, General Wiranto, of 7 April, which described the events in Liquisa the previous day, and stated that the police and a TNI special forces unit had immediately 'backed-up' the pro-integration militia.[49] The involvement of the TNI in the crimes committed in Liquisa was corroborated by Father Rafael dos Santos, who testified that the attack was launched from the front of the Liquisa Military Command post, that tear gas canisters fired by security forces were aimed at the residence where refugees were gathered inside the church compound, and that specific individuals he knew to be TNI had joined with the Besi Merah Putih in carrying out the attack. The Court stated clearly and explicitly that members of the TNI joined with the pro-integration militia in attacking refugees inside the compound.

Regarding the other four incidents, the Court did not find direct TNI participation but stated that with respect to each, Damiri's subordinates were aware of the attacks but did not act to prevent them or to investigate and punish the perpetrators.[50] In support of these conclusions, it relied on factual findings made in cases tried before other panels. Although the eighteen defendants were tried in separate proceedings, the Court wrote, the serious human rights abuses committed in East Timor constituted a single case. In considering the case against Damiri, therefore, it could take

[48] Putusan N. 09/PID.HAM/AD.HOC/2002/PN.JKT PST, p. 159. [49] Ibid., p. 156.
[50] Ibid., pp. 171–172.

account of facts that were proven in any of the other trials. In the trial of Endar Priyanto, District Military Commander for Dili, the judges found that members of the Maubara Military Command attacked Carrascalão's house, but because those troops were not from Priyanto's unit he was acquitted. Likewise, in the trial of Soedjarwo, it was proven that his withdrawal of the troops guarding Bishop Belo's residence facilitated an attack, and that Brigadier-General Noer Muis was found to have made a culpable omission in failing to anticipate clashes and violence.

There was nothing speculative or daring in the *Damiri* Court's analysis of the facts or the law. But the Judgment frames the events of 1999 in a way that points a finger of blame directly at the Indonesian military. In a section discussing expert testimony introduced at the trial, it rejected the argument of one of the experts that the systematic element of crimes against humanity requires proof of a formal state policy to violate the rights of citizens. After making the legal point that the systematic element can be proven circumstantially, it stated that based on the pattern and scale of the attacks and destruction in East Timor, it was clear that the militias were not solely responsible for the violence. In a later section of the Judgment discussing the 'indications' from the trial evidence, the Court pointed to the military as the likely instigator of the violence. It is undeniable, it wrote, that the armed forces, especially the TNI, had played a major if not determinative role in directing the policy of integration of East Timor as Indonesia's twenty-seventh province.[51]

While it is true that Indonesia would never have conducted prosecutions for crimes committed in East Timor had it not been coerced into doing so by the threat of an international tribunal, this is not the whole story. Some of those involved in the process refused to bow to the inevitable. The judges who decided the *Damiri* case no doubt strongly suspected that he would never be punished for his crimes. Yet despite the close attention being paid to the trial by the military authorities, and the physical presence of the soldiers in the courtroom, and the lack of public backing at home, and the disintegration of support abroad, they went ahead and convicted him anyway.

Conclusion

None of the defendants was ever punished for their crimes. The guilty verdicts against the four military and police defendants were reversed by

[51] Ibid., pp. 156–157.

the High Court in August 2004, and these decisions were upheld by the Supreme Court. The conviction of Abilio Soares was initially upheld by both the High Court and the Supreme Court but finally overturned when the Supreme Court reviewed the case a second time. Eurico Guterres was unsuccessful in his initial appeals, but the Supreme Court invalidated the conviction in March 2008, citing newly discovered evidence presented by his lawyers.

The lesson that emerges from the proceedings before the Human Rights Court is the nearly total irrelevance of facts and law. Neither the reality of what happened in East Timor, nor the law on crimes against humanity or command responsibility, constrained the decisions. The most naked demonstration of this irrelevance was the decision by the Court that reversed Adam Damiri's conviction. Citing the testimony of twenty-two named witnesses, all of whom were members of the armed forces or the Indonesian government, the Court stated that it was not proven either that the people under his command and control were involved in the East Timor clashes or that he did not exercise effective control over those who were involved. It further noted that neither Damiri nor his subordinates were guilty of failing to prevent the clashes, because the geographical distribution of violence and the limited resources available to them made it impossible to do this.[52] Without considering the evidence supporting the verdict of guilty, it reversed Damiri's conviction.

One reason the Court deciding the appeal could so completely ignore what had happened at the trial was that its decision was never made public. A court need not feel constrained to reconcile its decisions with an external understanding of law or fact if the grounds for its decisions are not subject to scrutiny. Of course, the *Damiri* appeal was the focus of greater interest than most decisions, so the Court was particularly concerned that it not be made public. What happened in this case is not out of the ordinary, though. There is no tradition of transparency in the Indonesian legal system and no norm that judicial decisions should be made public. The presumption is that court judgments are the internal work of the judiciary; no explanation is required for declining to make them available.

The sorry state of the Indonesian legal system is partly to blame for the failure of the East Timor prosecutions. But the circumstances in which the trials were conducted would strain any legal system. The proceedings

[52] Putusan No. 01 PID.HAM/AD.HOC/2004/PT.DKI, pp. 20–21.

before the Human Rights Court come into clearer focus when viewed in the context of the subsequent story of Munir Said Thalib, a member of KPP-HAM and founder of the human rights organisation KontraS. On 7 September 2004, Munir boarded a Garuda flight bound for Amsterdam, where he was to begin a graduate programme at the University of Utrecht. He became ill during the flight and died two hours before the plane landed. The Dutch authorities carried out an autopsy and found that he had died of arsenic poisoning. An off-duty Garuda pilot named Pollycarpus Priyanto was tried and convicted for his murder in 2005.

Few believe that Pollycarpus had acted on his own. Evidence from the trial and other sources pointed to officials within the State Intelligence Agency, Badan Intelijen Nasional. In 2008 Muchdi Purwoprandjono, the former deputy chief of Badan Intelijen Nasional, was charged with having solicited Pollycarpus to murder Munir. Muchdi, a Major-General in the Indonesian Army, had been the Commander of KOPPASUS during the months preceding the resignation of Suharto in 1998. It was believed that Muchdi killed Munir in retaliation for his having exposed KOPPASUS's role in the disappearance of democracy activists under his watch. In December 2008, Muchdi was tried in South Jakarta District Court for the murder of Munir. He was found not guilty.

9

Asia as the laboratory of the superior responsibility doctrine

REHAN ABEYRATNE[1]

On 7 December 1945, Yamashita Tomoyuki, the Commanding General of the Fourteenth Army Group of the Imperial Japanese Army, was found guilty by an American court for atrocities carried out under his command in the Philippines towards the end of the Second World War. At his trial, Yamashita did not deny that many of these crimes had occurred; he claimed instead that under American assault he had lost contact with his own troops.[2] His defence counsel argued that there was no evidence that he had either ordered or known of the crimes being committed, and could not be held criminally responsible for them.[3] The Court disagreed and found him guilty on the then-novel theory of failing to exercise his authority over subordinates who had committed major crimes.

While the *Yamashita* Judgment has been criticised for its indistinct *mens rea*, and lack of legal precedent, it is nonetheless an important milestone in the development of international criminal law. Since then, subsequent international criminal tribunals have looked to the superior responsibility doctrine, with refinements and clarifications, to hold leaders accountable for the crimes of their subordinates. Today, it is a well-established mode of liability, enshrined in various courts' founding documents, including the Statute of the International Criminal Court.[4]

The *Yamashita* Judgment is significant not only for this doctrinal innovation but also for the context in which it was decided. The development of international criminal law is often viewed through a

[1] The author wishes to thank Kirsten Sellars for invaluable guidance, and C. Mohanakrishna for excellent research assistance.

[2] United Nations War Crimes Commission, *Law reports of trials of war criminals*, 15 vols. (London: HMSO, 1947–1949), vol. 4, p. 27.

[3] Ibid., vol. 4, pp. 28, 29.

[4] Article 28, Rome Statute of the International Criminal Court: treaties.un.org.

Eurocentric lens, with a heavy emphasis on jurisprudence arising from the Nuremberg trials, and, more recently, the Yugoslavia Tribunal and the other Hague-based courts. The spotlight of international criminal law jurisprudence and scholarship is currently pointed at the International Criminal Court's investigations in Africa.[5] By contrast, the Asian experience is somewhat neglected. Yet *Yamashita* and other proceedings serve as a reminder that Asia too has been a testing ground for the development of international criminal law.

This chapter, which examines the development of superior responsibility since the Second World War, shows that the doctrine has largely emerged out of trials convened in Asia and dealing with wars that have taken place in Asia.[6] Beginning with *Yamashita*, it shows how superior responsibility was extended to civilian leaders at the Tokyo Tribunal, clarified in the subsequent Toyoda trial, and, after the Vietnam War, refined by 1977's Additional Protocol I to the 1949 Geneva Conventions. More recently, the Extraordinary Chambers in the Courts of Cambodia (ECCC) has applied superior responsibility to former leaders of the Khmer Rouge. Given that the doctrine was announced, refined and crystallised into its current form in Asia, the chapter concludes with some thoughts as to why the region has served as a laboratory for this important idea.

The case against Yamashita

General Yamashita was arraigned before a United States Military Commission in Manila on 8 October 1945. The charges against him stated:

> Tomoyuki Yamashita, General Imperial Japanese Army, between 9th October, 1944 and 2nd September, 1945, at Manila and at other places in the Philippine Islands, while a commander of armed forces of Japan at war with the United States of America and its allies, unlawfully disregarded and failed to discharge his duty as commander to control the operations of the members of his command, permitting them to commit brutal atrocities and other high crimes against people of the United States and of its allies and dependencies, particularly the Philippines; and he, General Tomoyuki Yamashita, thereby violated the laws of war.[7]

5 A. Triponel and S. Pearson, 'African states and the International Criminal Court: a silent revolution in international criminal law', *Journal of Law & Social Challenges* 12 (2010), pp. 65–106.

6 For an account of the development of the doctrine worldwide, see W.H. Parks, 'Command responsibility for war crimes', *Military Law Review* 62 (1973), 1–104.

7 UNWCC, *Law reports*, vol. 4, pp. 3–4.

In addition to these general charges, the prosecution, led by Captain Robert Kerr, submitted a Bill of Particulars that accused Yamashita of committing sixty-four specific offences, followed by a Supplemental Bill of Particulars that set forth an additional fifty-nine allegations. These covered the starvation, execution or massacre of civilian internees and prisoners of war; the torture, rape, murder and mass execution of civilians; and the burning and destruction of property including churches, schools and hospitals. The prosecutors sought first to establish that the crimes committed by Japanese forces under Yamashita's command had been widespread and systematic. Based on this, it pursued two arguments: first, that Yamashita had secretly ordered his forces to carry out the crimes, and, second, if he had not issued such orders, he had wilfully 'permitted' the commission of crimes by failing to exercise control over the forces under his command.

The prosecution lawyers gravitated towards the more straightforward, and less controversial, position that Yamashita had simply ordered his forces to commit the atrocities. They stated that these crimes – which they contended were carefully planned and methodically executed – were *commanded.*[8] But where was the evidence? They cited, among others, Narciso Lapus, private secretary to the by-then deceased Filipino nationalist General Artemio Ricarte, who claimed that Ricarte had told him that Yamashita had ordered all his commanders to destroy Manila and 'wipe out the whole Philippines, if possible'.[9] They also cited Joaquin Galang, a friend of Ricarte, who stated that Ricarte had asked Yamashita to rescind that order, and that Yamashita had refused.[10] But this second-hand evidence was refutable: the defence produced Ricarte's grandson and interpreter, Bislumino Romero, who denied that the latter exchange between Ricarte and Yamashita had taken place.[11]

So, as well as alleging that Yamashita had *ordered* the commission of atrocities, the prosecutors advanced a more innovative argument: if the atrocities had occurred, someone had *permitted* them to occur.[12] Who was that? 'Obviously the man whose duty it was to prevent such an orgy of planned and obviously deliberate murder, rape and arson – the commander of those troops!'[13] According to this theory, Yamashita had failed to uphold his responsibility as a commander to protect non-combatants – a responsibility, the prosecution averred, equal to his responsibility to combat the enemy.[14] Compelled by laws such as

[8] Ibid., p. 30. [9] Ibid., p. 19. [10] Ibid. [11] Ibid., p. 21. [12] Ibid., p. 84. [13] Ibid.
[14] Ibid., p. 30.

Article 1 annexed to the Hague Convention IV (requiring belligerents to be 'commanded by a person responsible for his subordinates'),[15] the prosecution stated that

> [A]ny man who, having the control of the operation of a dangerous instrumentality, fails to exercise that degree of care which under the circumstances should be exercised to protect third persons, is responsible for the consequences of his dereliction of duty. We say, apply that in this case![16]

Following up with quotes from Moore's *International Law Digest* (unless a commanding officer can control his soldiers, 'he is unfit to command them') and Wharton's *Criminal Evidence* (if a person's ignorance is negligent or culpable 'then ignorance is no defence'),[17] the prosecution claimed that if Yamashita did not know about the crimes, he, as the commander, *ought to have known* about them, and taken measures to prevent them. His failure to exercise his authority was tantamount to a violation of the laws of war.

The defence counsel, led by Colonel Harry Clarke, did not deny that most of the atrocities had occurred, but they challenged the idea that Yamashita should be held responsible for either acting or failing to act. He neither ordered, nor 'permitted', nor even knew about the atrocities, because the American assault had cut him off from his own forces. How, under battle conditions, could he have acquired this knowledge? Furthermore, the 'Rape of Manila', which formed the core of the charge against him, was carried out by *naval* troops, led by officers unknown to him, far from his own position, who had only been added to his command the previous month, and over whom he had little authority. As a telling example, Yamashita's Chief-of-Staff Mutō Akira stated that he was unaware of Yamashita's order to destroy Manila – he claimed instead that Yamashita had ordered the Japanese evacuation of the city, but, as a result of insubordination and lack of transport, this was not carried out.[18]

The defence's case did not persuade the Commission, presided over by Major-General Russell B. Reynolds. Instead of focusing on Yamashita's lack of knowledge (as the defence might have hoped), it concentrated on the widespread perpetration of the crimes, and Yamashita's failure to exert control over his troops. The findings, delivered on 7 December 1945, stated, '[W]here murder and rape and vicious, revengeful actions are widespread offences, and there is no effective attempt by a commander to discover and control the criminal acts, such a commander may be

[15] Hague Convention IV, Annex, Article 1 (1907).

[16] UNWCC, *Law reports*, vol. 4, p. 32. [17] Ibid., p. 33. [18] Ibid., p. 21.

held responsible, even criminally liable, for the lawless acts of his troops, depending upon their nature and the circumstances surrounding them.'[19] There was nothing new about holding a commander to account for issuing criminal orders to subordinates – various national field manuals, including the US Army's *The rules of land warfare*, addressed precisely this issue. What was novel was holding a commander responsible for his failure to compel subordinates to desist from committing international crimes. Focusing on *actus reus*, but not spelling out *mens rea*, the Commission concluded that atrocities had been committed throughout the Philippines, and that Yamashita, who had 'failed to provide effective control' over his troops, was guilty as charged, and sentenced to death.[20] It was this stark decision that gave birth to the modern doctrine of command responsibility for international crimes.

Stone, Rutledge, Murphy

Yamashita's defence team did not let the matter rest. It petitioned the US Supreme Court, which reviewed the case, *In re Yamashita*, on 7–8 January 1946. The main substantive issue was whether, as was claimed, 'the charge preferred against petitioner fails to charge him with a violation of the law of war'.[21] As Chief Justice Harlan Stone's majority opinion indicated, this issue was bound up with the question of superior responsibility. Since the Commission had found Yamashita guilty even though he had not ordered his subordinates to commit the crimes, the question, Stone stated, was 'whether the law of war imposes on an army commander a duty to take such appropriate measures as are within his power to control the troops under his command for the prevention of the specified acts which are violations of the law of war'.[22] He argued that the laws of war presupposed this,[23] citing the aforementioned Article 1 annexed to Hague Convention IV (requiring commanders to be responsible for their subordinates), as well as other provisions within the Geneva and Hague Conventions (compelling commanders to uphold the conventions and occupying forces to stay within the law).[24] The purpose of the laws of war, Stone concluded, was 'to protect civilian populations and prisoners of war from brutality', and that this would 'largely be defeated if the commander of an invading army could, with impunity, neglect to take reasonable measures for their protection'.[25] The Supreme Court's

[19] Ibid., p. 35. [20] Ibid. [21] *In re Yamashita*, 327 US 1 (1946), p. 6. [22] Ibid., pp. 14–15.
[23] Ibid., p. 15. [24] Ibid., pp. 15–16. [25] Ibid., p. 15.

majority opinion thus gave its legal imprimatur to the Commission's approach to superior responsibility.

In separate dissents, Justices Wiley Rutledge and Frank Murphy took issue with Stone's analysis. Rutledge's dissent focused on procedural defects in the Commission's operation, but also commented on the vagueness of the judgment against Yamashita. He wrote,

> [T]he commission's ultimate findings draw no express conclusion of knowledge, but state only two things: (1) the fact of widespread atrocities and crimes; (2) that petitioner 'failed to provide effective control . . . as required by the circumstances.' This vagueness, if not vacuity . . . affects the very gist of the offense – whether that was willful, informed and intentional omission to restrain and control troops known by petitioner to be committing crimes, or was only a negligent failure on his part to discover this and take whatever measures he then could to stop the conduct.[26]

Murphy took a different line in his dissent. First, giving credence to the defence petition, he observed that nowhere in the charge or bills of particulars 'was it alleged that the petitioner personally committed any of the atrocities, or that he ordered their commission, or that he had any knowledge of the commission thereof by members of his command'.[27] He added that the Military Commission's findings 'bear out this absence of any direct personal charge against the petitioner'.[28] Second, he pointed out the unprecedented nature of the superior responsibility theory advanced by *Yamashita*. In his view, international law made 'no attempt to define the duties of a commander of an army under constant and overwhelming assault, nor does it impose liability under such circumstances for failure to meet the ordinary responsibilities of command'.[29] The international conventions cited by Chief Justice Stone were thus not relevant to *Yamashita* because they did not pertain to commanders 'under constant and devastating attacks by a superior reinvading force'.[30] Murphy was not opposed to the punishment of commanders, but argued that charges against them had to be made in accordance with established international law: the charge against Yamashita, by contrast, was 'clearly without precedent in international law or in the annals of recorded military history'.[31]

The US Supreme Court rejected the defence petition on 4 February 1946 and, following an unsuccessful appeal to General MacArthur to commute his sentence, Yamashita was hanged on 23 February. The approach taken

[26] Ibid., pp. 51–52. [27] Ibid., p. 34. [28] Ibid. [29] Ibid., p. 35. [30] Ibid., pp. 36–37.
[31] Ibid., p. 40.

to superior responsibility at his trial has been the subject of much criticism. First, it has been argued that the Commission's *mens rea* standard was too harsh – adopting a strict liability standard by which a commander would be held criminally responsible for the crimes of troops under his authority regardless of the circumstances.[32] In reality, though, the Judgment did not set out such an exacting standard. It made clear that the standard was context-specific, whereby a commander 'may be held responsible . . . for the lawless acts of his troops, depending upon their nature and the circumstances surrounding them'.[33] Noting that these crimes were widespread and methodically supervised, it did not hold Yamashita strictly liable but rather imputed knowledge to him from these circumstances.[34]

A second criticism is that the Commission's standard was too vague. In his dissent, Justice Rutledge argued that it did not spell out in any detail, or with clear constituent elements, when commanders would be held liable for their subordinates' crimes.[35] The fogginess on *mens rea* was especially notable. The third criticism is that the Commission did not base its superior responsibility doctrine on established legal authority. While the Judgment did not cite international legal sources, Chief Justice Stone cited articles from the Hague and Geneva Conventions in his Supreme Court opinion. In his dissent, Justice Murphy replied that these provisions were not relevant to the adverse battle conditions in which Yamashita was operating, and did not hold a commander *criminally* responsible for crimes that had not been ordered, but which had been committed by subordinates in such circumstances.[36] This criticism of the *Yamashita* Judgment has some merit.

Broadening the doctrine at Tokyo

If the *Yamashita* trial first articulated the doctrine of superior responsibility, two trials in Tokyo clarified this message shortly after. The first of these was the International Military Tribunal for the Far East, before which all twenty-eight Japanese leaders were charged with conspiring to commit and committing crimes against peace; and many with murder, war crimes and, nominally, crimes against humanity.[37] The final count,

[32] See, for example, R.L. Lael, *The Yamashita precedent: war crimes and command responsibility* (Wilmington: Scholarly Resources Inc., 1982), p. 141.

[33] UNWCC, *Law reports*, vol. 4, p. 35. [34] Parks, 'Command responsibility', 87.

[35] *In re Yamashita*, 327 US, pp. 51–52. [36] Ibid., pp. 36–38.

[37] International Military Tribunal for the Far East, *The Tokyo major war crimes trial*, R.J. Pritchard (ed.), 124 vols. (Lewiston: Edwin Mellen Press, 1998), Indictment, vol. 2, pp. 1–14.

Count 55, which addressed breaches of the laws of war in the treatment of prisoners, raised the issue of superior responsibility. Twenty-six of the accused were charged with having, by virtue of their offices, 'deliberately and recklessly disregarded their legal duty to take adequate steps to secure the observance and prevent breaches thereof, and thereby violated the laws of war'.[38]

The Majority Judgment set forth the legal standard that it would apply to the accused on Count 55. Defendants would be held criminally liable only if they 'had knowledge that such crimes were being committed, and having such knowledge they failed to take such steps as were within their power to prevent the commission of such crimes in the future'.[39] Liability would also attach to defendants who 'failed to acquire such knowledge'.[40] This is similar to the *Yamashita* concept of superior responsibility, though it made clear that negligence was the operative *mens rea* standard.

The Tribunal also expanded the doctrine to encompass superiors who improperly relied on assurances from others that crimes were not taking place. It stated that a commander would not be exonerated if he had accepted the assurances from other commanders with more direct control 'if having regard to the position of those others, to the frequency of reports of such crimes, or to any other circumstances he should have been put upon further enquiry as to whether those assurances were true or untrue'.[41] In a nod to *Yamashita*, the Tribunal further noted, 'That crimes are notorious, numerous and widespread as to time and place are matters to be considered in imputing knowledge.'[42]

The Tribunal found several of the accused guilty under Count 55. Significantly, and for the first time after the Second World War, this included civilian leaders outside the chain of military command. Thus, Shigemitsu Mamoru, who served as Foreign Minister from April 1943 to April 1945, was found guilty for failing to investigate atrocities that were reported to him by agencies other than the military. The Tribunal noted that the Geneva Conventions' 'protecting powers' sent 'grave protests' to the Japanese Foreign Office regarding, *inter alia*, the inhumane treatment of prisoners of war and the powers' lack of access to them.[43] It found that Shigemitsu had not taken adequate measures in response to this information: '[H]e, as a member of the government, bore overhead responsibility for the welfare of the prisoners. He should have pressed the matter, if

[38] Ibid., p. 13. [39] IMTFE, Majority Judgment, vol. 101, pp. 48444–48445.
[40] Ibid., p. 48445. [41] Ibid. [42] Ibid. [43] IMTFE, Majority Judgment, vol. 103, p. 49829.

necessary to the point of resigning, in order to quit himself of a responsibility which he suspected was not being discharged.'[44]

Hirota Kōki, Foreign Minister during the 'Rape of Nanking' in December 1937 to February 1938, was found guilty on a similar theory. Hirota, on hearing of the atrocities, had sought and received assurances from the War Ministry that the atrocities would be stopped, but reports of further abuses continued to come in for at least another month after that. The Tribunal therefore held that, '*Hirota* was derelict in his duty in not insisting before the Cabinet that immediate action be taken to put an end to the atrocities, failing any other action open to him to bring about the same result. He was content to rely on assurances which he knew were not being implemented ... His inaction amounted to criminal negligence.'[45]

These two verdicts show that the Tribunal not only applied the doctrine to civilian leaders but also held these leaders criminally liable for failing to investigate atrocities, or for relying on false assurances that atrocities had stopped. Moreover, the crimes for which they were convicted were committed by troops emphatically *not* under their control. Compare Hirota, for instance, to Yamashita: the Tokyo Tribunal held the former, as Foreign Minister based in Tokyo, liable for crimes committed by military forces commanded by others, in China, another country altogether, while the Commission held Yamashita liable for crimes committed by troops under his command in the same country. Given the criticisms levelled at the Tokyo Tribunal on this point, more recent jurisprudence acknowledges that the superior responsibility doctrine 'extends to civilian superiors only to the extent that they exercise a degree of control over their subordinates which is similar to that of military commanders'.[46]

The Tokyo Tribunal's verdicts with respect to military leaders, however, closely tracked the *Yamashita* Judgment. Kimura Heitarō was Commander-in-Chief of the Burma Area Army from August 1944 until Japan's surrender in 1945.[47] The evidence showed that soldiers under his command had mistreated prisoners in Burma, including on the Burma-Siam Railway. Kimura did not deny this, but argued in his defence that on his arrival to Burma he issued orders to his troops 'to conduct themselves in a proper soldierly manner and to refrain from ill-treating prisoners'.[48]

[44] Ibid., p. 49831. [45] Ibid., p. 49791.

[46] *Prosecutor* v. *Delalić, Mucić, Delić and Landžo* (*Celebici* case), IT-96-21-T, Trial Chamber Judgment (16 November 1998), par. 378.

[47] IMTFE, Majority Judgment, vol. 103, p. 49809. [48] Ibid.

The Tribunal found this insufficient, noting: 'The duty of an army commander in such circumstances is not discharged by the mere issue of routine orders ... His duty is to take such steps and to issue such orders as will prevent thereafter the commission of war crimes.'[49] As with Yamashita, Kimura's proximity to the crimes militated against him. The Tribunal found that he was negligent in his duty to enforce the laws of war '[i]n view of the nature and extent of the ill-treatment of prisoners, in many cases on a large scale within a few miles of his headquarters'.[50]

One of the most interesting verdicts against a military officer was issued in the case of Mutō Akira, who served as an officer on General Matsui Iwane's staff in China from November 1937 to July 1938 (the period covering the 'Rape of Nanking'), and later as General Yamashita's Chief-of-Staff in the Philippines, from October 1944 until September 1945. On Nanking, the Tribunal found Mutō's superior, Matsui, guilty under Count 55, because he had failed to stop his troops from committing atrocities,[51] but it found Mutō not guilty on this charge, because he had occupied a 'subordinate position', and therefore 'could take no steps' to prevent the crimes taking place, even though he knew of them.[52] On the Philippines, though, it was a different story for Mutō, who was found guilty under Count 55 for failing to stop atrocities committed by Japanese troops under Yamashita's command. With respect to these crimes, the Tribunal held that

> During his tenure of office as such Chief-of-Staff a campaign of massacre, torture and other atrocities was waged by the Japanese troops on the civilian population, and prisoners of war and civilian internees were starved, tortured and murdered. *Muto* shares responsibility for these gross breaches of the Laws of War. We reject his defense that he knew nothing of these occurrences. It is wholly incredible.[53]

This finding is difficult to square with the Tribunal's earlier conclusion that Mutō had no power to halt the atrocities at Nanking. While it observed that he had greater power under Yamashita than he did under Matsui, it is also likely that it was unwilling to contradict the *Yamashita* Judgment, which imputed knowledge to Yamashita, and found him guilty – despite his professed ignorance of the crimes.

The Toyoda acquittal

The trial of Admiral Toyoda Soemu, which opened in Tokyo on 29 October 1948, added further refinements of the doctrine. Toyoda was

[49] Ibid. [50] Ibid. [51] Ibid., p. 49816. [52] Ibid., p. 49820. [53] Ibid., pp. 49820–49821.

Japan's highest-ranking naval officer during the latter stages of the Second World War, being the Commander-in-Chief of the Japanese Combined Fleet from May 1944 onwards, and then Chief of the Naval General Staff from May 1945 to the end of the war. Like Yamashita, Toyoda was charged under a theory of superior responsibility for crimes that occurred in the Philippines, particularly for the atrocities committed in Manila in February 1945. Because the charges were similar to those against Yamashita, the Tribunal reviewed the evidence from that trial and from thirty-one other trials that it believed might be relevant in Toyoda's case.[54] Recall that one of the principal contentions of Yamashita's defence team was that Yamashita had no authority or control over the naval land forces that committed many of the atrocities in Manila.[55] Defence counsel for Toyoda seized on this point and asked the Tribunal to take judicial notice of the *Yamashita* Judgment, which had concluded that Yamashita (not Toyoda) was responsible for the crimes of the naval forces in Manila.[56]

The quasi-international Tribunal, presided over by an Australian judge, John O'Brien, but hearing an American case, largely agreed with the *Yamashita* Judgment's findings on the chain of command in the Philippines: 'The Tribunal is convinced – as were the Commissions in the trials of Yamashita, Muto and Yokoyama, with the conclusions of which this Tribunal can find no point of major issue – that these navy personnel were both legally and in fact commanded by the Japanese Army at the times and under the conditions here under consideration.'[57] On 6 September 1949, the Tribunal therefore acquitted Toyoda of all charges. In doing so, it also provided a unified standard of superior responsibility that took into account the reasoning and judgments of previous cases, including those from Nuremberg. It stated:

> In the simplest language it may be said that this Tribunal believes the principle of command responsibility to be that, if this accused knew, or should by the exercise of ordinary diligence have learned, of the commission by his subordinates, immediate or otherwise, of the atrocities proved beyond a shadow of a doubt before this Tribunal or of the existence of a routine which would countenance such, and, by his failure to take any

[54] Parks, 'Command responsibility', 70–71. [55] UNWCC, *Law reports*, vol. 4, pp. 21.

[56] Trial transcript, *United States* v. *Soemu Toyoda* (Tokyo: General Headquarters, Supreme Commander for the Allied Powers, 1949), pp. 1119–1123.

[57] 'Judgement of the GHQ war crimes tribunal in the case of *U.S.A.* v. *Toyoda Soemu*' (Tokyo: General Headquarters, Supreme Commander for the Allied Powers, 1949), p. 5011.

> action to punish the perpetrators, permitted the atrocities to continue, he has failed in his performance of his duty as a commander and must be punished.[58]

This was the clearest statement on superior responsibility from any post-war case: it clarified the *mens rea* required (namely, that a superior 'knew, or should by the exercise of ordinary diligence have learned'); and it specified that a superior would be punished if 'by his failure to take any action to punish the perpetrators [he] permitted the atrocities to continue'.[59]

The Medina trial and 'knowledge'

Despite a four-decade pause in international criminal law after the conclusion of the post-war trials, important doctrinal developments of superior responsibility took place in the 1970s, again spurred by events in Asia – this time, the Vietnam War. But while the post-war cases were defined by judicial activism, the later initiatives are characterised by judicial retrenchment.

The *Medina* trial[60] arose out of the My Lai massacre, in which a US Army Company under the command of Captain Ernest Medina killed between 175 and 400 unarmed civilians, raped several women, and set fire to the hamlet of My Lai on the morning of 16 March 1968.[61] Even though there was no proof that Medina intentionally ordered his soldiers to kill non-combatants, it was established by the evidence that he was only a few hundred yards away while most of the crimes were carried out.[62] The prosecution, invoking the command responsibility doctrine, charged Medina, among other things, with intentional murder – on the basis that he knew that his subordinates were committing crimes, and that he had the means to prevent them from doing so but chose not to. In his testimony, Medina admitted that his company had burned My Lai, but denied seeing 'any indiscriminate killing' of Vietnamese people.[63]

[58] Ibid., p. 5006. [59] Ibid. [60] *United States* v. *Medina* CM 427 162 (ACMR 1971).

[61] For casualty figures, see *Report of the Department of the Army review of the preliminary investigations into the My Lai incident* (Washington, DC: Department of the Army, 1970), pp. 2–3.

[62] W.G. Eckhardt, 'Command criminal responsibility: a plea for a workable standard', *Military Law Review* 97 (1982), 12.

[63] Testimony of Captain Ernest L. Medina, pp. 268, 270: www.internationalcrimesdatabase.org/Case/1132/Medina.

This, Chief Prosecutor William Eckhart later wrote, was a 'classic case of command criminal responsibility'.[64]

The Presiding Judge, Kenneth Howard, thought otherwise. He rejected the theory and reduced the charges to involuntary manslaughter:

> [A] military superior in command is responsible for and required, in the performance of his command duties, to make certain the proper performance by his subordinates of their duties as assigned by him … Furthermore, a commander is also responsible if he has actual knowledge that troops or other persons subject to his control are in the process of committing or are about to commit a war crime and he wrongfully fails to take the necessary and reasonable steps to insure compliance with the law of war. You will observe that these legal requirements placed upon a commander *require actual knowledge plus a wrongful failure to act. Thus mere presence at the scene without knowledge will not suffice.* That is, the commander-subordinate relationship alone will not allow an inference of knowledge. While it is not necessary that a commander actually see an atrocity being committed, *it is essential that he know that his subordinates are in the process of committing atrocities or are about to commit atrocities.*[65]

This standard of superior responsibility was substantially more favourable to the defendant than that to which Yamashita and other Japanese defendants had been held, because it required a commander to have actual knowledge of crimes occurring under his command: no liability attached to commanders who 'should have known' of their subordinates' crimes. The discrepancy between *Yamashita* and *Medina* on this issue did not go unremarked: Medina's attorney F. Lee Bailey said, 'I don't think that what is done to a jap hanged in the heat of vengeance after World War II can be done to an American on an imputed theory of responsibility.'[66]

The US Army's manual – *The law of land warfare* (1956) – set out guidelines to the American forces. The section on 'Responsibility for acts of subordinates' held that a commander was responsible 'if he has actual knowledge, or should have knowledge, through reports received by him or through other means, that troops or other persons subject to his control are about to commit or have committed a war crime and he fails to take the necessary and reasonable steps to insure compliance with the law of war or to punish violators thereof'.[67] This statement of superior

[64] Eckhardt, 'Command criminal responsibility', 13. [65] Ibid., 15. Emphasis added.

[66] L.P. Rockwood, *Walking away from Nuremberg: just war and the doctrine of command responsibility* (Amherst: University of Massachusetts Press, 2007), p. 126.

[67] Department of the Army field manual *FM 27–10: the law of land warfare* (Washington, DC, US Department of the Army, 1956), par. 501.

responsibility, particularly the phrase 'should have knowledge, through reports received by him or through other means', drew from both *Yamashita* and the refinements made by subsequent post-war judgments. But while *The law of land warfare* aimed to provide 'authoritative guidance' to American forces on their obligations in both treaty and customary international law,[68] it did not create any basis for criminal liability in domestic courts martial.[69]

Instead, in keeping with American military practices, all the charges against Medina arose out of the Uniform Code of Military Justice, a domestic American statute, and not from international criminal law. The Uniform Code does not set forth a clear standard of superior responsibility, and, as Eckhardt explained, the prosecution had to resort to 'bootstrapping' from other sources to establish this standard.[70] Moreover, the Code requires knowledge to hold defendants accountable. Medina was charged under Article 119 for involuntary manslaughter, and under Article 77 as a 'principal'. Article 77 imposes criminal liability as a 'principal' on any individual who '(1) commits an offense punishable by this chapter, or aids, abets, counsels, commands, or procures its commission; or (2) causes an act to be done which if directly performed by him would be punishable by this chapter'.[71] This implies a knowledge requirement and does not hold commanders liable for their omissions.

The 1969 *Manual for courts-martial United States*, which provides commentary on the Uniform Code, nevertheless suggests that principal liability can be imposed in certain situations where the accused had a duty to intervene but failed to do so. It states, 'While merely witnessing a crime without intervention does not make a person a party to its commission, if he had a duty to interfere and his noninterference was designed by him to operate and did operate as an encouragement to or protection of the perpetrator, he is a principal.'[72] This explanation perhaps clarifies the standard used in the Medina trial. Captain Medina would have had a duty to intervene and prevent crimes occurring under his command only if he knew of or encouraged their commission.

68 Ibid., par. 1.

69 M.L. Smidt, 'Yamashita, Medina, and beyond: command responsibility in contemporary military operations', *Military Law Review* 164 (2000), 186.

70 Eckhardt, 'Command criminal responsibility', 14.

71 Article 77, Uniform Code of Military Justice, reprinted in *Manual for courts-martial United States* (Washington, DC: US Government Printing Office, rev. edn., 1969), appx. 2, p. 'A2-27'.

72 Ibid., chap. 28, p. '28-4'.

As Judge Howard later explained, '[I]f the commander gains actual knowledge and does nothing, then he may become a principal in the eyes of the law in that by his inaction he manifests an aiding and encouraging support to his troops, thereby indicating that he joins in their activity and wishes the end product to come about.'[73] The Court found that the evidence did not prove that Medina had such knowledge and acquitted him of all charges.

Thus, relying on the Uniform Code, *Medina* announced a new standard of superior responsibility. The fact that the American military applied a less burdensome *mens rea* standard on one of its own citizens than it did on Japanese commanders in the post-war tribunals provoked much criticism. One of the most damning statements came from retired US Army Brigadier-General Telford Taylor, who had served as the Chief Prosecutor at the 'subsequent' American trials at Nuremberg. The *New York Times* quoted him saying in a TV interview that if America's Vietnam War commanders, such as the US Army's Chief-of-Staff General William Westmoreland, were held to the same standard as Yamashita, 'there would be a very strong possibility that they would come to the same end as he did'.[74]

Stung by this criticism, the US Army instructed Lieutenant General William Peers to head the formal inquiry into the My Lai massacre. After a detailed investigation that included visits to the site, testimony from military personnel and interviews with survivors, Peers produced a Department of the Army Report on the 'My Lai incident' on 14 March 1970.[75] Later, introducing the book *The My Lai inquiry*, he wrote,

> The My Lai incident was a black mark in the annals of American military history. In analyzing the entire episode, we found that the principal breakdown was in leadership. Failures occurred at every level within the chain of command, from individual noncommissioned-officer squad leaders to the command group of the division. It was an illegal operation in violation of military regulations and of human rights, starting with the planning, continuing through the brutal, destructive acts of many of the men who were involved.[76]

[73] K.A. Howard, 'Command responsibility for war crimes', *Journal of Public Law* 21 (1972), 22.

[74] N. Sheehan, 'Taylor says by Yamashita ruling Westmoreland may be guilty', *New York Times* (9 January 1971), 3.

[75] *Report of the Department of the Army review of the preliminary investigations into the My Lai incident* (Washington, DC: Department of the Army, 1970).

[76] R.W. Peers, *The My Lai inquiry* (New York: Norton, c. 1979), p. xi.

General Westmoreland responded promptly to the 'Peers Inquiry'. In April 1970, a month after the report was released, he directed the Army War College Commandant to initiate a study that would examine 'several unfavourable events' that called into question the 'discipline, integrity, morality, ethics, and professionalism of the Army'.[77] This led to the War College's *Study on military professionalism*, which accused Army leaders and the institution itself of failing to live up to its own standards.

The Geneva Protocol's approach

It was against the backdrop of the Vietnam War and its aftermath that the United States sent a delegation to the Geneva Diplomatic Conference (1974–1977), which was convened to modify the Geneva Conventions of 1949 in order to more effectively protect non-combatants, and to address guerrilla warfare and non-international armed conflicts. The four conference sessions resulted in two draft Additional Protocols, the first addressing the protection of victims of international armed conflicts, and the second the protection of victims of non-international armed conflicts.[78] The American experience in Vietnam cast a long shadow over the proceedings and strongly influenced the US delegation's approach to superior responsibility. In a turnaround from *Medina*, it pushed – and eventually won support – for a slightly more rigorous version of military command responsibility deriving from antecedents in international law.

Two articles in the Protocol address directly this issue: Article 86 ('Failure to act') and Article 87 ('Duties of commanders').[79] Draft Article 76, which became Article 86, purported to codify the Nuremberg and Tokyo standard of superior responsibility, not the *Medina* standard. It read:

> 1. The High Contracting Parties undertake to repress breaches of the Conventions or of the present Protocol resulting from a failure to perform a duty to act.
> 2. The fact that a breach of the Conventions or of the present Protocol was committed by a subordinate does not absolve his superiors from

77 Rockwood, *Walking away from Nuremberg*, p. 134.

78 Y. Sandoz, C. Swinarski and B. Zimmermann (eds.), *Commentary on the Additional Protocols of 8 June 1977 to the Geneva Conventions of 12 August 1949* (Geneva: ICRC, 1987).

79 Protocol Additional to the Geneva Conventions of 12 August 1949, and Relating to the Protection of Victims of International Armed Conflicts: www.icrc.org.

> penal responsibility if they knew or should have known that he was committing or would commit such a breach and if they did not take measures within their power to prevent or repress the breach.[80]

In March 1974, the Syrian delegate introduced an amendment to delete the words 'should have known' from the text; and in May 1976, the Syrians raised the issue a second time, this time supported by the Argentinian delegate.[81] The proposal did not gain enough support, however, which could be seen as a rejection of the *Medina* standard. All the same, delegates were concerned that the draft Article was too harsh on superiors, and, prompted by the Americans, took steps to soften the provision: it was revised to remove the word 'penal', to replace 'should have known' with the more accommodating 'should reasonably have known in the circumstances at the time', and to state that superiors would commit a breach only if they did not take 'reasonable' measures.[82]

While this seemed to cover superior responsibility, the American delegation proposed an additional provision at the Fourth Session of the Conference in 1977: Article 76 bis, which became Article 87. This proposal, after some revision, stated:

> 1. The High Contracting Parties and the Parties to the conflict shall require military commanders, with respect to members of the armed forces under their command and other persons under their control, to prevent and, where necessary, to suppress and to report to competent authorities breaches of the Conventions and this Protocol.
> 2. In order to prevent and suppress breaches, High Contracting Parties and Parties to the conflict shall require that, commensurate with their level of responsibility, commanders ensure that members of the armed forces under their command are aware of their obligations under the Conventions and this Protocol.
> 3. The High Contracting Parties and parties to the conflict shall require any commander who is aware that subordinates or other persons under his control are going to commit or have committed a breach of the Conventions or the present Protocol, to initiate such steps as are necessary to prevent such violations of the Conventions or this

80 International Committee of the Red Cross, *Draft Additional Protocols of the Geneva Conventions of August 12, 1949: commentary* (Geneva: ICRC, 1973), pp. 95–96.

81 H.S. Levie, *Protection of war victims, Protocol 1 of the Geneva Conventions*, 4 vols. (Dobbs Ferry, NY: Oceana Publications, 1979–1981), vol. 4, pp. 302, 306–307.

82 United States, 'Draft Protocol I, Article 76, Draft Amendment' (c. 21 March 1975): FCO 61/1373, The National Archives, UK (TNA); Levie, *Protection of war victims*, vol. 4, p. 303.

> Protocol, and, where appropriate, to initiate disciplinary or penal action against violators thereof.[83]

It was clear to the other delegates why the Americans wanted to lay down an unambiguous statement on command responsibility: as the British observed, it 'clearly has its origins in the US experiences in Vietnam'.[84] Paragraphs 2 and 3, in particular, appeared to be influenced by the fallout caused by *Medina*, because they required commanders to educate their troops on the laws of war, to organise a system for reporting breaches and to take appropriate disciplinary action.[85]

Some other states had reservations about the draft. The British, for example, expressed a concern that these same paragraphs, which arose out of a peculiarly American disciplinary and command structure, would be 'inappropriate' for broader application.[86] In particular, they felt that Paragraph 3 was 'unnecessary and undesirable', because existing procedures already placed commanders under a duty to follow their obligations under law.[87] As one official argued, 'To single out Article 76 [bis] for special attention would imply in other contexts, where there is no equivalent of para 3, that the duty of enforcement is somehow less.'[88] Nevertheless, they decided that there was nothing in the American proposal that was 'seriously objectionable' and decided not to oppose it in light of the 'wide breadth of support it apparently enjoys'.[89] After all, as the Ministry of Defence noted, the Article 'in effect codifies existing law and is compatible with UK practice'.[90] The British delegation therefore eventually supported its adoption, as did most other states, by a vote of seventy-two in favour, no votes against and two abstentions.[91] This pleased the American delegates, who noted that it gained 'wide support, in particular from Arab Group'.[92]

83 'Duties of commanders' (sent out for comment on 2 May 1977): DEFE 24/1748, TNA.
84 'Draft Protocol', Article 76 bis (15 February 1977): DEFE 24/1746, TNA.
85 Defence Policy Staff and Defence Secretariat, 'Diplomatic Conference . . .' (21 June 1977), Article 76 bis, p. 9: DEFE 24/1238, TNA.
86 Foreign and Commonwealth Office, 'Brief for the UK delegation' (7 April 1977), p. 141: DEFE 24/1748, TNA.
87 Smallwood, 'Humanitarian law' (11 May 1977): DEFE 24/1237, TNA. 88 Ibid.
89 UK Geneva Mission, 'Humanitarian law in armed conflict' (27 April 1977), p. 1: DEFE 24/1748, TNA.
90 Defence Policy Staff and Defence Secretariat, 'Diplomatic Conference . . . ' (21 June 1977), Article 76 bis, p. 9: DEFE 24/1238, TNA.
91 US Geneva Mission to State Department, 'Diplomatic Conference on International Humanitarian Law' (29 April 1977), p. 1–2: 1977GENEVA03249, Access to Archival Databases (AAD), National Archives Records Administration, United States.
92 US Geneva Mission to State Department, 'Diplomatic Conference on International Humanitarian Law' (22 April 1977), p. 1: 1977GENEVA03017, AAD.

The provision gathered this support because there was little new about it. It did not purport to change the existing law on superior responsibility, but simply to codify existing, albeit broader, obligations under the 1949 Geneva Conventions – specifically Article 45 of the First Convention and Article 46 of the Second (on the execution of the Conventions), Article 127 of the Third, and Article 144 of the Fourth (on the dissemination of the Conventions).[93] The ICRC's 1987 Commentary to Additional Protocol 1 supported this view: 'The recognition of the responsibility of superiors who, without any excuse, fail to prevent their subordinates from committing breaches of the law of armed conflict is . . . by no means new in treaty law.'[94]

Widespread approval of the provisions in the Protocol indicates that the international community largely accepted the standard of superior responsibility articulated by *Yamashita* and then refined by Tokyo and *Toyoda*. By the same token, it rejected the more lenient standard set forth in *Medina*, which had been heavily criticised in the United States and did not gain traction in the international sphere.

The ICC's Rome Statute adds a further refinement to the post-war judgments. It recognises that the requirement of effective control applies differently to military and civilian leaders, and therefore makes separate provisions for each. In the military context, Article 28(a) provides that a commander is responsible for 'crimes . . . committed by forces under his or her effective command and control'; while in the civilian context, Article 28(b) and (b)(ii) states that a superior is responsible for 'crimes . . . committed by subordinates under his or her effective command and control' where these crimes 'concerned activities that were within the effective responsibility and control of the superior'.[95] In other words, the Statute recognises that non-military superiors tend to have a broader range of responsibilities than their military counterparts.

The recurring Asian motif

The modern superior responsibility doctrine has been largely shaped by events in Asia, from the Asia-Pacific War, to the war in Vietnam, to the 'killing fields' of Cambodia. The Extraordinary Chambers in the

[93] Foreign and Commonwealth Office, 'Fourth session of the Diplomatic Conference . . . ', Annex B, Article 87 (1 December 1977): FCO 58/1128, TNA.

[94] Sandoz, Swinarski and Zimmermann (eds.), *Commentary on the Additional Protocols*, p. 1011.

[95] Articles 28(a), (b)(ii), Rome Statute.

Courts of Cambodia, established in 2004 to try the Khmer Rouge leadership for crimes committed from 1975 to January 1979, is just one of the latest in a series of trials established to hold military and civilian leaders responsible for international crimes. On superior orders, the 'Law on the Establishment of the ECCC' sits squarely within the tradition established at Manila and Tokyo. The third stanza of Article 29 provides that

> The fact that any of the acts . . . were committed by a subordinate does not relieve the superior of personal criminal responsibility if the superior had effective command and control or authority and control over the subordinate, and the superior knew or had reason to know that the subordinate was about to commit such acts or had done so and the superior failed to take the necessary and reasonable measures to prevent such acts or to punish the perpetrators.[96]

This definition essentially adopts the *Yamashita* standard, by holding superiors responsible when they 'had reason to know' of their subordinates' crimes, and, if circumstances permit, imputing knowledge to the accused. It also follows the Tokyo Judgment, which held superiors responsible if they 'failed to take such steps as were within their power to prevent the commission of such crimes in the future';[97] and the *Toyoda* Judgment, which added liability in situations in which there was a 'failure to take any action to punish the perpetrators'.[98] The ECCC Statute criminalises both omissions and uses the phrase 'necessary and reasonable measures' instead of Tokyo's formulation, 'such steps as were within their power'.[99]

In July 2010, the ECCC Trial Chamber for Case 001 found Kaing Guek Eav, alias 'Duch', guilty of crimes against humanity and war crimes based, *inter alia*, on superior responsibility.[100] It derived three elements from Article 29: first, a superior–subordinate relationship in which the former has effective control over the latter; second, a superior's knowledge, direct or inferred from the circumstances, that a subordinate was about to commit or had committed a crime; and third, a superior's failure to take necessary and reasonable measures to prevent the crime or to punish

[96] Law on the Establishment of the Extraordinary Chambers in the Courts of Cambodia for the Prosecution of Crimes Committed during the Period of Democratic Kampuchea, NS/RKM/1004/006 (as amended 27 October 2004) (ECCC Law).

[97] IMTFE, Majority Judgment, vol. 101, p. 48445.

[98] *United States* v. *Soemu Toyoda*, Judgment, p. 5006. [99] Article 29, ECCC Law.

[100] *Duch*, 001/18-07-2007/ECCC/TC, Trial Chamber Judgment (26 July 2010), pars. 548–549.

the perpetrator.[101] Duch, it stated, had 'exercised effective control over the rest of the S-21 staff, knew that his subordinates were committing crimes, and failed to take necessary or reasonable measures to prevent their commission or punish their perpetrators'.[102] Yet when concluding this, the Court relied exclusively on the case law emerging from the ad hoc tribunals on former Yugoslavia and Rwanda[103] – most likely because this offered refinements on the jurisprudence arising from the post-war trials. The first element, for example, makes clear that to be held liable, a superior must have *effective* control over his subordinates. This improves on *Yamashita* (where the facts indicated that Yamashita had lost contact with, and therefore effective control over, his troops), and, of course, on Tokyo (which held Foreign Minister Hirota responsible for crimes committed by military forces not under his control).

A few months later, the ECCC Pre-Trial Chamber issued two decisions in response to appeals from the accused in Case 002. These appeals contended that superior responsibility was not recognised by international law during the Khmer Rouge era of 1975–1979, and that the application of this doctrine to them violated the principle of legality. The Pre-Trial Chamber rejected this argument, concluding instead that superior responsibility for both civilian and military leaders had crystallised into customary international law by 1975.[104] These decisions, unlike the *Duch* Judgment, discussed Asian antecedents. The Decision on Ieng Sary's Appeal, for instance, stated that 'it is without question that *Yamashita* serves as precedent for the notion that a superior may be held criminally responsible under international law with respect to crimes committed by subordinates'.[105] It also analysed the Tokyo and *Toyoda* decisions[106] to support its conclusion that superior responsibility was an established mode of liability by the 1970s.[107] Neither of the Pre-Trial Chamber decisions mentioned Additional Protocol I, possibly because it only came into force in December 1978, a month before the Khmer Rouge regime was ejected from power.

101 Ibid., par. 538. 102 Ibid., par. 549. 103 Ibid., pars. 538–547.

104 *Nuon et al.*, 002/19-09-2007-ECCC/OCIJ (PTC75), Decision on Ieng Sary's Appeal against the Closing Order (*Nuon* PTC Decision 002) (11 April 2011), par. 460; *Nuon et al.*, 002/19-09-2007-ECCC/OCIJ (PTC 145 & 146), Pre-Trial Chamber Decision on Appeals by Nuon Chea and Ieng Thirith against the Closing Order (15 February 2011), par. 232.

105 *Nuon* PTC Decision 002, par. 427. 106 Ibid., pars. 444–457. 107 Ibid., par. 458.

Conclusion

What accounts for Asia's prominence in the development of the superior responsibility doctrine? The common thread between the aforementioned cases and initiatives – *Yamashita*, Tokyo, *Toyoda*, *Medina* and Additional Protocol I – is heavy American involvement.

The first three cases were manifestations of American power and legal activism in Asia. At the end of the Asia-Pacific War, the United States exploited its power to create new jurisdictions and to indulge in legal experimentation, far from home and relatively unfettered by the usual restraints. In the process, it created a new international doctrine of superior responsibility, and tested it out in several iterations against both Japanese civilian and military leaders at the trials of Yamashita, Toyoda and the Japanese leaders at Tokyo.

The next two initiatives were expressions of American retrenchment in Asia, and judicial caution when it came to handling its own citizens. This is especially evident in *Medina*, where an American court martial departed from the *Yamashita* standard by requiring a military commander to have actual knowledge of his subordinates' crimes to be held criminally liable. The *Medina* standard failed to gain traction within the American military and was rejected at the Geneva Diplomatic Conference. Instead, in light of the post-*Medina* experience at home, the United States proposed a new article which required commanders to assume greater responsibility in instructing troops on their obligations under international law and to report violations to the appropriate authority. While this provision was more detailed than past articulations of superior responsibility, it did not substantively advance the doctrine. Rather, it was explicitly intended to codify existing legal obligations that were implicit within the 1949 Geneva Conventions.

So far, the United States, responding to Asian events, has been the major protagonist in the creation of the superior responsibility concept in international law. Asia has been merely the laboratory for those doctrinal developments. What role *Asian* protagonists will play in the further refinement of the idea remains to be seen.

10

The two approaches to the superior orders plea

BING BING JIA

Although well established in international criminal law, the plea of superior orders is still not free of the controversy that has enshrouded it almost since it came into existence. The controversy is a fundamental one, namely, whether the plea may ever be applied as a separate defence, excluding individual criminal responsibility, or whether it may be applied only as a mitigating factor in sentencing. The latter is often called the 'absolute liability' approach, meaning that the plea cannot absolve the defendant of their responsibility for the result of carrying out the order, whereas the former is commonly known as the 'conditional liability' mode, in that the plea can exclude the responsibility of the defendant, subject to various conditions.

Somewhere in between lies the doctrine that a mixture of the superior orders plea with other less contentious pleas may result in a complete defence. Here, the question arises as to whether the plea has any independent worth, since being subsumed by those other pleas would spell its end as a stand-alone category. Even a cursory reading of materials shows that all of these approaches are clearly discernible in statutory international law and the jurisprudence of the war crimes trials held after the Second World War. As a result, the outcomes for the defendants and defence counsel have been unpredictable. This highlights the urgent need to develop a clear and predominant rule that injects certainty into future cases in this field.

In view of the prior development of those three approaches in the practice – absolute liability, conditional liability and a mixture of pleas – they should perhaps be divided into two pairs for ease of analysis and comparison. The first pair consists of the two forms of the plea as either a defence or a mitigating factor. The second comprises the two forms of the plea as either a defence in its own right or as a factor that is to be considered in conjunction with other, less controversial pleas.

The first pair has already been comprehensively analysed in the literature.[1] The aim here, however, is to show that the two facets of the plea in this pair can *both* stake a claim to reflect customary law. To say that they can coexist is clearly not conducive to the certainty of law, and the two forms may eventually fight it out for ultimate recognition as part of positive law. For now, though, there are two traditions, which have developed in parallel, and which both reflect customary law. It is also argued that the pendulum seems to be swinging back to the position where the plea can be applied as a defence, rather than simply as a ground for mitigation of punishment. The approach to the plea contained in the ICC's Rome Statute, which accepts it as a defence, currently has the edge – not least because it has survived one of the longest and most serpentine series of diplomatic negotiations in history.

The second pair of approaches to the superior orders plea is either that it is a defence in its own right or that it is a component of other defences such as mistake of law or duress. The question here is that if the plea is merely another dimension of the other pleas, then why is it necessary to preserve its status as a plea in its own right? For the past seven decades, jurists seeking to express abhorrence to war crimes, without usurping military discipline and the rights of the defendant, have grappled with these difficult issues. Here, we revisit the doctrinal debates, paying special attention to the debates and programmes that evolved at trials convened in Europe and Asia.

Developments in military law before 1945

The idea that the superior orders plea is a complete defence can be traced back to nineteenth-century German military law. This claim may appear to be simplistic, considering the layers of nuance added to the plea by state practice in the intervening years. Nonetheless the fact remains that the concept, complete with the idea that a subordinate would be protected unless the order was manifestly illegal, emerged in this body of

[1] See, for example, Y. Dinstein, *The defence of 'obedience to superior orders' in international law* (Oxford University Press, 2012); O. Triffterer, 'Article 33', in O. Triffterer (ed.), *Commentary on the Rome Statute of the International Criminal Court: observers' notes, article by article* (Munich: C.H. Beck-Hart-Nomos, 2nd edn., 2008), pp. 915–929; A. Zimmermann, 'Superior orders', in A. Cassese *et al.* (eds.), *The Rome Statute of the International Criminal Court: a commentary*, 2 vols. (Oxford University Press, 2002), vol. 1, pp. 957–974; P. Gaeta, 'The defence of superior orders: the Statute of the International Criminal Court *versus* customary international law', *European Journal of International Law* 10 (1999), 172–191.

law in 1882,[2] and was referred back to in future debates of international interest. It was taken into consideration (although not admitted as a defence) at the trial convened in Leipzig in 1921 to deal with war crimes arising from the sinking of the *Llandovery Castle* during the First World War.[3] And it was cited again at the United Nations War Crimes Commission (UNWCC) in 1944, when delegates addressed the question of superior orders in anticipation of the work of a future inter-Allied court. In August that year, the Chinese UNWCC representative Liang Yuen-Li submitted a report suggesting that the German rule be applied with a view to assisting both the proposed court and national courts, in cases involving superior orders.[4] As an alternative to that, he suggested adopting the wording of a previous draft submitted by the American delegate Lawrence Preuss:

> 1. The plea of superior orders shall not constitute a defence against a charge arising under Article 1 [of the draft] if the order was so manifestly contrary to the laws of war that a person of ordinary sense and understanding would know or should know, given his rank or position and the circumstances of the case, that such an order was illegal.
> 2. It shall be for the Tribunal and its Divisions to consider to what extent irresistible compulsion shall be a ground for mitigation of the penalty or for acquittal.[5]

This rule left open the possibility that the plea could become a full defence if the order in question was not manifestly illegal. It would then be a self-contained defence. The test laid down in the first paragraph was the manifest illegality of the order.

The second paragraph was less straightforward because it seemed to treat the 'irresistible compulsion' accompanying a superior order, and the *extent* of that irresistible compulsion, as being either a defence or a mitigating factor for sentencing purposes, the choice being left to the court.[6] (It should

[2] L.C. Green, 'Superior orders and command responsibility', *Canadian Yearbook of International Law* 27 (1989), 176–177.

[3] For the *Llandovery Castle* trial, see: *Annual Digest of Public International Law Cases* 2 (1923–1924), 437.

[4] Liang Y.-L., 'Report on the plea of obedience to superior orders', Committee III, United Nations War Crimes Commission (UNWWC) (28 August 1944) pp. 5: www.legal-tools.org.

[5] Ibid.

[6] A remaining question was whether under this paragraph, the plea could still constitute a factor in support of another defence.

be noted that this scenario involving compulsion arose only in some cases; in others involving superior orders, the accused may have carried out an order without any compulsion, or with resistible compulsion.) Taking the two articles as a whole, if a given order were manifestly illegal under the law of war, and obedience to it involved extensive 'irresistible compulsion', this would not entail acquittal, but might result in a mitigated sentence.

The British change tack

While UNWCC was considering these options, the British decided to amend the section on superior orders in the *Manual of military law 1929* – a reference work on military law published under the auspices of the War Office. This change would reveal the uncertainty of the applicable law, and open up debates about the expectations placed upon serving members of the armed forces during the course of a war. From the beginning of the century, Paragraph 443 of Chapter 14 of an earlier version of the *Manual*, drafted by J.E. Edmonds and Lassa Oppenheim, had declared that

> [M]embers of the armed forces who commit such violations of the recognized rules of warfare as are ordered by their Government or by their commander are not war criminals and cannot therefore be punished by the enemy. He may punish the officials or commanders responsible for such orders if they fall into his hands, but otherwise he may only resort to the other means of obtaining redress[7]

According to Hugh Bellot, writing in 1916, this approach had not been so settled as to form an authoritative rule in *all* circumstances, but it seemed to represent the prevailing view within the British armed forces at the time.[8] It did not go unchallenged, however, even by jurists closely connected to the Service Departments. At the end of the First World War, for example, two prominent jurists, J.H. Morgan and Frederick Pollock, who were considering prosecuting alleged German war criminals, questioned the basis for the Edmonds/Oppenheim approach.[9] Yet no change was made. The editors of the next edition of the *Manual of military law*,

[7] War Office, *Manual of military law . . . 1914* (London: HMSO, 1914), ch. 14, par. 443.

[8] H.H.L. Bellot, 'War crimes: their prevention and punishment', *Transactions of the Grotius Society* 2 (1916), 47.

[9] Morgan, 'The plea of superior orders', 23 December 1918 (pp. 36–53), and Pollock, 'A note on the defence of superior orders', 30 December 1918 (pp. 53–55), as part of *First interim report from the committee of enquiry into breaches of the laws of war*: CAB 24/85, The National Archives, United Kingdom (TNA).

published in 1929, decided to retain the old formula, with its protection for subordinates operating under orders, and it remained in place until the latter stages of the Second World War.

The official change to the British approach to the superior orders plea finally occurred in April 1944. This took the form of 'Amendment No. 34' to Paragraph 443 of Chapter 14, drafted by Hersch Lauterpacht, and dispatched to military judges and commanders to insert into copies of the *Manual*.[10] Lauterpacht's Amendment read,

> The fact that a rule of warfare has been violated in pursuance of an order of the belligerent Government or of an individual commander does not deprive the act in question of its character as a war crime; neither does it in principle, confer upon the perpetrator immunity from punishment by the injured belligerent. Undoubtedly, a court confronted with the plea of superior orders adduced in justification of a war crime is bound to take into consideration the fact that obedience to military orders, not obviously unlawful, is the duty of every member of the armed forces and that the latter cannot, in conditions of war discipline, be expected to weigh scrupulously the legal merits of the order received. The question, however, is governed by the major principle that members of the armed forces are bound to obey lawful orders only and that they cannot therefore escape liability if, in obedience to a command, they commit acts which both violate unchallenged rules of warfare and outrage the general sentiment of humanity.[11]

This revision shut the door to pleading superior orders as a complete defence. Henceforth, any criminal act carried out in pursuance of an illegal order would be deemed exactly that – a criminal act.

The Amendment reflected the immediate priorities of the Service Departments and Law Offices at the end of the Second World War. British ministers and officials, spurred by the Moscow Declaration of November 1943, were contemplating trials against alleged 'minor' German war criminals after the war, and anticipating the defence objections that might be raised on grounds of double standards. The revision, drafted in timely manner before the end of the war, pre-empted this possibility with regard to superior orders. More broadly, it reflected the prevailing view among the jurists and Service chiefs at the time concerning the appropriate balance between military discipline and breaches of

[10] War Office, *Manual of military law 1929* (London: HMSO, 7th edn., reprinted December 1939, published 1940), altered by Amendment No. 12 of 1936 and Amendment No. 34 of 1944.

[11] Ibid., Ch. 14, par. 443.

the laws of war. In retrospect, though, the Amendment's significance – far beyond the realm of purely national law – is that it anticipated, and possibly influenced, the approach taken by the drafters of the Nuremberg Charter a year later. In other words, it effectively heralded the plea's entry into international law as one subject to the test of manifest illegality.

Nuremberg's innovative approach

The International Military Tribunal for the 'trial and punishment of the major war criminals of the European Axis'[12] was established by the London Agreement of 8 August 1945. The annexed Nuremberg Charter offered a radical new approach to the superior orders plea, which was set out in Article 8. This stated that:

> The fact that the defendant acted pursuant to order of his Government or of a superior shall not free him from responsibility, but may be considered in mitigation of punishment if the Tribunal determine that justice so requires.[13]

This Article was adopted at the London Conference as a compromise between the United States and the Soviet Union – the Americans initially proposing the plea as a possible defence, and the Soviets rejecting this, proposing instead an 'absolute liability' position.[14] The quite distinct original positions of the two parties can be discerned in documents submitted before the opening of the meeting. The Americans had earlier presented a draft to foreign ministers at the San Francisco Conference in April 1945 which proposed: 'The fact that a defendant acted pursuant to order of a superior or government sanction shall not constitute an absolute defense but may be considered either in defense or in mitigation of punishment if the tribunal before which the charges are being tried determines that justice so requires.'[15] The Soviets submitted a counter-proposal in June 1945, which explicitly rejected obedience to orders as a justification, and omitted to consider it as mitigation of punishment, stating, 'The fact that the accused acted under orders of his superior or his government will not be considered as justifying the guilt circumstance.'[16]

[12] International Military Tribunal, *Trial of the major war criminals before the International Military Tribunal*, 'The Blue Series', 42 vols. (Nuremberg: IMT, 1947–1949), Charter, vol. 1, p. 10.

[13] Ibid., p. 12.

[14] For a discussion of the American and Soviet positions, see Dinstein, *Defence*, pp. 109–117.

[15] Report of Robert H. Jackson, *United States representative, to the International Conference on Military Trials* (Washington DC, Department of State, 1949), p. 24.

[16] Ibid., p. 62.

The compromise between the two positions that appeared in Article 8 crucially retained the Soviet proposal to reject obedience to orders as any sort of grounds, but acceded to the American proposal to allow it in mitigation of punishment. The significance of the Article is that it broke the link with national military law by repudiating superior orders as a defence, and thereby set in motion a new legal approach to the plea.

At the end of the Nuremberg trial, the Tribunal, which accepted the premise of Article 8, added its own embellishment in the Judgment, by introducing the 'moral choice' test. Addressing the defence argument that most of the defendants had acted under Hitler's orders and therefore could not be held responsible for crimes committed in obedience to them, it stated:

> That a soldier was ordered to kill or torture in violation of the international law of war has never been recognized as a defense to such acts of brutality, though, as the Charter here provides, the order may be urged in mitigation of the punishment. The true test, which is found in varying degrees in the criminal law of most nations, is not the existence of the order, but whether moral choice was in fact possible.[17]

As this indicates, the Tribunal did not consider the plea to be a defence, only a mitigation of punishment, as laid down by Article 8. But it might be argued that unlike Article 8, the Tribunal admitted the possibility that the defendant might *not* have had moral choice, which would amount to duress. Did it consider a defence of duress in its discussion of superior orders? This is not the interpretation that comes most naturally from the Judgment. Rather, the Tribunal seemed to suggest that the plea would not constitute a defence, and that it did not necessarily constitute a mitigating factor, if there were a moral choice. The plea could serve to reduce a sentence, but only if the recipient of the order had no choice but to comply with the order in question. (In Keitel's case, for example, it held that 'Superior orders, even to a soldier, cannot be considered in mitigation where crimes as shocking and extensive have been committed consciously, ruthlessly, and without military excuse or justification.'[18]) The stringency of the Nuremberg Judgment in respect of the function of the plea of superior orders is unmistakable.

The Tokyo discrepancy

While the Nuremberg Charter arose out of negotiations between the four major allies, the Tokyo Charter was more of an American production,

[17] IMT, Judgment, vol. 1, p. 224. [18] Ibid., p. 291.

and this was reflected in a revised approach to superior orders. The drafters of the latter did not replicate Article 8, but instead amalgamated Nuremberg's provisions on command responsibility and superior orders to create Article 6, which read:

> *Responsibility of accused.* Neither the official position, at any time, of an accused, nor the fact that an accused acted pursuant to order of his government or of a superior shall, of itself, be sufficient to free such accused from responsibility for any crime with which he is charged, but such circumstances may be considered in mitigation of punishment if the Tribunal determines that justice so requires.[19]

It is likely, as Yoram Dinstein has argued, that this divergence from the Nuremberg Charter was driven by the Americans' desire to throw off the straightjacket of the Soviets' absolute liability approach and return to the more flexible formula they had originally proposed to the foreign ministers at the San Francisco Conference.[20] Thus, while Article 8 removed superior orders as a defence, Tokyo's Article 6 merely stated that obedience to orders was not *of itself* sufficient as a justification – thus leaving open the possibility that obedience to orders, if combined with other factors such as duress and mistake of law, might still constitute a defence.[21] Yet as it transpired, the defence were unable to exploit this more accommodating approach, because they were constrained in their interpretation of the plea by the Nuremberg Judgment (which, it may be recalled, endorsed Article 8), which was released in October 1946, before they had started making their case at Tokyo.

Bearing this restriction in mind, the defence adopted a three-pronged strategy: first, to establish that the defendants were not free agents, but rather had been ordered to embark on a particular course by their superiors; second, that they were unaware that the orders they had received were illegal; and third, that they would have faced drastic consequences had they not carried them out. This was designed to cover all eventualities, the first two prongs being designed to meet the 'manifest illegality' test, and the third prong being designed to meet the 'moral choice' test. The argument put forward by the defence team for Matsui Iwane, the Japanese Army commander-in-chief charged with crimes against peace and war crimes, exemplified this approach. With

[19] International Military Tribunal for the Far East, *The Tokyo major war crimes trial*, R.J. Pritchard (ed.), 124 vols. (Lewiston: Edwin Mellen Press, 1998), Amended Charter, vol. 2, p. 3.

[20] Dinstein, *Superior orders*, p. 157. [21] Ibid.

respect to the crimes against peace charge, it was stated that Matsui believed that Japan was using force in self-defence, and that being charged with having planned, prepared, instigated and waged a war of aggression 'was a surprise to him'.[22] It was further argued that, 'If the General had declined such designation and disobeyed the order of the Central Authorities, he would have been punished severely.'[23]

The defence returned to the superior orders plea in the closing speeches. It recounted the duties of subordinates that appeared in the Japanese Criminal Code, the Japanese Army Criminal Code and the Japanese Navy Criminal Code, all of which demanded obedience to orders. Then, casting the net wider, it cited German and French jurists who had discussed the extent of the protection offered to subordinates. Then, finally, playing its trump card, it turned to the Chinese approach to superior orders. It observed that Paragraph 2 of Article 21 of the then-current Chinese Criminal Code of 1935 stated, 'No act is punishable, which is done in the course of an official duty under the order of one's superior officer, *except the case of a person who has known clearly the illegality of such order.*'[24] In other words, a subordinate could not be held responsible for carrying out their superior's order, unless they *knew* it to be illegal. This Article, the defence counsel argued,

> sweeps away any doubts by stating that punishment will be imposed only upon a subordinate who has acted with a clear knowledge of illegality of his superior's order. It follows, therefore, that in case there existed any ambiguity as to illegality of the order, he shall not be responsible, even if he carried out the order. Since the basic principle of officialdom lies in the chain of command and subjugation, especially in the case of the army and navy, it is according to the thinking of Chinese law, unreasonable to expect him to act contrary to his superior's order, even when he was not quite sure of its being either legal or illegal.[25]

In response, the prosecution flatly responded, '[S]uperior orders are not recognized as a defense in international law. The Charter specifically provides that they shall not be so considered but that they can be considered in mitigation.'[26] Nuremberg's Article 8 *redux*.

This position was fully justified when considered in the light of the 'Law Governing the Trial of War Criminals' promulgated by the Chinese government on 24 October 1946 for the purposes of prosecuting the

[22] IMTFE, vol. 97, pp. 47198–47199. [23] Ibid., p. 47198.
[24] IMTFE, vol. 98, p. 47553. Original emphasis. [25] Ibid., pp. 47555–47556.
[26] IMTFE, vol. 100, p. 48372.

Japanese accused of war crimes who were in its custody.[27] Article 1 stated that this law would prevail over Chinese criminal law, including the Criminal Code, which would be applied in conjunction with it,[28] while Article 8 declared that superior orders in themselves would not constitute a defence.[29] This Law was deemed by UNWCC to be in line with the Nuremberg and Tokyo charters and Control Council Law No. 10.[30] Whichever edition of the Criminal Code the defence relied on, the end result would still be the one tersely declared by the prosecution.

When drafting the Tokyo Judgment, the majority of judges, like the prosecutors, were also reluctant to depart from legal principles set down by the Nuremberg Judgment, stating that, 'In view of the fact that in all material respects the Charters of this Tribunal and the Nuremberg Tribunal are identical, this Tribunal prefers to express its unqualified adherence to the relevant opinions of the Nuremberg Tribunal rather than by reasoning the matters anew in somewhat different language to open the door to controversy by way of conflicting interpretations of the two statements of opinions.'[31] In fact, Nuremberg's Article 8 and Tokyo's Article 6 were far from 'identical'. But the Chinese member of the Tribunal, Mei Ru'ao, insisted that they were based on the same guiding principle. He later wrote:

> The reason why the Charters of the two tribunals adopted this position [on the plea] is because an individual should only act in accordance with lawful orders, and not follow unlawful, criminal orders. If he violates a clear, indisputable law of war in carrying out an order, he cannot escape responsibility. If the rule were otherwise, and only the superior officer who had issued the order were held responsible, then at the end of the day, only the head of the state or a few high-ranking officials would be held responsible for war crimes. This would severely damage the enforcement of laws of war.[32]

The impact on the subsequent trials

While both the international military tribunals ultimately followed the line set down by the Nuremberg Charter, some, but not all, of the Allied

27 United Nations War Crimes Commission, *Law reports of trials of war criminals*, 15 vols. (London: HMSO, 1947–1949), vol. 14, pp. 152–160.

28 Ibid., p. 152. 29 Ibid., p. 157. 30 Ibid.

31 IMTFE, Majority Judgment, vol. 101, p. 48439.

32 Mei Ru'ao, *Yuan Dong Guo Ji Jun Shi Fa Ting (The International Military Tribunal for the Far East)* (Beijing: Law Press, 1988), p. 26.

tribunals convened to try the lower-ranking war crimes suspects followed a more conventional route. The twelve American-run 'subsequent' tribunals, conducted pursuant to Control Council Law No. 10, were a case in point.

These tribunals widely considered the plea of superior orders,[33] and, like the Tokyo Charter, reverted to the original American position set out at the San Francisco Conference. In the *Einsatzgruppen* case of 1947, for example, the Tribunal set out various criteria that had to be met to activate the plea as a defence. It stated that the accused could not plead innocence to a criminal act ordered by his superiors if 'he himself approved of the principle involved in the order'.[34] His objection to the order had to have been 'constant'.[35] It was not enough for the accused to claim that he had mentally rebelled against the order; he had to demonstrate some tangible action to counter it, such as releasing a victim.[36] And if after receiving the order he had at any time acquiesced in the order's 'illegal character', the superior orders defence would be denied him.[37] This accumulation of factors, which seemed to require a subordinate's unwavering opposition to an order in the face of threats of severe punishment, more closely resembled a defence of duress. Even so, after the stringency of Article 8, the court was prepared to readmit by the back-door the idea of a superior orders defence, provided that a subordinate put up enough resistance to the order in question.

The British war crimes trials were more disposed to follow the Nuremberg line, however. This was partly due to the lineage between Lauterpacht's amendment to the *Manual of military law 1929* and the Nuremberg Charter, and partly because the British war crimes trials were established and conducted under the terms of the Royal Warrant, dated 14 June 1945, and its appended 'Regulations for the Trial of War Criminals'.[38] There is no need to recount here the appropriateness of using a Royal Warrant, as distinct from a statute, to found the jurisdiction

[33] K.J. Heller, *The Nuremberg military tribunals and the origins of international criminal law* (Oxford University Press, 2011), p. 301, states, 'With the exception of the *Pohl* tribunal, then, all of the tribunals adopted a conditional liability approach to the defense of superior orders.'

[34] *Trials of war criminals before the Nuernberg Military Tribunals under Control Council Law No.10*, 'The Green Series', 15 vols. (Nuremberg: US Government Printing Office, October 1946–April 1949), vol. 4, pp. 480.

[35] Ibid., p. 481. [36] Ibid. [37] Ibid.

[38] War Office, Royal Warrant: Regulations for the Trial of War Criminals (Army Order 81/1945) (London: HMSO, signed 14 June 1945, promulgated 18 June 1945): LCO 53/102, TNA.

of British military courts.[39] The prerogative instrument contained an important provision: 'The Court shall take judicial notice of the laws and usages of war.'[40] This put international law, absorbed into British law, at the heart of the trials. Yet the Royal Warrant makes no reference to the plea of superior orders, despite its prominence in many of the cases.[41] The plea must therefore be construed from the then-international law, and from the *Manual of military law 1929* as amended in 1944.

A few examples will suffice. At the Hong Kong trials, defence lawyers, who pinned little hope on being able to use the plea as a complete defence, advanced the plea as a mitigation of punishment. In *Tamura Teiichi, Hirano Noburo and Fujino Masazo*, heard in May and June 1947, the defendants were charged with war crimes for their part in the execution without trial of a British airman at Ichinomiya, with Hirano allegedly ordering the execution, and Fujino carrying it out under Tamura's command. The court, having found the defendants guilty, sentenced Hirano and Tamura to death, and Fujino to fifteen years' imprisonment. Reviewing the court's decision, the Judge Advocate stated, 'Superior orders are not of course a ground of defence for an offence such as this but the Court evidently considered that they afforded some mitigation in the case of [Fujino] and according refrained from sentencing him to death.'[42]

In the case of *Tokunaga Isao et al.*, the five defendants were charged with war crimes for the ill treatment and death of prisoners of war and civilians in Hong Kong camps under their jurisdiction from January 1942 to August 1945. Three of them pleaded superior orders as a defence: Tsutada Itsuo and Harada Jotaro, who were accused of having beaten Dutch and British prisoners of war, and Tokunaga Isao, who was accused of executing Canadian prisoners who had either escaped or had attempted to escape. The defence argued that superior orders had to be obeyed. But in line with the common practice at the Hong Kong trials, and as noted by the Judge Advocate, the plea 'could only influence the court in mitigation of sentence'.[43] So it came to pass, because on review, Tokunagu's death sentence was commuted to life imprisonment. The Judge Advocate thought that this decision had likely

[39] A.P.V. Rogers, 'War crimes trials under the Royal Warrant: British practice 1945-1949', *International and Comparative Law Quarterly* 39 (1990), 788–789.

[40] Royal Warrant, Regulation 8 (iii).

[41] See, for example, UNWCC, *Law reports*, vol. 15, p. 157, stating that the plea was 'raised by the Defence in war crime trials more frequently than any other'.

[42] Judge Advocate's Report, *Tamura Teiichi, Hirano Noburo and Fujino Masazo* (27 August 1947), p. 2: WO 235/1021, TNA.

[43] Judge Advocate's Report, *Tokunaga Isao et al.* (9 May 1947), p. 3: WO 235/1012 (pt. 1), TNA.

been influenced by a petition from Selwyn Clarke, the British Chief Medical Officer in Hong Kong, affirming that the defendant had done what he could under the circumstances to alleviate the prisoners' lot.[44]

Divisions over the Nürnberg Principles

Six weeks after the Nuremberg Judgment was handed down, and while the Tokyo Tribunal and some of the subsequent trials were in progress, the UN General Assembly passed Resolution 95(I), the 'Affirmation of the Principles of International Law Recognized by the Charter of the Nürnberg Tribunal' (Nürnberg Principles).[45] A year later, on 21 November 1947, the General Assembly established the International Law Commission (ILC) by Resolution 174(II),[46] and requested that it formulate those principles and start work on what would become the draft 'Code of Offences against the Peace and Security of Mankind' by Resolution 177(II).[47] The debates on the Nürnberg Principles and the draft Code within the Commission gave rise to substantial differences of opinion about the nature of the superior orders plea.

When the ILC submitted the proposed Nürnberg Principles to the General Assembly in 1950, Principle IV provided that

> The fact that a person acted pursuant to order of his Government or of a superior does not relieve him from responsibility under international law, provided a moral choice was in fact possible to him.[48]

A contrary reading of this principle would strongly suggest that the plea *could* be a defence if no moral choice was possible. As a result, the Principle's juxtaposition of moral choice with superior orders was not consistent with the Nuremberg Judgment, because, some claim, the latter allowed a lack of 'moral choice' only in mitigation of punishment, not as a defence.

This reading of the Judgment has been criticised in some quarters.[49] It seems, however, that the English text suggests this interpretation,[50]

44 Judge Advocate to Attorney General's Office, *Tokunaga Isao et al.* (14 July 1947), p. 1: WO 235/1012 (pt. 1), TNA.

45 UNGA Resolution 95(I) (11 December 1946): research.un.org/en/docs/ga/quick/regular/1.

46 UNGA Res. 174(II) (21 November 1947): research.un.org/en/docs/ga/quick/regular/2.

47 UNGA Res. 177(II) (21 November 1947): research.un.org/en/docs/ga/quick/regular/2.

48 Principles of International Law Recognized in the Charter of the Nürnberg Tribunal and in the Judgment of the Tribunal (1950): www.un.org/law/ilc.

49 Dinstein, *Defence*, p. 149.

50 See, for example, ibid., pp. 235–236 (referring to Spiropoulos' opinion).

especially in light of the actual wording of Article 8 of the Charter, which allowed the Tribunal to mitigate punishment 'if the Tribunal determine that justice so requires'. In the course of that determination, factors must be considered in the interest of justice. Coercion of any degree would seem to be such a factor. Yet it would be rather strange for the Tribunal to reopen the possibility of the plea being treated as a defence after it already said immediately before that the plea 'has never been recognized as a defense to such acts of brutality'. It explained further that the plea 'may be urged in mitigation of the punishment'. The question would be with what varying effect it may be urged for that purpose. The variation in the availability of the moral choice would probably account for that variation in effect of the plea for mitigating purposes.

This approach seems to be consistent with the view expressed at the subsequent American tribunals at Nuremberg. In the *Einsatzgruppen* case, for example, the defence of necessity in the sense of duress was raised in connection with superior orders.[51] With respect to their participation in the mass killings, the defendants pleaded obedience to military orders because they had acted under duress and lacked independent will.[52] The court responded that those subject to military discipline were not obliged to carry out other illegal acts, such as stealing, and nor were they automatons, since they were reasoning beings.[53] It further stated that if the defendant 'accepts a criminal order and executes it with a malice of his own' he could not claim superior orders in mitigation.[54] As for duress, the court stated that the harm to the victim caused by carrying out the order must not be much greater than the harm caused to the subordinate by disobeying the order – for example, it was not acceptable for soldiers to obey an order to kill a person known to be innocent just because they risked a few days' imprisonment for refusing to do so.[55]

If, however, the Nuremberg Tribunal really meant to include the defence of duress in its determination, it would have represented a significant departure from Article 8. As Greenspan had written,

> If the tribunal's statement implies that a person who has no moral choice in carrying out an illegal order is free from guilt, then this implication is contrary not only to Article 8 of the tribunal's charter ... but also to international law as exemplified in the *Llandovery Castle* line of cases.[56]

[51] NMTs, *Einsatzgruppen* case, vol. 4, pp. 480–483. [52] Ibid., p. 470. [53] Ibid.
[54] Ibid., p. 471. [55] Ibid.
[56] M. Greenspan, *The modern law of land warfare* (Berkeley: University of California Press, 1959), p. 494.

Returning to Principle IV of the Nürnberg Principles, the existence of the (illegal) superior order and the lack of moral choice on the part of the recipient combined to produce a defence. The ILC's discussion on 14–15 June 1950 indicates the drift of the debate. The chair, Georges Scelle, suggested that Principle IV could do with 'the addition of a few words expressing the idea that the court could take account of the fact that a person committing a crime had acted on the order of a government or of a superior, not only to mitigate punishment but also as grounds for acquittal, if justice so required'.[57] In what became known as the 'Brierly amendment', James Brierly suggested adding the words: 'Provided a moral choice was in fact possible to him.'[58] He later explained, 'Where there was no moral freedom there could be no guilt'[59] – in other words, the plea could sometimes take the form of a defence. Jesús María Yepes immediately added that 'in certain cases, a superior order could be an absolute defence'.[60]

But Brierly's amendment raised opposition connected with a simmering dispute over whether the Nürnberg Principles should replicate or interpret the Charter and Judgment. J.P.A. François stated that Principle VI should not diverge from Article 8, and accused Brierly of 'endeavouring to camouflage this decision [to do otherwise] under a formula which did not decide the issue'.[61] Richard Córdova argued that the Commission was exceeding its terms of reference because neither Charter nor Judgment regarded a superior order to be a defence, and Jean Spiropoulos added that the Judgment was 'categorical' on this question.[62] Gilberto Amado countered that what had really been rejected by the Charter was the plea as an *absolute* defence, with the mere existence of an order exonerating a subordinate in all circumstances, and Faris el-Khoury explained that by contrast to this scenario, Brierly's amendment was based on two tests, both of which had to be satisfied: the existence of the order and the lack of 'moral choice' to disobey.[63] The only question left was whether the plea could still constitute a defence without any role played by moral choice – a dilemma for another time.

The debate over the plea in the Commission and, later, the Sixth Committee of the General Assembly shows that just a few years after Nuremberg had closed, confidence in the plea's existence in international law, as defined in its Charter and Judgment, was already dwindling. Not

[57] ILC, *Yearbook of the International Law Commission*, vol. 1, p. 42. [58] Ibid., p. 46.
[59] Ibid., p. 45. [60] Ibid. [61] Ibid., p. 46. [62] Ibid. [63] Ibid.

only was there a sharp division of opinion in these fora,[64] but the General Assembly in 1950 chose not to endorse the Nürnberg Principles; instead, it passed them back to the ILC to be taken into account when drawing up the draft Code of Offences against the Peace and Security of Mankind.[65] (It is overhitting it to claim, as some have done, that the General Assembly's earlier affirmation of the Nürnberg Principles in 1946 was evidence of their customary law status; at the time, the delegates did not have the text of the yet-to-be-formulated Principles in front of them.) With the suspension in 1954 of the ILC's work on the draft Code, the superior orders plea was left in abeyance, at least as a subject of multilateral negotiations, for another two decades.

The Lords reappraise the Amendment

While the Nürnberg Principles were in the process of being shelved at the United Nations, the House of Lords in London, contemplating the publication of *Manual of military law* (1951), engaged in two telling debates, in 1950 and 1952, about the superior orders plea. Both considered motions sponsored by the Earl of Cork and Orrery, a former Admiral of the Fleet, which aimed to overturn Lauterpacht's 'Amendment No. 34' of Paragraph 443 on superior orders. The motions' supporters, led by former military commanders, and motivated equally by fears of ideologically driven prosecutions brought by communist powers and domestic prosecutions of soldiers involved in Britain's colonial wars, made the case for greater legal protection for serving members of the armed forces. The opponents to the motions, led by the Law Lords, argued that the Amendment reflected the prevailing international view in the wake of the Nuremberg Tribunal, and that it should be retained in the next edition of the *Manual*, as indeed it was.

What, then, did the motions say? The 1950 motion contended that the Amendment was 'inimical to military discipline, is unjust to all serving in the Armed Forces when under active service conditions, and should be revised'.[66] It narrowly fell by a vote of nineteen for and twenty-one against. The 1952 motion, raised just before the 1951 *Manual of military*

64 For a summary of the debate in the Sixth Committee, see Liang Y.-L., 'Notes on legal questions concerning the United Nations', *American Journal of International Law* 45 (1951), 515–517.

65 Res. 488 (V), 12 December 1950: research.un.org/en/docs/ga/quick/regular/5.

66 *The Parliamentary debates (Hansard)*, House of Lords (London, HMSO, 19 July 1950), vol. 168, cols. 347–348.

law was due to be published, called for a reconsideration of the principles of Chapter 14 (of which the Amendment was a part) 'by a competent tribunal before the publication of the revised edition'.[67] It was withdrawn after promises of consultation with the Service Departments. The debates illustrated the different priorities of commanders and jurists, with the former laying greater emphasis on military discipline, the latter on developments in international law. Indeed, Lord Ogmore was moved to remark: 'It is not often, even in your Lordships' House, that our most distinguished Service chiefs are bowlers and our most distinguished lawyers are batsmen. This has been a Homeric encounter.'[68]

Introducing the 1950 motion, Lord Cork stated that the Edmonds/Oppenheim Paragraph 443, which had been 'swept away' by Lauterpacht's Amendment, had in reality expressed 'the considered views of Great Britain, the Dominions and the U.S.A.'.[69] He explained that obedience to orders was 'the keystone of all military activity'.[70] 'When everything is going wrong,' he continued, 'then is the time for officers and men to hold fast to those military virtues and for an officer or man to do his utmost, to the end of his strength and resolution, to carry out the orders of his seniors and not to enter into an argument whether the orders that have been given are legal of not.'[71] He added that as soon as responsibility for decision-making was divided between superiors and subordinates, this system would break down.[72] A single man, he said, 'could disrupt a whole battalion by arguing with his officer – and that is the right which he is now given'.[73]

Further, Lord Wilson, speaking on behalf of the Army in the later debate, pointed out that there were 'ominous' inadequacies in both Amendment No. 34 and the 1949 Geneva Convention with respect to military necessity – inadequacies which provided a wide scope for potential charges.[74] He claimed that it was axiomatic that a British commander had the right to take whatever action was necessary and reasonable for the safety or security of his command.[75] It followed that only the superior officer issuing an order had to be well informed about the reasons behind it. But what would happen, asked Wilson, if a junior officer drew a different conclusion and refused to carry out the commander's order – could he

[67] *The Parliamentary debates (Hansard)*, House of Lords (London, HMSO, 14 May 1952), vol. 176, col. 956.
[68] *Parliamentary debates*, 1952, col. 1006. [69] *Parliamentary debates*, 1950, col. 441.
[70] Ibid., col. 443. [71] Ibid., col. 444. [72] Ibid. [73] *Parliamentary debates*, 1950, col. 445.
[74] *Parliamentary debates*, 1952, col. 964. [75] Ibid.

justifiably plead that there was insufficient military necessity, even though he was not in possession of all of the facts?[76]

It might be mentioned that in the course of these contributions, Lauterpacht himself came in for criticism – some of it mildly unfair (Cork: 'we shall be told that [the new edition] has been carefully revised by Professor Lauterpacht and that Professor Lauterpacht agrees with the views of Professor Lauterpacht!'),[77] and some of it positively unsavoury (Cork again: it was preferable to have British or Dominions lawyers looking after 'the interests of the British people' rather than Lauterpacht, who was 'out of place').[78]

On the lawyers' side, Lord Chancellor Viscount Jowitt, taking up Cork's arguments on obedience, countered, 'The noble and gallant Earl . . . has enunciated doctrines which, to my mind, are so shocking and so utterly immoral that I am glad to have this opportunity of exposing them. I do not believe that any soldier or sailor, by putting on a uniform and obeying orders, completely dissociates himself from all his responsibility as a citizen and as a human being.'[79] He added that 'if he accepts this doctrine he is accepting entirely what is called the "*Fuerer prinzip*" – that every man, so long as he obeys the orders given by his superior, is free'.[80] The former Lord Chancellor Viscount Simon contended that the pre-Amendment editions of the *Manual* did not reflect the correct law on the matter, thus creating precisely the issues for the debate.[81] It was in his view 'astonishing that it should for so long have contained a statement which was wrong and which it has taken so long to correct'.[82] Needless to say, Lord Cork was having none of this. 'Great admirer as I am of lawyers,' he said, 'they do sometimes make mistakes.'[83]

The rejection of the plea

Before commenting on the significant developments in the 1990s, a word should be said about the rejection of a proposal to provide for the plea of superior orders at the Diplomatic Conference on Humanitarian Law in Armed Conflict (1974–1977) that produced Additional Protocol I to the 1949 Geneva Conventions. During the debate over Article 77 on 'superior orders' in Committee I, some delegations opposed 'the inclusion of

[76] Ibid. [77] Ibid., cols. 961–962. [78] Ibid., col. 962.
[79] *Parliamentary debates*, 1950, col. 447. [80] Ibid., col. 449.
[81] *Parliamentary debates*, 1952, col. 1004. [82] Ibid. [83] Ibid., col. 1023.

the principles' set forth in the Article from the beginning.[84] When Committee I adopted Article 77, as amended,[85] at the 70th meeting on 28 April 1977,[86] it read as follows:

> 1. The High Contracting Parties undertake to ensure that their internal law penalizing disobedience to orders shall not apply to orders that would constitute grave breaches of the Conventions and this Protocol.
> 2. The mere fact of having acted pursuant to an order of an authority or a superior does not absolve an accused person from penal responsibility, if it be established that in the circumstances at the time he knew or should have known that he was committing a grave breach of the Conventions or of this Protocol. It may, however, be taken into account in mitigation of punishment.[87]

The vote was thirty-eight for, twenty-two against, with fifteen abstentions.[88] There was no outright rejection of the plea as a defence, although pleading it successfully would have to satisfy the knowledge requirement, which depended on the manifest illegality test. Besides, even if the recipient knew about the illegality of the order in relation to the grave breaches, the order, if carried out by him, might still be considered as a mitigating factor.[89]

On 30 May 1977, the Plenary Meeting of the Diplomatic Conference voted on Article 77 as submitted by Committee I, and the result was thirty-six in favour, twenty-five against and twenty-five abstaining.[90] Because the Article failed to gain a two-thirds majority, it was rejected, and Additional Protocol I contains no rule on the matter of superior orders. Prior to the vote, the delegates of both the United Kingdom and Mexico pointed out that the draft Article should without distinction apply to both the grave breaches and other breaches of international humanitarian law, with the UK's delegate further suggesting that the matter be left for existing rules of international law to deal with, which

[84] *Official records of the Diplomatic Conference on the reaffirmation and development of international humanitarian law applicable in armed conflicts* (Bern: Federal Political Department, 1978), vol. 10, p. 187.

[85] Ibid., vol. 3, pp. 331–332 (amendments proposed by Syria, Australia, Switzerland and the United States).

[86] At the 69th meeting, on 27 April 1977, Committee I took a roll-call vote on a motion to retain an article on superior orders in draft Additional Protocol I, and the result was thirty-four for, nine against and thirty-five abstaining: ibid., vol. 9, pp. 387–388.

[87] Ibid., vol. 10, 262. [88] Ibid., 188.

[89] This was what the United States proposed: ibid., vol. 3, p. 332. This view was also shared by Canada: ibid., vol. 6, 330 (after voting for Article 77 in the plenary meeting).

[90] Ibid., vol. 6, p. 308.

were 'well understood and clearly explained in existing manuals on the law of armed conflict'.[91] There was no reference to the Nuremberg or Tokyo charters.

After the vote, a number of states explained their positions. Of those who had voted against the provision, Syria considered that it might incite disobedience to military orders,[92] while Yemen[93] and Sudan[94] expressed similar concerns about the implications for military discipline. Argentina stated that, 'The main difficulty . . . lies in deciding, according to rank, the extent to which orders may be questioned and the consequent penal responsibility of the agent.'[95] The United States explained that 'this basic unwillingness to provide a defence to combatants who refuse to commit an obviously illegal act is one that does not augur well for the future implementation of the Protocol'.[96] Of those who had voted in favour, Canada saw the retention of the Article as not in any way contrary to the maintenance of military discipline,[97] a view also favoured by the Holy See.[98] The latter further stated that the rejection of Article 77 was like a writing off of the principles applied in Nuremberg, thus taking 'humanitarian law back a step'.[99] Israel[100] and Poland,[101] which also both voted in favour, regarded Article 77 as reflecting customary law as enunciated in the Nürnberg Principles (and, Israel added, embodied in Article 125 of the Israel Military Justice Law).

The 1977 Diplomatic Conference's rejection of Article 77 was clear evidence that Article 8 of the Nuremberg Charter was not seen as representing customary law at the time, and the question of superior orders was far from settled. Consequently, the practice after the Diplomatic Conference, just like the practice prior to 1977, would follow any of the three views of the effect of superior orders: as a defence, as a mitigating factor or as a factor in support of another defence.

The ICC and Nuremberg

The drafters of the Rome Statute aimed to provide a comprehensive codification and clarification of international criminal law. When it came to the plea of superior orders, they had before them two traditions, which had been developing in parallel over the previous half century. The older of these, which could trace its genealogy back to the end of the

[91] Ibid., p. 308. [92] Ibid., p. 309. [93] Ibid., p. 332. [94] Ibid., p. 339. [95] Ibid., p. 330.
[96] Ibid., p. 339. [97] Ibid. [98] Ibid., p. 333. [99] Ibid., p. 334. [100] Ibid., p. 336.
[101] Ibid., p. 309.

nineteenth century, was the approach to the plea set out in national military law or war crimes legislation. This tradition encompassed the idea that the plea was an independent defence and emphasised the manifest illegality of orders. The newer approach was embodied in the Nuremberg and Tokyo judgments, which denied the idea that the plea was a separate defence, and laid stress on moral choice. The Rome Statute plumped for the older approach, with a few add-ons by way of compromise.

At the beginning of the 1990s, it might not have been anticipated that the drafters of the Rome Statute would endorse the older tradition. When anticipating the establishment of the International Tribunal for the former Yugoslavia in 1993, the UN Secretary-General Boutros Boutros-Ghali confidently stated that the Nuremberg Charter, including Article 8, had 'without doubt' become part of customary international law.[102] Shortly after, Article 7(4) of the ICTY's Statute provided that, 'The fact that an accused person acted pursuant to an order of a Government or of a superior shall not relieve him of criminal responsibility, but may be considered in mitigation of punishment if the International Tribunal determines that justice so requires'[103] – a formulation that hews close to the line followed by Nuremberg's Article 8. Similar Nuremberg-influenced articles appeared in the statutes for the courts established on Rwanda in 1994 and Sierra Leone in 2000.[104] There was therefore a clear conceptual thread running between the Nuremberg Charter and the statutes of the first ad hoc tribunals established by the UN Security Council.

This reaffirmation of Article 8 may have been due to the lack of ready rules to hand when the ad hoc courts were established. But the question of whether it reflected customary law at the time might not have been as clear-cut as the Secretary-General believed. Looking back, the debates of the 1950s in the International Law Commission and the Sixth Committee reveal several possible understandings of Article 8. As previously discussed, the 'Brierly amendment' of 1950, dealing with the reading of the

[102] *Report of the Secretary-General pursuant to Paragraph 2 of Security Council Resolution 808 (1993)*, S/25704, 3 May 1993, par. 35.

[103] Statute of the International Tribunal for the Prosecution of Persons Responsible for Serious Violations of International Humanitarian Law Committed in the Territory of the Former Yugoslavia since 1991, S/25704 (3 May 1993), adopted by Security Council, S/RES/827 (25 May 1993).

[104] Article 6(4), Statute for the International Criminal Tribunal for Rwanda; Article 6(4), Statute of the Special Court for Sierra Leone.

Nuremberg Judgment on superior orders and other issues, drew almost as much criticism as support from the members of the ILC, and, when it came to a vote, did not gain unanimous support.[105] If there were doubts about Article 8's customary law status in the 1950s, the doubts were revived in the 1990s, and they were transmitted into the negotiations over the Rome Statute governing the International Criminal Court, adopted in 1998.

The outcome of the debates at the Rome Conference was Article 33, which indicates that delegates did *not* consider Article 8 to be part of customary international law. Instead, it reverts to the position of preserving the plea as a defence, with the test of manifest illegality to be applied in tandem. It has also finally rid itself of the connection with moral choice. It states:

> 1. The fact that a crime within the jurisdiction of the Court has been committed by a person pursuant to an order of a Government or of a superior, whether military or civilian, shall not relieve that person of criminal responsibility unless:
>   (a) The person was under a legal obligation to obey orders of the Government or the superior in question;
>   (b) The person did not know that the order was unlawful; and
>   (c) The order was not manifestly unlawful.
> 2. For the purposes of this article, orders to commit genocide or crimes against humanity are manifestly unlawful.[106]

The plea and 'manifest illegality'

Existing practice has been wavering between moral choice and manifest illegality in assessing the effect of the plea of superior orders. The former was emphasised in the Nuremberg and Tokyo judgments, while the latter has been consistently, though not necessarily uniformly, set out in national military law or war crimes legislation. The Rome Statute opted for the manifest illegality approach.

The test of manifest illegality of a superior order appears in Article 33 (1). This has been a feature of the plea from its inception in German military law to the various national regulations put into place at the end

[105] ILC, *Yearbook of the International Law Commission* (1950), vol. 1, 47. The Amendment was eventually adopted by a vote of nine to three. The concurrent vote on the text of Principle IV on superior orders, as amended, showed a similar pattern: eight in favour, two against and two abstaining (ibid.).

[106] Rome Statute of the International Criminal Court: treaties.un.org.

of the Second World War.[107] It is therefore notable that it did not appear in Article 8 of the Nuremberg Charter (or in its successors in the statutes of the ad hoc tribunals). Article 8 could probably stake a claim to having started a new trend in international law, while Article 33, with its stress on manifest illegality, can be seen as sustaining the older tradition within national military law, with the two approaches running along parallel tracks. It might also be noted here that while Article 8's claim to reflect custom is questionable, Article 33's long pedigree with respect to manifest illegality does indeed entitle it to be considered as part of customary international law.

That said, Article 33 does contain two innovative elements that national military law, as of 1998, did not cover so far as manifest illegality is concerned. These appear in Articles 33(1)(c) and 33(2). Article 33(1)(c) introduces an objective test for the International Criminal Court to assess the manifest illegality or unlawfulness of the superior order in question. If a defendant intends to rely on Article 33 as a defence, one must do more than establish that they 'had no personal knowledge of the illegality of the order'. (By contrast, national military law or legislation on war crimes would deem it sufficient, under rules similar to Article 33(1)(b), to allow the plea of superior orders as a defence.) The defendant at the ICC must not only establish that they did not know an order was illegal but also, as an additional step, try to negate the point of manifest illegality, or at least raise a reasonable doubt on the point, in order to establish a defence.

Article 33(2), meanwhile, excludes the commission of genocide and crimes against humanity, as defined in the Rome Statute, from the defence of superior orders. This exclusion had not been familiar heretofore in either international jurisprudence or national military law, except in the Rome Conference's Preparatory Committee[108] – although its incorporation into Article 33 seems to have been less controversial than the incorporation of Article 33(1).

It might be added here that Article 33, while upholding certain traditions found in national military law, does not follow this body of law in all its variations. It does not, for example, recognise some countries' earlier practice of precluding enemy nationals from using a superior orders defence.[109] This is entirely to be expected. For one thing, the practice

[107] For the regulations put into place by the 'Big Four' Allies in the immediate post-war period, see Greenspan, *Modern law*, pp. 490–492.

[108] Triffterer, 'Article 33', p. 919. [109] Gaeta, 'Defence', 179 and fn. 22.

was not general, and for another, the modern trend was in the other direction: Article 2(2) of Control Council Law No. 10, for instance, defined the scope of the law as covering 'Any person without regard to nationality or the capacity in which he acted.'[110] Finally and most importantly, it would be rather unlikely for an international tribunal to discriminate between nationals and non-nationals, including enemy personnel, if all were involved in the commission of war crimes.

While one major distinction between the Nuremberg jurisprudence and the Rome Statute is Article 33's emphasis on manifest illegality, the other major distinction is that Article 33 has abandoned the Nuremberg Judgment's test of moral choice. This test seemed to fade out of international discourse in the early 1990s, making a final appearance in the draft Code of Crimes against the Peace and Security of Mankind of 1991.[111] There was no superior orders provision in the draft Code of 1994 (despite the Special Rapporteur's attempt to retain the moral choice principle).[112] By 1996, Article 5 of the draft Code stated: 'The fact that an individual charged with a crime against the peace and security of mankind acted pursuant to an order of a Government or a superior does not relieve him of criminal responsibility, but may be considered in mitigation of punishment if justice so requires.'[113] It is likely that the omission of moral choice was intended to disengage the plea from other defences, including duress.

The plea of superior orders may still be a factor in the application of Article 32(2) of the Rome Statute, which states, among other things, that mistake of law may be 'a ground for excluding criminal responsibility if it negates the mental element required by such a crime, or as provided for in article 33'.[114] But it is not necessary for the application of Article 32(2) in all cases. Sometimes the plea may have little to do with the negation of the *mens rea* on the strength of such a mistake of law as envisaged under

[110] T. Taylor, *Final report to the Secretary of the Army on the Nuernberg war crimes trials under Control Council Law No. 10* (Washington, DC: US Government Printing Press, 1949), Appendix D, p. 251.

[111] ILC, *Report of the International Law Commission on the work of its forty-third session* (29 April-19 July 1991), UNGA, Official Records, 46th Session, Supplement No. 10 (A/46/10), 100.

[112] *Report of the International Law Commission on the work of its forty-sixth session* (2 May-22 July 1994), UNGA, Official Records, 49th Session, Supplement No. 10 (A/49/10), 83.

[113] *Report of the International Law Commission on the work of its forty-eighth session* (6 May-26 July 1996), UNGA, Official Records, 51st Session, Supplement No. 10 (A/59/10), 23.

[114] Rome Statute of the International Criminal Court: treaties.un.org.

Article 32(2). It can instead exclude criminal liability of the defendant in its own way, as defined in Article 33.[115]

The plea as an independent defence

The independent status of the defence of superior orders, accepted in many national military and war crimes legislations or cases,[116] has been confirmed in Article 33. That may not settle the debate among lawyers, though. One prominent objector, Yoram Dinstein, who rejects the plea either as a defence or a mitigating factor, states that

> the fact of obedience to orders constitutes not a defence *per se* but only a factual element that may be taken into account in conjunction with the other circumstances of the given case within the compass of a defence based on lack of *mens rea*, that is, mistake of law or compulsion.[117]

By this he proposes a new answer to the question of the nature of the plea of superior orders, and he calls this 'the *mens rea* principle'.[118]

There is strong logic in his proposal, which fits with the commonly known effect of a defence of mistake or duress. A considerable part of the jurisprudence of post-war war crimes trials, together with the aforementioned discussions in the course of drafting the Nuremberg Charter, shows support for it. The question, though, is whether his proposal merely addresses the method of application, rather than the actual status of the plea, in a context of criminal proceedings.

At the common law at least, 'defences' are understood as being 'some justifying or excusing circumstance',[119] or at a pinch, 'failure of proof' arguments.[120] It is for the prosecution to disprove a plea or circumstance raised by the defendant on fact and law. Otherwise, the case falls apart as the plea successfully negates the *mens rea* or, in a broader sense, the fault of the defendant. The point would therefore seem to be that the prosecution would need to train arguments and proof on a target, namely, a plea raised by the defence. If the plea of superior orders cannot be raised as an independent ground, there may be no need for the prosecution to direct its firepower at it. For the plea would be like any other circumstances in support of a plea of duress or mistake of law. It can certainly be one of

[115] On similar doubts, see Zimmermann, 'Superior orders', p. 966.
[116] UNWCC, *History*, pp. 280–288. [117] Dinstein, *Defence*, p. 88. [118] Ibid.
[119] D. Ormerod, *Smith & Hogan criminal law* (Oxford University Press, 11th edn., 2005), p. 247.
[120] A. Ashworth, *Principles of criminal law* (Oxford University Press, 5th edn., 2006), p. 202.

those circumstances, depending on the factual background of the given case. But can it be more than that? After all, not every case of duress or mistake of law results from a manifestly illegal order. The drafters of the Rome Statute clearly thought as much, which is why they created Article 33.

The problem with dismissing the plea as a separate defence lies in the plain fact that Article 33 stands alone in the Rome Statute. It may be relevant as a mistake of law defence under Article 32(2), but only if the *mens rea* of the defendant is obliterated by that mistake. In that case, it is no longer an independent defence, but part of another self-contained defence. It is absorbed in that new defence. But where it is not identified with a mistake of law, the plea of superior orders has an independent role to play as a defence, as Article 33 explicitly recognises.

In addition, as already noted, the plea had been applied as an independent defence by almost all American tribunals established under Control Council Law No. 10. The conditional liability approach has persisted since then in the practice of military law in the United States.[121] The American tilt towards a defence of superior orders was particularly felt during the negotiations of Article 33 of the Rome Statute.[122]

Moreover, the independence of the plea of superior orders is likely due to the unique character of armed forces, to which general principles of criminal law may not be readily applicable. Some of the delegates who voted against Article 77 on superior orders at the 1977 Diplomatic Conference made this point. In 1991, the ILC considered 'the question of superior order and its effect on the responsibility of a subordinate', and took the view 'that the importance of the question and its relationship with the issue of responsibility of the superior' justified covering it in Article 11 of the draft Code of Crimes, which dealt with the orders of a government or superior, rather than in Article 14, which provided comprehensively for the issue of defences in proceedings without singling out any particular defence.[123] Whether its relations with superior responsibility are so important as to guarantee its independence as a rule was not discussed, but it does confirm that the superior orders, like superior responsibility, is a distinctive feature of the law governing international crimes.

[121] L.C. Green, *Superior orders in national and international law* (Leiden: A.W. Sijthoff, 1976), pp. 134–153.

[122] Zimmermann, 'Superior orders', p. 967.

[123] ILC, *Report of . . . its forty-third session*, 100.

Conclusion

At present, customary law seems to recognise two approaches to the issue of superior orders and has yet to settle on either. It would follow that it is unnecessary for the ICC to bring its practice into line with the parallel version of the rule on superior orders exemplified by the Nuremberg Charter and the statutes of the ICTY and ICTR.[124] After all, Article 33 of the Rome Statute simply addresses the plea from a different, but equally valid, perspective. First, it recognises the plea of superior orders as an independent defence, but imposes substantial limitations on its scope, excluding genocide and crimes against humanity. Second, it does not recognise the relevance of moral choice, but does recognise the manifest illegality of the order. Both points support the argument here that the plea of superior orders may be independently invoked either as a defence or as a mitigating factor.[125]

All the same, the debate over the state of customary law regarding the plea of superior orders will linger on. To indicate some of the difficulties that lie ahead, the ICRC's 2005 study, *Customary international humanitarian law*, states: 'Obeying a superior order does not relieve a subordinate of criminal responsibility if the subordinate knew that the act ordered was unlawful or should have known because of the manifestly unlawful nature of the act ordered.'[126] This immediately suggests the *a contrario* view that the plea would be a defence if the subordinate did not know of the unlawful nature of the order or if the order were not manifestly unlawful. These issues are unresolved, and it may depend on which tradition is called upon: that of Article 8 and the ad hoc tribunals or that of national military law and the Rome Statute. The fact that the latter has given the ICC the opportunity to develop a new line of case law[127] in contradistinction to the Nuremberg tradition will, of course, provide further challenges to legal thinking.

124 See also, R. Cryer *et al.*, *An introduction to international criminal law and procedure* (Cambridge University Press, 2nd edn., c. 2010), pp. 416–417. For emphasis on the problems with this, see Dinstein, *Defence*, pp. xx–xxi; and Gaeta, 'Defence', 190.

125 Article 78 of the Rome Statute; and Rule 145(1)(b) and 145(2)(a)(i) of the ICC's Rules of Procedure and Evidence.

126 J.-M. Henckaerts and L. Doswald-Beck, *Customary international humanitarian law*, vol. 1, Rules (Cambridge University Press, 2005), Rule 155, p. 565.

127 See, for example, *Prosecutor* v. *Lubanga and Ntaganda*, ICC-01/04-120-Red, OTP Document in Support of the Appeal (28 January 2011), par. 40(a).

11

The joint criminal enterprise doctrine at the Extraordinary Chambers in the Courts of Cambodia

NEHA JAIN[1]

Joint criminal enterprise (JCE) liability, first articulated by the Appeals Chamber of the International Criminal Tribunal for the former Yugoslavia in *Prosecutor* v. *Tadić*, comprises three categories – JCE I, JCE II and JCE III.[2] The *actus reus* elements, common to all three categories, are a plurality of persons; the existence of a common plan, design or purpose which amounts to or involves the commission of a crime provided for in the Statute; and participation of the accused in the common design.[3] The *mens rea* element differs for each category. For JCE I, the accused must share the intent to perpetrate a certain crime. For JCE II, the accused must know of the system of ill treatment and intend to further it. For JCE III, the accused must intend to participate in and further the criminal purpose of the group. In addition, they will be liable for a crime other than the one envisaged in the common plan if the crime was a foreseeable consequence of the common plan and they willingly took that risk.[4]

Initially developed by the International Criminal Tribunal for the former Yugoslavia (ICTY) based upon a controversial interpretation of 'commission' liability in Article 7(1) of its Statute, JCE has come to occupy pride of place in prosecutions before international and hybrid tribunals around the world. Nevertheless, academics remain sceptical about its possibilities and limitations, ranging from an outright

[1] Material for this chapter originally appeared in N. Jain, *Perpetrators and accessories in international criminal law: individual modes of responsibility for collective crimes* (Oxford: Hart Publishing, 2014).

[2] *Prosecutor* v. *Tadić*, IT-94-1-A, Appeals Chamber Judgment (15 July 1999) (*Tadić* Appeals Judgment), par. 195.

[3] Ibid., par. 227. [4] Ibid., par. 228.

denunciation of JCE as a device for 'just convict[ing] everyone'[5] to pleas for curtailing its scope and applicability.[6] Recent years have witnessed the first rumblings of discontent with JCE within the international criminal law community, where courts such as the International Criminal Court (ICC)[7] and prominent academics[8] now propose indirect perpetration and co-perpetration as doctrinally richer alternatives to JCE.

The Extraordinary Chambers in the Courts of Cambodia (ECCC) is the only international tribunal to have expressly rejected JCE III on the basis that it does not have a firm foundation in customary international law.[9] The ECCC's pronouncement thus constitutes a significant departure from established JCE jurisprudence and has important consequences, both for the evolution of modes of participation at other tribunals and for the interpretation of perpetration responsibility at the ECCC. This chapter outlines the evolution of the concept of JCE in international criminal law and its interpretation by the ECCC.

Innovations at the Yugoslavia Tribunal

Duško Tadić was a member of an armed Serbian group that had attacked the village of Jaskici in Bosnia-Herzegovina and killed five Bosnian Muslim men. He was charged under Article 7(1) of the ICTY Statute

[5] M.E. Badar, '"Just convict everyone!" – joint perpetration: from Tadić to Stakić and back again', *International Criminal Law Review* 6 (2006), 302.

[6] See, for example, H. Olásolo, 'Reflections on the treatment of the notions of control of the crime and joint criminal enterprise in the Stakić Appeal Judgment', *International Criminal Law Review* 7 (2007), 157–161; E. van Sliedregt, 'Joint criminal enterprise as a pathway to convicting individuals for genocide', *Journal of International Criminal Justice* 5 (2007), 205–206; A.M. Danner and J.S. Martinez, 'Guilty associations: joint criminal enterprise, command responsibility, and the development of international criminal law', *California Law Review* 93 (2005), 134–146.

[7] See *Prosecutor* v. *Lubanga*, ICC-01/04-01/06, Pre-Trial Chamber I Decision on the Confirmation of Charges (29 January 2007) (*Lubanga* Decision), pars. 322, 339–341; *Prosecutor* v. *Katanga and Chui*, ICC-01/04-01/07, Pre-Trial Chamber I Decision on the Confirmation of Charges (30 September 2008) (*Katanga* Decision), pars. 488–499.

[8] See, for example, K. Ambos, 'Joint criminal enterprise and command responsibility', *Journal of International Criminal Justice* 5 (2007), 159; H. van der Wilt, 'Joint criminal enterprise: possibilities and limitations', *Journal of International Criminal Justice* 5 (2007), 91.

[9] *Nuon et al.*, 002/19-09-2007-ECCC-OCIJ, Pre-Trial Chamber Decision on the Appeals against the Co-Investigative Judges Order on Joint Criminal Enterprise (JCE) (20 May 2010) (*Nuon* PTC JCE Decision), par. 83; *Nuon et al.*, 002/19-09-2007/ECCC/TC, Trial Chamber Decision on the Applicability of Joint Criminal Enterprise (12 September 2011) (*Nuon* Trial Chamber JCE Decision), par. 35.

with thirty-one counts of crimes against humanity, war crimes and grave breaches, including the killings. Although Tadić had been a member of the group and played an active role in the attack, the Trial Chamber was not satisfied beyond reasonable doubt that he had participated in the killings of the five men.[10] The prosecution appealed against this decision, arguing that Tadić should have been held responsible for the killings in accordance with the doctrine of 'common purpose', since the killings were a natural and foreseeable consequence of the attack and occurred in the context of a broader policy to ethnically cleanse the region of Prijedor of non-Serbs.[11] As there was no proof that Tadić had personally killed the men, the Appeals Chamber had to decide whether he could be held responsible because of his participation in the acts of the group that had committed the killings.[12]

The Appeals Chamber analysed Tadić's responsibility under Article 7(1) of the ICTY Statute, which deals with modes of participation.[13] It interpreted the concept of 'commission' in the context of the inviolability of the principle of personal culpability in criminal law,[14] by situating it within the object and purpose of the ICTY Statute,[15] and based on the inherent nature of international crimes.[16] According to the Chamber, the ICTY had a mandate to bring to justice *all* those who were responsible for serious violations of international humanitarian law committed in former Yugoslavia, regardless of the manner of their participation.[17] Thus, an accused who contributed to the commission of a crime enumerated under the Statute in pursuance of a common criminal purpose could, in certain circumstances, also be held responsible.[18] The Appeals Chamber claimed support for this category of collective criminality from customary international law – mainly cases from domestic courts and international legislation.[19]

[10] *Prosecutor* v. *Tadić*, IT-94-1-T, Trial Chamber Judgment (7 May 1997), par. 373.

[11] 'The second ground of cross-appeal by the prosecution', *Tadić* Appeals Judgment, par. 175.

[12] Ibid., par. 183.

[13] Article 7(1) of the ICTY Statute states, 'A person who planned, instigated, ordered, committed or otherwise aided and abetted in the planning, preparation or execution of a crime referred to in articles 2 to 5 of the present Statute, shall be individually responsible for the crime.'

[14] *Tadić* Appeals Judgment, par. 186. [15] Ibid., pars. 189–190. [16] Ibid., pars. 191.

[17] Ibid., par. 190. [18] Ibid. [19] Ibid., par. 194.

JCE I: common design

The first category of cases identified by the Chamber is where all the perpetrators, acting pursuant to a common design, possess the same criminal intent. The accused must voluntarily participate in one aspect of the common design, and intend the object of the common design.[20] To establish the customary international law basis of JCE I, the Chamber cited cases decided by the Allied Military courts set up in the aftermath of the Second World War, but its reliance on these cases is questionable on various grounds.

First, early cases convened by the British, such as the *Almelo*[21] and *Schonfeld* [22] trials, were decided under Regulation 8(ii) of the Royal Warrant: this was an evidentiary rule which was not based on any notion of common design liability.[23] Second, in other cases, the basis for attribution of liability is unclear – either the decisions did not explicitly state what mode of responsibility was being applied (such as in the American-run *Einsatzgruppen* case)[24] or they used vague terminology such as being 'concerned in the commission of the crime', which is capable of multiple meanings, including liability for aiding and abetting (such as the later British-run *Feurstein* and *Jepsen* trials).[25] Third, quite a few of the cases

20 Ibid., par. 196.

21 *The trial of Otto Sandrock et al.* (*Almelo* case), British Military Court, Almelo (24–26 November 1945) in United Nations War Crimes Commission, *Law reports of trials of war criminals*, 15 vols. (London: HMSO, 1947–1949), vol. 1.

22 *Trial of Franz Schonfeld et al.*, British Military Court, Essen (11–26 June 1946) in UNWCC, *Law reports*, vol. 11, p. 71.

23 Royal Warrant: Regulations for the Trial of War Criminals (Army Order 81/1945) (London: HMSO, signed 14 June 1945, promulgated 18 June 1945): LCO 53/102, National Archives, UK (TNA). Regulation 8(ii) states, 'Where there is evidence that a war crime has been the result of concerted action upon the part of a unit or group of men, then evidence given upon any charge relating to that crime against any member of such unit or group may be received as *prima facie* evidence of the responsibility of each member of that unit or group for that crime.'

24 *United States* v. *Ohlendorf et al.* (*Einsatzgruppen* case), US Military Tribunal Judgment, in *Trials of war criminals before the Nuernberg Military Tribunals under Control Council Law No. 10*, 'The Green Series', 15 vols. (Nuremberg: US Government Printing Office, October 1946–April 1949), vol. 4. The *Tadić* Appeals Chamber erroneously relies on a statement of law from the *Einsatzgruppen* prosecution's closing statement rather than from the Judgment (par. 200).

25 *Trial of Feurstein et al.* (*Ponzano* case), Judgment (24 August 1948), cited by *Tadić Appeals Judgment*, par. 199; *Trial of Gustav Alfred Jepsen et al.*, Judgment (24 August 1946), cited by *Tadić Appeals Judgment*, par. 198. The *Tadić Appeals Judgment* quote from *Jepson*, purportedly in support of common design, is ambiguous; it is not clear whether Jepsen was being held responsible for the acts committed by his agents, under his directions, and with his active participation, or for being part of the 'common enterprise'.

cited involve a very small group of people who are familiar with each other and physically present at the commission of the offences.[26] This is a much narrower category of cases than those at which JCE I liability is aimed. Indeed, given its reliance on these cases, the ICTY Appeals Chamber concluded its analysis of JCE I on a surprising note: 'It should be noted that in many post-World War II trials held in other countries, courts took the same approach to instances of crimes in which two or more persons participated with a different degree of involvement. However, they did not rely upon the notion of common purpose or common design, preferring to refer instead to the notion of co-perpetration.'[27]

The Chamber's distinction between 'common purpose or common design' and 'co-perpetration', and its non-reliance on cases concerning the latter category, is mystifying, given that most of the cases it cites would indeed be more akin to a notion of co-perpetration, which was first articulated by the ICTY in *Prosecutor* v. *Furundžija*.[28] In this trial, the Trial Chamber distinguished between two separate modes of liability in international criminal law: co-perpetrators who participate in a joint criminal enterprise, and aiders and abettors.[29] It defined common design liability to comprise participation in a joint criminal enterprise (*actus reus*) with the intent to participate (*mens rea*).[30] It further held that the accused would be held guilty as a co-perpetrator (of torture) if he participated in an integral part of the crime (torture) and partook of the purpose behind the crime (torture).[31] While the *Furundžija* Trial Chamber made no clear distinction between co-perpetration and joint criminal enterprise, it actually endorsed these two separate categories of liability.[32] Since the accused played an integral role in the torture, it convicted him as a co-perpetrator.[33] The concept of joint criminal enterprise was not developed any further.

The cases cited by the *Tadić* Appeals Chamber in support of JCE I fit into the concept of co-perpetration articulated in *Furundžija*.[34] In almost

[26] See Danner and Martinez, 'Guilty associations', 111.

[27] *Tadić* Appeals Judgment, par. 201.

[28] *Prosecutor* v. *Furundžija*, IT-95-17/I-T, Trial Chamber Judgment (10 December 1998) (*Furundžija* Trial Judgment).

[29] Ibid., par. 216. [30] Ibid., par. 249. [31] Ibid., par. 257.

[32] G. Boas, J.L. Bischoff and N.L. Reid, *International criminal law practitioner library series*, vol. 1: *Forms of responsibility in international criminal law* (Cambridge University Press, 2007), pp. 13–14.

[33] *Furundžija* Trial Judgment, pars. 267, 268.

[34] Boas *et al.*, *Forms of responsibility*, pp. 18–19.

all these cases, the accused is not merely part of a large undefined group whose members he may never have met but with whom he is presumed to share a common intention. Rather, he is relatively close to the scene of the crime and provides active assistance.

JCE II: concentration camp cases

JCE II, labelled as a 'variant' of JCE I,[35] comprises concentration camp cases where crimes are committed by 'members of military or administrative units ... i.e., by groups of persons acting pursuant to a concerted plan'.[36] Whereas the *actus reus* elements are common to all forms of JCE, the *mens rea* differs. For JCE II, the accused must know of the system of ill treatment and intend to further it. In support of this category, the Chamber relied on two cases, one decided by a British military court, the other by an American military court, sitting in Germany: *Belsen*[37] and *Dachau*.[38] In both cases, the defendants, who occupied important positions in concentration camps, were charged with committing various offences against camp detainees in pursuance of a common design.

In *Dachau*, the crux of the prosecution case was reliance on a common design that required proof of a system to ill-treat the prisoners and commit the crimes, the accused's awareness of the system, and the accused's encouragement and abetment in enforcing this system.[39] The defence challenged this notion of common design on several counts, the most notable of which was the vagueness of the term and the difficulty in distinguishing it from a charge of conspiracy.[40]

The military court did not find it necessary to distinguish between conspiracy and common design, although from the evidence adduced by the prosecution and the conviction based upon this, it can be surmised that the burden of proof was lower than it would be in a conspiracy charge.[41] There was no evidence to show that the accused had ever come together to form an agreement to kill and ill-treat the detainees, they did not necessarily know each other, and they were not even all at Dachau at the same time.[42] The conviction was based on the fact that there was

[35] *Tadić* Appeals Judgment, par. 203. [36] Ibid., par. 202.

[37] *Trial of Josef Kramer et al.* (*Belsen* case), British Military Court, Luneberg (17 September-17 November 1945) in UNWCC, *Law reports*, vol. 2.

[38] *Trial of Martin Gottfried Weiss et al.* (*Dachau Concentration Camp* case), General Military Government Court of the US Zone, Dachau (15 November-13 December 1945) in UNWCC, *Law reports*, vol. 11.

[39] Ibid., p. 13. [40] Ibid., p. 14. [41] Ibid. [42] Ibid.

a general system of cruelty in place in the camp, which was practised with the active knowledge and participation of the accused. Everyone who took part in this common design was guilty of a war crime, with the differing degrees of participation being reflected in the different sentences imposed (from five years' imprisonment to death).[43] It is difficult, however, to state unreservedly that the court was even conscious of convicting the accused pursuant to a mode of liability that was distinct from conspiracy.

This is also true of *Belsen*, where, the United Nations War Crimes Commission (UNWCC) reported, the prosecution charged the accused with being 'parties to a general conspiracy' (with alternative expressions being 'concerted action', 'joint action', or 'unit') to ill-treat the camp prisoners.[44] There is no explicit statement in the decision on what mode of responsibility was used to finally convict the accused. Further, in his summary of the case, the Judge Advocate specified that in assessing responsibility for participation in the administration of the camp, a person's mere presence on the staff would not suffice; there had to be a deliberate commission of a war crime.[45]

The *Tadić* Appeals Chamber relied on these cases to derive the elements of JCE II liability. These consist of 'active participation in the enforcement of a system of repression, *as it could be inferred from the position of authority* and the specific functions held by each accused'.[46] In addition, the accused must have known of the nature of the system and have had the intent to further the common design of ill treatment.[47] The Chamber emphasised that the intent element can be inferred from the accused's position of authority, which may, on its own, indicate an awareness of the common design.[48]

This is a troubling extrapolation from *Dachau* and *Belsen*. It contradicts the caveat introduced by the Judge Advocate in *Belsen* (one of the only two cases cited by the Chamber) that the mere position on the staff of a concentration camp is insufficient to establish criminal responsibility. In the *Tadić* Chamber's formulation, a position of authority serves as inferential evidence for establishing both the *actus reus* and the *mens rea* elements of JCE II. This gives the position of the accused far more weight in establishing responsibility than what a fair reading of *Belsen* would indicate. It also casts doubt on the Chamber's claim that JCE II is merely a variant of JCE I. For JCE I, the *mens rea* requirement is that the accused should have

[43] Ibid. [44] *Belsen* case, p. 108. [45] Ibid., pp. 120–121.
[46] *Tadić* Appeals Judgment, par. 203. Emphasis added. [47] Ibid. [48] Ibid.

intended (along with the co-perpetrators) to perpetrate a certain crime.[49] If this intent element in JCE II can be inferred from the position of the accused in the hierarchy, and if this position can make him liable for all crimes that may be part of the concentration camp operation despite his lack of express knowledge, then the *mens rea* element in JCE I is watered down to a considerable degree. Indeed, it comes to more closely resemble JCE III.[50]

JCE III: the extended form

JCE III, also referred to as the 'extended form of joint criminal enterprise' in subsequent ICTY jurisprudence,[51] comprises cases 'involving a common design to pursue one course of conduct where one of the perpetrators commits an act which, while outside the common design, was nevertheless a natural and foreseeable consequence of the effecting of that common purpose'.[52] The accused must have been aware that the actions of the group were most likely to lead to the killing, and have chosen to take that risk; in other words, the mental state is not one of mere negligence, but advertent recklessness, or *dolus eventualis*.[53]

The Chamber based its analysis of the requirements for JCE III liability on a series of cases. The first of these are situations of mob violence, where several participants carry out the common unlawful purpose, but the precise role of each perpetrator is unclear, or it is difficult to determine the exact causal connection between individual perpetrators' acts and the harm suffered.[54] The *Tadić* Chamber referred particularly to the *Essen Lynching*[55] and *Borkum Island*[56] cases, decided respectively by

[49] Ibid., par. 228.

[50] See also, S. Powles, 'Joint criminal enterprise: criminal liability by prosecutorial ingenuity and judicial creativity?', *Journal of International Criminal Justice* 2 (2004), 609–610.

[51] *Prosecutor* v. *Blaškić*, IT-95-14-A, Appeals Chamber Judgment (29 July 2004), par. 33.

[52] *Tadić* Appeals Judgment, par. 204.

[53] Ibid., par. 220. As critics point out, the Chamber uses different formulations to describe the *mens rea* applicable to JCE III: the consequence not covered in the common plan could be predicted and the accused was indifferent to the risk; *dolus eventualis*; *culpa* (negligence); and that the crime was not only foreseeable but, additionally, the accused willingly took that risk. (See M. Sassòli and L.M. Olson, 'The judgment of the ICTY Appeals Chamber on the merits in the *Tadić* case', *International Review of the Red Cross* 82 (2000), 749–750.)

[54] Ibid., par. 205.

[55] *Trial of Erich Heyer et al.* (*Essen Lynching* case), British Military Court, Essen (18–19, 21–22 December 1945) in UNWCC, *Law reports*, vol. 1.

[56] *United States* v. *Kurt Goebell et al.* (*Borkum Island* case), cited in *Tadić* Appeals Judgment, par. 210.

a British military court and a US military court. These involved Germans being charged with war crimes for having taken part in the repeated assault on, and ultimate death of, British and American prisoners of war.

In *Essen Lynching*, the prosecution had argued that 'every person who, following the incitement to the crowd to murder these men, voluntarily took aggressive action against any one of these three airmen, was guilty in that he was concerned in the killing'.[57] The accused were all held guilty. The *Tadić* Chamber relied on this conviction to infer that though not all the accused intended to kill, they were nevertheless found guilty for being concerned in the killing. Thus, those who struck a blow or incited the murder were guilty of murder because they could have foreseen that this would result in the killing of the prisoners.[58] The Chamber's reliance on a summary of the case that fails to state the legal basis of the verdict is of dubious value.[59] It is moreover contestable whether the *Essen Lynching* prosecution relied on any theory of common design.[60] On the contrary, it cited several theories of liability in the course of its argument, including holding the accused responsible as accessories before the fact or as principal parties to the crime.[61] Further, even if the court did resort to some notion of common design, it is difficult to see why JCE I cannot be applied to the case – the common design was evidently to kill the prisoners, and the various accused played different roles in that common design with the intent to accomplish this objective.

The same objection can be raised against *Tadić*'s reference to *Borkum Island*. Here, the prosecution had developed a notion of common design which stressed the role of each of the accused as a cog in the wheel of the common design and their responsibility for the prisoners' murders on the basis of their participation in the violence that led to the killing. The *Tadić* Appeals Chamber acknowledged that this conception was closer to JCE I rather than JCE III.[62] Yet it contended that since some of the accused had been found guilty of assault, whereas others had been convicted for murder without any evidence that they had actually killed the prisoners, this must have been on the basis of the latter's ability to

57 *Essen Lynching* case, p. 89. (A different version of this quote, taken from the transcript, appears in *Tadić* Appeals Judgment, par. 208.)
58 *Tadić* Appeals Judgment, par. 209.
59 Danner and Martinez, 'Guilty associations', 110–111.
60 Ibid., 111; see also R.C. Clarke, 'Return to *Borkum Island*: extended joint criminal enterprise responsibility in the wake of World War II', *Journal of International Criminal Justice* 9 (2011), 851.
61 *Essen Lynching* case, pp. 89–90.
62 *Tadić* Appeals Judgment, pars. 210–211.

predict that the assault would result in the killings.[63] This is a misleading conclusion. One can argue that if JCE III was the basis for convicting some of the accused of murder, it should possibly have been applied to hold everyone in the group guilty of murder rather than assault.

The *Tadić* Chamber then turned to a number of Italian cases dealing with crimes committed during the Second World War. The only pertinent case cited for the proposition that a person may be held criminally responsible for the acts of a group which were not part of the original criminal purpose is *D'Ottavio et al.*[64] In this case, four armed civilians attempted to capture two former Yugoslav prisoners who had escaped from a concentration camp. One of the civilians shot at the prisoners, resulting in their death. The Italian Court of Cassation applied Article 116 of the Italian Criminal Code to uphold the trial court's conviction of the accused for manslaughter.[65] While the result in *D'Ottavio* aligns with an application of JCE III, the legal basis is quite different. Unlike *Tadić*, the decision in *D'Ottavio* is based on a mode of liability provided specifically in the aforementioned Article 116. The rationale for liability under this Article is the concurrence of independent causes: the cause of a cause is also the cause of the thing caused.[66] This differs from the notion of collective responsibility in JCE doctrine. *D'Ottavio* also applies the causation nexus of foreseeability within the context of a very small closed group of people who work in concert. By contrast, JCE III liability has no ostensible temporal or geographic limitation, and can extend to individuals who had no prior contact with each other and/or were unaware of each other's exact actions.

JCE after *Tadić*

Since the *Tadić* trial, there have been important developments in JCE doctrine at the ICTY. Three in particular – the development of the 'fluid

[63] Ibid., pars. 212–213.

[64] *D'Ottavio et al.*, no. 270, Italian Court of Cassation, Criminal Section I, Judgment (12 March 1947) (trans. A. Cassese) in *Journal of International Criminal Justice* 5 (2007), 232–234. The relevance of the other Italian cases is less obvious; for example, *Aratano et al.* deals with exculpatory factors for attributing liability to a group of persons acting together when the crime committed by one of them goes beyond the intended object – and so adds nothing to the issue of the attribution of criminal responsibility (*Tadić* Appeals Judgment, pars. 216–217).

[65] According to *D'Ottavio* (233), Article 116 states, 'Whenever the crime committed is different from that willed by one of the participants, also that participant answers for the crime, if the fact is a consequence of his action or omission.'

[66] Ibid.

JCE' idea, the redefinition of the 'common plan' concept and the requirement of 'significant contribution' – will be relevant to how JCE doctrine may evolve at the ECCC, especially because they relate to problems concerning the attribution of responsibility to high-level leaders who are remote from the scene of the crime.

The first development is the emergence of the idea of a 'fluid' JCE. In *Krajišnik*, the Trial Chamber embraced the notion of a common plan which is fluid in its criminal means: the accused may be held responsible for crimes that were initially not part of the plan if leading JCE members have information about the additional crimes due to an expansion of the criminal objective and do not prevent their recurrence.[67] In this situation, the accused's contribution towards these additional crimes is not likely to be significant, yet he will be responsible for them not because of his own conduct but because of the conduct of leading JCE members.

To illustrate this concept, if leading JCE members accept crimes that are not initially part of the plan (say unlawful detentions, killings), they can be regarded as an expansion of the means of achieving the aim of the JCE (forcible transfer and deportation).[68] Using this logic, the accused can be convicted under JCE I rather than under JCE III, which undermines the shared intent requirement for JCE I and elides the distinction between JCE I and JCE III.[69] The *Krajišnik* Appeals Chamber attempted to distinguish between the fluid JCE I category and JCE III on the basis that in the case of the former, the accused is responsible for crimes after they have become part of the common objective, and not beforehand (on the basis that they were a natural and foreseeable consequence under JCE III).[70] It also demanded a more rigorous factual evaluation of when and how leading JCE members became aware of the expanded crimes, and if they failed to take preventative measure and persisted in their implementation.[71]

[67] *Prosecutor* v. *Krajišnik*, IT-00-39-T, Trial Chamber Judgment (27 September 2006) (*Krajišnik* Trial Judgment), par. 1098.

[68] Ibid., pars. 1098, 1126, 1182; see also *Prosecutor* v. *Popović et al.*, IT-05-88-T, Trial Chamber II Judgment (10 June 2010) (*Popović* Trial Judgment), par. 1028; *Prosecutor* v. *Dordević*, IT-05-87/1-T, Trial Chamber Judgment (23 February 2011) (*Dordević* Trial Judgment), par. 1862.

[69] E. van Sliedregt, *Individual criminal responsibility in international law* (Oxford University Press, 2012), p. 137.

[70] *Prosecutor* v. *Krajišnik*, IT-00-39-A, Appeals Chamber Judgment (17 March 2009) (*Krajišnik* Appeals Judgment), pars. 164–167.

[71] Ibid., par. 172.

Despite these safeguards, the creation of a fluid JCE I category leads to an expansion in the scope of JCE liability. As the Appeals Chamber noted, there is no clarity on who is a 'leading JCE member'[72] – an acceptance of the expanded crimes by 'leading members' such as zealous mid-level participants who go beyond the policy formulated initially by political leaders may thus form part of the fluid plan, for which the latter can be responsible under JCE I. Moreover, the broader the definition of the initial expanded JCE, the easier it is to build a case for even further crimes under JCE III occurring as a natural and foreseeable consequence of this evolving JCE I.

The second development at the ICTY post-*Tadić* is the redefinition of the common plan or agreement. In *Brdanin*, the Trial Chamber attempted to qualify the extent of common purpose when it decided that in order to establish JCE liability, there must be an understanding between the accused and the *physical perpetrators* of the crime to commit that particular crime, or a crime that is a natural and foreseeable consequence of the crime agreed upon.[73] It is not sufficient to show an agreement between the accused and the person in control of a military or similar unit committing the crime.[74] This mutual understanding to commit a crime can be established through direct evidence, or it may be inferred from the fact that the accused and the physical perpetrators acted in unison to implement the common plan, though only when this is the sole inference possible from the evidence.[75] A necessary implication of this definition of an agreement is that the physical perpetrator must be a member of the JCE.[76] The Chamber also cautioned that given the 'extraordinarily broad' nature of the case and the structural remoteness of the accused from the commission of the crimes, JCE might not be an appropriate mode of liability to describe the accused's responsibility.[77]

This requirement of an agreement between the physical perpetrators of the crime and the accused was overturned by the *Brdanin* Appeals Chamber, which concluded that in order to establish JCE liability it is not important whether the physical perpetrator of the crime is a JCE member, but whether the particular crime in question forms part of the

72 Ibid.

73 *Prosecutor* v. *Brdanin*, IT-99-36-T, Trial Chamber Judgment (1 September 2004) (*Brdanin* Trial Judgment), pars. 344, 347.

74 Ibid., par. 347. 75 Ibid., pars. 352–353.

76 *Prosecutor* v. *Brdanin*, IT-99-36-A, Appeals Chamber Judgment (3 April 2007) (*Brdanin* Appeals Judgment), pars. 389–391.

77 *Brdanin* Trial Judgment, par. 355.

common purpose.[78] This may be inferred from various circumstances, including whether some members of the JCE closely cooperated with the physical perpetrator to further the common criminal purpose. It is not essential that the latter knows of the existence of the JCE.[79] Regardless of whether the physical perpetrator is a JCE member, an express agreement between him and the JCE members is not necessary.[80] The crime must be imputable to a JCE member who, in using the physical perpetrator, acts according to the common plan.[81] The determination of this connection depends on the individual facts of the case. If a JCE member explicitly or implicitly requests, instigates, orders, encourages or otherwise avails himself of a non-JCE member to commit the crime, this is indicative of the requisite link.[82] The most important factor is the existence of a criminal purpose that is not merely the same, but common, to all the persons acting together within the enterprise. Even if the contribution of the accused to this purpose is not substantial, it must be significant for the crimes for which he is found responsible.[83]

The third development post-*Tadić* is the requirement of significant contribution to a JCE. Participation for JCE only requires the accused to have performed some act that is *in some way directed to the furtherance of the common plan or purpose*. This act may even be in the form of an omission that contributes to the common criminal purpose.[84] Yet recent ICTY decisions present a confused picture as to whether a *substantial* contribution is required. In *Kvočka*, the Appeals Chamber partially overruled the Trial Chamber's determination[85] that the accused's participation must be substantial.[86] The Appeals Chamber held that the fact that the accused can be easily replaced and that the criminal purpose can therefore be achieved without his participation is of little relevance.[87] There are, however, special cases where proof of a substantial contribution becomes necessary: for instance, opportunistic visitors who are not staff members in a detention camp but who enter the camp and commit

[78] *Brdanin* Appeals Judgment, par. 418. [79] *Dordević* Trial Judgment, par. 1866.

[80] *Brdanin* Appeals Judgment, pars. 415–418.

[81] Ibid., par. 413; and *Dordević* Trial Judgment, par. 1866.

[82] *Krajišnik* Appeals Judgment, par. 226; *Dordević* Trial Judgment, par. 1866.

[83] *Brdanin* Appeals Judgment, par. 430.

[84] *Prosecutor* v. *Kvočka et al.*, IT-98-30/1-A, Appeals Chamber Judgment (28 February 2005) (*Kvočka* Appeals Judgment), par. 187; *Dordević* Trial Judgment, par. 1863.

[85] *Prosecutor* v. *Kvočka et al.*, IT-98-30/1-T, Trial Chamber Judgment (2 November 2001), par. 309 (holding that the accused's participation must be 'significant', – i.e., it made the enterprise 'efficient or effective').

[86] *Kvočka* Appeals Judgment, par. 187. [87] Ibid., par. 193.

crimes will be held liable for participation in a JCE only if they make a substantial contribution to the overall effect of the camp.[88]

The absence of the requirement of a substantial contribution by the accused does not sit well with the notion of equal culpability that lies at the heart of JCE liability. The accused in a JCE is not merely responsible, but equally responsible, as the other participants for all acts carried out pursuant to the common criminal plan.[89] It is difficult to see how this can be reconciled with the requirement of a significant contribution, which is predicated on different levels of contribution – some significant, some not. Making a special exception for opportunistic visitors to detention camps only confuses the issue further. On what basis can one distinguish between a low-level staff cook in the detention camp who is aware of the activities carried out in the camp and an opportunistic visitor who is not a staff member but enters the camp to commit crimes? The Appeals Chamber's reasoning makes the cook liable regardless of a substantial contribution, since it is not necessary for him to be irreplaceable as a staff member or for the camp's criminal purpose to be unachievable without his participation. If the cook is held liable for merely being a staff member, it is to a standard that disturbingly resembles guilt by association.

JCE at the Khmer Rouge trials

The doctrine of JCE has had a long and troubled history at the Extraordinary Chambers in the Courts of Cambodia. The first significant pronouncement on its application at the Court was the 2009 JCE Order by the Office of the Co-Investigating Judges (OCIJ) in Case 002, which relied on the reasoning and sources in *Tadić* to hold that JCE was a recognised mode of liability in customary international law.[90] Since the ECCC possessed the indicia of an international court, and the existence of JCE in customary international law satisfied the tests of foreseeability and accessibility to the accused, the ECCC was justified in applying JCE in Case 002.[91] However, JCE was a specifically international mode of

88 Ibid., par. 599.

89 On equal culpability, see J.D. Ohlin, 'Three conceptual problems with the doctrine of joint criminal enterprise', *Journal of International Criminal Justice* 5 (2007), 85–88.

90 *Nuon et al.*, 002/19-09-2007-ECCC-OCIJ, Office of the Co-Investigating Judges Order on the Application at the ECCC of the Form of Liability Known as Joint Criminal Enterprise (8 December 2009) (*Nuon* OCIJ 2009 Order), pars. 13, 21.

91 Ibid., pars. 19–21.

participation developed to capture the unique features of international crimes where the individuals who bore the greatest responsibility were often far removed from their physical commission. Thus, applying the French doctrine of autonomous legal 'regimes', the OCIJ held that JCE was limited to international crimes and did not extend to Cambodian national crimes under the ECCC Law.[92]

This ruling was partially overturned by the Pre-Trial Chamber, which confirmed that the ECCC was authorised to apply JCE I and JCE II, which were firmly established in customary international law, but was unable to find similar support for JCE III.[93] The basic concept of JCE (JCE I and JCE II) required a shared *mens rea* for the crime and contribution to its commission. This concept had traditional civil law counterparts, including in the 1956 Cambodian Penal Code, which was applicable during the temporal jurisdiction of the ECCC.[94] The basic form of JCE could be likened to liability for 'co-perpetration' under Cambodian criminal law, even though it had broader application to situations where the accused was more remote from the physical perpetration of the *actus reus* of the crime. Actions that fell outside the common purpose could, however, only be punishable as 'complicity' under Cambodian law.[95]

In its analysis of JCE I and JCE II, the Pre-Trial Chamber did not confine itself to the sources cited in *Tadić*, but also relied on post-war cases decided under Control Council Law No. 10, in particular the *Justice* case and the *RuSHA* case.[96] It dismissed *Tadić*'s reliance on international instruments and case law to establish JCE III, holding that these either did not support the extended form of JCE[97] or failed to indicate the precise mode of liability being applied.[98] Moreover, the Italian judgments cited by *Tadić* were decisions by domestic courts applying domestic law and were not appropriate precedents to establish customary international law.[99]

The Pre-Trial Chamber also rejected the contention that the OCIJ Order incorrectly restricted the application of JCE to the domain of international crimes. It noted that Article 29 of the ECCC Law on modes of responsibility did not distinguish between domestic crimes defined in Article 3(new) of the Law and international crimes provided

92 Ibid., par. 22; Law on the Establishment of the Extraordinary Chambers in the Courts of Cambodia for the Prosecution of Crimes Committed during the Period of Democratic Kampuchea, NS/RKM/1004/006 (as amended 27 October 2004) (ECCC Law).

93 *Nuon* PTC JCE Decision, pars. 57–58, 69, 83. 94 Ibid., par. 41. 95 Ibid.

96 Ibid., pars. 57, 65–69. 97 Ibid., par. 78. 98 Ibid., pars. 79–81. 99 Ibid., par. 82.

in Articles 4 to 7.[100] Domestic forms of co-perpetration recognised in the applicable law and JCE were thus both forms of commission under Article 29.[101] However, the parties had failed to demonstrate any error in holding that JCE, which was a form of liability recognised in customary international law, should apply to international crimes alone.[102]

In July 2010, the Trial Chamber affirmed the Pre-Trial Chamber's reasoning on JCE I and JCE II in its first Judgment in the case of *Duch*,[103] but refrained from commenting on JCE III since the co-prosecutors had relied on it only in the alternative in their final trial submissions.[104] This was followed by the Office of the Co-Investigating Judges' Closing Order of September 2010 in Case 002, where the OCIJ, on the facts of the case, considered JCE I to be the most suitable form of liability for characterising the conduct of the accused.[105]

The OCIJ established that senior leaders of the Democratic Kampuchea regime, who were members of the Communist Party of Kampuchea, had a common purpose to implement a socialist revolution in Cambodia through a 'great leap forward' and to defend the Party against enemies 'by whatever means necessary'.[106] It was further stated that, 'The purpose itself was not entirely criminal in nature but its implementation resulted in and/or involved the commission of crimes within the jurisdiction of the ECCC.'[107] The Party leaders designed and implemented five policies to achieve this purpose: population movements from urban to rural areas, establishment of cooperatives and work sites, 're-education' of bad elements and enemies, targeting of groups perceived as opposed to the revolution and regulation of marriage.[108] These policies resulted in or involved the commission of crimes by JCE members and non-members, that comprised several counts of crimes against humanity, genocide and war crimes – including murder, extermination, torture, deportations, imprisonments, persecution, rape, enslavement, unlawful confinements, wilful killings and causing serious injury and other inhumane acts.[109] The members of the JCE included members of the Standing Committee (including accused Nuon Chea and Ieng Sary), members of the Central Committee (including accused Khieu Samphan), heads of Communist Party Ministries (including accused Ieng Thirith), zonal and sector secretaries and heads of military divisions.[110]

[100] Ibid., par. 102. [101] Ibid. [102] Ibid.
[103] *Duch*, 001/18-07-2007/ECCC/TC, Trial Chamber Judgment (26 July 2010), par. 512.
[104] Ibid., par. 513.
[105] *Nuon et al.*, 002/19-09-2007-ECCC-OCIJ, Office of the Co-Investigating Judges Closing Order (15 September 2010) (*Nuon* OCIJ Closing Order), par. 1541.
[106] Ibid., par. 1524. [107] Ibid. [108] Ibid., par. 1525. [109] Ibid. [110] Ibid., par. 1529.

A return to the 1940s

The Pre-Trial Chamber's JCE decision breaks new ground in rejecting the customary international law basis of JCE III through a sophisticated and critical analysis of the sources referenced in *Tadić*. The *Tadić* Appeals Chamber referred primarily to summaries of cases decided by military courts set up by the Allied powers in the aftermath of the Second World War, and on domestic prosecutions for war crimes in countries like Italy, to argue that JCE liability had a basis in customary international law. The Appeals Chamber's analysis, in particular its conclusions on JCE III, might have been strengthened if it had conducted a more in-depth analysis of the case law of the military tribunals.[111] The ECCC Pre-Trial Chamber's decision is open to the same criticism, and its rejection of JCE III would have been more convincing had it taken into account a wider array of war crimes prosecutions after the Second World War.[112]

For instance, Robert Clarke's recent piece on the war crimes trials mounted by the Australians in Rabaul, Papua New Guinea, references the Judge Advocate's directions in a few cases to argue that concepts similar to JCE III were used to convict the accused.[113] The *Hatakeyama*[114] and *Matsumoto*[115] trials dealt with Japanese defendants held responsible for torturing and beating to death Chinese residents of Nauru and Lumburua. In *Hatakeyama*, the Judge Advocate cited English law, which provided that if several persons combine to carry out an unlawful act, including in the face of opposition, and if one of them kills the victim in its execution, then all are guilty of murder.[116] In *Matsumoto*, the Judge Advocate made a reference to the Australian *Manual of military law*, which held each of the accused 'responsible

[111] See, for example, Clarke, 'Return to *Borkum Island*', 853–855, arguing that a perusal of the transcripts and recommendations by the reviewing officers in certain American military trials points to the use of concepts cognate to JCE III, particularly the cases of *Tashiro* (*United States* v. *Tashiro et al.*, US Military Commission, Yokohama, 1948), and *Rüsselsheim* (*United States* v. *Hartgen et al.*, US Military Commission, 1945).

[112] See, for example, S. Linton, 'Rediscovering the war crimes trials in Hong Kong, 1946–48', *Melbourne Journal of International Law* 13 (2012), 315–317.

[113] Clarke, 'Return to *Borkum Island*', 856–858.

[114] *Hatakeyama Yosutaki et al.* (1–2 May 1946): A471, 80982, National Archives of Australia (NAA).

[115] *Matsumoto Tsijigi, Ueno Koichi and Shinaki Jinichi* (19 March 1946): A471, 80728, NAA.

[116] Clarke, 'Return to *Borkum Island*', 856–857, discussing Judge Advocate's address at *Hatakeyama*, sheet 17, which cited: T.R. Fitzwalter Butler and M. Garsia, *Archbold's pleading, evidence & practice in criminal cases* (London: Sweet & Maxwell, 1943), p. 1430.

for every offence committed by any one of them' in pursuance of a common unlawful purpose.[117] As an example, it mentioned the responsibility of the occupants of a house who resist the arrest of one of them by a police officer and his assistant, in the course of which the assistant is killed.[118]

These cases pose similar challenges as the ones cited by the *Tadić* Chamber for establishing JCE III. In the Rabaul trials, the Judge Advocates relied on specific principles of domestic criminal law, which constituted fairly limited evidence of a broader recognition of doctrines similar to JCE III.[119] An even more important limitation, which Clarke does not acknowledge sufficiently, is the lack of clarity about whether the accused were convicted on the basis of the actions performed by one of them as a foreseeable consequence of the common unlawful purpose, or due to their joint participation in acts of torture that ultimately resulted in the victims' deaths. For this reason it is difficult to ascertain whether these decisions truly support the use of JCE III as a form of principal responsibility.

One can argue that given the limitations of this case law, the ECCC Pre-Trial Chamber's conclusions on JCE III would have likely been the same, even if it had conducted a broader survey of war crimes trials in other jurisdictions. Nonetheless, given that this was the first decision by an international tribunal rejecting JCE III, by confining itself largely to the sources cited in *Tadić*, the Chamber missed an opportunity to definitively challenge its customary international law basis.

Moreover, the absence of the distinction between principal and secondary responsibility in these cases may not have been conclusive for the ECCC Pre-Trial Chamber. In its discussion of JCE II, for instance, the Chamber relied heavily on post-war cases decided under Control Council Law No. 10,[120] in particular the *Justice* case[121] and the *RuSHA* case.[122] The indictments in these two cases, however, charged the accused as principals as well as accessories and the judgments did not distinguish

[117] Clarke, 'Return to *Borkum Island*', 856–857 discussing Judge Advocate's address, *Matsumoto*, sheet 19, which cited: Military Board, *Australian edition of manual of military law 1941* (Canberra: Commonwealth Government Printer, 1941), ch. 7, par. 17.

[118] Ibid. [119] Clark, 'Return to *Borkum Island*', 859, 860.

[120] *Nuon* PTC JCE Decision, pars. 57, 65–69.

[121] *United States* v. *Altstoetter et al.* (*Justice* case), US Military Tribunal Judgment (3–4 December 1947), in *NMT*, vol. 3.

[122] *United States* v. *Greifelt et al.* (*RuSHA* case), US Military Tribunal Judgment (10 March 1948), in *NMT*, vols. 4–5.

between various modes of responsibility.[123] Thus, if the Pre-Trial Chamber had been willing to accept these as evidence of JCE II as a mode of principal responsibility, it would have needed to at least justify why the same logic should not apply to concepts similar to JCE III which had been embraced in earlier war crimes trials.

The significance of common purpose

While the Pre-Trial Chamber may have rejected the application of JCE III, it is arguable that the OCIJ Closing Order of 15 September 2012 reintroduces a version of JCE III into ECCC jurisprudence through its definition of a common purpose. In this Order, the OCIJ linked the accused to the crimes in a series of moves: the accused shared the (non-criminal) purpose to achieve a socialist revolution and to defend the Party against enemies. They designed policies that were not necessarily criminal by nature to attain these ends, the execution of which resulted in or involved international crimes. Further, the accused were held responsible under JCE I (and not JCE III) for their contribution to this non-criminal purpose. This formula does not meet JCE I's requirement of a shared intent to commit a criminal offence.

In interpreting the common purpose in this fashion, the OCIJ falls into the same trap as the Special Court for Sierra Leone. Initially, in the *AFRC* case, the SCSL Trial Chamber dismissed the JCE pleading in the Indictment on the basis that the common purpose of taking 'any actions necessary to gain and exercise political power and control over the territory of Sierra Leone' was not inherently criminal.[124] This was overturned by the Appeals Chamber, which ruled that 'the requirement that the common plan, design or purpose of a joint criminal enterprise is inherently criminal means that it must either have as its objective a crime within the Statute, *or contemplate crimes* within the Statute as the means of achieving its objective'.[125] Thus, even though the ultimate objective of

123 It is worth noting that the *Justice* and *RuSHA* cases, by themselves, are insufficient to establish customary international law; see van Sliedregt, *Individual criminal responsibility*, p. 163. For reliance on the *Justice* case to establish liability under JCE for crimes physically committed by other persons, see also *Prosecutor* v. *Rwamakuba*: ICTR-98-44-AR72.4, Appeals Chamber, Decision on Interlocutory Appeal Regarding Application of Joint Criminal Enterprise to the Crime of Genocide (22 October 2004), pars. 19, 24, 26.

124 *Prosecutor* v. *Brima, Kamara, and Kanu*, SCSL-04-16-T, Trial Chamber II Judgment (20 June 2007), par. 67.

125 *Prosecutor* v. *Brima, Kamara, and Kanu*, SCSL-04-16-A, Appeals Chamber Judgment (22 February 2008) (*AFRC* Appeals Judgment), par. 80. Emphasis added.

the common plan alleged in the Indictment – gaining and exercising political power and control over the territory of Sierra Leone – may not be criminal, the means to achieve this contemplated by the accused, such as unlawful killings, forced labour and physical and sexual violence, were crimes within the SCSL Statute.[126]

The *AFRC* Appeals Chamber's standard of the accused's 'contemplation' of crimes as a means of achieving the non-criminal JCE objective arguably expands the limits of JCE in a manner unsupported by ICTY jurisprudence. Contemplating a crime can potentially be likened to involving, or amounting to, a crime, which does not pose any problems as such. However, another way to read the requirement is that the accused must merely foresee the crimes as a possible result of accomplishing the JCE's non-criminal objectives.[127] This undermines the shared criminal intent for a common purpose that is a prerequisite for JCE liability.[128] The SCSL has abandoned the requirement of a 'necessary relationship between the objective of a common purpose and its criminal means'; it suffices that 'the latter are "contemplated to achieve" the former'.[129] Thus, if the accused cooperates with other individuals who share the common (lawful) objective of gaining political power over territory, and each of them independently foresees the possibility that crimes may be committed in the accomplishment of this lawful objective, they can all be held liable for the commission of crimes pursuant to a common criminal enterprise.[130]

This new JCE standard not only abandons the distinction between JCE I and JCE III but also unduly stretches the bounds of JCE III liability.[131] This is demonstrated in the SCSL's conviction of RUF commander Augustine Gbao under JCE I, despite the determination that he lacked the shared intent to commit all the crimes that were within the common

126 Ibid., pars. 82–84.

127 C. Rose, 'Troubled indictments at the Special Court for Sierra Leone: the pleading of joint criminal enterprise and sex-based crimes', *Journal of International Criminal Justice* 7 (2009), 362–363. See also, W. Schabas, 'Special Court for Sierra Leone rejects joint criminal enterprise' (*The trial of Charles Taylor*, 25 June 2007): charlestaylortrial.org.

128 W. Jordash and P. van Tuyl, 'Failure to carry the burden of proof: how joint criminal enterprise lost its way at the Special Court for Sierra Leone', *Journal of International Criminal Justice* 8 (2010), 603.

129 *Prosecutor* v. *Sesay, Kallon, and Gbao*, SCSL-04-15-A, Appeals Chamber Judgment (26 October 2009) (*RUF* Appeals Judgment), par. 296.

130 Jordash and van Tuyl, 'Failure', 603–604.

131 *RUF* Appeals Judgment, Partially Dissenting and Concurring Opinion of Justice Shireen Avis Fisher (Fisher Opinion), pars. 17–19.

criminal purpose.[132] Instead, his liability was based on the fact that he shared the (non-criminal) common objective to control parts of the country's territory and intended or could foresee that other JCE members or individuals used by them may commit crimes in this pursuit.[133]

Returning to the ECCC, the OCIJ repeats the problems with the SCSL's acceptance of the accused's contribution to a non-criminal purpose where he merely foresees the commission of the crimes. Indeed, the OCIJ's standard is potentially broader than the SCSL's, since the common plan may only result in the crimes being committed. It is unclear what, if any, *mens rea* the accused must possess towards these crimes. And while the Trial Chamber's 'JCE Decision' of 12 September 2011 limits the OCIJ's definition of common purpose by citing SCSL jurisprudence that the common plan must at least 'contemplate crimes' as the means of achieving the non-criminal objective,[134] this merely means that the problems with the SCSL's common purpose standard will also be manifested in ECCC jurisprudence.

The legal 'regimes' limitation

The Pre-Trial Chamber upheld the concept of autonomous legal 'regimes' introduced by the 2009 OCIJ Order in Case 002. However, the decision did not provide any rationale for the confinement of JCE to international crimes under the ECCC Law. The failure to cite any justification for this limitation is highly unsatisfactory given that there is no proper basis for relying on the French concept of autonomous legal 'regimes' to interpret ECCC Law. Further, Article 29 of the ECCC Law itself makes no such distinction between domestic and international crimes.[135] This is in contrast to Article 6(5) of the Statute for the Special Court for Sierra Leone, which explicitly provides that individual criminal responsibility for crimes under Sierra Leonean law will be determined by applying domestic law principles.[136] One can argue that the application of uniquely international forms of responsibility that have no equivalent in domestic law to

[132] *Prosecutor* v. *Sesay, Kallon, and Gbao*, SCSL-04-15-T, Trial Chamber I Judgment (2 March 2009) (*RUF* Trial Judgment), pars. 2019, 2040; Fisher Opinion, pars. 14–16.

[133] *RUF* Trial Judgment, pars. 2010–2014, 2060; *RUF* Appeals Judgment, Fisher Opinion, pars. 17–19.

[134] *Nuon* Trial Chamber JCE Decision, par. 17.

[135] See K. Gustafson, 'ECCC tackles JCE: an appraisal of recent decisions', *Journal of International Criminal Justice* 8 (2010), 1323, 1330.

[136] Statute of the Special Court for Sierra Leone, 16 January 2002, 2178 UNTS 138, 145, art. 6(5).

prosecute purely domestic crimes violates the legality principle.[137] The Chamber, however, makes no such determination.

Other forms of commission

The Pre-Trial Chamber likened JCE I to co-perpetration, which already existed as a form of participation in domestic Cambodian criminal law applicable during the temporal jurisdiction of the ECCC. Given the existence of co-perpetration as a mode of responsibility in national law, it is surprising that the ECCC has chosen to follow the JCE jurisprudence of the *ad hoc* tribunals rather than looking to the version of co-perpetration outlined by the ICTY in *Furundžija* or to the adoption of co-perpetration by the ICC.

The ICC first specified the objective and subjective elements of co-perpetration in the *Lubanga* Decision on Confirmation of Charges, and these have formed a template for subsequent iterations of the elements by the Pre-Trial Chamber. The objective elements consist of, first, an agreement or a common plan between two or more persons. This plan can be implicit and should include an element of criminality, even though it need not be directed specifically at the commission of a crime.[138] The second required objective element is coordinated essential contribution by each perpetrator resulting in the realisation of the objective elements of the crime; this contribution is not limited to the execution stage and may be at any stage of the crime.[139] The Pre-Trial Chamber has identified essential contributions to include activating mechanisms by leaders that lead to automatic compliance with their orders and the commission of the crime, such as designing an attack and providing institutional, financial and logistical support.[140]

[137] For a similar argument raised in relation to the Special Tribunal for Lebanon, see M. Milanovic, 'An odd couple: domestic crimes and international responsibility in the Special Tribunal for Lebanon', *Journal of International Criminal Justice* 5 (2007), 1142.

[138] *Lubanga* Decision, pars. 343–345. [139] Ibid., pars. 346–348.

[140] See, for example, *Katanga* Decision, pars. 524–526 (giving examples of essential contribution as activating mechanisms by leaders that lead to automatic compliance with their orders, including designing an attack, supplying ammunition and coordinating the activities of troops); *Prosecutor* v. *Muthaura, Kenyatta and Ali*, ICC-01/09-02/11, Pre-Trial Chamber II Decision on the Confirmation of Charges (23 January 2012) pars. 404–406 (stating that the contribution was essential, since in the absence of activating mechanisms by the accused – which included giving orders for the commission of the crimes, and institutional and financial support – the common plan to commit the crimes would have been frustrated).

The subjective elements of co-perpetration were also identified first in the ICC Pre-Trial Chamber's *Lubanga* decision, but there has been a significant amount of controversy about the requirements in subsequent decisions. According to this decision, the first subjective element is the accused's fulfilment of all subjective elements of the crime with which he is charged, including the specific intent for crimes such as genocide. For most crimes under the jurisdiction of the ICC, this would mean meeting the 'intent' and 'knowledge' requirements in Article 30(1) of the Rome Statute.[141] The second subjective element is that all co-perpetrators must be mutually aware of and accept that the execution of the common plan may result in the realisation of the objective elements of the crime. If there is a substantial likelihood that the objective elements of the crime would occur, this mutual acceptance can be inferred from the co-perpetrators' awareness of this likelihood and their decision to implement the plan despite such awareness. If, on the other hand, the risk is low, the co-perpetrators must have expressly accepted that implementing the plan would result in the realisation of the objective elements of the crime.[142] The third subjective factor is the accused's awareness of the factual circumstances enabling him to jointly control the crime – that is, that his role is essential in the implementation of the common plan and that he can frustrate its realisation by failing to perform his function.[143]

The second subjective element defined by the *Lubanga* Pre-Trial Chamber incorporates the *mens rea* of *dolus eventualis*, which is unlikely to meet the 'intent' and 'knowledge' test required under Article 30 of the Rome Statute. This is precisely the ground on which it was challenged and ultimately rejected by the *Bemba* Pre-Trial Chamber.[144] This Pre-Trial Chamber reformulated the second subjective element to require that the co-perpetrators must be mutually aware that the implementation of the plan will result in the commission of the crime, and should nonetheless carry out their actions either with the purpose to commit the material elements of the crime or with the awareness that their fulfilment will, in the ordinary course of things, be a 'virtually certain consequence'

[141] Rome Statute of the International Criminal Court: treaties.un.org. See, for example, *Prosecutor* v. *Bemba*, ICC-01/05-01/08, Pre-Trial Chamber II Decision on the Charges (15 June 2009) (*Bemba* Decision), par. 351.

[142] See, for example, *Lubanga* Decision, pars. 361–365; *Katanga* Decision, pars. 533, 537.

[143] See, for example, *Prosecutor* v. *Banda and Jerbo*, ICC-02/05-03/09, Pre-Trial Chamber I Decision on the Confirmation of Charges (7 March 2011) (*Banda* Decision), pars. 150, 160–161.

[144] *Bemba* Decision, pars. 352–369.

of their actions.[145] The *Lubanga* Trial Chamber also rejected the *dolus eventualis* standard as incompatible with Article 30's requirement of intent or knowledge.[146] Thus, the co-perpetrators 'must know the existence of a risk that the consequence will occur', that is, they must be aware that the consequence will occur 'in the ordinary course of events'.[147]

The International Criminal Court's jurisprudence, while still in its formative stages, reveals clear differences between JCE as developed by the ICTY and co-perpetration. Co-perpetration requires an essential contribution by each co-perpetrator, whereas JCE jurisprudence on the extent of contribution required by the accused still vacillates between significant contributions to the crime with which the accused is charged and to the common plan as a whole. In any event, there is no mention of an 'essential' contribution. In contrast, at the ECCC, the Office of the Co-Investigating Judges has merely followed the ICTY's lead in holding that the accused need not make a necessary or substantial contribution, but that it should be a significant contribution to the crimes for which he is charged.[148] The ECCC Trial Chamber has failed to clarify the extent of participation required for JCE liability, merely stating that 'it is sufficient to show that the Accused participated in some way in the JCE'.[149]

It is also unlikely that the fluid JCE I common plan can be encompassed within the doctrine of co-perpetration. The OCIJ and the ECCC Trial Chamber appear to have accepted a slightly different version of an evolving common criminal plan, which expands to cover additional crimes for which the accused is held liable. In the context of assessing the *mens rea* for the crime of genocide, the OCIJ's[Amended] Closing Order 15 September 2010 held that from 1997 onwards, '[T]he members of the JCE knew that the implementation of the common purpose expanded to include the commission of genocide of these protected groups. Acceptance of this greater range of criminal means, coupled with persistence in implementation, amounted to an intention of the JCE members to pursue the common purpose through genocide.'[150] This

145 Ibid., par. 370. See also, *Prosecutor* v. *Ruto, Kosgey and Sang*, ICC-01/09–01/11, Pre-Trial Chamber II Confirmation of Charges (23 January 2012), pars. 334–336 (concurring with the rejection of *dolus eventualis*); *Banda* Decision, par. 159 (determining that the accused were mutually aware that the implementation of the common plan would result, in the ordinary course of events, in the fulfilment of the material elements of the crime).

146 *Prosecutor* v. *Lubanga*, ICC-01/04-01/06, Trial Chamber I Judgment (14 March 2012), par. 1011.

147 Ibid., par. 1012. 148 *Nuon* OCIJ Closing Order, par. 1522.

149 *Nuon* Trial Chamber JCE Decision, par. 17.

150 *Nuon* OCIJ Closing Order, par. 1527.

was endorsed, without comment, by the Trial Chamber.[151] It is difficult to ascertain the exact *mens rea* required of the accused for crimes committed pursuant to an expansion of the common plan's objectives, but depending on how this is interpreted in subsequent ECCC jurisprudence, it may not satisfy the *mens rea* elements for co-perpetration liability.

It could very well be that the Cambodian domestic concept of co-perpetration, which is based on French criminal law, is different from the ICC's conception, which relies on the control theory developed in German criminal law. Nonetheless, it highlights the need for the ECCC to clarify the relationship between JCE I and co-perpetration, what is the correct understanding of co-perpetration under the ECCC Law and why the ECCC should give precedence to a mode of participation that is controversial in international criminal law, rather than develop its own jurisprudence on co-perpetration.

Conclusion

The doctrine of JCE has undergone various transformations at the *ad hoc* and hybrid tribunals, and its recent interpretation by the ECCC represents yet another important step in its evolution. The challenge to JCE III by the ECCC can be interpreted in one of two ways. On the one hand, it can be regarded as a mere symptom of diversification in international law, where different tribunals interpret and apply the same basic doctrine or concept in different ways. On this account, JCE III's rejection by the ECCC can be dismissed as an anomaly that does not materially affect the jurisprudence of other international tribunals; indeed, this is the view that appears to have been adopted by the Special Tribunal for Lebanon, which dismissed the ECCC's approach to JCE III on relatively flimsy grounds.[152] On the other hand, the Pre-Trial Chamber's careful consideration of case law in its analysis of JCE III may truly have made an impact upon JCE III's status in international criminal law. It may also serve as a general cautionary tale to tribunals contemplating the development of other criminal law doctrines. It is nevertheless regrettable that an equally sophisticated interpretative exercise was not undertaken for JCE I and JCE II and that the Pre-Trial Chamber missed an opportunity

[151] *Nuon* Trial Chamber JCE Decision, par. 20.

[152] *Interlocutory decision on the applicable law: terrorism, conspiracy, homicide, perpetration, cumulative charging*, STL-11-01/I, Appeals Chamber (16 February 2011), par. 239, fn. 360.

to include jurisprudence from a broader range of war crimes trials conducted in other jurisdictions.

The ECCC's JCE jurisprudence also reveals the delicate situation the tribunal finds itself in at this juncture in the evolution of international criminal law. Currently, the ICC and the *ad hoc* tribunals, in particular the ICTY, represent two very different approaches to modes of commission responsibility for international crimes. The ECCC occupies an uncomfortable position where, at the point of time when the initial prosecution case was constructed and the first few decisions were handed down, JCE seemed to have a firm foothold in international criminal law, and constituted the only possible option for attributing perpetrator responsibility to high-level accused. With the advent of the ICC's jurisprudence on co-perpetration and indirect perpetration, the ECCC has alternative models of commission liability available to it, which may moreover have counterparts in domestic Cambodian law. The ECCC will have to consider carefully which path it should follow, as a matter of domestic as well as international law, and what consequences this might have for the cases currently before the tribunal.

12

Trials for international crimes in Bangladesh

Prosecutorial strategies, defence arguments and judgments

M. RAFIQUL ISLAM

Few matters in Bangladesh have attracted such national and global attention as the trials of those accused of orchestrating and committing international crimes during the war of national liberation of 1971. During the course of Bangladesh's secession from the Federation of Pakistan, Pakistani troops, local auxiliary forces and political collaborators perpetrated international crimes against pro-independence civilians, involving mass killings, atrocities, torture, disappearances, rape and the destruction of towns and villages.[1]

Following its independence, the Bangladesh government introduced three important bodies of law pertaining to these crimes. First, under Article 38(2) of the newly enshrined Constitution, it banned the religious party Jamaat-e-Islami, whose members had actively collaborated with Pakistani troops in committing these crimes.[2] Second, it enacted the 'International Crimes (Tribunals) Act, 1973', which provided for the establishment of special war crime tribunals to try those who had committed, directly or indirectly, genocide, crimes against humanity, and other international crimes.[3] And third, it promulgated the 'Bangladesh Collaborators (Special Tribunals) Order 1972', which provided for

1 International Commission of Jurists, *The events in East Pakistan, 1971* (Geneva: ICJ Secretariat, 1972), pp. 24–45; A. Mascarenhas, *The rape of Bangla Desh* (Delhi: Vikas Publications, 1971); W. Akmam, 'Atrocities against humanity during the liberation war in Bangladesh', *Journal of Genocide Research* 4 (2002), 543–559; Y. Saikia, 'Beyond the archive of silence: narratives of violence of the 1971 liberation war of Bangladesh', *History Workshop Journal* 58 (2004), 275–287.

2 Article 38(2) of the Constitution of the People's Republic of Bangladesh (1972) stated, 'No person shall have the right to form or be a member or otherwise take part in the activities of any communal or other association or union which in the name or on the basis of any religion has for its object or pursues a political purpose.'

3 The International Crimes (Tribunals) Act, 1973: bdlaws.minlaw.gov.bd.

tribunals to try local perpetrators and collaborators for 'political' crimes (opposing independence from Pakistan) and connected 'ordinary' crimes, such as rape, attempted murder, murder and arson.[4] Between 1972 and 1975, the authorities arrested as many as 37,400 people under the 1972 Order[5] – including senior political figures – although there are wide discrepancies in the figures about how many were held, or were subsequently tried or released.[6] The authorities also revoked the citizenship of individuals who had gone abroad in 1971 to campaign against the formation of Bangladesh as an independent state.

All three initiatives soon stalled. With the consolidation of the People's Republic of Bangladesh, the government on 30 November 1973 declared a general amnesty for those who had opposed independence from Pakistan as a matter of principle (although it expressly excluded those suspected of having committed or collaborated to commit crimes). This led to the release of between 26,000 and 35,000 local detainees.[7] The remaining prisoners were retained to face trial. It is not clear how far the trial programme advanced, but it came to an abrupt halt after the assassination of President Sheikh Mujibur Rahman, and the ouster of his Awami League government by military coup on 15 August 1975. The military oligarchy that assumed power revoked the 1972 Order on 31 December 1975,[8] released the prisoners, and rehabilitated them by restoring citizenships and allowing people back into government positions. It also reversed the banning of Jamaat-e-Islami, allowing it to register and function as a political party.

Over the same period in the early 1970s, the Bangladesh government also addressed the issue of war crimes committed by the Pakistani forces. After the fall of East Pakistan (Bangladesh) on 16 December 1971, the Indian Army took 82,000 Pakistani prisoners of war into custody. Among them were 195 alleged war criminals. On 28 August 1973 India and

[4] Bangladesh Collaborators (Special Tribunals) Order, 1972, President's Order No. 8 of 1972.

[5] See, for example, C. Reiger, *Fighting past impunity in Bangladesh: a national tribunal for the crimes of 1971* (International Center for Transnational Justice, 2010), p. 3.

[6] For comments about the numbers, see S. Linton, 'Completing the circle: accountability for the crimes of the 1971 Bangladesh war of liberation', *Criminal Law Forum* 21 (2010), 205.

[7] Reiger, *Fighting past impunity*, p. 4; A. Ziauddin, 'The case of Bangladesh: bringing to trial the perpetrators of the 1971 genocide', in A.J. Jongman (ed.), *Contemporary genocides: causes, cases, consequences* (Leiden: PIOOM, 1996), p. 99.

[8] Bangladesh Collaborators (Special Tribunals) (Repeal) Ordinance, 1975: bdlaws.minlaw.gov.bd.

Pakistan came to an agreement about the repatriation of the prisoners of war to Pakistan, but left open the question of the alleged war criminals.[9] Bangladesh was not a party to this bilateral agreement, but it maintained pressure on India and Pakistan to turn them over to Bangladesh to stand trial. On 9 April 1974, under the terms of the tripartite Simla Agreement between India, Pakistan and Bangladesh, it was agreed, in the name of 'reconciliation, peace and friendship in the sub-continent', that the alleged war criminals would be returned to Pakistan.[10]

Unfinished business

Because there was not a legal reckoning for the crimes of 1971, popular demands for the trial of those responsible have been a perennial feature of national life ever since. So when on 29 December 2008 the Awami League made an election pledge to hold trials, the mandate was overwhelming, and the party was swept into government. In January 2009, the Parliament adopted a formal resolution to mount trials and turned to Sections 3(1) and 6(1) of the 1973 Act, which authorised it to establish, by gazette notification, tribunals to try international crimes committed in 1971. The two special International Crimes Tribunals it convened – ICT-1 and ICT-2[11] – are both absolutely domestic in composition and orientation. As stated in the *Molla* Judgment, and echoed in others, 'Merely for the reason that the Tribunal is preceded by the word "international" and possessed jurisdiction over crimes such as Crimes against Humanity, Crimes against Peace, Genocide, and War Crimes, it will be wrong to assume that the Tribunal must be treated as an "International Tribunal."'[12]

The two tribunals are governed by the 1973 Act, which has been in force since its enactment, and was amended on 14 July 2009 and 17

[9] H.S. Levie, 'The Indo-Pakistani Agreement of August 28, 1973', *American Journal of International Law* 68 (1974), 95, 96.

[10] Agreement on the Repatriation of Prisoners of War and Civilian Internees, *Treaties and Agreements: Bangladesh-India-Pakistan, International Legal Materials* 13 (1974), 504.

[11] ICT-1 was formed on 25 March 2010 and became operational on 26 March 2010; and ICT-2 was formed on 22 March 2012 and became operational on 25 March 2012.

[12] *Chief Prosecutor* v. *Abdul Quader Molla*, ICT-BD Case No. 02 of 2012, Judgment (5 February 2013) (*Molla* Judgment), par. 5. See also, *Chief Prosecutor* v. *Delwar Hossain Sayeedi*, ICT-BD Case No. 01 of 2011, Judgment (28 February 2013) (*Sayeedi* Judgment), par. 16; *Chief Prosecutor* v. *Muhammad Kamaruzzaman*, ICT-BD Case No. 03 of 2012, Judgment (9 May 2013) (*Kamaruzzaman* Judgment), par. 5; *Chief Prosecutor* v. *Ali Ahsan Muhammad Mujahid*, ICT-BD Case No. 04 of 2012, Judgment (17 July 2013) (*Mujahid* Judgment), par. 4.

February 2013.[13] Section 26 overrides all other laws in force in the event of any inconsistency between them, and Section 22 allows both tribunals to formulate their own rules of procedure.[14] The tribunals have jurisdiction over those accused of committing genocide, war crimes, crimes against humanity, crimes against peace, and other crimes under international law. According to the 2009 amendment to Section 3(1) of the Act, they have the power 'to try and punish any individual or group of individuals, or organisation, or any member of any armed, defence or auxiliary forces, irrespective of his nationality, who commits or has committed, in the territory of Bangladesh, whether before or after the commencement of this Act' any of aforementioned crimes.

The two tribunals, which deal with international, not domestic, crimes, are not bound by technical rules of evidence and can flexibly adopt and apply expeditious and non-technical procedures. Thus, under Section 19(1), the court may admit any evidence with probative value, including 'reports and photographs published in newspapers, periodicals and magazines, films and tape-recordings and other materials'; and, under Section 19(4), it may recognise the evidentiary value of official government documents, reports by the United Nations and its subsidiaries, and reports by other international bodies such as NGOs. These tribunals are composed of professional judges who have the judicial capacity to administer the admissibility test of given evidence. Expeditious trials through less technical rules and noncomplex procedures for the admission of evidence are preferred, so as to avoid unreasonable delays and the broaching of irrelevant issues.

In particular, the tribunals, under Rule 56(2) of the Rules of Procedure, have the discretion to consider hearsay evidence. This issue was addressed in the *Azad* Judgment, which stated that the Tribunal 'is not bound by the strict rules of evidence'.[15] It added that the 'probative value of testimony of even a single witness is to be weighed', and that accordingly, 'acceptance of and reliance upon uncorroborated evidence, *per se*, does not constitute an error in law, in finding an accused guilty under the Act of 1973'.[16]

[13] International Crimes (Tribunals) (Amendment) Act, 2009 (Act No. LV of 2009), (2009 Amendment); International Crimes (Tribunals) (Amendment) Act, 2013 (Act No. III of 2013) (2013 Amendment).

[14] International Crimes Tribunal Rules of Procedure, 2010 (amended on 28 October 2010, and 28 June 2011); and International Crimes (Tribunal-2) Rules of Procedure, 2012.

[15] *Chief Prosecutor* v. *Moulana Abul Kalam Azad (Absconded)*, ICT-BD Case No. 05 of 2012, Judgment (21 January 2013) (*Azad* Judgment), par. 143.

[16] Ibid.

The *Molla* Judgment also observed that circumstantial and hearsay evidence, if considered 'with caution' and assessed for 'reasonable probative value', was 'not inadmissible *per se*'.[17]

The tribunals may take judicial notice of facts of common knowledge, which cannot reasonably be disputed, without requiring any proof. For example, the *Kamaruzzaman* Judgment took judicial notice of the common knowledge that paramilitary groups 'e.g Razaker Bahini, Al-Badar Bahini, Peace Committee, Al-Shams were formed as accessory forces of the Pakistani occupation armed force for providing moral supports, assistance and they substantially contributed to the commission of atrocities through[ ]out the country'.[18] Judicial notice is an effective tool for reducing the repetition of evidence and conclusions, and the tribunals invariably take judicial notice of documentary evidence and adjudicated facts arising from previous proceedings on the same matters.

In the name of expeditious proceedings, the tribunals have sometimes imposed restrictions on the number of witnesses that can be called. This is usually in response to the defence counsel's dilatory tactics to prolong the trials, which have included submitting almost endless lists of witnesses,[19] and failing to attend court hearings. (Defence lawyers involved in several of the cases have been fined for their unexplained and unreasonable absences.)[20] On 20 February 2013, ICT-2 in the *Kamaruzzaman* case, when presented with a list of over a thousand defence witnesses, imposed a limit of four witnesses for the establishment of an alibi.[21] It reasoned that neither the 1973 Act nor the Rules of Procedure gave the defence the unfettered right to submit such a lengthy list: 'In a criminal trial either in our domestic court or in any international *adhoc* tribunal established for prosecuting and trying crimes against humanity, such kind of action on part of the accused . . . never happens.'[22] It concluded, 'Furnishing list of more than thousand defence witnesses itself demonstrates an ulterior intention to somehow haul the trial and disposal of the case which the Tribunal by passing necessary order shall have right to prevent.'[23]

17 *Molla* Judgment, par. 70. 18 *Kamaruzzaman* Judgment, par. 95.

19 For example, the ICT-1 received a list of 2,939 defence witnesses in the *Azam* case: *Chief Prosecutor* v. *Professor Ghulam Azam*, ICT-BD Case No. 06 of 2011, Judgment (15 July 2013) (*Azam* Judgment), par. 35. And the ICT-2 received a list of 3,328 defence witnesses in the *Alim* case: *Chief Prosecutor* v. *Md. Abdul Alim*, ICT-BD Case No. 01 of 2012, Judgment (9 October 2013) (*Alim* Judgment), par. 25.

20 See, for example, 'Counsels for Ghulam Azam, Alim fined for absence', *Daily Star*, 12 March 2013: archive.thedailystar.net.

21 *Kamaruzzaman* Judgment, pars. 2, 14. 22 Ibid., par. 8. 23 Ibid., par. 11.

The rights of defendants, victims and witnesses

The 1973 Act recognises certain rights of the accused. They are entitled to be given notice of the formal charge and the accompanying documents a reasonable time before the start of the trial (Section 16). They have the right to offer an explanation relevant to the charge against them, conduct their own defence or rely on the assistance of counsel, present evidence in support of their defence, and cross-examine prosecution witnesses (Section 17). State defence counsel are appointed to defend the accused who have absconded – for example, Azad, Ashraf and Mueen[24] – under Section 10A(2) or the accused who refuse to participate in the preparation of the case – for example, S.Q. Chowdhury.[25] The accused have the right to appeal against any conviction and sentence (Section 21). In 2011, ICT-1 amended the Rules of Procedure so as to uphold by Rule 43(1) the presumption of innocence, protection against being tried twice, entitlement to a fair and public hearing, the right to a trial without undue delay, protection against compulsion to confess guilt and the right to be heard before punishment.[26]

The tribunals have been mindful of certain basic principles set out in the International Covenant on Civil and Political Rights (ICCPR) concerning the rights of the accused, from the arrest of the suspect through to the conclusion of trial. Despite the polarisation of opinion over fair-trial issues arising from the tribunals, nearly all of the judgments have categorically raised and extensively addressed the rights of the accused recognised by the ICCPR, and drawn attention to corresponding provisions in the 1973 Act and Rules of Procedure.[27] There is one notable deviation from the ICCPR, however: the provision for the death penalty in Section 20(2) of the Act. It may be noted, though, that internationally, capital punishment, no matter how undesirable, is yet to be outlawed; there are many jurisdictions around the world that continue to practise such punishment.

Still on the subject of safeguards, victims and witnesses also need adequate protection. Neither the 1973 Act nor the Rules of Procedure originally provided for their needs, but as the trials progressed, it became

[24] *Azad* Judgment, par. 21; *Chief Prosecutor* v. *Ashrafuzzaman Khan (Absconded) and Chowdhury Mueen Uddin (Absconded)*, ICT-BD Case No. 01 of 2013, Judgment (3 November 2013) (*Ashraf and Mueen* Judgment), par. 22.

[25] *Chief Prosecutor* v. *Salauddin Quader Chowdhury*, ICT-BD Case No. 02 of 2011, Judgment (1 October 2013) (*S.Q. Chowdhury* Judgment), par. 3.

[26] International Crimes Tribunal Rules of Procedure (Amendment), 2011.

[27] See, for example, *Azad* Judgment, pars. 15, 25.

apparent that such provisions were needed, especially in the cases involving rape. Sexual violence is a sensitive issue in many countries, including Bangladesh, where rape victims are unlikely to testify in public for fear of humiliation and social stigma, which, along with the crime itself, may haunt them for the rest of their lives. So ICT-1 amended the Rules of Procedure, incorporating new safeguards in Rule 58A.[28] On their own initiative, or on an application from either party, the tribunals can pass an order directing the appropriate authorities to provide for the 'protection, privacy and well-being' of witnesses and victims on both sides. If court sessions are held in camera, both sides are obliged to maintain confidentiality about the proceedings and the identity of witnesses, with breaches being prosecuted under Section 11(4) of the Act. ICT-2 has repeatedly iterated the internationally recognised rights of victims in ICCPR Article 2(3).[29]

Prosecutorial strategies

How has the prosecution constructed its cases? The onus, of course, is on the prosecution to prove beyond reasonable doubt that the accused had directly or indirectly participated in the commission of the charged crimes. During the course of the trials, it has provided documentary and physical evidence to establish the existence of mass graves, the killing fields at Rayerbazaar and the 'torture camp' in the Mohammadpur Physical Training Institute. It has quoted speeches of the accused encouraging local paramilitary groups to operate as death squads or *Azrail* (Islam's angel of death) to exterminate pro-liberation Bangalees. It has offered evidence showing that the accused had systematically planned and targeted attacks against pro-liberation political parties, the Hindu community, freedom fighters and eminent intellectuals. And it has elicited statements from witnesses and testimonies from victims and their family members. One of the cornerstones of the prosecution's strategy has been its focus on widespread rape and other gender crimes.

The prosecution's charges have usually alleged that the accused, as an individual or as an active member of local paramilitary force, has committed crimes against humanity and any other international crimes listed in section 3(2) of the 1973 Act. In the process, they have advanced a number of legal theories connecting individuals to the crime. These

[28] International Crimes Tribunal Rules of Procedure (Amendment), 2011.

[29] See, for example, *Kamaruzzaman* Judgment, pars. 66–67; *Mujahid* Judgment, pars. 46–47.

include five addressed here: the doctrines of superior responsibility, joint criminal enterprise, aiding and abetting, complicity and, finally, incitement.

One of the most prominent theories advanced by the prosecution is the doctrine of superior responsibility. Civilian leaders in particular do not usually commit crimes through direct participation – instead, their responsibility emanates from their authority over subordinates who have committed crimes and complicity in sustaining the culture of impunity. Section 4(2) of the 1973 Act, read in conjunction with its amended Section 3(1), has given the tribunals jurisdiction over both military and civilian superiors with direct or indirect involvement in the commission of crimes. The *Mujahid* Judgment, for example, held that under the Act, a superior will be held responsible for their subordinates' actions regardless of whether or not they had any 'actual' (knew) or 'constructive' (should have known) knowledge about the subordinates' crimes.[30]

The tribunals have articulated the following elements to be proven in order to subject the accused to superior responsibility: that the crimes designated under Section 3 of the 1973 Act were committed; that the crimes were perpetrated by someone other than the accused; that there was 'a superior-subordinate relationship', however informal, so long as there was *de facto* authority over the perpetrators; that the accused had the material ability, or direct influence, or effective controlling authority, over the activities of the subordinate perpetrators; and that the accused failed to prevent the principal perpetrators from committing the crime.[31]

The *Azam* Judgment in particular made an extensive survey of the conditions of the superior–subordinate relationship and developments within international jurisprudence, in order to explain the rationale behind the doctrine. It stated that the international criminal justice system has placed upon superiors 'a greater responsibility than that of their subordinates in ensuring that the law is not violated', and, furthermore:

> Superiors, by virtue of their elevated position in the hierarchy, have an affirmative duty to ensure that IHL [international humanitarian law] is duly respected and that breaches are appropriately repressed. Their failure to do so can be interpreted as acquiescence in the unlawful acts of their subordinates, thereby encouraging further breaches and developing a culture of impunity.[32]

[30] *Mujahid* Judgment, par. 454.
[31] *Kamaruzzanan* Judgment, par. 620; *Mujahid* Judgment, pars. 178, 183.
[32] *Azam* Judgment, par. 340.

In addition to examining the general features of the doctrine, the *Azam* Judgment, pronouncing on the case of a religious leader, specifically addressed the issue of civilian superior command responsibility. It concluded that the application of the doctrine to civilian leaders had become a part of customary international law;[33] that the crucial question is not the civilian status of the accused but the degree of authority they exercised over their subordinates;[34] and that a civilian superior must have 'effective control' over their subordinates to prevent them from committing the crimes.[35] Finally, the Judgment specified that 'superiors are liable to be awarded heavier sentences . . . than that of the actual perpetrators'.[36] This was because the consequences of someone's actions are necessarily more serious if they are at the top of a political hierarchy,[37] and because a failure to prevent or punish subordinates' crimes 'creates an impression of tolerance, acquiescence or even approval' of such actions.[38]

Turning to another theory of liability, the prosecution argued that Section 4(1) of the 1973 Act contains liability for 'common plan of collective criminality', which corresponds to the joint criminal enterprise (JCE) doctrine. (This Section states that when any crime specified under the Act 'is committed by several persons, each of such person is liable for that crime in the same manner as if it were done by him alone'.) In the *Mujahid* case specifically, it was asserted that the accused – being the leader of the paramilitary group Al-Badr, which was responsible for the massacre of the intellectuals in December 1971 – 'was also a party to the common plan and purpose of collective criminal enterprise in accomplishing the crime of abduction of intellectuals for causing their death'.[39]

The *Mujahid* Judgment agreed, stating that the killings of the intellectuals were indeed 'diabolical collective criminal acts',[40] which could constitute JCE within the meaning of Section 4(1):

> JCE is a form of co-perpetration that establishes personal criminal liability . . . The expression *'committed'* occurred in section 4(1) of the Act includes participation in JCE. Section 4(1) tends to cover the necessary elements of JCE, especially JCE category 1 and 3. In line with the recognized principles almost common to all legal systems, a person who takes 'consenting part' in the commission of the crime or who is found to be 'connected with plans or enterprise' involved in the commission of crime . . . or who is found to 'belong an organisation or group' engaged in the activities of committing crime, is guilty together with the 'principals'.[41]

[33] Ibid., par. 331. [34] Ibid. [35] Ibid., par. 332. [36] Ibid., par. 343. [37] Ibid., par. 342.
[38] Ibid., par. 341. [39] *Mujahid* Judgment, par. 442. [40] Ibid., par. 429.
[41] Ibid., pars. 443–444.

In another case dealing with the abduction and killing of the intellectuals, the *Ashraf and Mueen* Judgment concluded that the secret nature of the large-scale abduction with a view to killing warranted the conclusion that the crimes were perpetrated by a collective 'murderous enterprise'.[42]

Abetment, complicity, incitement

Unlike joint criminal enterprise, 'abetting' is a specified crime under Section 3(2)(g) of the 1973 Act. The prosecution has frequently alleged that Jamaat-e-Islami as an organisation, and the accused as its members, by helping to create auxiliaries to the Pakistani Army, abetted the commission of the crimes in the name of protecting Pakistan and Islam. The *Molla* Judgment, drawing on International Criminal Tribunal for Rwanda and Special Court for Sierra Leone decisions, observed that 'abetting' (along with 'conspiracy') is sufficient to render an individual criminally liable 'for any of these unlawful acts that substantially facilitated the commission of offence enumerated in section 3(2)'.[43] The *actus reus* of abetting requires 'assistance, encouragement or moral support which has a substantial effect on the perpetration of the crimes'.[44] The *mens rea* 'need not be explicit, it may be inferred from the circumstances':

> Indeed, as *mens rea* is a state of mind, its proof is typically a matter of inference. The standard of proof dictates, of course, that it be the only reasonable inference from the evidence and relevant and surrounding circumstances. In the case in our hand, we are to perceive that the accused acted having 'awareness' coupled with his conscious decision to accompany the principals to the crime site.[45]

Complicity, another mode of liability proposed by the prosecution, is, like abetting, an independent crime under the 1973 Act – Section 3(2)(h) refers to 'complicity in or failure to prevent commission of any such crimes'. The *Azam* Judgment explained the liability regime of this doctrine:

> [C]omplicity ... operates to hold persons criminally responsible for the acts of others. Complicity encompasses accessorial and conspiratorial liability. Accessorial liability is frequently referred to as accomplice liability. An accomplice is a person who helps another person to commit a crime, accomplice liability involves primary actors who actually participates in the commission of the crime and secondary actors who aid and

[42] *Ashraf and Mueen* Judgment, par. 237. [43] *Molla* Judgment, par. 121.
[44] Ibid., par. 358. [45] Ibid., par. 135.

> encourage the primary actors. The aid can be either physical or psychological. The secondary actors are called accomplices.[46]

According to the *Azam* Judgment (which was discussing complicity in relation to genocide), the doctrine encompasses: an accomplice procuring the means, such as weapons, for the commission of crimes in the knowledge that the means would be used to commit crimes; knowingly aiding and abetting a perpetrator in the planning or enablement of crimes; and intentionally instigating crimes through 'gifts, promises, threats, abuse of authority or power, machinations or culpable artifice'.[47] On *mens rea*, the *Molla* Judgment stated that complicity presupposes that the accomplice 'must have acted knowingly . . . and he was aware of the consequences of his act'.[48] Thus in that case, the timing and pattern of the accused's conduct at the crime site, as well as before the commission of the crime, was 'the best indication of his conscious option to commit a crime'.[49] It added that, 'Intent, coupled with affirmative action, is evidence of the highest degree of imputative responsibility.'[50]

Several judgments have observed that the term 'complicity' covers 'culpable association' with the principal perpetrators, proving encouragement and moral support,[51] and that the terms 'complicity' and 'accomplice' may describe conduct that is broader than 'aiding' and 'abetting'.[52] Nevertheless, it was also noted that the mere fact that an accused had close associations with the Pakistani Army, and visited the Army's facilities, 'does not *ipso facto* prove his liability'.[53] Criminal liability only arises when the accused is present at, and is supportive and encouraging of, the accomplishment of a crime carried out by the principals, thus forming part of the crime – for example, willingly accompanying the principals to killing sites and helping them to identify members of a targeted group.[54]

Finally, the prosecution alleged that Ghulam Azam, the *Ameer* (President) of Jamaat-e-Islami, had made public statements and speeches *inciting* his followers to commit crimes. Incitement is not specifically mentioned as a crime under Section 3(2) of the 1973 Act, so the prosecution charged him under Section 3(2)(f), covering 'any other crimes under international law'. The *Azam* Judgment examined the status of incitement as a crime in international law and found that 'direct and public incitement to commit crime[s] against humanity and genocide is a recognised crime

[46] *Azam* Judgment, par. 220. [47] Ibid., par. 218. [48] *Molla* Judgment, par. 250.
[49] Ibid., par. 365. [50] Ibid. [51] Ibid., par. 245. [52] *Kamaruzzaman* Judgment, par. 609.
[53] *Azad* Judgment, par. 209. [54] Ibid., par. 138.

under customary international law and as such the offence of incitement is a crime under international law'.[55] It also set out the elements of this crime in relation to genocide: that the accused 'incited others to commit genocide', that 'the incitement was direct', that 'the incitement was public', that the accused 'had the specific intent to commit genocide' and that the incitement was 'complete when uttered or published'.[56]

Issues raised by the defence

Charge-specific defences aside, the defence arguments have been by and large similar in all the cases so far, and have focused on five themes: that there was a four-decade delay in prosecution after the crimes were committed, that the 1973 Act was primarily enacted to prosecute 195 Pakistani alleged war criminals exonerated by the Simla Agreement, that the amendments to the 1973 Act were retroactive enactments, that defendants tried as collaborators in 1972 could not be retried, and that the 1973 Act's definition of crimes against humanity is inadequate compared to international definitions.

The first argument usually advanced by the defence was that there had been an undue delay in prosecution. They have argued that the trials were held four decades after the event, that they had not been sufficiently explained, and that there were doubts about their fairness.[57] The tribunals have stated that criminal trials are not time-barred because the passage of time does not wash away the guilt of the perpetrators.[58] If anything, the trials are making up lost ground, because 'justice delayed is no longer justice denied'.[59] The 1973 Act contains no time limit for the prosecution of the crimes under its remit – nor does the 1948 Genocide Convention or the 1949 Geneva Conventions, dealing with genocide and war crimes respectively.[60] The 1968 Convention on the Non-Applicability of Statutory Limitations to War Crimes and Crimes against Humanity has gone a step further in guarding against the application of limitations on prosecution for international crimes.[61] This explains why

[55] *Azam* Judgment, par. 135. [56] Ibid., par. 137.

[57] See, for example, *Azad* Judgment, par. 40; *Molla* Judgment, pars. 80–81; *S.Q. Chowdhury* Judgment, par. 52.

[58] See, for example, *Molla* Judgment, par. 91.

[59] See, for example, *S.Q. Chowdhury* Judgment, par. 69.

[60] See, for example, *Sayeedi* Judgment, par. 55; *S.Q. Chowdhury* Judgment, par. 68; *Alim* Judgment, par. 76.

[61] UN General Assembly Resolution 2391(XXIII) of 26 November 1968.

the Nazi war criminals are still being prosecuted in various courts of the world,[62] and why trials for crimes committed under the Pol Pot regime in Cambodia in the 1970s are ongoing.[63]

Some judgments also considered the political climate, which imposed restraints on holding trials in the post-independence period.[64] A complex interplay of national and international politics prevented the early pursuit of justice. Initially, the Awami League government was too preoccupied with post-war reconstruction and national security to convene trials under the 1973 Act, not least because the United States, China and the major Muslim countries continued to support Pakistan and oppose Bangladesh. Later, after the assassination of President Sheikh Mujibur Rahman in the military coup in 1975, military dictators who camouflaged themselves in democratic garb, including some of the accused, governed Bangladesh. In 1978, the leader of the 1975 coup, Ziaur Rahman, formed a political party, the Bangladesh Nationalist Party, which in 1991 and 2002 came to power in coalition with Jamaat-e-Islami, the main collaborator in the 1971 crimes. It was only in 2008 that the returned Awami League government, responding to popular pressure, pledged to conduct the trials.

The second argument put forward by the defence also referred back to the post-independence period. The defence counsel argued that the 1973 Act has been enacted to prosecute 195 Pakistani alleged war criminals who had been exonerated under the 1974 Simla Agreement, and that without prosecuting the alleged Pakistani principals, the accused could not be brought to justice as aiders and abettors.[65] The tribunals took judicial notice of common knowledge that Pakistani troops and their local associates were involved in the commission of genocide, crimes against humanity and war crimes. Because the prohibition of these crimes is recognised as a *jus cogens* norm of international law, trials cannot be set aside by the Simla Agreement or by the acquiescence of its parties. The tribunals therefore held that this Agreement constituted no legal barrier to trying alleged local perpetrators[66] – indeed, the *Molla* Judgment stated that it was

[62] In a recent case, the 92-year-old Dutch-born Siert Bruins, an SS volunteer during the Second World War, was tried in a German court for the killing of Aldert Klaas Dijkema, a Dutch resistance fighter, in 1944. He was released on grounds of insufficient evidence.

[63] See, for example, *Azad* Judgment, par. 44; *Molla* Judgment, par. 83; *Azam* Judgment, par. 59.

[64] See, for example, *Molla* Judgment, par. 88.

[65] See, for example, *Kamaruzzaman* Judgment, par. 97; *Mujahid* Judgment, par. 86; *Ashraf and Mueen* Judgment, par. 35.

[66] See, for example, *Sayeedi* Judgment, pars. 47, 48; Azam Judgment, pars. 49–51; *Ashraf and Mueen* Judgment, par. 52.

voided by Article 53 of the 1969 Vienna Convention on the Law of the Treaties (which states that '[a] treaty is void if . . . it conflicts with a peremptory norm of general international law').[67]

It may further be observed that declining to commence trials of alleged local perpetrators because it is not possible to try the Pakistani principals is the same as arguing that since all criminals cannot be brought to justice, none should be. The 'all-or-none' approach is neither a legal standard nor subsumable into any justice system. It defeats the very purpose of justice. Not to try those available would simply reinforce the *status quo* in Bangladesh, which has been based on the long-standing evasion of justice and the perpetuation of post-traumatic stress for the surviving victims and relatives.[68] In short, a failure to mount trials would 'allow old wounds to fester'.[69] It was for this reason, among others, that the UN Transitional Authority in East Timor decided to try local perpetrators before the Special Panel for Serious Crimes despite its inability to prosecute some of the Indonesian Army personnel who had orchestrated or carried out the most serious atrocities in East Timor.

Retroactivity, double jeopardy, flawed definitions

Turning to the legal framework for the trials, the defence claimed that the 2009 amendment of Section 3(1) of the 1973 Act was a retroactive enactment. The unamended text read: 'A Tribunal shall have power to try and punish *any person* irrespective of his nationality who, *being a member of any armed, defence or auxiliary forces* commits or has committed in the territory of Bangladesh, whether before or after the commencement of this act, any of the following crimes.'[70] The amendment replaced the words 'any person irrespective of his nationality who, being a' with 'any individual or group of individuals or', thereby enlarging the tribunal's jurisdictional scope to encompass civilians as well as 'members of armed, defence or auxiliary forces'.[71] The defence contended that this

67 *Molla* Judgment, par. 109.

68 Ibid., par. 89, which cited the UN Commission on Human Rights Special Rapporteur Theo von Boven, who wrote: '[I]t is well established that for many victims of gross violations of human rights, the passage of time has no attenuating effect; on the contrary, there is an increase in post-traumatic stress' ('Study concerning the right to restitution, compensation and rehabilitation for victims of gross violations of human rights and fundamental freedoms', E/CN.4/Sub.2/1993/8 (2 July 1993), p. 135).

69 Ibid. 70 Emphases added.

71 2009 Amendment. Another amendment, added in 2013, but applicable to cases dating back to 2009, added the words 'or organisations' (2013 Amendment).

amendment was expressly designed to capture local civilian leaders after the event, whereas the 1973 Act's original intent had simply been to prosecute members of the Pakistani Army and its auxiliaries.[72] They thus argued that the tribunals had no lawful jurisdiction over civilian individuals and groups of individuals.[73]

The tribunals declared that it was the obligation of the state to bring to justice anyone accused of committing international crimes, even if only as an individual, and that the 1973 Act had been amended accordingly.[74] They also stated that the amended Article 47A(2) of the Constitution of Bangladesh removed the right of the accused to question the tribunals' jurisdiction over international crimes.[75] It might further be noted that if the defence argument is legally tenable, then all ad hoc international crimes trials based on charters or statutes adopted after the commission of crimes would be called into question. The tribunals found that the 1973 Act and its subsequent amendments did not represent an exception to the accepted worldwide practice. Instead, they observed that the ad hoc tribunals for former Yugoslavia and Rwanda and the Special Court for Sierra Leone were all convened retrospectively, and that only one court – the International Criminal Court – was convened prospectively.[76]

Another argument put forward by the defence relates to the *ne bis in idem* principle. They maintained that if the accused had been prosecuted between 1972 and 1975 under the Bangladesh Collaborators (Special Tribunals) Order 1972 for committing crimes in concert with Pakistani troops, then their prosecution for the same crimes before the current tribunals was barred on grounds of double jeopardy.[77] As already noted, people were imprisoned under the terms of the Order, but it is not clear how many were charged, convicted and punished. If charged, they were not charged for the international crimes under the 1973 Act, and they were freed without trial after the 1975 military coup.[78] This factual position led the tribunals to reject the argument of double jeopardy.

[72] See *Molla* Judgment, pars. 92–94.

[73] See, for example, *Azad* Judgment, par. 40; *Mujahid* Judgment, par. 86; *Alim* Judgment, par. 73.

[74] See, for example, *Kamaruzzaman* Judgment, par. 110; *Alim* Judgment, par. 83.

[75] See, for example, *Azad* Judgment, par. 59; *Kamaruzzaman* Judgment, par. 111; *Sayeedi* Judgment, par. 54.

[76] See, for example, *Sayeedi* Judgment, par. 52; *Azam* Judgment, par. 55.

[77] See, for example, *Mujahid* Judgment, par. 86; *Sayeedi* Judgment, par. 44; *Alim* Judgment, par. 73.

[78] See, for example, *Kamaruzzaman* Judgment, par. 126; *Alim* Judgment, par. 110; *Ashraf and Mueen* Judgment, par. 57.

Finally, the defence claimed that the definition of crimes against humanity provided by the 1973 Act was inadequate because it failed to incorporate the 'widespread or systematic' component of the crime found in Article 7 of the ICC's Rome Statute.[79] The tribunals have gone to great lengths to show that the definition is consistent with international criminal law. They have surveyed the modern definitions of the crime and observed that 'there is no "consistency" among definitions' – although they share the same spirit, they differ in the 'nitty-gritty'.[80] For example, Article 5 of the ICTY Statute differs from both Article 3 of the ICTR Statute and Article 7 of the Rome Statute in that it does not require 'widespread or systematic attack' (or the presence of 'knowledge') as a condition for crimes against humanity. Referring to Article 10 of the Rome Statute, which states that the definitions of crimes contained within are 'for the purpose of the Statute', the *Molla* Judgment observed that the Statute's drafters 'were not only aware of, but recognized that the definitions were not the final and definitive interpretations, and that there are others'.[81] Consequently, the Rome Statute 'is not binding upon this Tribunal for resolving the issue of elements requirement to constitute the offence of crimes against humanity'.[82] Given their comparative analysis definitions, the tribunals found the 1973 Act to be 'fairly compatible with current international standards'.[83]

It may also be noted that Section 3(2)(a) of the 1973 Act, which sets out the elements of crimes against humanity, alludes to the 'systematic' or 'widespread' nature of attack in the phrases 'committed against any civilian population' or 'persecutions on political, racial, ethnic or religious grounds'. The *Azam* Judgment expanded on the approach to these elements of crimes against humanity. First, the terms 'systematic' and 'widespread' are 'a disjunctive, rather than cumulative requirement'; in other words, like the Rome Statute's approach, they are alternative conditions and the presence of either of them is enough to qualify.[84] Second, 'systematic' is a qualitative element that describes the organised nature of the attack as the 'non-accidental repetition of similar criminal conduct on a regular basis', while 'widespread' is a quantitative element indicating 'the large-scale nature of the attack which is primarily reflected in the

[79] See, for example, *Molla* Judgment, par. 122; *Kamaruzzaman* Judgment, par. 127; *Mujahid* Judgment, par. 116.

[80] *Sayeedi* Judgment, par. 19. [81] *Molla* Judgment, par. 129. [82] Ibid.

[83] *Sayeedi* Judgment, par. 32. See also, *Azad* Judgment, par. 79; *S.Q. Chowdhury* Judgment, par. 38.

[84] *Azam* Judgment, par. 32.

number of victims'.[85] Third, the 'widespread' or 'systematic' attack implies that there must be 'some form of governmental, organizational or group policy to commit these acts'.[86] Fourth, the attack must be against a 'civilian population' rather than 'civilians', indicating that 'the individual [is] being victimized not because of his individual attributes but rather because of his membership of a targeted civilian population'.[87]

Conclusion

International crimes, though prohibited in all forms and manifestations, can in some cases stigmatise their victims more than their perpetrators. The reversal of the stigma is long overdue in Bangladesh. The tribunals represent humankind's quest to combat international crimes and prosecute their perpetrators through a collective resolve to ensure a dignified existence. The holding of the trials is imperative for the rendering of post-conflict justice. No ad hoc international crimes trials, past or present, have been without shortcomings, and the Bangladesh trials are no different. They have suffered from teething problems and have had to operate within the resource constraints of a less developed country. But their achievement in breaking the protective garb of impunity and delivering justice to many victims should not be gainsaid. They are the first exclusively national trials of international crimes to be convened in the era of the International Criminal Court, and it is hoped that they may usher in a reform agenda based on the harmonious functioning of the ICC along with national jurisdictions on the basis of complementarity.

[85] Ibid. [86] Ibid. [87] Ibid.

13

Theories of joint criminal responsibility at the Asian tribunals

Hong Kong, East Timor and Cambodia

NINA H.B. JØRGENSEN

Joint Criminal Enterprise (JCE) and co-perpetratorship are both methods of attributing responsibility when two or more perpetrators jointly commit crimes. Historically, JCE has its origins in the common law, while co-perpetratorship, as understood in international criminal law, is viewed as deriving from civil law systems. The proceedings before the latest tribunals in Asia have exposed some of the controversies relating to the suitability and application of JCE and co-perpetratorship. At the Extraordinary Chambers in the Courts of Cambodia (ECCC), the prosecution adopted elements of the JCE doctrine (even though co-perpetratorship is recognised in Cambodian law), while the Pre-Trial Chamber rejected the third form of JCE because it was not customary international law during Khmer Rouge rule.[1] By contrast, the Special Panels for Serious Crimes dealing with cases in East Timor did little to clarify the relationship between JCE and co-perpetration, using the concepts more or less interchangeably. It remains to be seen whether future regional tribunals will follow the lead of the International Criminal Court (ICC), where a unique form of co-perpetratorship has emerged as a competitor to JCE doctrine in fulfilling the same function of describing decision-makers' participation in international crimes despite their physical detachment from the actual commission of those crimes.

This chapter considers the possible reasons why prosecutors and courts, with the exception of the ICC, have tended to view JCE as being especially appropriate as a mode of liability relevant to international

[1] *Nuon et al.*, 002/19-09-2007-ECCC-OCIJ, Pre-Trial Chamber Decision on the Appeals against the Co-Investigative Judges Order on Joint Criminal Enterprise (JCE) (20 May 2010) (*Nuon* PTC JCE Decision).

crimes. Is the main justification tied to the customary law status of JCE, or does JCE simply capture the magnitude of mass atrocity crimes in a manner that cannot be achieved by any other method of attributing responsibility? The hybrid tribunals in Asia provide an ideal starting point for a study of these questions because they are built on the domestic foundations of the civil law and in principle place JCE and a form of co-perpetratorship side by side. Tentative conclusions may therefore be drawn as to the coexistence, scope of application, and future evolution of JCE and co-perpetratorship as modes of liability in international criminal law.

JCE's origins in the Asian context

At the International Military Tribunal for the Far East, which opened in Tokyo in May 1946, the Preamble of the Indictment against twenty-eight high-ranking defendants referred to the policies of a 'criminal militaristic clique'.[2] The first five counts, addressing all of the defendants jointly, concerned a 'common plan or conspiracy' to wage aggressive war with the object of securing Japan's domination over East Asia and the Pacific and Indian Oceans.[3] Under these charges – set out in accordance with Article 5 of the Tokyo Charter [4] – all defendants would be 'responsible for all acts performed by themselves or by any person in execution of such plan'.[5] In its Judgment, the Tribunal explained that: 'A conspiracy to wage aggressive or unlawful war arises when two or more persons enter into an agreement to commit that crime.'[6] Using expressions that are reminiscent of modern JCE liability, the Tribunal went on to say:

> These far-reaching plans for waging wars of aggression and the prolonged and intricate preparation for and waging of these wars of aggression were not the work of one man. They were the work of many leaders acting in pursuance of a common plan for the achievement of a common object. That common object, that they should secure Japan's domination by preparing and waging wars of aggression, was a criminal object.[7]

It was found that the concrete common plan of the conspirators in terms of territorial domination was more limited than alleged in the Indictment

[2] International Military Tribunal for the Far East, *The Tokyo major war crimes trial*, R.J. Pritchard (ed.), 124 vols. (Lewiston: Edwin Mellen Press, 1998), Indictment, vol. 2, p. 1.
[3] Ibid., Indictment, pp. 2–4. [4] Ibid., Amended Charter, pp. 2–3.
[5] Ibid., Indictment, pp. 2–3. [6] Ibid., Majority Judgment, vol. 101, p. 48477.
[7] Ibid., Majority Judgment, vol. 103, pp. 49768–49769.

but that within the reduced charge, the criminal conspiracy to wage wars of aggression had been proved.[8] When it came to a consideration of individual criminal responsibility for participation in the long-running conspiracy, apparently little more had to be demonstrated than approval for, and active support at the political level of, Japan's aggressive aims. Conspiracy was not treated wholly as an inchoate offence since, according to the Tribunal, 'All of those who at any time were parties to the criminal conspiracy or who at any time with guilty knowledge played a part in its execution are guilty of the charge contained in Count 1.'[9] In the result, this included all but two of the accused against whom verdicts were issued. The Tribunal's approach has been criticised for its reliance on a concept of inchoate conspiracy known to Anglo-American law but not to international law,[10] and the broad and flexible manner in which it was applied without paying proper attention to the requirements of individual liability.[11] Significantly, it has also been asserted that 'the majority judgment is a shadowy precedent for the basic form of joint enterprise'.[12]

The Tokyo Tribunal's Majority Judgment referenced the attack on Hong Kong, which fell to the Japanese forces on 25 December 1941.[13] Following Japan's surrender in September 1945 and the capture of suspected war criminals, the British established war crimes courts in Hong Kong, functioning under the Royal Warrant of 18 June 1945.[14] A total of 46 trials of 123 accused were held.[15] The charges in these cases were framed broadly, describing the accused's responsibility in terms of being 'concerned in' or 'together concerned in' the relevant crime.[16] For example, in the case of *Kishi Yasuo et al.*, the Indictment alleged that the accused in violation of the laws and usages of war at Lantau Island between 18 and 26 August 1945 were 'together concerned in' the beating,

[8] Ibid., p. 49770, [9] Ibid.

[10] See N. Boister and R. Cryer, *The Tokyo International Military Tribunal: a reappraisal* (Oxford University Press, 2008), pp. 220.

[11] Ibid, pp. 218–219. [12] Ibid, p. 225. [13] IMTFE, Majority Judgment, vol. 103, p. 49573.

[14] War Office, Royal Warrant: Regulations for the Trial of War Criminals (Army Order 81/1945) (London: HMSO, signed 14 June 1945, promulgated 18 June 1945): LCO 53/102, The National Archives, United Kingdom (TNA).

[15] See Hong Kong's War Crimes Trials Collection at: hkwctc.lib.hku.hk/exhibits/show/hkwctc/home.

[16] N.H.B. Jørgensen, 'On being "concerned" in a crime: embryonic joint criminal enterprise?', in S. Linton (ed.), *Hong Kong's war crimes trials* (Oxford University Press, 2013), pp. 137–167.

torture and maltreatment of inhabitants of the Silver Mine Bay district and in the killing of nine of those inhabitants.[17]

The Hong Kong cases did not directly apply a common intent doctrine, although this featured in the British *Manual of military law 1929*, which provided the procedural framework for the trials.[18] But on some occasions prosecutors attempted to read a concept akin to common purpose liability into Regulation 8(ii) of the list appended to the Royal Warrant,[19] which stated that 'where there is evidence that a war crime has been the result of concerted action upon the part of a unit or group of men, then evidence given upon any charge relating to that crime against any member of such unit or group may be received as prima facie evidence of the responsibility of each member of that unit or group for that crime'.[20] This regulation was invoked in the *Kishi Yasuo et al.* case, where the prosecutor echoed the Tokyo Tribunal's language in maintaining that the execution of so many villagers 'was not a one-man show'.[21]

Overall, the prosecutors and judges in the Hong Kong cases made efforts to individualise guilt within the expansive scope of the charges. While the cases do not align themselves strictly with either a common purpose or co-perpetration theory, the influence of English law is readily apparent. The use of open-ended charges illustrates a practice common at that time when dealing with lower-level, more direct perpetrators alleged to have participated to varying degrees in the commission of crimes. International law theories of liability were only just emerging, and even command responsibility, also captured by the charge of being 'concerned in' a crime, was still a relative novelty.

Three decades later, the Tokyo Tribunal's language of 'cliques' also made its way into the allegations before the People's Revolutionary Tribunal (PRT) established in Cambodia in 1979 after the Vietnamese forces drove out the Khmer Rouge.[22] Pol Pot and Ieng Sary were both

[17] *Kishi Yasuo et al.*, Judgment (c. 25 April 1946), p. 528: WO 235/993, TNA. Emphasis added.

[18] War Office, *Manual of military law 1929* (London: HMSO, 7th edn., reprinted December 1939, published 1940), amended by Amendment No. 12 of 1936 and Amendment No. 34 of 1944.

[19] Royal Warrant, Regulation 8(ii).

[20] *Kishi Yasuo et al.*, 'Final address of prosecuting officer' (c. 25 April 1946), pp. 524–525: WO 235/993, TNA.

[21] Ibid., p. 522.

[22] See, for example, Decree Law No. 1, in H.J. De Nike, J. Quigley and K.J. Robinson (eds.), *Genocide in Cambodia: documents from the trial of Pol Pot and Ieng Sary* (Philadelphia: University of Pennsylvania Press, 2000), p. 45.

charged with being 'the instigator and planner of genocide'.[23] The Judgment echoed the idea of planning at the highest policy level, finding that: 'Pol Pot and Ieng Sary have a record of collusion with each other to oppose the Kampuchean revolution; that they jointly mapped out extremely reactionary domestic and foreign policies and organized and directed the implementation of these policies.'[24] They were held liable as instigators and planners and therefore found to be responsible for all the consequences of their genocidal acts. Subsequent proceedings before the Extraordinary Chambers in the Courts of Cambodia have highlighted certain deficiencies of the 1979 Tribunal.[25] Nonetheless, the PRT's process in the immediate aftermath of the Khmer Rouge rule is illustrative of the evolution of methods used to link the highest-level perpetrators with a wide spectrum of crimes.

Modern expressions of JCE

It is well known that the modern crystallisation of JCE occurred with the ICTY Appeals Chamber's Judgment in the case of *Prosecutor* v. *Tadić*.[26] It is also well known that JCE liability may be divided into three categories. The first 'basic' category refers to the situation in which all co-accused, acting pursuant to a common design, possess the same criminal intention, where proof is required that the accused voluntarily participated in one aspect of the common design and, even if not physically committing the crime, nevertheless intended the planned result.[27] The second 'systemic' form is based on proof of active participation in the enforcement of a system of repression combined with knowledge of the nature of the system and the intent to further the common concerted design to ill-treat inmates in a concentration camp setting.[28] The third 'extended' category, the one in fact applied in *Tadić*, concerns cases involving a common design to pursue one course of conduct where one of the perpetrators commits an act which, while outside the common design, was nevertheless a natural consequence of putting that design

[23] Ibid., Indictment, p. 487. [24] Ibid., Judgment, p. 548.

[25] See, for example, *Nuon et al.*, 002/19-09-2007/ECCC/TC, Decision on Ieng Sary's Rule 89 Preliminary Objections (Ne Bis In Idem and Amnesty and Pardon) (3 November 2011), par. 23; *Nuon et al.*, 002/19-09-2007-ECCC/OCIJ (PTC75), Decision on Ieng Sary's Appeal against the Closing Order (11 April 2011), pars. 174–175.

[26] *Prosecutor* v. *Tadić*, IT-94-1-A, Appeals Chamber Judgment (15 July 1999) (*Tadić* Appeals Judgment).

[27] Ibid., pars. 196–200. [28] Ibid., pars. 202–203.

into effect. The subjective element in the last category is foreseeability – specifically, foreseeing that a crime other than the one agreed upon might be perpetrated, and still willingly taking that risk.[29] Criminal responsibility for participating in a JCE in any of its three forms is considered to be within the ambit of 'committing' a crime under Article 7(1) of the ICTY Statute.[30] Thus, a participant in a JCE is not an accessory to the person who 'materially performs the criminal act' but rather a type of 'co-perpetrator'.[31] The Appeals Chamber in *Tadić* identified the objective and subjective elements of the three categories of JCE by reference to customary international law.[32]

The International Criminal Court has made painstaking efforts to give clarity to the forms of individual criminal responsibility listed in Article 25 of the Rome Statute.[33] It regards the form of co-perpetration that it applies as being uniquely tailored to the needs of international law. The majority of charges before the ICC are brought under Article 25(3)(a) of the Rome Statute, which states that a person will be individually criminally responsible if he or she 'Commits such a crime, whether as an individual, jointly with another or through another person, regardless of whether that other person is criminally responsible.'[34] Less frequently invoked is an alternative mode of liability set out in Article 25(3)(d), that a person will be held responsible if he or she 'In any other way contributes to the commission or attempted commission of such a crime by a group of persons acting with a common purpose.'[35]

In contrast to co-perpetration, which is considered to be a way of committing a crime as a principal, contributing to a common purpose is seen as an accessorial form of liability.[36] For the ICC, co-perpetration is the preferred means of including within the notion of principals 'those who, in spite of being removed from the scene of the crime, control or mastermind its commission because they decide whether and how the offence will be committed'.[37] In the *Lubanga* case, the Pre-Trial Chamber explained that the concept of co-perpetration was based on the idea that

[29] Ibid., pars. 204–219, 228.
[30] Updated Statute of the International Criminal Tribunal for the former Yugoslavia, September 2009 (originally adopted by Security Council Resolution 827 on 25 May 1993); *Tadić* Appeals Judgment, par. 190.
[31] *Tadić* Appeals Judgment, ibid., par. 192. [32] Ibid., par. 194.
[33] Rome Statute of the International Criminal Court: treaties.un.org. [34] Ibid. [35] Ibid.
[36] See, for example, *Prosecutor* v. *Mbarushimana*, ICC-01/04-01/10-465-Red, Pre-Trial Chamber I Decision on the Confirmation of Charges (16 December 2011), par. 278.
[37] See, for example, *Prosecutor* v. *Lubanga*, ICC-01/04-01/06, Pre-Trial Chamber I Decision on the Confirmation of Charges (29 January 2007) (*Lubanga* Decision), par. 330.

'when the sum of the co-ordinated individual contributions of a plurality of persons results in the realisation of all the objective elements of a crime, any person making a contribution can be held vicariously responsible for the contributions of all the others and, as a result, can be considered as a principal to the whole crime'.[38] The concept of co-perpetration thus described is based on the notion of joint control over the crime:

> [It] ... is rooted in the principle of the division of essential tasks for the purpose of committing a crime between two or more persons acting in a concerted manner. Hence, although none of the participants has overall control over the offence because they all depend on one another for its commission, they all share control because each of them could frustrate the commission of the crime by not carrying out his or her task.[39]

Outlining the elements for co-perpetratorship based on joint action by two or more individuals, the Trial Chamber in *Lubanga* confirmed that there must be a common plan or agreement between the co-perpetrators.[40] This need not be specifically directed at the crime in question. Rather, the implementation of the common plan must embody a sufficient risk that, in the ordinary course of events, a crime will be committed, coupled with the individual perpetrator's awareness of these circumstances.[41] While the offence may be the result of the combined actions of the co-perpetrators, the contribution of each must be essential according to the division of tasks. A direct physical link in the sense of presence or participation between the accused and the crime is not required provided control is established.[42] The Trial Chamber explained its reasoning by reference to the framework of the ICC Statute and the distinctions drawn between principals and accessories in Article 25(3)(a), and (b) to (d).

> It would be possible to expand the concept of principal liability (or 'commission' or 'perpetration'), to make it more widely applicable, by lowering the threshold that the accused's contribution be essential. However, lowering that threshold would deprive the notion of principal liability of its capacity to express the blameworthiness of those persons who are the most responsible for the most serious crimes of international concern. Instead, a notion of co-perpetration that requires an essential

[38] Ibid., par. 326. [39] Ibid., par. 342.

[40] *Prosecutor* v. *Lubanga*, ICC-01/04-01/06, Trial Chamber I Judgment (14 March 2012) (*Lubanga* Trial Judgment), par. 981.

[41] Ibid., pars. 984, 987. The elements are listed in full at par. 1018.

[42] Ibid., pars. 1003–1004.

contribution allows for the different degrees of responsibility to be properly expressed and addressed.[43]

Judge Fulford filed a Separate Opinion arguing that the Trial Chamber's approach was not supported by the ICC Statute and imposed 'an unnecessary and unfair burden on the prosecution'.[44] In his view, the modes of liability in Article 25(3) 'were not intended to be mutually exclusive' and less still intended to reflect a hierarchy of seriousness.[45] He favoured a 'plain text reading' of Article 25(3)(a), which would avoid hypothetical inquiries into what might have occurred without the accused's essential contribution.[46]

By comparison with the ad hoc tribunals, the ICC has been less concerned with custom, preferring to rely on general principles and legal theory while stressing that the Rome Statute is the primary source of law. In *Lubanga*, the defence presented an argument that the prosecutor's theory of liability was not supported by customary international law or by general principles of law, but the Pre-Trial Chamber did not conduct an analysis similar to the one in *Tadić*, being content to conclude that the concept of control over the crime that was put forward by the prosecutor is 'applied in numerous legal systems'.[47] Similarly in *Katanga*, the defence argued that the concept of co-perpetration as defined in *Lubanga* was not supported by customary international law, but the Pre-Trial Chamber, citing various sources, concluded that '[t]he control over the crime approach has been applied in a number of legal systems, and is widely recognised in legal doctrine'.[48] The Trial Chamber in the *Lubanga* case observed that although 'both the Romano Germanic and the Common Law legal systems have developed principles about modes of liability', these systems were never intended to address 'the most serious crimes of concern to the international community as a whole'.[49] Judge Fulford, however, has pointed out the irony in the fact that the control of the crime doctrine developed in the ICC jurisprudence is derived from German law. In his view isolated jurisprudence from the

43 Ibid., par. 999.

44 *Prosecutor* v. *Lubanga*, ICC-01/04-01/06–2842, Separate Opinion of Judge Adrian Fulford (14 March 2012) (Fulford Opinion), par. 3.

45 Ibid., pars. 7–8. 46 Ibid., par. 17.

47 See *Prosecutor* v. *Lubanga*, ICC-01/04-01/06, Pre-Trial Chamber I Decision on the Confirmation of Charges (29 January 2007) (*Lubanga* Decision), pars. 324 and 330.

48 *Prosecutor* v. *Katanga and Chui*, ICC-01/04-01/07, Pre-Trial Chamber I Decision on the Confirmation of Charges (30 September 2008) (*Katanga* Decision), par. 485 and fn. 647.

49 *Lubanga* Trial Judgment, par. 976.

ICTY and ICTR, itself relying heavily on the German legal system, unduly influenced the development of the ICC's theory of co-perpetration.[50]

The four manifestations of co-perpetration based on the notion of control of the crime (direct perpetration, perpetration through another person or indirect perpetration, co-perpetration based on joint control, and indirect co-perpetration[51]) have been subjected to ever more sophisticated interpretations by the ICC. For example, in the case of *Al Bashir*, the Pre-Trial Chamber has found that indirect co-perpetration, whereby all the co-perpetrators carry out their respective essential contributions to a common plan through another person,[52] includes the use of the state apparatus in a coordinated manner. The Pre-Trial Chamber found reasonable grounds to believe that Al Bashir either played an essential role in coordinating the design and implementation of the common plan through his roles as *de jure* and *de facto* President of the State of Sudan and Commander-in-Chief of the Sudanese Armed Forces,[53] or that he did not simply coordinate but was in full control of all the relevant branches of the apparatus of the state and used this control to implement the common plan.[54]

The ICC theory of co-perpetration is still somewhat in a state of flux but will become more certain as it is applied in a growing number of cases. It differs from JCE in focusing on the essential contribution of the accused as an objective element as opposed to the common intent amongst the co-perpetrators as a subjective element. While the underlying notion of co-perpetration may be a candidate for recognition as a general principle or a norm of customary international law, the ICC is developing a concept tailored specifically to international criminal law applied at the international level. The ICC appears to be encouraging the concept to break out of the bubble of its German law genesis, but it may be difficult to transplant such a sophisticated notion back into a domestic context, even where international crimes are concerned. The cases heard in East Timor illustrate the challenges that may be presented.

[50] Fulford Opinion, referring to the ICTY Trial Chamber Judgment in the *Stakić* case, and ICTR Appeal Judge Schomburg's Separate Opinion in the *Gacumbitsi* case (par. 10). Judge Fulford also notes that unlike the ICC, the sentencing range in the German legal system is determined by the mode of liability (par. 11).

[51] *Prosecutor* v. *Al Bashir*, ICC-02/05-01/09, Pre-Trial Chamber 1 Decision on the Prosecution's Application for a Warrant of Arrest (4 March 2009), par. 210.

[52] Ibid., par. 213. [53] Ibid., par. 221. [54] Ibid., par. 222.

JCE in the East Timor cases

The Special Panels for Serious Crimes (SPSC) in East Timor, established by Regulation 2000/15 in 2000,[55] dealt with serious criminal offences, including genocide, war crimes, crimes against humanity, torture, murder and sexual offences (the last two categories being governed by the Indonesian Penal Code in force at the time). Section 14 of this Regulation borrows the description of individual criminal responsibility directly from Article 25 of the Rome Statute. Thus Regulation Section 14.3(a) copies Article 25.3(a) in stating that liability will ensue if a person 'commits . . . a crime, whether as an individual, jointly with another or through another person, regardless of whether that other person is criminally responsible'.[56] Section 14.3(d) virtually replicates Article 25 (3)(d) in describing residual common purpose liability.[57]

The Regulation therefore left various options open to the SPSC in terms of how to address joint criminal responsibility. The Special Panels might have followed the ICC model, although at the time there was little jurisprudence to serve as a guide. Alternatively they could have interpreted Sections 14.3(a) and (d) in a manner reflective of domestic law. The Criminal Code of Indonesia, applicable to East Timor at the time of the relevant conduct, provides in Article 55 that 'those who perpetrate, cause others to perpetrate, or take a direct part in the execution of the act' shall be punishable as principals.[58] Provoking the execution of the act is also punishable,[59] as is complicity by aiding or deliberately providing the 'opportunity, means or information for the commission of the crime'.[60]

Tadić-style joint criminal enterprise quickly made its way into the jurisprudence of the SPSC although it was applied in a rather haphazard manner, which suggests some confusion over the content of this theory of liability. In the *Marques et al.* case, various references were made to ICTY and ICTR precedents. The prosecutor presented an argument as to co-perpetration, suggesting that Section 14.3(a) included the notion of several participants acting pursuant to a common design with the same criminal intention.[61] Confusingly, Section 14.3(d) was described by the

[55] United Nations Transitional Administration in East Timor, Regulation 2000/15 'On the Establishment of Panels with Exclusive Jurisdiction over Serious Criminal Offences' (6 June 2000).

[56] Ibid., Section 14.3(a). [57] Ibid., Section 14.3(d).

[58] Article 55, *Kitab Undang-Undang Hukum Pidana* (Criminal Code). [59] Ibid.

[60] Ibid., Article 56.

[61] *Prosecutor* v. *Marques et al.*, 09/2000, Trial Chamber Judgment (11 December 2001), p. 38.

prosecutor as encompassing the three forms of JCE liability described in *Tadić*.[62] The Judgment did not explain the role and basis for responsibility of each accused in clear terms and neither co-perpetration nor JCE seemed to provide an explicit foundation for a conviction.

In the *Cardoso* case, responsibility was grounded in the concept of joint criminal enterprise in accordance with Section 14.3(a) of Regulation 2000/15.[63] But it has been noted that the Judgment nowhere explains 'why the conduct of the accused which it describes should be characterised as participation in a joint criminal enterprise, rather than simple commission, or even co-perpetration'.[64] In this case the JCE notion seems to have been misunderstood, its use being described as a 'conceptual overkill'[65] with respect to someone who was apparently 'right in the thick of the criminal action'[66] and a more likely candidate for a direct form of liability.[67] Meanwhile in the *Pedro* case, it was simply held that the accused and another militia member each stabbed the victim 'according to a pre-conceived common design to kill him', thereby committing the crime against humanity '"jointly with another" in the sense of Sec. 14.3(a) Reg. 2000/15 (co-perpetration)'.[68]

The *Laku* case addressed the domestic offence of murder covered in Section 8 of Regulation 2000/15, with reference to Article 340 of the Criminal Code of Indonesia.[69] The Judgment found the accused to have participated directly in the operation that led to the death of the victim. Furthermore, even if he had not been the main perpetrator, Section 14.3 (b) of the Regulation (ordering, soliciting or inducing the commission of a crime) was held to apply.[70] In the *Leki* case, also dealing with murder, it was suggested without explanation that even if the accused was not the main perpetrator of murder, he was still responsible under Section 14.3(d).[71] Similarly in the case of *Tavares*, it was held without further

[62] Ibid., p. 40.

[63] *Prosecutor* v. *Cardoso*, 04/2001, Trial Chamber Judgment (5 April 2003), par. 367.

[64] G. Boas, J.L. Bischoff and N.L. Reid (eds.), *International criminal law practitioner library series*, vol. 1: *Forms of responsibility in international criminal law* (Cambridge University Press, 2008), p. 135.

[65] A. Zahar, 'Commentary' on trial judgments of the East Timor Special Panels in the cases of José Cardoso Ferreira and Agustinho Atolan, in A. Klip and G. Sluiter (eds.), *Annotated leading cases of international criminal tribunals*, vol. 13: *Timor Leste: the Special Panels for Serious Crimes 2001–2003* (Antwerp, Intersentia, 2008), p. 765.

[66] Ibid. [67] Ibid.

[68] *Prosecutor* v. *Pedro*, 1/2001, Trial Chamber Judgment (14 April 2005), p. 6.

[69] *Prosecutor* v. *Laku*, 8/2001, Trial Chamber Judgment (25 July 2001). [70] Ibid., p. 11.

[71] *Prosecutor* v. *Leki*, 05/2000, Trial Chamber Judgment (11 June 2001), p. 9.

clarification that even if the accused was not the main perpetrator he would be responsible under Section 14.3(c) and (d).[72] Thus, the 'international' modes of liability were in principle found to be applicable also in respect of the domestic crimes but there is no reasoning to explain how this was seen to operate. The SPSC jurisprudence throws little light on the relationship between JCE and co-perpetration as derived from the ICC Statute and, indeed, mixes the two concepts. Any apparent favouring of JCE as a method of addressing joint criminal responsibility may stem from the fact that there was little else in the arena of international criminal law to serve as a guide at the time.

JCE in the Khmer Rouge cases

The Extraordinary Chambers in the Courts of Cambodia have partially subscribed to the JCE doctrine while refraining from developing any alternative theory of co-perpetration even with respect to the domestic offences falling within the Court's jurisdiction. Like the ICTY, the ECCC has been concerned to identify the applicable customary international law with reference to the time frame relevant to the charges. When considering the JCE doctrine, the Pre-Trial and Trial Chambers have generally reinforced the status of the basic and systemic categories of JCE (JCE I and II), but have sharply repudiated the extended category, JCE III, at least with respect to conduct pre-dating the *Tadić* decision.

According to Article 29 of the ECCC Law, individual criminal responsibility will be established in the case of anyone who 'planned, instigated, ordered, aided and abetted, or committed' the crimes set out therein, including genocide, crimes against humanity, war crimes, destruction of cultural property, crimes against internationally protected persons, and, under Article 3 (new), the domestic crimes of homicide, torture and religious persecution.[73] The 1956 Penal Code is the basis for the crimes under domestic law, and it defines and distinguishes between the concepts of co-perpetration and complicity.[74] The perpetrator (*auteur*) is the

[72] *Prosecutor* v. *Tavares*, 02/2001, Trial Chamber Judgment (28 September 2001), par. 52.

[73] Law on the Establishment of the Extraordinary Chambers in the Courts of Cambodia for the Prosecution of Crimes Committed during the Period of Democratic Kampuchea, NS/RKM/1004/006 (as amended 27 October 2004) (ECCC Law).

[74] *Nuon* PTC JCE Decision, par. 41, referring to Kai Ambos' amicus curiae brief; *Duch*, 001/18-07-2007-ECCC/OCIJ (PTC 02) Doc. D99/3/42, Pre-Trial Chamber Decision on Appeal against Closing Order Indicting ... Duch (5 December 2008) (*Duch* PTC Decision), par. 114, and fn. 73.

person who commits the crime, while co-perpetration (*co-action*) requires a common agreement between the co-perpetrators, and complicity covers indirect participation.[75] According to the ECCC Trial Chamber, the modes of liability in Article 29, which expressly apply to the domestic crimes set out in Article 3 (new), were known under the 1956 Code, with the exception of planning and superior responsibility (although planning was criminalised by specific provisions).[76]

JCE quickly became a contentious issue in the proceedings before the ECCC. The co-prosecutors set out a theory of JCE liability in their Introductory Submission of July 2007, triggering the judicial investigation into the conduct of the five original detainees: Nuon Chea, Ieng Sary, Ieng Thirith, Khieu Samphan and Kaing Guek Eav (alias Duch).[77] The *Duch* case was subsequently severed for a separate trial, becoming known as Case 001.[78] In their Final Submission in Case 001 of July 2008, the co-prosecutors put forward a modified JCE theory ('S-21 JCE') to describe an organised system of repression within the notorious S-21 detention centre, of which Duch was Deputy and then Chairman.[79] When the co-investigating judges issued a Closing Order (indictment) in the case against Duch,[80] no reference was made to JCE, prompting an appeal by the co-prosecutors before the Pre-Trial Chamber.

In its decision on the appeal, the Pre-Trial Chamber noted that the co-investigating judges should have reasoned why they had turned down the co-prosecutors' proposal to include the allegation of a JCE within S-21.[81] Nevertheless, the Chamber rejected this aspect of the appeal. JCE was found to be unique in allowing 'individual responsibility at the level of a co-perpetrator to be attributed to participants in collective criminal action even though they may be physically divorced from the actual offences'.[82] In its view, the use of the JCE theory to indict Duch would consequently change the perception of the level and extent of his responsibility from the description given in the Closing Order, in fact expanding

75 *Duch* PTC Decision, par. 114 and fn. 73.

76 *Duch*, 001/18-07-2007/ECCC/TC, Trial Chamber Judgment (26 July 2010) (*Duch* Trial Judgment), par. 474.

77 Introductory Submission Pursuant to ECCC Internal Rule 53 (18 July 2007) (confidential); *Duch* PTC Decision, par. 118–121.

78 *Duch*, D-18, Co-Investigating Judges' Separation Order (19 September 2007).

79 *Duch*, 002/14-08-2006/ECCC/OCP, Public Information by the Co-Prosecutors Pursuant to Rule 54 (18 July 2008), pars. 244, 250–253.

80 *Duch*, 002/14-08-2006, Closing Order Indicting Kaing Guek Eav alias Duch (public redacted version) (8 August 2008).

81 *Duch* PTC Decision, par. 115. 82 Ibid., par. 136.

the type of conduct attributable to him.[83] Since the S-21 JCE did not constitute a part of the factual basis for the investigation, and since Duch had not been informed of the allegation relating to his participation in such a JCE prior to the Final Submission, the Pre-Trial Chamber declined to add it to the Closing Order.[84]

The JCE doctrine was nevertheless to reappear in the Trial Chamber's final judgment in Case 001. At the initial hearings of the trial in February 2009, the co-prosecutors had notified the Chamber and the parties that they would request the application of JCE to the charges against Duch.[85] Four months later they followed this up with a written request that the Trial Chamber declare that all three forms of JCE be generally applicable before the ECCC, and specifically applicable in the case.[86] The Trial Chamber postponed a ruling on this request until the judgment stage. It produced its Judgment in July 2010, and, when addressing the JCE question, it relied upon ECCC Internal Rule 98(2), which provides that although judgment must be limited to the facts in the Closing Order, the Chamber may 'change the legal characterisation of the crime as set out in the Indictment, as long as no new constitutive elements are introduced'.[87] The parties had agreed that Rule 98(2) referred to both crimes and forms of responsibility,[88] and the Trial Chamber therefore used this to enable itself 'to change the legal characterisation of facts contained in the Amended Closing Order to accord with a new form of responsibility provided that it does not go beyond those facts'.[89] At the same time, it acknowledged the need to respect the accused's fair trial rights and ensure that the mode of liability was applicable before the ECCC.[90]

The Trial Chamber referred to the 1956 Cambodian Penal Code to support its conclusions as to the applicability of JCE, but not to consider co-perpetration as an alternative mode of liability. It noted that under Article 82 of the Code, reference is made to co-perpetration as a form of responsibility deriving from direct participation, and, further, that it provides that direct or indirect voluntary participants may be equally liable with the principal of the crime.[91] Observing that the Code was modelled on its French counterpart, it stated that 'references to national legislation and case law only serve to illustrate that the notion of joint criminal enterprise (or common purpose) upheld in international criminal law has an underpinning in many national systems, including that of Cambodia'.[92] The

[83] Ibid. [84] Ibid., par. 141. [85] *Duch* Trial Judgment, par. 489. [86] Ibid.
[87] Ibid., par. 492. [88] Ibid., par. 493. [89] Ibid., par. 496. [90] Ibid. [91] Ibid., par. 510.
[92] Ibid.

Chamber went on to say that JCE in its basic and systemic forms and co-perpetration under Code were similar but not identical and, citing the Pre-Trial Chamber, that although both require a shared intent on the part of the perpetrators, 'participation in a JCE, even if it has to be significant, would appear to embrace situations where the accused may be more remote from the actual perpetration of the *actus reus* of the crime than the direct participation required under domestic law'.[93] It nevertheless concluded that JCE as applied before the ECCC was found to follow from customary international law rather than from national law.[94]

The Trial Chamber held that JCE was included as a form of commission of a crime in Article 29 (new) of the ECCC Law.[95] In addition, it affirmed the status of the basic and systemic forms of JCE in customary law, took account of JCE's 'resonance with the Cambodian law concept of co-perpetration applicable at the time', and found that JCE liability was accessible and foreseeable to the accused.[96] Duch was thus found to bear individual criminal responsibility for a range of crimes against humanity and war crimes on the basis of his participation in a systemic JCE (in other words, JCE II) at S-21.[97] The Supreme Court Chamber's Judgment on appeal did not challenge JCE II as the chosen mode of liability.[98] Furthermore, while agreeing that the 1956 Penal Code was the applicable law from 1975 to 1979,[99] the Supreme Court Chamber did not evaluate Duch's responsibility under the Code for that period for the crimes of premeditated murder and torture. Essentially, this was because the Trial Chamber had previously failed to secure the minimum of four affirmative votes from the judges required by Article 14 (new) of the ECCC Law, in an earlier decision as to whether prosecution for the domestic crimes was time-barred.[100] In that decision the international judges were unable to conclude that the limitation period applicable to domestic crimes had been suspended between 1979 and 1993 and found that prosecution was no longer possible after the promulgation of Articles 3 and 3 (new) of the ECCC Law.[101] This meant that this aspect of the proceedings against

[93] Ibid, citing *Nuon* PTC JCE Decision, par. 41. [94] *Duch* Trial Judgment, par. 510.
[95] Ibid., par. 511. [96] Ibid., par. 512. [97] Ibid., par. 516.
[98] *Duch*, 001/18-07-2007-ECCC/SC, Supreme Court Chamber Appeal Judgment (3 February 2012) (*Duch* Appeal Judgment), par. 91.
[99] Ibid., par. 92.
[100] *Duch*, 001/18-07-2007/ECCC/TC, Trial Chamber Decision on the Defence Preliminary Objection Concerning the Statute of Limitations of Domestic Crimes (26 July 2010), par. 56.
[101] Ibid., Opinion of Judges Silvia Cartwright and Jean-Marc Lavergne, pars. 39–55.

Duch had to be discontinued, and consequently there was no assessment of the relevant modes of liability.[102]

In Case 002, dealing with the remaining four suspects included in the July 2007 Introductory Submission of the Co-Prosecutors (Nuon Chea, Ieng Sary, Khieu Samphan and Ieng Thirith), the Closing Order asserted that all the modes of liability in Article 29 (new) of the ECCC Law were part of international law applicable in Cambodia at the relevant time, including commission by means of JCE I or II.[103] The Closing Order described the Communist Party of Kampuchea leaders' common purpose as the implementation of 'rapid socialist revolution ... in Cambodia through "a great leap forward"', and the defence of the Party 'against internal and external enemies, by whatever means necessary'.[104] While this purpose was not criminal as such, its implementation was alleged to have resulted in or involved the commission of crimes within the jurisdiction of the ECCC. The CPK leaders, including the four alleged members of the JCE, were accused of designing and implementing five policies to achieve the common purpose,[105] and contributing to its furtherance with the requisite intent as set out in the Closing Order.[106] Notably, the co-investigating judges held that the basic form of JCE (JCE I) best described the criminal responsibility of the (then) charged persons, and that JCE II need not be retained.[107] Facing the issue of how to address the offences under domestic law, the judges noted the procedural stalemate in Case 001, which they attributed in part to the hybrid nature of the Court.[108] They nonetheless ordered the inclusion in the Indictment of the charges of murder, torture and religious persecution, as defined and made punishable by the 1956 Penal Code.[109] The Pre-Trial Chamber upheld these charges when dealing with appeals against the Closing Order.[110] In its decision on Ieng Sary's appeal, the Pre-Trial Chamber also affirmed the co-investigating judges' conclusion that all charged modes of liability existed in law at the time of the alleged offences.[111]

[102] *Duch* Trial Judgment, par. 678.

[103] *Nuon et al.*, 002/19-09-2007-ECCC-OCIJ, Office of the Co-Investigating Judges Closing Order (15 September 2010), par. 1318.

[104] Ibid., par. 1524. [105] Ibid., pars. 1525–1526.

[106] Ibid., pars. 1533, 1535, 1537 and 1539. [107] Ibid., par. 1541. [108] Ibid., par. 1574.

[109] Ibid., par. 1576.

[110] *Nuon et al.*, 002/19-09-2007-ECCC/OCIJ (PTC75), Pre-Trial Chamber Decision on Ieng Sary's Appeal against the Closing Order (*Nuon* PTC Decision)(11 April 2011); *Nuon et al.*, 002/19-09-2007-ECCC/OCIJ (PTC 145 & 146), Pre-Trial Chamber Decision on Appeals by Nuon Chea and Ieng Thirith against the Closing Order (15 February 2011).

[111] *Nuon* PTC Decision, par. 260.

When considering domestic crimes, the Chamber substituted its own reasoning for what it considered to be inadequate reasoning by the judges and found that the limitation period applicable to these crimes had not expired and that there was no violation of the principle of legality in proceeding with the charges.[112] It noted that the judges had not specified the facts and modes of liability underlying the charges for the domestic crimes, yet it stated that a reading of the Closing Order as a whole made it clear that the factual basis for both national and international crimes was the same. The modes of liability were similarly identical 'save for [those] that the Co-Investigating Judges have said to be international, namely commission via a joint criminal enterprise, superior responsibility and instigation'.[113] The Pre-Trial Chamber was concerned only with the issue of the ECCC's jurisdiction to forward the case for trial in relation to these domestic crimes. The question of whether ultimately the facts of Case 002 could be characterised as murder, torture and religious persecution under the 1956 Penal Code was for the Trial Chamber to determine at a later stage.

In addressing preliminary objections brought by the defence at the start of the trial, the Trial Chamber noted that even though JCE was apparently viewed by both the co-investigating judges and the Pre-Trial Chamber as being exclusively applicable to international crimes, 'this form of responsibility is included in the Closing Order's disposition'.[114] The Trial Chamber regarded it as problematic that '[n]either the Closing Order nor the Pre-Trial Chamber explains how the Accused could be held responsible for domestic crimes as a member of a JCE'.[115] Having found defects in the manner in which the domestic crimes were charged, the Trial Chamber concluded that 'the charges in the Closing Order pertaining to offences in the 1956 Penal Code cannot form the basis of trial proceedings before the ECCC'.[116]

In the meantime, in May 2010, the Pre-Trial Chamber had rendered its decision, in which it found that the authorities relied upon in *Tadić* did not 'constitute a sufficiently firm basis to conclude that JCE III formed part of customary international law at the time relevant to Case 002'.[117] Two months later, the Trial Chamber handed down its Judgment in Case 001 and declined to pronounce on the customary law status of JCE III in the period 1975–1979 since the co-prosecutors had only sought

[112] Ibid., par. 287. [113] Ibid., par. 296.
[114] *Nuon et al.*, 002/19-09-2007-ECCC/TC, Decision on Defence Preliminary Objections (Statute of Limitations on Domestic Crimes) (22 September 2011), par. 15.
[115] Ibid. [116] Ibid., par. 23. [117] *Nuon* PTC JCE Decision, par. 83.

to apply the extended form of JCE in the alternative, which meant it became irrelevant to the decision in Case 001.[118]

A year later, the Trial Chamber rendered a decision in Case 002 in response to a co-prosecutor's motion to be allowed to use JCE III as an alternative mode of liability.[119] When referring back to the Pre-Trial Chamber's decision, and to its own Judgment in Case 001, the Trial Chamber saw no reason to depart from the ECCC's earlier analysis of JCE III.[120] Indeed, the Trial Chamber noted that the issue of the applicability of JCE III had already been 'extensively litigated before the ECCC'[121] and that it would not be in the interests of judicial economy to give extensive reasoning where 'it can find no cogent reasons to depart from the Pre-Trial Chamber's analysis and where it concurs in the result'.[122]

In this instance, the Trial Chamber did, however, offer its views on the post-war cases relied upon in *Tadić*[123] and the cases relied upon in a decision by the Appeals Chamber of the Special Tribunal for Lebanon in support of JCE III.[124] None of the available post-war authorities persuaded the Chamber that JCE III had emerged as a customary international law notion by 1975–1979.[125]

The Trial Chamber went on to consider whether JCE III could be supported as a general principle of law, a question that had not been answered directly by the Pre-Trial Chamber. It surveyed the law of a number of nations, including among others the United States, Germany, the Soviet Union, France and Cambodia, and concluded that there was a significant divergence of approach in these jurisdictions and that no general principle could be derived from domestic practice.[126] Thus, it agreed with *Tadić* that 'state practice in this area lacks sufficient uniformity to be considered a general principle of law'.[127] Regarding Cambodian law specifically, the Trial Chamber noted that none of the forms of responsibility in the 1956 Penal Code, applicable at the relevant time, supported the application of JCE III liability.[128]

118 *Duch* Trial Judgment, pars. 512–513.

119 *Nuon et al.*, 002/19-09-2007/ECCC/TC, Trial Chamber Decision on the Applicability of Joint Criminal Enterprise (12 September 2011) (*Nuon* Trial Chamber JCE Decision).

120 Ibid., pars. 22, 26. 121 Ibid., par. 26. 122 Ibid.

123 Ibid., pars. 30–31 (referring to the *Borkum Island* and *Essen Lynching* cases).

124 Ibid., pars. 32–33, and 34 (referring to the *Ulrich and Merkle* and *Wuelfert* cases).

125 Ibid., par. 35. 126 Ibid., par. 37. 127 Ibid. 128 Ibid., fn. 91.

The severance of Case 002

By the time of its decision on the applicability of JCE III, the Trial Chamber had issued a severance order in which it decided to proceed with a sub-trial of limited scope against the four individuals charged within Case 002 (Case 002/01), in the interests of a timely verdict.[129] Following an appeals process which resulted in the annulment of this order,[130] the Trial Chamber issued a second, extensively reasoned, decision on severance.[131] Even so, it still did not explain how the overarching JCE would be affected by the severance, except to indicate that it would consider the roles and responsibilities of the accused in relation to the policies relevant to the whole indictment in the severed case.[132] It also stressed that the core of Case 002 was 'a common purpose to implement radical socialist revolution by achieving a great leap forward and eliminating internal and external enemies by whatever means possible, in which all Accused are alleged to have participated'.[133] The co-prosecutors subsequently requested confirmation of the five policies forming part of the JCE that would be subject to definitive factual findings or legal conclusions in Case 002/01.[134] In response, the Trial Chamber issued a memorandum which referred to the factual themes of the sub-case

[129] 002/19-09-2007-ECCC/TC, Severance Order Pursuant to Internal Rule 89*ter* (22 September 2011), par. 8. The Co-Prosecutors appealed a subsequent decision on the scope of Case 002/01, and in February 2013, the Supreme Court Chamber decided to annul the original order: *Nuon et al.*, 002/19-09-2007-ECCC-TC/SC(18), Supreme Court Chamber Decision on the Co-Prosecutors' Immediate Appeal of the Trial Chamber's Decision Concerning the Scope of Case 002/01 (8 February 2013), pars. 48–49.

[130] The Co-Prosecutors appealed a decision on the scope of Case 002/01, which followed from the severance order. *Nuon et al.*, 002/19-09-2007-ECCC-TC/SC(18), Supreme Court Chamber Decision on the Co-Prosecutors' Immediate Appeal of the Trial Chamber's Decision Concerning the Scope of Case 002/01 (8 February 2013), pars. 48–49.

[131] *Nuon et al.*, 002/19-09-2007/ECCC/TC, Trial Chamber Decision on Severance of Case 002 Following Supreme Court Chamber Decision of 8 February 2013 (26 April 2013) (*Nuon* Trial Chamber Decision on Severance). The Co-Prosecutors and the accused Nuon Chea appealed against the second decision on severance, but the Supreme Court Chamber dismissed these, and ordered that evidentiary hearings in the second sub-case should commence as soon as possible after closing submissions in the first sub-case: *Case 002*, 002/19-09-2007-ECCC-TC/SC(28), Supreme Court Chamber Decision on Immediate Appeals against Trial Chamber's Second Decision on Severance of Case 002 (25 November 2013). See also, *Nuon et al.*, 002/19-09-2007-ECCC/TC, Trial Chamber Decision on Additional Severance of Case 002 and Scope of Case 002/02 (4 April 2014).

[132] *Nuon* Trial Chamber Decision on Severance, ibid, par. 16.

[133] Ibid, par. 92.

[134] *Nuon et al.*, 002/19-09-2007-ECCC/TC, Co-Prosecutors' Request for Clarification of Findings Regarding the Joint Criminal Enterprise alleged in Case 002/01 (7 August 2013).

(namely, forced movement and execution of purported enemies of the regime), and indicated that 'the presentation in general terms of all five policies was permissible to enable consideration of the manner in which the policy was developed'.[135]

The Trial Chamber delivered its judgment in Case 002/01 on 7 August 2014, by which time only Nuon Chea and Khieu Samphan remained as accused, after the death of Ieng Sary on 14 March 2013 and the earlier staying of proceedings against Ieng Thirith due to her unfitness to stand trial.[136] It unsurprisingly followed its own established jurisprudence on JCE: JCE I and II were available while JCE III was not applicable.[137] It also found that JCE as a mode of liability was foreseeable and accessible to the accused, considering their 'senior positions' as well as 'the customary nature of JCE I and JCE II by 1975'.[138] The evidence was considered to have established that in the time period relevant to Case 002/01 (17 April 1975 to December 1977), there was a plurality of persons who shared the common purpose 'to implement a socialist revolution in Cambodia'.[139] While it was acknowledged that this common purpose was not criminal *per se*, it was found that the 'population movements' policy and 'targeting' policy were preconceived and criminal in nature as they involved a consistent pattern of crimes such as 'forced transfers, murders, attacks against human dignity and political persecution' to achieve the goals of the JCE.[140] Nuon Chea and Khieu Samphan were convicted of committing through a JCE (basic form) the crimes against humanity of murder, extermination, political persecution and other inhumane acts in connection with the implementation of the policies under consideration in Case 002/01.[141]

[135] *Nuon et al.*, E284/5, Memorandum from President of the Trial Chamber on Co-Prosecutors' Request for Clarification of Findings Regarding the JCE Alleged in Case 002/01 (27 August 2013).

[136] *Nuon et al.*, 002/19-09-2007/ECCC/TC, Trial Chamber's Decision on Ieng Thirith's Fitness to Stand Trial (17 November 2011).

[137] *Nuon et al.*, 002/19-09-2007/ECCC/TC, Trial Chamber Judgment Case 002/01 (7 August 2014), (*Nuon* Judgment Case 002/01), par. 691.

[138] Ibid. When addressing planning, instigating, ordering, and aiding and abetting, the Judgment followed the same formula, stressing their customary nature by 1975: ibid., pars. 697, 699, 701 and 703.

[139] Ibid., par. 804.

[140] Ibid., in relation to the 'population movements' policy, and ibid., par. 835 in relation to the 'targeting' policy. See also legal findings at pars. 777–778.

[141] Ibid., pars. 940 and 1053.

Conclusion

Like some of the other Asian tribunals, the ECCC has proceeded down the road of JCE liability without any sustained consideration of an alternative model of co-perpetration, such as that provided in Cambodian law. This is despite the fact that the Trial Chamber has not hesitated to make reference to the distinction between common law and civil law notions in other areas, scrupulously emphasising the civil law genesis of the ECCC.[142] It is perhaps surprising that the ECCC has not adopted the same attitude to modes of liability as well. Instead, it has presented JCE as being a *type* of co-perpetration, stating that

> In spite of its unique nature, the concept of JCE, at least in its basic and systemic forms (JCE I & II), resembles accountability in traditional civil law in that it treats as co-perpetrators not only those who physically perform the *actus reus* of the crime, but also those who possess the *mens rea* for the crime and participate or contribute to its commission. In this sense, JCE has an underpinning in Cambodian law.[143]

The Special Tribunal for Lebanon, also noting that 'JCE is a mode of co-perpetration',[144] has nonetheless grappled more wholeheartedly with the relationship between Lebanese law and international law. While noting that JCE is unknown in Lebanese law, the STL Appeals Chamber found that domestic law and international law overlapped to such an extent in their application that both the first and third forms of JCE were potentially available to the Tribunal.[145] In the event of any future conflict, the source of law leading to the greatest protection for the rights of the accused should be applied.[146] It remains to be seen whether JCE will reign supreme in the practice of the Special Tribunal.

As the domestic offences under the ECCC's jurisdiction have fallen by the wayside for procedural reasons, the anticipated direct juxtaposition of JCE and co-perpetration as defined by the 1956 Penal Code has not so far occurred. The ECCC Chambers have failed to scrutinise the co-investigating judges' position that JCE is applicable solely to international crimes and is not relevant to the domestic crimes over which the ECCC

[142] In relation to procedure, for example, the *Duch* Trial Judgment, par. 495, asserted: 'It follows from the many structural differences between the international *ad hoc* tribunals and the ECCC that certain of the common law-inspired procedural mechanisms of the former have no counterpart in the civil law-oriented framework of the latter.'

[143] *Nuon* PTC JCE Decision, par. 41.

[144] *Interlocutory decision on the applicable law: terrorism, conspiracy, homicide, perpetration, cumulative charging*, STL-11-01/I, Appeals Chamber (16 February 2011), par. 236.

[145] Ibid., pars. 259–261. [146] Ibid., par. 262.

has jurisdiction. The reverse assertion, that a form of co-perpetration is applicable to the domestic crimes but not to international crimes, has similarly not been considered. The SPSC jurisprudence relating to the East Timor cases suggests that there may be no valid basis for such distinctions. The ECCC Civil Parties appealed against the part of the co-investigating judges' Order on JCE that referred to autonomous liability regimes for domestic and international crimes, meaning that JCE was applicable only to international crimes.[147] The Pre-Trial Chamber found that the arguments on appeal failed to demonstrate an error, however.[148]

The ECCC's readiness to adopt the common-law-inspired notion of JCE is presumably influenced by the fact that the doctrine is recognised under customary international law. Co-perpetration in its more elaborate manifestations, especially as applied by the ICC, does not currently enjoy the same status. Indeed, when the ICTY Appeals Chamber had to make a choice between JCE and another theory of co-perpetration in the *Stakić* case, it claimed that co-perpetration as defined by the Trial Chamber in that case 'does not have support in customary international law or in the settled jurisprudence of this Tribunal'.[149] However, the allure of JCE goes deeper than the dictates of custom. The ECCC Trial Chamber acknowledged that the concept allows for greater remoteness between the accused and the physical commission of the crime. The prosecution had urged the application of JCE before the ECCC on the basis that the crimes were not the isolated acts of individual cadres 'but the result of deliberate criminal policies designed and enforced by the *Khmer Rouge*'.[150] Further, it asserted that the ECCC could only realise its mandate to try senior leaders and those most responsible if it were able to assign criminal responsibility to those who created and oversaw the implementation of policies.[151] In the view of the prosecution, JCE is 'the mode of liability best suited to this task'.[152] The suggestion is that JCE is uniquely capable of providing the right framework for joint criminal responsibility in cases

147 *Nuon et al.*, 002/19-09-2007/ECCC/OCIJ(PTC37), Appeal Brief against the Order on the Application at the ECCC of the Form of Liability known as Joint Criminal Enterprise (8 January 2010), par. 11.

148 *Nuon* PTC JCE Decision, pars. 98–102.

149 *Prosecutor* v. *Stakić*, IT-97-24-A, Appeals Chamber Judgment (22 March 2006), par. 62.

150 *Nuon et al.*, 002/19-09-2007-ECCC/OCIJ, Co-Prosecutors' Response to Ieng Sary's Motion on Joint Criminal Enterprise (11 August 2008), par. 13.

151 Ibid., pars. 13–14.

152 *Nuon et al.*, 002/19-09-2007-ECCC/TC, Co-Prosecutors' Request for the Trial Chamber to Consider JCE III as an Alternative Mode of Liability (17 June 2011), par. 16.

involving systematic crimes orchestrated at the highest level of decision-making.

Even if the ECCC's approach to the issue of participation in collective crimes was warranted, the court faced the complex issue of how to approach an overarching JCE within the limited factual scope of Case 002/01. In the interests of fairness and in view of the age and health condition of the surviving accused, it might have been desirable to break the JCE down into smaller components. Indeed, the court had its own precedent in the form of the 'S-21 JCE'. The Judgment in Case 002/01 does attempt to focus on a limited range of policies that constituted the essence of the JCE applicable to the sub-case,[153] but its discussion of the origins and evolution of the common plan extends well beyond the framework of the precise factual allegations.[154] As a concept, JCE in its first and second forms becomes objectionable only when it is viewed as being overly expansive. If co-perpetration under Cambodian law is to be used to inform the approach to JCE, then it could also be seen to serve a restraining function. The ECCC has a special role in undertaking both an historical inquiry into international law as it was in 1975–1979 and in addressing issues at the cutting edge of international criminal law, especially concerning modes of liability. The emerging practice demonstrates that steps remain to be taken in uncovering the mysteries of overlapping modes of liability in order to provide a coherent yet contextually relevant approach to joint criminal responsibility at future trials.

[153] *Nuon* Judgment Case 002/01, par. 779. [154] Ibid., Section 14.1 (Common Purpose).

14

The tribunals in Bangladesh

Falling short of international standards

ABDUR RAZZAQ

The People's Republic of Bangladesh emerged as an independent state in 1971 after a nine-month war of liberation and an international conflict between India, Pakistan and Bangladesh. Some 82,000 members of the Pakistani armed forces and some 11,000 civilians were taken as prisoners of war or internees by the joint command of the Bangladesh and Indian forces. In July 1973, the Bangladesh Parliament passed the 'International Crimes (Tribunals) Act, 1973' to try 195 prisoners of war who were alleged to have committed war crimes. In February the following year, Pakistan recognised Bangladesh as an independent state and the relationship between the two countries improved. In April 1974, following a tripartite agreement between Bangladesh, India and Pakistan, Bangladesh granted clemency to the 195 suspects, and they were repatriated back to Pakistan.

Thirty-five years later, the Awami League government revived the idea of trials, declaring its intention to prosecute members of the political opposition for war crimes. In July 2009, it amended the 1973 Act in order to allow the prosecution of civilians, and eight months later, it established a three-member Tribunal, known as the International Crimes Tribunal. In August 2010, four leaders of the opposition party, Jamaat-e-Islami – Motiur Rahman Nizami, Ali Ahsan Muhammad Mujahid, Abdul Quader Molla and Muhammad Kamaruzzaman – were arrested not for war crimes (as had been threatened) but for crimes against humanity and genocide. In March 2012, a second Tribunal was set up to expedite the trials, dealing with both Jamaat-e-Islami and Bangladesh Nationalist Party indictees. Two death sentences were handed down in 2013, and the first sentence was carried out on 12 December that same year. While the international community has supported the trials in principle, organisations such as the UN Working Group on Arbitrary Detention,[1] the International Bar Association,[2] Amnesty International,[3] Human Rights Watch[4] and the Bar Human Rights Committee of England and Wales[5] have all criticised aspects of the legal framework and trial process.

This chapter examines the 1973 Act, the unique features of the Bangladesh trials, and the extent to which the trials meet acceptable standards. In particular, it asks whether the legal framework of the trials, the use of modes of liability and the definitions of crimes are consistent with the developments in international criminal law at the ad hoc tribunals and International Criminal Court.

Establishing the trials

The legislative framework for the trials consists of four elements: the 1973 Act; the 'Constitution (First Amendment) Act, 1973'; the 'Bangladesh National Liberation Struggle (Indemnity) Order, 1973'; and the rules of procedure framed by the tribunals.

The 1973 Act invests the tribunals with the authority to try and to punish any individual, group or organisation, irrespective of nationality, who commits or has committed in Bangladesh crimes against humanity, genocide, war crimes and crimes against peace 'whether before or after the commencement of this Act'.[6] While hailed by some as a worthy successor to the Nuremberg Tribunal (from which it drew inspiration), it has shortcomings that adversely affect the quality of justice provided. We here examine just a few of these issues.

[1] *Motiur Rahman Nizami et al.* v. *Bangladesh*, Working Group on Arbitrary Detention, Opinion No. 66/2011, U.N. Doc. A/HRC/WGAD/2011/66 (2011); *Azharul Islam et al.* v. *Bangladesh*, Working Group on Arbitrary Detention, Opinion No. 66/2012, U.N. Doc. A/HRC/WGAD/2012/66 (2012).

[2] International Bar Association opinion, *Consistency of Bangladesh International Crimes (Tribunals) Act 1973 with international standards* (29 December 2009): ictbd-defenceteam.org.

[3] Amnesty International, Letter to Mr Justice Md. Nizamul Huq (21 June 2011): ictbd-defenceteam.org.

[4] Human Rights Watch: *Bangladesh: guarantee fair trails for independence-era crimes* (11 July 2011): www.hrw.org.

[5] Bar Human Rights Committee of England and Wales, summary of proceedings, *Spotlight on the Bangladesh International Crimes Tribunal* (18 March 2013), p. 2.

[6] International Crimes (Tribunals) Act, 1973: bdlaws.minlaw.gov.bd.

The 1973 Act permits trials *in absentia*,[7] despite the assertion in the International Covenant on Civil and Political Rights of a person's right to be tried 'in his presence'.[8] The first *in absentia* trial in Bangladesh under its terms, conducted against Abul Kalam Azad, was especially notable for the inadequacy of the defence. The state defence counsel had just ten days to challenge the charges and twenty-two days to prepare the case. (He reportedly undertook no investigations on behalf of his client, instead basing his preparation on the papers provided by the prosecution.)[9] The absent Azad was condemned to death, and if he were to return to Bangladesh, he would be executed. This is because the period of limitation for filing an appeal has expired,[10] and because he – like those absconding accused convicted by the Special Tribunal for Lebanon[11] – does not enjoy the right to request a retrial.

The 1973 Act provides for appeal against the final verdict, but not for appeal against interlocutory orders.[12] This has allowed the tribunals to act with impunity at times, especially when dealing with applications for recusal. When, for example, the defence for Ali Ahsan Muhammad Mujahid sought recusal in 2012 against all three judges at the Tribunal for participating in a closed-door meeting with two prosecution witnesses, this application was heard by the same judges and rejected.[13] The same Tribunal later awarded the death penalty to the accused on the basis of the evidence provided by the two witnesses with whom the judges had met.

In 2009, the War Crimes Committee of the International Bar Association examined the 1973 Act for consistency with international

[7] Ibid. Section 10A states that the Tribunal with 'reason to believe that the accused person has absconded or concealed himself so that he cannot be produced for trial, may hold the trial in his absence'.

[8] Article 14(d) of the International Covenant on Civil and Political Rights: treaties.un.org.

[9] D. Bergman, 'Azad Judgement analysis 1: "in-absentia" trials and defence inadequacy' (26 January 2013): bangladeshwarcrimes.blogspot.com.

[10] An appeal must be filed within thirty days. (Prior to an amendment of 24 September 2012, it was sixty days.)

[11] Article 22(3) of the *Statute of the Special Tribunal for Lebanon* states, 'In case of conviction in absentia, the accused, if he or she had not designated a defence counsel of his or her choosing, shall have the right to be retried in his or her presence before the Special Tribunal, unless he or she accepts the judgement.'

[12] Ibid. Section 24 states, 'No order, judgement or sentence of a Tribunal shall be called in question in any manner whatsoever in or before any Court or other authority in any legal proceedings whatsoever except in the manner provided in section 21.'

[13] *Chief Prosecutor* v. *Ali Ahsan Muhammad Mujahid*, ICT-2 Order No. 24 (27 August 2012).

standards and made seventeen recommendations for change.[14] It suggested the deletion of Section 18 ('No excuse from answering any question') and Section 19(1) ('A Tribunal shall not be bound by technical rules of evidence'); the amendment of Section 11(2) so as to disallow the Tribunal from drawing a negative inference from the silence of the accused; the explicit provision for protection against self-incrimination; and the setting out of the duties of the prosecution and rights of suspects.[15] None of these recommendations has been implemented.

Defendants' rights under the Constitution

The 'Constitution (First Amendment) Act, 1973' added the first amendments to the Constitution of Bangladesh – Articles 47(3) and 47A – on 15 July 1973. Article 47(3) states that no law or provision providing for the detention, prosecution and punishment of any person accused of 'genocide, crimes against humanity or war crimes and other crimes under international law' could be declared void or unlawful on grounds of unconstitutionality – effectively protecting the 1973 Act from legal challenge before the Supreme Court.[16] Meanwhile, Article 47A denies any person to whom the 1973 Act applies the guarantees given to all other Bangladeshi citizens, for example, the right to protection of law (Article 31), safeguards over trial and punishment (Article 35) and the enforcement of fundamental rights (Article 44).[17] Article 47A also states that persons accused of 1973 Act offences are deprived of the 'right to move the Supreme Court for any of the remedies under this Constitution', such remedies including the right to seek judicial review and to enforce a person's fundamental human rights.[18] So a person loses their constitutional rights. Not only that, but according to the Rules of Procedure framed under the 1973 Act a person becomes 'an accused' as soon as an investigation commences against them, so they lose their constitutional rights as soon as an investigation opens.[19]

Jurists have sharply criticised these amendments. When the Jamaat-e-Islami MP Hamidur Rahman Azad recently sought opinions on the amendments, Soli Sorabjee, a former Attorney General of India, described the amendment as 'draconian',[20] while Michael Beloff QC,

[14] International Bar Association, *Consistency*. [15] Ibid.

[16] Constitution of the People's Republic of Bangladesh (Constitution): bdlaws.minlaw.gov.bd.

[17] Ibid. [18] Ibid. [19] Rule 2(1), as introduced by amendment on 28 October 2010.

[20] Opinion, S.J. Sorabjee (19 May 2010), p. 2: ictbd-defenceteam.org.

the British public law specialist, concluded that 'Article[s] 47(3) and 47A are unconstitutional in so far as they abrogate judicial review'.[21]

On 22 August 2010, the defence for two of the accused, Muhammad Kamaruzzaman and Abdul Quader Molla, jointly filed an application before the High Court Division of the Supreme Court challenging the constitutionality of Article 47(3) as introduced by the 'Constitution (First Amendment) Act, 1973'. During the preliminary hearing, when the judges decided whether there was a case for the government to answer, the Presiding Judge commented that 'independence comes only once in the life-time of a nation' and that a reasonable distinction could be drawn between the rights afforded to 'ordinary citizens' and to 'other citizens accused of war crimes'.[22] On the basis of the amendment, he therefore indicated that a mere accusation of war crimes was sufficient to deny essential rights, including the presumption of innocence, to the accused.

Finally, the tribunals constituted under the 1973 Act may only try crimes committed by one side of the 1971 conflict – the losing side. Under the 'Bangladesh National Liberation Struggle (Indemnity) Order, 1973', courts are barred from trying crimes committed by the liberating forces of Bangladesh. Article 2 thus states:

> No suit, prosecution or other legal proceeding shall lie in any Court against any person for or on account of or in respect of any act done during the period from the 1st day of March, 1971 to the 16th day of December, 1971, in connection with the struggle for national liberation or for maintenance or restoration of order up to the 28th day of February, 1972.[23]

In order to prevent any challenge to its constitutionality on the ground that it violates the equality clause of the Bangladesh Constitution,[24] the 1973 Order has been given protection under Article 46 of the Constitution, which gives Parliament the power to provide indemnity to those committing acts 'in connection with the national liberation struggle'.[25] This grant of selective indemnity under the 1973 Order violates Bangladesh's duties under Article 26 of the International Covenant on Civil and Political

21 Opinion, M.J. Beloff (21 December 2009), p. 30: ictbd-defenceteam.org.

22 For the latter comments, see also D. Bergman, 'Withdrawal of first amendment challenge' (23 August 2010): bangladeshwarcrimes.blogspot.com.

23 Bangladesh National Liberation Struggle (Indemnity) Order, 1973: bdlaws.minlaw.gov.bd.

24 Article 27 of the Constitution states, 'All citizens are equal before law and are entitled to equal protection of law.'

25 Ibid., Article 46.

Rights and Article 7 of the Universal Declaration of Human Rights, which both state that all are equal before the law.

Findings on joint criminal enterprise

In some cases before the Bangladesh tribunals, the prosecutors and judges have relied heavily upon the doctrine of joint criminal enterprise. One of these cases dealt with Ali Ahsan Muhammad Mujahid, a leader of the student front of Jamaat-e-Islami, Islami Chhatra Sangha (ICS). It is an historical fact that in 1971, Jamaat-e-Islami and the ICS opposed the liberation of Bangladesh and supported continuing unity with Pakistan, but they have always insisted that they never committed, supported or encouraged the atrocities committed to that end.

During the liberation struggle, the Pakistani Army set up a local auxiliary paramilitary force, the Razakar Force, with two wings, Al-Badr and Al-Shams. Al-Badr is alleged to have committed some of the worst atrocities, especially during the event known as the 'killing of intellectuals' between 10 and 16 December 1971 (just before the Pakistani Army's surrender), when hundreds of professors, journalists and professionals were brutally murdered and then dumped in a mass grave in Rayerbazaar, Dhaka.[26] The prosecution argued that Al-Badr was made up of ICS leaders and activists[27] and charged Mujahid with involvement in genocide and crimes against humanity.

The Tribunal held that in this case members of Al-Badr – a 'criminal organisation'[28] – were involved in a joint criminal enterprise (JCE) to 'cripple the Bengali nation'[29] by liquidating the intelligentsia, and thereby destroying the potential leadership of the new nation. The issue under consideration was whether Mujahid was associated with this criminal enterprise. According to the jurisprudence of the international criminal tribunals, the conduct of the JCE participant should 'take the form of assistance in, or contribution to, the execution of the common plan or purpose'.[30] The involvement of the JCE participant need not necessarily

[26] *Chief Prosecutor* v. *Ali Ahsan Muhammad Mujahid*, ICT BD 04 of 2012, ICT-2 Judgment (17 July 2013) (*Mujahid* Judgment), par. 401.

[27] Ibid., pars. 422–423. [28] Ibid., pars. 418, 440, 451. [29] Ibid., par. 434.

[30] *Prosecutor* v. *Tadić*, IT-94-1-A, Appeals Chamber Judgment (15 July 1999) (*Tadić* Appeals Judgment), par. 227; *Prosecutor* v. *Ntakirutimana and Ntakirutimana*, ICTR-96-10A and ICTR-96–17-A, Appeals Chamber Judgment (13 December 2004), par. 466.

be substantial,[31] but it has to be of a 'significant' nature.[32] The participant's conduct must also be such as to 'form a link in the chain of causation'.[33]

So the first question to arise in the Mujahid case was whether he was a leading member of Al-Badr, and the second question was whether the *actus reus* and *mens rea* requirements of the alleged JCE were met. According to international jurisprudence, the *actus reus* requirement would be fulfilled if the accused held a position of authority within an organisation set up to achieve criminal ends, and their contribution to the organisation's activities was significant. The *mens rea* requirement would be satisfied if the accused intended that certain crimes were committed as part of the organisation's activities, and, under JCE III doctrine, it could be foreseen that further crimes would likely result from the intended crimes.

The Bangladesh Tribunal was well aware of the jurisprudence of the international tribunals on JCE liability when considering these questions. It pointed out that Section 4(1) of the 1973 Act includes 'the necessary elements of JCE, especially JCE category 1 and 3',[34] and that it 'refers to JCE liability . . . as evolved through judicial pronouncement in the case of *Tadic* (ICTY)'.[35] So, when identifying the elements, it followed the *Tadić* Appeals Judgment in recognising that proof was required of: a plurality of persons; existence of a common plan, design or purpose to commit a crime; and participation of the accused in the common design.[36] It also cited the *Stakić* Appeals Judgment, which stated that participation 'may take the form of assistance in, or contribution to, the execution of the common purpose'.[37]

On the question of Al-Badr membership, the defence argued that there was no evidence to prove that all members of the ICS were members of Al-Badr, and that Mujahid, in his capacity as an ICS leader, was not in

31 Ibid.; *Prosecutor* v. *Kvočka et al.*, IT-98-30/1-A, Appeals Chamber Judgment (28 February 2005), par. 97.
32 *Prosecutor* v. *Brdanin*, IT-99-36-A, Appeals Chamber Judgment (3 April 2007), par. 430.
33 *Prosecutor* v. *Brdanin*, IT-99-36-T, Trial Chamber Judgment (1 September 2004), par. 263.
34 Ibid., par. 444.
35 Ibid., par. 443. According to Section 4(1) of the 1973 Act, 'When any crime as specified in section 3 is committed by several persons, each of such person is liable for that crime in the same manner as if it were done by him alone.'
36 *Tadić* Appeals Judgment, par. 227.
37 *Mujahid* Judgment, par. 450, citing *Prosecutor* v. *Stakić*, IT-97-24-A, Appeals Chamber Judgment (22 March 2006), par. 64.

any manner associated with Al-Badr.[38] It even elicited an admission from the Investigating Officer under cross-examination that he had found no evidence of the involvement of the accused with the Al-Badr forces.[39] Furthermore, even if Mujahid *had* been a member, the Tribunal still should have heeded the *Stakić* Judgment's warning that 'joint criminal enterprise can not be viewed as membership in an organisation because this would constitute a new crime not foreseen under the Statute and therefore amount to a flagrant infringement of the principle *nullum crimen sine lege*'.[40]

The Tribunal nevertheless decided – contrary to the defence arguments – that Mujahid had played a leading role in Al-Badr. Moreover, it considered his level of influence and authority within an organisation to be one of the defining elements of his participation in the JCE, noting that

> Conduct, act, behaviour and the level of influence and authority of the accused together . . . are thus qualified to be the constituent of '*participation*' too, in furtherance of common purpose, [and] the accomplishment of the crimes as it substantially contributed to, or have had a substantial effect on the perpetration of the crimes for which the accused has been charged with.[41]

The Tribunal thus held that Mujahid as 'the person in authority of Al-Badar' had sufficient reason to 'know the common purpose and plan and also the commission of crime alleged'[42] and was therefore part of the common plan to kill the intellectuals.[43] It also held that by dint of this authority, he had come to 'an understanding or agreement, express or implied' that 'a planned crime of killing selected intellectuals would be committed'.[44] In consequence, he was 'part of collective criminality' and incurred liability under Section 4(1) of the 1973 Act.[45] In other words he was held to be a JCE participant primarily on the basis of his purported position as an Al-Badr 'person in authority' without proof of his actual involvement in any common plan or design with other Al-Badr members to commit the specified offences.

Another issue is whether the *actus reus* requirements were met in establishing the accused's part in the JCE. Mujahid's contribution to the activities of Al-Badr – resulting, for example, in the killing of the

[38] Ibid., par. 172.
[39] *Chief Prosecutor* v. *Ali Ahsan Muhammad Mujahid*, Deposition by Investigating Officer, cross examination (22 April 2013).
[40] *Prosecutor* v. *Stakić*, IT-97-24-T, Trial Chamber II Judgment (31 July 2003), par. 433.
[41] *Mujahid* Judgment, par. 265. Original emphasis. [42] Ibid., par. 263. [43] Ibid.
[44] Ibid., par. 266. [45] Ibid.

journalist Seraj Uddin Hossain – had to be significant in order to fulfil these criteria. While it is not necessary to establish the existence of an actual agreement between Mujahid and the Al-Badr perpetrators of murder, it *is* necessary to present some evidence of a person's contribution to the activities carried out in furtherance of the JCE in order to show that it is of a significant nature. The defence argued that in this instance, the *actus reus* requirement for a *significant* contribution was not satisfied because there was insufficient evidence to establish a connection between Mujahid and Hossain.

The deployment of JCE III

Still on the *Mujahid* case, the Tribunal relied on the controversial 'extended' form of joint criminal – JCE III – which, in the *Tadić* Appeals Judgment's formulation, imputes criminal responsibility to 'all participants within the common enterprise where the risk of death occurring was both a predictable consequence of the execution of the common design and the accused was either reckless or indifferent to that risk'.[46] In line with this, it decided in relation to the killing of Hindu civilians at Bakchar village, Faridpur, that the evidence had shown that Mujahid had 'consciously and being aware of the foreseeable consequence of his acts and conducts aided, encouraged and provided moral support[ ] and approval to the principals for committing crimes alleged'.[47] More generally, it concluded that 'conscious conduct, culpable act, behaviour or omission to act of the accused Ali Ahsan Muhammad Mujahid knowing the foreseeable consequence, which have been convincingly proved, are thus qualified to be the constituent of "participation" too'.[48]

The Tribunal again had occasion to rely on the theory of JCE III in the case of Muhammad Kamaruzzaman, charged with a murder as a crime against humanity. It found that the accused, together with other members of Al-Badr, was responsible for abducting a civilian, Badiuzzaman, who they then handed over to the Pakistani Army at Ahmednagar Camp, who tortured him overnight and killed him the following morning.[49] The defence argued that the evidence did not show that Kamaruzzaman was party to any common design to murder Badiuzzaman, but the Tribunal rejected this, holding that 'the armed group of Al-Badars led by the

46 *Tadić* Appeals Judgment, par. 204. 47 *Mujahid* Judgment, par. 606.
48 Ibid., par. 597.
49 *Chief Prosecutor* v. *Muhammad Kamaruzzaman*, ICT BD 03 of 2012, ICT-2 Judgment (9 May 2013) (*Kamaruzzaman* Judgment), par. 218.

accused was aware of predictable consequence of their criminal acts that eventually resulted in killing of the victim', and that no member of this group could evade responsibility for the murder.[50] It decided that 'the act of the accused leading the gang of Al-Badars in abducting the victim [and taking him] to the camp is a "link" constituting the "chain"'[51] – the first and only reference to a nexus between the accused and the perpetrators.

The Tribunal in the *Mujahid* case quotes with approval the legal and moral justifications for the JCE doctrine with reference to Antonio Cassese's amicus brief in the case of *Duch* at the Extraordinary Chambers in the Courts of Cambodia (ECCC) in which he states: 'To obscure responsibility in the fog of collective criminality and let the crimes go unpunished would be immoral and contrary to the general purpose of criminal law of protecting the community from deviant behaviour that causes serious damage[ ] to the general interest.'[52] Yet the *Tadić* Appeals Chamber, of which Cassese was a member, also acknowledged the basic assumption rooted in international law (as well as in national systems) that 'the foundation of criminal responsibility is the principle of personal culpability: nobody may be held criminally responsible for acts or transactions in which he has not personally engaged or in some other way participated'.[53] While there are strong legal and moral foundations underpinning the JCE doctrine, to interpret the doctrine too liberally – by failing to establish a significant role for the participant, by inferring participation from formal function, or by establishing perfunctory links in the chain of causation – compromises the principle of *nulla poena sine culpa*.

Decisions on customary international law

The Bangladesh Tribunal's deployment of JCE III is all the more contentious in light of the preceding determination by the ECCC Pre-Trial Chamber that it did not consider JCE III to be customary international law during 1975–1979, when the Khmer Rouge was in power.[54] This issue is of course highly pertinent to the Bangladesh cases, which cover events that occurred several years earlier, in 1971. Yet the defence is currently

[50] Ibid., par. 240. [51] Ibid., par. 220. [52] *Mujahid* Judgment, par. 449.

[53] *Tadić* Appeals Judgment, par. 186.

[54] *Nuon et al.*, 002/19-09-2007-ECCC-OCIJ, Pre-Trial Chamber Decision on the Appeals against the Co-Investigative Judges Order on Joint Criminal Enterprise (JCE) (20 May 2010), par. 83.

unable to cite the ECCC decision because the Appellate Division of the Supreme Court of Bangladesh, which serves as the Appeals Chamber of the Bangladesh Tribunals, has declared that as far as the trials conducted under the 1973 Act are concerned, international customary law does not apply.

The Appellate Division's leading Judgment, delivered in September 2013 in the case of the *Government of the People's Republic of Bangladesh* v. *Abdul Quader Molla*, made various attempts to undermine the universal applicability of customary international law. First, in an Austinian attack, it held that international law 'cannot qualify as law since it lacks anything by way of sovereign legislature or of sanctions'.[55] It went on to describe the various processes by which laws are framed under the Bangladesh Constitution, and concluded that 'Nothing but the provision[s] falling within the . . . constitutional periphery can be law', and that 'any international obligation or responsibility under[taken] by the Government cannot have any force of law within the jurisdiction of Bangladesh'.[56] Thus,

> CIL cannot be applied by a domestic tribunal if those are inconsistent with an Act of Parliament or prior judicial decisions of final authority. The domestic courts have to make sure that what they are doing is consonant with the conditions of internal competence under which they must work. Thus the rule of international law shall not be applied if it is contrary to a statute.[57]

The leading Judgment's second attack on customary international law invoked Emmerich de Vattel's eighteenth-century treatise *The law of nations*, and Curtis Bradley and Mitu Gulati's recent article 'Withdrawing from international custom', when deciding that the rules of customary international law are only binding on a nation so long as the nation chooses to be bound.[58] It observed, 'Vattel, Professors Bradley and Gulati, the Eighteenth Century writers, draw upon three early Supreme Court cases to show that "customary international law rules were binding only on nations that continued to accept them."'[59] It concluded that it

[55] *Government of the People's Republic of Bangladesh* v. *Abdul Quader Molla* (Criminal Appeal No. 24–25 of 2013), Appellate Division of the Supreme Court of Bangladesh Judgment (17 September 2013) (*Molla* Appeals Judgment), p. 128.

[56] Ibid., p. 130. [57] Ibid., p. 131.

[58] *Molla* Appeals Judgment, p. 109, citing: *The law of nations or the principles of natural law applied to the conduct and to the affairs of nations and of sovereigns* (Indianapolis: Liberty Fund, 2008); 'Withdrawing from international custom', *Yale Law Journal* 120 (2010), 202–407.

[59] Ibid.

was a 'generally accept[ed] principle that international law cannot bind states without their consent' and that 'CIL binds a state only if that particular state accepts that rule of CIL is a bi[n]ding obligation'.[60] Having thus called into question the universal application of custom, the leading Judgment not only implicitly repudiated custom-based claims (such as objections to the application of JCE III to 1970s cases) but also explicitly rejected the international definition of crimes against humanity as having no applicability to trials convened under the 1973 Act.

The leading Judgment thus dismissed defence submissions outlining the standard elements of a crime of humanity within international jurisprudence as being 'not only misleading but also foreign to the Act, 1973'[61] – these elements being *inter alia* that there must be an attack,[62] that the accused must have nexus with the attack,[63] that the attack must be against a civilian population,[64] that the attack needs to be widespread or systematic,[65] and that it must be on national, political, ethnic, racial or religious grounds.[66] In the Appeals Chamber's view, the judgments of the international ad hoc tribunals had been made in light of their own statutes, and therefore had 'no manner of application in this case'.[67] Yet while rejecting the international approach to crimes against humanity, it did not attempt to provide an alternative – an omission that will undoubtedly lead to much confusion in future trials.

Still on the subject of crimes against humanity, the Bangladesh tribunals have expanded the definition (set out in the statutes of the international ad hoc tribunals) of one of its elements – namely, 'other inhumane acts'. According to the international jurisprudence, an inhumane act is one of 'similar gravity and seriousness' to other offences listed as crimes against humanity (for example, murder, rape or enslavement)[68] – one example

[60] Ibid., p. 111. [61] Ibid., p. 159.

[62] See, for example, *Nahimana et al.* v. *The Prosecutor*, ICTR-99–52-A, Appeals Chamber Judgment (28 November 2007), pars. 917–918.

[63] See, for example, *Prosecutor* v. *Kunarac, Kovač and Vuković*, ICTY-IT-96-23 & IT-96-23/1-A, Appeals Chamber Judgment (12 June 2002), par. 99.

[64] See, for example, *Prosecutor* v. *Bisengimana*, ICTR-00–60-T, Trial Chamber-II Judgment (13 April 2006), pars. 48–53.

[65] See, for example, *Prosecutor* v. *Kordić and Čerkez*, IT-95-14/2-A, Appeals Chamber Judgment (17 December 2004), pars. 93–94.

[66] See, for example, *Prosecutor* v. *Akayesu*, ICTR-96–4-T, Trial Chamber I Judgment (2 September 1998), par. 595.

[67] *Molla* Appeals Judgment, p. 159.

[68] *Prosecutor* v. *Kayishema and Ruzindana*, ICTR-95–1-T, Trial Chamber Judgment (21 May 1999), pars. 154, 583.

being sexual mutilation. The provision should not be treated as an all-encompassing 'catch all' category,[69] and nor should these acts be lesser-order offences.[70] Yet in the *Kamaruzzaman* case, the Tribunal held that parading Syed Abdul Hannan, the Principal of Sherpur College, around town after having shaved his head and smeared his face with ash constituted an inhumane act.[71] It was undoubtedly a crime, but not a crime on a par with murder, rape or enslavement; instead, it might be argued that the Tribunal diluted the gravity of crimes against humanity.[72]

The issue of command responsibility

The theory of superior or command responsibility has been discussed in recent judgments passed by the Bangladesh tribunals. The jurisprudence of the international criminal tribunals indicates that a 'superior–subordinate' relationship exists if a superior possesses 'effective control' over the perpetrators of offences punishable under international criminal law – in other words, the superior has the material ability to prevent, or punish a subordinate for commission of, such an offence.[73] *De jure* authority is not the same as 'effective control'.[74] Such a 'superior–subordinate' relationship is characterised by the power to issue orders and to punish perpetrators of offences punishable under international criminal law.[75] The power to *influence* the subordinate perpetrator – short of 'effective control' amounting to a material ability to prevent, and punish a subordinate for committing, offences – is not sufficient.[76]

Returning to the *Mujahid* case, the Bangladesh Tribunal adopted the jurisprudence relating to command responsibility set out by the 1973 Act

[69] Ibid., par. 583. [70] Ibid. [71] *Kamaruzzaman* Judgment, par. 287.

[72] Under the Bangladesh Penal Code, the accused would have faced a maximum sentence of imprisonment of one month for wrongful restraint and three months for the use of criminal force. The Tribunal awarded ten years' imprisonment to Muhammad Kamaruzzaman on this count.

[73] *Prosecutor* v. *Kajelijeli*, ICTR-98-44A, Appeals Chamber Judgment (23 May 2005), par. 86.

[74] *Prosecutor* v. *Orić*, IT-03-68-A, Appeals Chamber Judgment (3 July 2008), par. 91.

[75] *Prosecutor* v. *Delalić, Mucić, Delić and Landžo* (*Celebici* case), IT-96-21-T, Trial Chamber Judgment (16 November 1998), par. 810; *Prosecutor* v. *Limaj, Bala and Musliu*, IT-03-66-T, Trial Chamber II Judgment (30 November 2005), par. 715; *Prosecutor* v. *Strugar*, IT-01-42-T, Trial Chamber II Judgment (31 January 2005), pars. 395–398.

[76] *Prosecutor* v. *Delalić, Mucić, Delić and Landžo* (*Čelebići* case), IT-96-21-A, Appeals Chamber Judgment (20 February 2001), par. 266; *Prosecutor* v. *Hadzihasanovic and Kubura*, IT-01-47-T, Trial Chamber Judgment (15 March 2006), par. 80.

and developed by the international criminal tribunals. Section 4(2) of the Act states,

> Any commander or superior officer who orders, permits, acquiesces or participates in the commission of any of the crimes specified in section 3 or is connected with any plans and activities involving the commission of such crimes or who fails or omits to discharge his duty to maintain discipline, or to control or supervise the actions of the persons under his command or his subordinates, whereby such persons or subordinates or any of them commit any such crimes, or who fails to take necessary measures to prevent the commission of such crimes, is guilty of such crimes.[77]

In interpreting these statutory provisions relating to superior responsibility, the Tribunal made extensive reference to the judgments of the ICTY and ICTR, thus holding that no formal letter of appointment was required to establish a 'de facto superior position',[78] that a formal position or designation as a commander was not required,[79] that the key to establishing the existence of a 'superior–subordinate' relationship was the existence of 'effective control' over the actions of alleged subordinates,[80] and that the indicators of 'effective control' are more a matter of evidence than of substantive law.[81] Yet, while recognising the settled jurisprudence of the international ad hoc tribunals, the Bangladesh Tribunal appears to depart from the case law that it so faithfully reproduced in its judgments when discussing the indicia of 'effective control' in determining a 'superior-subordinate' relationship.

In the *Mujahid* case, the Tribunal placed reliance on three elements when concluding that the accused acted as an Al-Badr 'superior': his speeches, his political power and his visits to Al-Badr headquarters. With respect to his speeches, the Tribunal relied in particular on Mujahid's statement that '[t]he youths of the Razakars and Al-Badar forces and all other voluntary organizations have been working for the nation to protect it from the collaborators and agents of India'.[82] It held that this was sufficient for it to infer that the accused 'had a position of authority on the Al-Badar force'.[83] In similar vein, it referred to speeches during

[77] Section 4(2), 1973 Act.

[78] *Mujahid* Judgment, par. 181 (citing *Blagojević and Jokić* Trial Chamber I Judgment), and par. 182 (citing *Zigiranyirazo* Trial Chamber III Judgment).

[79] Ibid., par. 194 (citing *Milutinović* Trial Chamber III Judgment).

[80] Ibid., par. 195 (citing *Bagilishema* Appeals Chamber Judgment).

[81] Ibid., par. 196 (citing *Blaškić* Appeals Chamber Judgment).

[82] *Mujahid* Judgment, par. 187. [83] Ibid., par. 188.

which Mujahid had urged ICS workers 'to form Al-Badar at different levels asking them to ensure that no person of un-Islamic attitude gets access in the Al-Badar bahini',[84] and had proclaimed that 'Al-Badr is the Azrail (Angel of death) in presence to the "Indian agents" or the "miscreants"'.[85] These comments were held to have shown that Mujahid had 'substantial authority and control'[86] and a 'significant level of authority'[87] within Al-Badr. Elaborating, the Tribunal held that 'Mujahid possessed power by virtue of his political position that he occupied during the war of liberation in 1971 [as leader of ICS] within the territory of Bangladesh' and that 'he was entrusted with political power of addressing the Al-Badar men, although he was not the sole leader of the Al-Badar force'.[88] In short, Mujahid's statements *about* Al-Badr were held by the Tribunal to be sufficient to establish that he held a position of authority *within* Al-Badr.

The Tribunal also placed much reliance on the evidence that Mujahid visited Al-Badr headquarters. It cited testimony that he 'used to come to the Al-Badar head quarter, sometimes being accompanied by the top brasses of JEI and ICS', and concluded from this that 'in exercise of his position of authority the accused visited Al-Badar head quarter to co-ordinate the activities of Al-Badar'.[89] For example, after observing that paramilitaries had been taking intellectuals, artists and lawyers to the Al-Badr headquarters where they were tortured to death in the dining hall, the Tribunal, in a leap of logic, concluded, 'This barbaric portrayal sufficiently offers the culpable purpose of visit of AB HQ by the accused Ali Ahsan Muhammad Mujahid.'[90]

The *Mujahid* Judgment thus shows a significant expansion of the indicia of 'effective control' from which a 'superior–subordinate' relationship may be inferred. In its view, merely holding an important position in a political group (ICS), being in a position to deliver speeches to members of that group, and visiting the headquarters of Al-Badr are sufficient to establish a superior–subordinate relationship between the accused and members of the latter organisation. While such evidence may be sufficient to establish the accused's association with Al-Badr, it is difficult to understand how it establishes his ability to prevent and punish the commission of specific offences by its members.

In the case of Ghulam Azam, the Tribunal again had occasion to consider the theory of command responsibility. Azam was the chief of

[84] Ibid., par. 198. [85] Ibid., par. 199. [86] Ibid., par. 198. [87] Ibid. [88] Ibid., par. 189.
[89] Ibid., par. 191. [90] Ibid.

East Pakistan Jamaat-e-Islami from 1969 to 1971, touring the area and delivering speeches in support of unity with Pakistan. The Tribunal quoted with approval four elements of the doctrine of superior responsibility set out in the ICTY's *Orić* case, namely, that the crime is committed by someone other than the accused, that there was a 'superior–subordinate' relationship between the accused and the perpetrator, that the accused knew or had reason to know the perpetrator had committed or was going to commit the crime, and that the accused did nothing to prevent or punish the perpetrator for so doing.[91] Citing more authorities, the Tribunal went on to hold that *de facto* (as well as *de jure*) commanders may incur criminal responsibility provided they exercised 'effective control';[92] that the military doctrine of command responsibility is equally applicable to civilian superiors;[93] and that it is not the civilian status of the accused, but the degree of authority the accused exercised over subordinates, that is significant.[94]

Yet in Azam's case, as in Mujahid's, the Tribunal departed from the settled international jurisprudence in determining the indicia of 'effective control' as a means of inferring a 'superior–subordinate' relationship. It observed that Azam was 'the Ameer (Head) of the then East Pakistan Jamaat-e-Islami', that he was 'a prominent member of the [pro-Pakistan] 140-member central peace committee', 'a member of the 21-member Executive committee of the said central peace committee' and 'a member of the 6-member sub-committee of the said Executive committee'.[95] For all its citing of international jurisprudence, the Tribunal relied on Azam's formal designations of 'Ameer of Jamaat-e-Islami' and his memberships within the Peace Committees to conclude that he was the *de facto* civilian administrator of East Pakistan, and that as such, he had effective control over military subordinates committing international crimes.

In particular, the Tribunal inferred Azam's superior status from his position within Jamaat-e-Islami, deciding that he had used this to exercise control over his subordinates in the party, by, for example, compelling 'his two subordinate party leaders' to join the Cabinet of Ministers and insisting that 'people belonging to Jamaat-e-Islami' form paramilitary forces to resist the independence of Bangladesh.[96] Whatever his status within the party, no evidence was brought on record or discussed in the Judgment to show that he had the authority to prevent and punish

[91] *Chief Prosecutor* v. *Professor Ghulam Azam*, ICT BD 6 of 2011, ICT-1 Judgment, (15 July 2013) (*Azam* Judgment), par. 312.

[92] Ibid., pars. 313, 319. [93] Ibid., pars. 318, 321. [94] Ibid., par. 331. [95] Ibid., par. 355.

[96] Ibid., par. 364.

the commission of offences either by members of the Pakistani Army or by members of local paramilitary forces. Yet the Tribunal concluded that Azam was responsible in his capacity as 'de[ ]facto administrator'[97] for the atrocities committed in 1971, stating that he 'had superior responsibility over his subordinates but he failed to prevent them from committing atrocities as contemplated in section 4(2)' of the 1973 Act.[98]

Finally, in the case of Kamaruzzaman, the Tribunal relied on evidence of his *influence* in the district of Sherpur in northern Bangladesh to infer that he exercised 'effective control' over members of Al-Badr. It quoted a witness – who had said that 'Kamaruzzaman ... was a high flyer' who 'could have turned Sherpur upside down' – to demonstrate his superior position in the locality, not least 'over the Al-Badar members of the camp in Sherpur including the Pakistani occupation army'.[99] It also relied on a 1971 *Daily Sangram* news report identifying Kamruzzaman as the 'chief organiser of Al-Badar force'[100] to establish his purported authority over its members (notwithstanding the Investigation Officer's admission under cross-examination that there was no such post in Al Badr's command structure[101]). Despite the doctrine's recognition of the insufficiency of the *influence* short of 'effective control', and despite the absence of evidence of Kamruzzaman's ability to impose it, the Tribunal simply expanded the indicia of control by focusing on his alleged position of 'chief organiser' and his local standing in Sherpur.

The theory of superior responsibility developed by the Bangladesh tribunals in the cases of Mujahid, Azam and Kamruzzaman clearly sanctions 'guilt by association'. Accordingly, someone could be deemed to be a 'superior' in a criminal organisation by associating with its members (such as visiting or referring to them in speeches), or by holding a position of authority within an associated political party, or by holding a position of influence in a particular locality. In these cases, there was no attempt to prove the material ability of the accused to prevent crimes by, or punish members of, the criminal organisation. This expansion of the doctrine of command responsibility beyond the contours contemplated by international jurisprudence upsets the balance between the principle of personal culpability and the need for superiors' accountability for crimes committed by subordinates.

[97] Ibid., par. 356. [98] Ibid., par. 386. [99] *Kamaruzzaman* Judgment, par. 296.
[100] Ibid., par 154.
[101] *Chief Prosecutor* v. *Muhammad Kamaruzzaman*, Cross-examination, 20 February 2013.

Before concluding on 'superior responsibility', it should be noted that Section 4(2) of the 1973 Act does not specify the requisite *mens rea* of the 'superior'. The prosecution argued that the Tribunal should not read *mens rea* into the law if the law is silent on the issue.[102] Rejecting this contention, the Tribunal held that 'it would be highly repugnant to common sense and natural justice to hold some one responsible for the crimes committed by his subordinates which was unknown to him'.[103] It went on to hold that 'Judges of the common law shall supply the omission of the legislature' and that it was 'competent to import an additional element of knowledge' if doing so would be 'conforming to natural justice and customary international laws'.[104] So as far as identifying the *mens rea* of the superior is concerned, the Tribunal's jurisprudence corresponds to international jurisprudence. Its interpretation of Section 4(2) is a progressive development and ensures a fair application of the *mens rea* requirement of the command responsibility doctrine.

Conclusion

There can be no doubt that there should be an end to the culture of impunity. War criminals should be brought to justice. Yet care should be taken that further injustice is not perpetrated in the process. Purely domestic tribunals are not necessarily appropriate forums for trials of international crimes, particularly in countries that have gained their independence through revolutions and wars, where there is always the danger that a politically motivated executive and prosecution and a less-than-independent judiciary may be inclined to ignore the rights of the defendants.

The Bangladesh experience shows that a lack of sound knowledge of, and rigorous training in, international criminal law may result in the expansion of modes of responsibility and definitions of crimes beyond the parameters considered acceptable in contemporary international criminal law. Even more disconcerting is the manner in which the principle of *nulla poena sine culpa* – firmly rooted in national and international criminal jurisprudence – has been compromised. The law laid down by the Bangladesh tribunals can hardly be said to have contributed in any meaningful manner to the existing jurisprudence developed by the international criminal tribunals.

[102] *Azam* Judgment, par. 336. [103] Ibid. [104] Ibid., par. 338.

A number of widely reported incidents have further eroded the credibility of the tribunals in Bangladesh. Ministers have made speeches threatening defence witnesses.[105] A Judge was found to have acted as an investigator against the person he was trying.[106] A defence witness disappeared from the steps of the Tribunal and turned up six months later in a neighbouring country's jail, alleging abduction by the police.[107] And the Chairman of one of the tribunals was found to be relying on someone outside the court to prepare the Judgment before all the evidence had been heard, and had been offered inducements to wrap up cases by a certain time – revelations which eventually led to his resignation.[108]

The domestic trial process in Bangladesh, while paying lip-service to the principles and standards of international law, has failed to apply them correctly, to the detriment of the defendants. Not only that, but it has proven to be susceptible to executive pressure and nationalistic fervour. The proper recourse is to hold such trials under international supervision – for without it, there is the likelihood of further miscarriages of justice.

[105] Agriculture Minister Matia Chowdhury warned defence witnesses in the district of Sherpur against giving evidence in favour of the accused, Muhammad Kamaruzzaman. A contempt petition was disposed of with a warning to the Minister. See, for example, 'Matia asked to explain by Sept 19', *Daily Star* (7 September 2012): www.thedailystar.net.

[106] Delwar Hossain Sayedee sought recusal against the then Tribunal Chairman Justice Md. Nizamul Huq, on the grounds that he was on the Secretariat of the People's Inquiry Commission investigating war crimes allegations against him in 1993–1994; the application was rejected by *Prosecutor* v. *Sayedee*, ICT-1 Order No. 29 (14 November 2011). See, for example, 'Tribunal won't pass order on Justice Nizamul', *Daily Star* (15 November 2011): archive.thedailystar.net.

[107] Shukhoranjan Bali was due to appear as a defence witness in the case of Delwar Hossain Sayedee; he reappeared six months later in Dum Dum jail in Kolkata, claiming to have been kidnapped by Bangladesh police. See, for example, Human Rights Watch, *India: protect Bangladesh war crimes trial witness* (16 May 2013): www.hrw.org/news.

[108] Skype calls between Justice Md. Nizamul Huq and Dr Ahmed Ziauddin, the Brussels-based Director of the Bangladesh Centre for Genocide Studies, leaked to *The Economist*, revealed, among other things, that the draft Judgment in the *Sayedee* case was being prepared by Dr Ziauddin (not the Tribunal) when defence lawyers were still presenting their case, and that Justice Huq had been offered promotion upon disposal of as many as three cases by December 2012. See, for example, 'Trying war crimes in Bangladesh', *Economist* (15 December 2012): www.economist.com.

INDEX

For EU product safety concerns, contact us at Calle de José Abascal, 56–1°, 28003 Madrid, Spain or eugpsr@cambridge.org.

www.ingramcontent.com/pod-product-compliance
Lightning Source LLC
LaVergne TN
LVHW011529200926
848484LV00001B/205
* 9 7 8 1 1 0 7 1 0 4 6 5 5 *